OXFORD HISTORICAL MONOGRAPHS

Elite Women in English Political Life *c.*1754–1790

ELAINE CHALUS

CLARENDON PRESS · OXFORD

OXFORD
UNIVERSITY PRESS

Great Clarendon Street, Oxford OX2 6DP

Oxford University Press is a department of the University of Oxford.
It furthers the University's objective of excellence in research, scholarship,
and education by publishing worldwide in

Oxford New York

Auckland Cape Town Dar es Salaam Hong Kong Karachi
Kuala Lumpur Madrid Melbourne Mexico City Nairobi
New Delhi Shanghai Taipei Toronto

With offices in

Argentina Austria Brazil Chile Czech Republic France Greece
Guatemala Hungary Italy Japan Poland Portugal Singapore
South Korea Switzerland Thailand Turkey Ukraine Vietnam

Published in the United States
by Oxford University Press Inc., New York

First published 2005

British Library Cataloguing in Publication Data
Data available

Library of Congress Cataloging in Publication Data
Data available

Typeset in Ehrhardt by
SPI Publisher Services, Pondicherry, India
Printed in Great Britain on acid-free paper by
Biddles Ltd.
King's Lynn, Norfolk.

ISBN 0–19–928010–X

1 3 5 7 9 10 8 6 4 2

ACKNOWLEDGEMENTS

Without the financial support of the Arts and Humanities Research Board, the Social Sciences and Humanities Research Council of Canada, the Committee for Graduate Studies at the University of Oxford, the Friends of the Essex Record Office, and Wolfson College, this project would not have been possible. Special thanks must also go to Charles Philpin, Joanna Innes, Chris Wickham, and rest of the editorial board of *Past & Present*, who were encouraging and understanding while I was finishing the doctoral dissertation from which this monograph comes. Without the support of Fiona Montgomery, Alan Marshall, and my colleagues at Bath Spa University College, the task of transforming the dissertation into a monograph would have been yet further delayed.

I would like to acknowledge the generosity of the dukes of Beaufort and Northumberland, Sir Edward Dashwood, Bt., and the Trustees of the Chatsworth Settlement for the use of their collections. I would also like to thank the Rector and Fellows, Exeter College, Oxford, for permission to use the Bray Papers. Permission to use the Gordon Papers is by courtesy of the Trustees of the Goodwood Collections. The County Archivist and the West Sussex Record Office were very helpful with these papers and those of the Du Cane Manuscripts. The Wentworth Woodhouse Muniments are courtesy of Olive, Countess Fitzwilliam's Wentworth Settlement Trustees and the Director. Lady Stafford's letters are used courtesy of the University of Birmingham, with special thanks to Christine Penney and the library staff for being exceptionally helpful to a visiting researcher at the end of a long hot summer day.

This monograph includes some material which has appeared elsewhere in various other forms: '"That epidemical Madness": Women and Electoral Politics in the Late Eighteenth Century', in Hannah Barker and Elaine Chalus (eds.), *Gender in Eighteenth-Century England: Roles, Representations and Responsibilities* (Harlow, 1997), 151–78; '"*My Minerva* at my Elbow": The Political Roles of Women in Eighteenth-Century England', in Richard Connors, Clyve Jones, and Stephen Taylor (eds.), *Hanoverian Britain and Empire: Essays in Memory of Philip Lawson* (Cambridge, 1998), 210–28; 'Women, Electoral Privilege and Practice in the Eighteenth-Century', in Kathryn Gleadle and Sarah Richardson (eds.), *Women in British Politics, 1760–1860: The Power of the Petticoat* (Basingstoke, 2000), 19–38; 'Elite Women, Social Politics and the Political World of Late Eighteenth-Century England', *Historical Journal*,

43: 3 (Sept. 2000), 669–97; '"To Serve My Friends": Women and Political Patronage in Eighteenth-Century England', in Amanda Vickery (ed.), *Women, Privilege and Power: British Politics, 1750 to the Present* (Stanford, Calif., 2001); 'How Lady Susan Wooed the Voters', *BBC History Magazine*, 2: 6 (June 2001), 44–6. I would like to thank, respectively, Longman (Peason Education), the Boydell Press, the Macmillan Press, the *Historical Journal*, the Board of Trustees of the Leland Stanford Jr. University, and the *BBC History Magazine* for their permission to use this material.

Any project which takes as long as this one has builds up enormous debts in terms of people, as well as sources, and, despite my best intentions, it is inevitable that I will forget to thank someone who has played a part. Archivists and librarians across Britain have invariably been helpful and occasionally insightful. I was extremely fortunate to be at Oxford with a particularly challenging and supportive community of young historians who gathered there during the 1990s: in particular, Hannah Barker, Sue Brown, Philip Carter, Kimberly Crouch, Cindy McCreery, Amanda Foreman, Stephen Howard, Alexandra Shepherd, Susan Skedd, Kim Reynolds, and Roey Sweet all deserve thanks for everything from debates, discussions, and shared references to publishing projects, conferences, symposia, dinners, and cups of coffee. Hannah and Roey have been outstanding, reading drafts of this manuscript and providing feedback and support over the years. John Brewer, Neil Cartlidge, Linda Colley, Penny Corfield, Matthew Cragoe, Richard Connors, Stephen Farrell, Tim Hitchcock, Kathryn Gleadle, Martin Ingram, Angela John, Peter Mandler, Alan Marshall, Ann Milovic, Colm O'Reardon, Carolee Pollock, Steve Poole, Jane Potter, Mark Pottle, Sarah Richardson, Jane Rendall, Debbi Simonton, Stephen Taylor, Amanda Vickery, Dror Wahrman, Barbara White, Susan Whyman, and David Wilkinson have all helped me to hone specific ideas. Special tribute must be reserved for Joanna Innes and Paul Langford, though, for their consistent support, academic generosity, and wisdom have been invaluable throughout. Despite these acknowledgements, however, I take entire responsibility for the intrepretation of women's involvement in the eighteenth-century English political world that follows—and for any errors or omissions it might include.

This project would never have been attempted if it had not been for the keen sense of history that my parents instilled in me. The friendship and gentle encouragement of Stephen Abrahall, Don Jones, Gaynor

Kavanagh, Cate Nelson-McDermott, Carrie Shemanko, Graeme Standen, and Barbara White have played a vital part in ensuring that it was completed. And I must not forget Moorland: her joy in long walks and her unshakeable belief in the importance of frisbees have often reminded me of the need to keep everything in perspective. I must, however, end sombrely. The fact that this is a monograph about eighteenth-century women and politics is a testimony to Philip Lawson, his teaching, and his fascination with the period and the subject. Phil was very excited about this project and followed its progress eagerly; unfortunately, he did not live to see it completed. It is to his memory that this monograph is dedicated.

CONTENTS

Introduction

There is something inherently fascinating, even titillating, in the very idea of eighteenth-century elite women's political involvement—the imagination, conditioned perhaps by the knowledge that the formal political world of parliament and policy was closed to women at the time, conjures up instead images redolent of the marquise de Merteuil from *Les Liaisons dangereuses*. Ghosts of silken-gowned women appear, knowingly, calculatingly operating 'behind the scenes' out of ambition or for purely personal political ends, deftly combining wit and charm with liberal doses of flirtatious sexuality and the attractions of ample white bosoms. The whiff of influence and corruption hangs in the air with the attar of roses . . . While it would be wrong to say that this highly coloured romantic tableau is entirely a figment of the imagination, the reality is—as realities often are—significantly more mundane; it is, nevertheless, also much more intricate, extensive, and interesting.

Back in 1990 when I began the research for my doctoral dissertation, from which this monograph stems, the shape, detail, and extent of eighteenth-century elite women's involvement in English political life was still so little known that there was some question as to whether there would be enough source material to make a viable dissertation, never mind a larger publication. There was no immediately apparent starting-point for the research, no pre-established framework to follow, and few obvious collections of manuscript sources. I was convinced, however, that there was a story to tell, if I could only find a way to get at it. The process was slow, but what I found fascinated me and, like all good research, lured me on, encouraging me to do always that little bit more before I risked writing things up and drawing conclusions.

My interest in eighteenth-century elite women and politics had originally been piqued by discrepancies I had noted while studying—separately—eighteenth-century political and women's history. A variety of important publications have been particularly useful in contributing to our understanding of the vitality and dynamism of eighteenth-century political culture, and, in some cases, beginning to suggest how it was gendered,[1] but it was only too possible in 1990 to echo Karl von den

[1] For the vitality of eighteenth-century political culture, see: John Brewer, *Party Ideology and Popular Politics at the Accession of George III* (Cambridge, 1976); also *The Sinews of*

Steinen's conclusions of 1979: 'one must now choose between politics without women or women without politics.'[2] With separate-spheres ideology approaching the height of its popularity in women's history, there was little encouragement to examine women's involvement in the public sphere. Moreover, assumptions about women and politics, about

Power: War, Money and the English State, 1688–1783 (London, 1989); Linda Colley, *Britons: Forging the Nation, 1707–1837* (London, 1992); David Eastwood, *Governing Rural England: Tradition and Transformation in Local Government, 1780–1840* (Oxford, 1994); also *Government and Community in the English Provinces, 1700–1870* (London, 1997); Paul Langford, *A Polite and Commercial People: England 1727–1783* (Oxford, 1990); also *Public Life and the Propertied Englishman, 1689–1798* (Oxford, 1991); Frank O'Gorman, *Voters, Patrons, and Parties: The Unreformed Electoral System of Hanoverian England, 1734–1832* (Oxford, 1991); also 'Campaign Rituals and Ceremonies: The Social Meaning of Elections in England, 1780–1860', *Past & Present*, 135 (May 1992), 79–115; John A. Phillips, *Electoral Behavior in Unreformed England: Plumpers, Splitters, and Straights* (Princeton, 1982); Nicholas Rogers, *Whigs and Cities: Popular Politics in the Age of Walpole and Pitt* (Oxford, 1989); also *Crowd, Culture and Politics in Georgian Britain* (Oxford, 1998). Gender-sensitive accounts include Donna Andrew, '"The Passion for Public Speaking": Women's Debating Societies', in Valerie Frith (ed.), *Women and History: Voices of Early Modern England* (Toronto, 1995); Amanda Foreman, *Georgiana: Duchess of Devonshire* (London, 1998); Kathryn Gleadle and Sarah Richardson (eds.), *Women in British Politics, 1760–1860: The Power of the Petticoat* (Basingstoke, 2000); Harriet Guest, *Small Change: Women, Learning and Patriotism, 1750–1810* (London, 2000); Margaret Hunt, *The Middling Sort: Commerce, Gender and the Family in England, 1680–1780* (London, 1996); Susan Kingsley Kent, *Gender and Power in Britain, 1640–1990* (London, 1999); Renata Lana, 'Women and Foxite Strategy in the Westminster Election of 1784', *Eighteenth-Century Life*, 26 (Winter 2002), 46–69; K. D. Reynolds, *Aristocratic Women and Political Society in Victorian Britain* (Oxford, 1998); Sarah Richardson, 'The Role of Women in Electoral Politics in Yorkshire During the 1830s', *Northern Hist.*, 32 (1996); Hilda L. Smith (ed.), *Women Writers and the Early Modern British Political Tradition* (Cambridge, 1998); Anne Stott, '"Female Patriotism": Georgiana, Duchess of Devonshire, and the Westminster Election of 1784', *Eighteenth-Century Life*, 17 (Nov. 1993); Naomi Tadmor, *Family and Friends in Eighteenth-Century England: Household, Kinship and Patronage* (Cambridge, 2001); Stella Tillyard, *Aristocrats: Caroline, Emily, Louisa and Sarah Lennox, 1740–1832* (London, 1992); Amanda Vickery (ed.), *Women, Privilege and Power: British Politics 1750 to the Present* (Stanford, Calif., 2001); also *The Gentleman's Daughter: Women's Lives in Georgian England* (London, 1998); James Vernon, *Politics and the People: A Study in English Political Culture, c.1815–1867* (Cambridge, 1993); Rachel Weil, *Political Passions: Gender, the Family and Political Argument in England, 1680–1714* (Manchester, 1999); Susan Whyman, *Sociability and Power in Late Stuart England: The Cultural Worlds of the Verneys, 1660–1720* (Oxford, 1999); Kathleen Wilson, *The Sense of the People: Politics, Culture and Imperialism in England, 1715–1785* (Cambridge, 1995); also 'Citizenship, Empire, and Modernity in the English Provinces, *c.*1720–1790', *Eighteenth-Century Studies*, 29 (1995–6), 69–96; and *The Island Race: Englishness, Empire and Gender in the 18th Century* (London, 2002).

[2] Karl von den Steinen, 'The Discovery of Women in Eighteenth-Century English Political Life', in Barbara Kanner (ed.), *The Women of England: From Anglo-Saxon Times To the Present* (Hamden, Conn., 1979), 247. See also his 'The Fabric of an Interest: The First Duke of Dorset and Kentish and Sussex Politics, 1705–1765', Ph.D. dissertation, University of California, Los Angeles (1969).

women's political history, and about the very definition of politics would need to be modified and extended if eighteenth-century women's involvement was to be viewed comprehensively and understood in its own right, not merely as a precursor in some way to the woman's movement and the grand Whig narrative of women's eventual enfranchisement.

At the time, both women's and political historians tended to assume that the customary political constraints which prevented eighteenth-century women from holding most places, voting, or sitting in parliament also precluded them from becoming political actors. While women of the lower sort might be mentioned for their involvement in quasi-political group actions, such as food riots, only a very few unquestionably outstanding elite women received attention—the duchesses of Marlborough and Devonshire at opposite ends of the century being the two most likely candidates. When the political involvement of elite women was considered at all, it was usually assumed to be anomalous, unaccountable, personal, and often at least slightly salacious. At best, a few exceptional women proved the rule, operating indirectly 'behind the scenes', astutely manipulating men and situations. Their activities and their social and personal approach to politics symbolized the lack of accountability and 'corruption' of the unreformed political system. Their political participation was assumed to have reached its apotheosis in 1784. The vicious press campaign against the duchess of Devonshire during the 1784 Westminster election and then, subsequently, the abhorrence of political women engendered by the French Revolution was assumed to have driven elite women out of politics and into the home.[3]

However, this image of increasingly constrained domestic femininity sat precariously alongside more recent research which revealed elite women as playing an increasingly important social role, particularly in the development of the new, mixed-sex, conversation-based polite society.[4]

[3] There are numerous discussions of women's exclusion from the political arena: Alice Browne, *The Eighteenth-Century Feminist Mind* (Brighton, 1987), 136–8; Leonore Davidoff and Catherine Hall, *Family Fortunes: Men and Women of the English Middle Class, 1780–1850* (London, 1992); Natalie Zemon Davis, 'Women in Politics', in id. and Arlette Farge (eds.), *A History of Women in the West. Vol. 3: Renaissance and Enlightenment Paradoxes* (Cambridge, Mass., 1993), 167–83; Catherine Hall, 'Private Persons versus Public Someones: Class, Gender and Politics in England', in *White, Male and Middle Class: Explorations in Feminism and History* (Cambridge, 1992), 151–71; Joan Landes, *Women and the Public Sphere in the Age of the French Revolution* (Ithaca, NY, 1987); Vernon, *Politics and the People*.

[4] Langford, *A Polite and Commercial People*, 109–16; G. J. Barker-Benfield, *Culture of Sensibility: Sex and Society in Eighteenth-Century Britain* (London, 1992), pp. xvii–xxxiv; Philip Carter, *Men and the Emergence of Polite Society: Britain 1660–1800* (Harlow, 2001), 66–70; Anna Bryson, *From Courtesy to Civility* (Oxford, 1998), 127–8. For elite women's role

Furthermore, while it was a historical commonplace that women were brought up to please men and to put the interests of their husbands and families first—something tediously and repeatedly encouraged by conduct-books throughout the century—it was simultaneously a commonplace that eighteenth-century politics was highly personal and familial, especially in the localities. Give or take the existence of party, historians acknowledged the importance of family, connexion, interest, influence, and patronage, both to the structure of the political elite and its machinations. Seemingly disparate, these pieces of information, once put together, were intriguing: they suggested a familial political world where a good deal of the actual political manoeuvring depended upon personal and social skills, and took place in social situations. This challenged any notion of hard-and-fast separate spheres, and implied instead that the personal, social, and political arenas were interwoven. Given that the eighteenth century saw parliamentary service take on ever-increasing *cachet*, and given that an individual's (and thus a family's) economic and social advancement still owed far more to patronage than to merit, they also posed some interesting questions. What was there to prevent women who had been born into politically active families, married into yet other politically active families, and then raised politically active families of their own, from becoming politicized? What stopped them from using their social skills for political ends out of a sense of duty to family, if nothing else?

Trawling through the texts and footnotes of generations of political histories led me to suspect that this was exactly what often happened. These texts revealed a significant scattering of elite women as political actors and commentators. Historians referred to them individually or cited their letters and journals to support arguments, but, because their interest was focused elsewhere, paid scant attention to the women themselves and seldom examined their political motivations, methods, or understanding.[5] Fragmentary and tantalizing as the references were, they begged further examination: these women were neither apolitical

in setting the limits of acceptable society, see Leonore Davidoff, *The Best Circles: 'Society', Etiquette and the Season* (London, 1986).

[5] Examples can be found in political histories across the century. See e.g. Frank O'Gorman, *The Rise of Party in England: The Rockingham Whigs 1760–82* (London, 1975); John Ehrman, *The Younger Pitt: The Years of Acclaim* (London, 1969); Philip Lawson, *George Grenville: A Political Life* (Oxford, 1984); Leslie Mitchell, *Charles James Fox* (Oxford, 1992); Lewis Namier, *The Structure of Politics at the Accession of George III* (London, 1929); J. H. Plumb, *Sir Robert Walpole*, 2 vols. (London, 1956); Lewis M. Wiggin, *The Faction of Cousins: A Political Account of the Grenvilles, 1733–1763* (New Haven, Conn., 1958).

nor uninformed. It seemed unlikely that they were all exceptions. But, if they were not, how did they fit in? What was needed was a more comprehensive picture of the political life of the elite, one that paid heed to the personal, familial, and social aspects of politics and, in doing so, reintegrated women.

This entailed looking beyond a definition of politics as the 'science' of governance—that is, as a concentration on the specific mechanics of parliament and policy, and such forth—important as those aspects of high politics are. Given the nature of eighteenth-century politics, it seemed more sensible to think about politics as the 'art' of governance—to recognize that both hard and soft politics played a part in creating and maintaining what was a remarkably stable and enduring elite political culture. What political scientists such as Lorraine Culley have recognized as important in evaluating modern women's political involvement is even more relevant when applied to a time when women were not enfranchised:

> The view that women are not interested in politics or not active in politics, in fact rests on a very narrow conception of what counts as 'politics'... In assessing women's active participation in politics, if we shift our focus from governments and offices in political parties and unions to other political arenas we find that women are not inevitably 'unpolitical'... There are many kinds of activity which seek to influence the making and execution of public policy and the distribution of resources, outside of fully institutionalised spheres.[6]

This meant taking social politics seriously, giving patronage its due weight, and recognizing that the electoral process included aspects of each and was in effect a socio-political cycle. This also meant restoring the all-too-frequently forgotten link between politics and society. As Sean Wilentz has argued, politics is 'a realm of social experience and action in its own right—a realm partly (but never entirely) independent of other social realms'.[7] As a result, it can never be completely disentangled from the conventions, hopes, and fears of the society from which it comes.

Eighteenth-century women's political involvement was often problematic: it could be violently criticized as well as highly praised. If women's involvement in politics was both distinct from and yet shaped by prevailing beliefs and concerns about class and gender, then the

[6] Lorraine Culley, *Women and Power* (Leicester, 1986), 2.

[7] Sean Wilentz, 'Introduction: Teufelsdröckh's Dilemma: On Symbolism, Politics, and History', in id. (ed.), *Rites of Power: Symbolism, Ritual, and Politics Since the Middle Ages* (Philadelphia, 1985), 3.

customs and constraints that governed women's political behaviour might well have been somewhat different from those that obtained in other areas of their lives. This in turn would be revealing of the degree to which women were accepted as political actors in their own rights and the way that their political activities were understood at the time. For instance, during contested elections rituals of social inversion and acceptance of excess became the norm for the men of the political elite: was there a similar loosening of social sanctions for elite women? And, if so, was it manifested in the same way(s)? Where and how was the line drawn between acceptable and unacceptable female political behaviour(s)?

Hence, my approach to women's *political* involvement is inclusive and my research is situated at the point where women's history, political history, and social history should intersect. While I am interested in finding out what difference, if any, women made in eighteenth-century politics, this question can only become meaningful if we first know what it was that women did, how they fitted into political culture, and how contemporaries (male and female) responded to their involvement. To do this comprehensively, it would be necessary to re-create the world of the eighteenth-century political elite. This, of course, is impossible; however, by concentrating on social politics, patronage, and the electoral process—key interlinked aspects of political life—it is possible to achieve a useful three-dimensional understanding of the political world and of women's part(s) in it.

The women who form the bulk of my research are primarily the mothers, wives, sisters, and daughters of the oligarchy that governed England in the second half of the eighteenth century. Not only were they were the closest to political power of all eighteenth-century women, but also, given the personal and familial nature of eighteenth-century politics, they were the women who were most likely to be involved. Many were the female counterparts of Sir Lewis Namier's 'inevitable Parliament men'.[8] Their politics was primarily familial, occasionally factional; it was not feminist. They were members of an elite that was English in political identification and orientation, but not exclusively so in terms of nationality. It included Scots, Welsh, and that small group of Irish who saw London and Westminster as the centre of their political world.[9]

[8] Namier, *The Structure of Politics at the Accession of George III*, 2nd edn. (London, 1960), 2.

[9] Ireland had its own distinct parliament and its political culture was shaped by the unique conditions that obtained under the Anglo-Irish ascendancy: the part played by elite women in Irish political life needs to be examined in its own right.

The political elite was wealthy and landed, but it was not large and its political power tended to be concentrated in relatively few hands. It was made up of aristocrats and gentry, leavened by the occasional merchant prince or nabob, and bound together by a spiderweb of bonds of kinship, friendship, obligation, clientage, and allegiance. At its most extensive it probably numbered no more than 20,000 families, even at the end of the eighteenth century.[10] Social and political prestige was attached to parliamentary service, but only approximately 600 men sat in the Commons and usually less than 200 in the Lords. The most important positions of power and influence were held by little more than a handful of men. The familial nature of the politics was reflected in the extensive family connexions that linked the various political arenas together: in 1760–1, for instance, Lord Hardwicke had one son-in-law in the Lords (notably the first lord of the Admiralty) and another son-in-law, four sons, and two of his wife's nephews in the Commons.[11] This does not include other parliamentary connexions made through his sons' wives, or any which might have existed among that scattering of men who held important positions at Court or in the administration of the state, the army, the law, or the diplomatic service.

The women of the political elite may not have been included in the formal institutions of politics, but they were members of political families and frequently they were the physical links between them. Indeed, they reflect the shape as well as the diversity of the political elite. The women who people this book come from families that were often, but by no means always, aristocratic, and, while predominantly landed, some were also the daughters of new urban, commercial, and imperial wealth. Some were almost entirely London-based; others seem never to have left their localities; many split their time and their politics between the metropolis and the country. Young or old, confident or diffident, they range from women for whom politics was a personal passion, through those for whom it was an omnipresent fact of life—to those for whom it was an occasional duty or even a trial, to be avoided whenever possible. Some are remarkable women by any criteria: they include some of the century's best-known political hostesses, wits, intellectuals, and leaders of society and style. Many are much more ordinary. They are the dutiful or ambitious wives, mothers, and daughters, and that host of formidable widows and matriarchs who people eighteenth-century conversation pieces, novels, and plays.

[10] O'Gorman, *Long Eighteenth Century*, 106.

[11] Namier, *Structure of Politics*, 3.

This is not to suggest that all elite women were formally or consistently involved in politics: by no means. Neither were all men. The closer they were to political power and events, in London or the provinces, and the more politically active their families of birth or marriage, the more likely they were to be involved to some degree at some point in their lives. While youth and beauty and charm were useful attributes for political women, charm superseded the others. The most active and effective political women were not necessarily the youngest, but those who had the personal and social skills necessary to work effectively with people from differing social groups and achieve results. The most successful female politicians were confident, assertive, intelligent, and approachable women who understood how politics worked and were interested in and excited by it for any number of reasons.

In a society where playing the political game well mattered—where gracious attention to the rituals of hospitality and social obligation in the country was recognized as affecting the outcome of elections, and where an individual's or family's social and economic advancement could depend upon the skilled use of the patronage system—politics was important, self-interested, and highly competitive, involving and affecting whole families. Elite society itself had a consistent undercurrent of politics, a wary mindfulness that no longer exists today. Elections, specific political events, or crises increased the voltage until politics temporarily dominated everything, sweeping aside all other concerns and interests. It was impossible to be a member of this society and not be politically aware; for women from politically active families, politics was a fact of life and some kind of political activity was almost inescapable. Different families had different expectations of female political involvement, and while, overall, more women were involved in the informal and social dimensions of politics than in the more formal aspects of patronage or electoral politics, women were active in each of these areas, and the demands of expediency or the excitement of the moment could serve as a great spur to occasional participants. It is not necessary to look behind the scenes to discover women in eighteenth-century political life; as soon as our focus is adjusted to include social politics and patronage, and to look at the electoral process holistically, they appear openly. Women had various points of political access and modes of involvement, and, at least for those women from politically active families, they often used these flexibly and knowingly.

Such conclusions are based on the accretion of evidence obtained from the study of several hundreds of women's and men's correspondences.

Even so, they are necessarily impressionistic: quantifying women's political involvement in any meaningful way is almost impossible. Simply finding a way into the topic initially posed a significant challenge. There is no readily identifiable collection of sources on women and eighteenth-century politics; moreover, many of the sources that do survive are sketchy and anecdotal. It is rare to find a lifetime's worth of papers from a highly political woman: we would be much the richer if the collections left by Lady Stafford, the duchess of Devonshire, and her mother, Lady Spencer, were matched by the equivalent from women like Lady Salisbury, the duchesses of Northumberland, Bedford, or Gordon (both the 4th and 5th duchesses), to name only a few. What is more, in order to gain a fuller understanding of the nature and extent of women's involvement in political life, I knew I had to go beyond the women at the apex of political society and access those who were removed from the centre, either by distance, connexion, or status. I also needed to find out how their activities were received by male and female contemporaries, and especially by male politicians, if I was to understand how politically active women 'fitted' into eighteenth-century politics and society.

To begin with, it was necessary to find out what sources were available. I cast my net as widely as possible in the dual hope of circumventing any possible shortage of sources and achieving a broad cross-section of the political elite. The land-tax records for five significantly different counties—Derbyshire, Dorset, Essex, Lancashire, and Oxfordshire—and for two important election years—1754 and 1784—supplied an initial list of political families.[12] These were supplemented by the families of the hundred most active parliamentary speakers for the second half of the century, in an effort to include families who were most likely to be politicized and regularly in London for the parliamentary season. Since politicians of both sexes were inveterate correspondents, with contacts that spanned the country, I chose to concentrate on personal, general, and political correspondences. As sources proliferated and I discovered and followed various networks of correspondents, the research developed two strands: a vertical strand that focused on women's involvement in the most public and formal aspects of politics, as revealed through their correspondence with leading politicians, especially first lords; and a horizontal strand that emerged from reading across political families' correspondence networks and cast light on the workings of politics and

[12] I must thank Paul Langford for his generosity in sharing the land-tax information from which this comes, which is taken from his unpublished research.

the way that women were integrated into political life as a whole. Politicians' collections proved surprisingly useful. Not only did they call attention to the more formal aspects of women's political involvement, particularly the part they played in borough management and patronage, but they also demonstrated that there were women besides the 'usual suspects', those with the highest status and the best political pedigrees, who were involved in even the most elevated of politicians' correspondences. Indeed, politicians' letters furnished glimpses of an unexpected number of women, many of whom appear to have left little or no other historical record. They also served to guard against asymmetry by putting women's political involvement into context.

This prosopographical and familial approach to women and politics has led some historians to label my work Namierite or neo-Whig.[13] Elite women's political involvement sits uncomfortably with any grand Whig narrative of women's politicization and progress towards enfranchisement and liberation. Indeed, eighteenth-century society drew on traditions and expectations of political involvement for elite women that looked backwards rather than forwards. While their overall political participation was more extensive and well-established than has previously been imagined, and their activities, as long as they did not threaten the political status quo, were more likely to be accepted and praised than criticized, their motivations, methods, and goals were predominantly familial and/or factional, rather than personal. They accepted the political system as it was and used the avenues that were available to them—openly and often effectively—to work within its confines: enfranchisement was simply not an issue. In addition, I would argue that elite women's political involvement, at least at the top of the political elite, continues into the nineteenth century. It did not end with the French Revolution or electoral reform in 1832; however, neither was it transmogrified neatly into the nineteenth-century woman's movement. By fostering an intimate political dialogue which encouraged a sense of self-identification that bound the political elite together, women were vitally important in creating and sustaining a remarkably stable and enduring politicized society: one that—arguably—survived at elite levels

[13] Peter Mandler, 'Namier in Petticoats?' (Feb. 1999), review of K. D. Reynolds, *Aristocratic Women and Political Society in Victorian Britain* (Oxford, 1998): http://www.history.ac.uk/ihr/Focus/Victorians/mandler.html; Anna Clark (Sept. 1998), review of Amanda Vickery, *The Gentleman's Daughter: Women in Georgian England* (London, 1998). http://www.history.ac.uk/reviews/paper/anna.html.

right into the twentieth century.[14] The personal political world of influence and connexion that elite eighteenth-century women inhabited appears to have adapted to changing times and the formation of party rather than disappeared: Winston Churchill's repeated requests to his mother to use her influence and her political connexions to forward his career, and her repeated attempts to do so (sometimes successful, at other times not), differ little from those of other political mothers and sons in the eighteenth century.[15] I would suggest instead that elite women's political involvement ran in tandem with the developing women's movement during the nineteenth century, the two groups separated largely by class and proximity to power, and that they only very gradually came together.

By concentrating on individuals and families, and on the personal and social dimensions of politics as I do, it is inevitable that my work will be viewed as Namierite in some quarters. Ironically, some aspects of Namier's vision of politics are perhaps more appropriate when applied to eighteenth-century women than to men; however, even women's politics was not solely the politics of self- (or family-) interest. While it is impossible to extract the ideological dimension entirely, the second half of the eighteenth century was only beginning to see the revival of party and, on the whole, both elite men and women shared basic Whig political beliefs and were parts of political groupings that were still fluid and differed only subtly. Consequently, ideological differences were slighter and mattered less then (for men or women) than they did during periods of high party feeling. Yet they did exist and they were played out in women's lives in a variety of ways. It was, for instance, differences in ideology that put paid to Lady Rockingham's friendship with Lady Susan Stewart (later Lady Stafford) when the Rockinghams come to power in 1765.[16] This is not to say that political beliefs could not shape women's lives. There were always a few women who were implacably ideological: Lady Susan Keck's lifelong dedication to the Whig cause and

[14] Despite the rise of party, the political world in which Lady Londonderry moved in the late nineteenth and early twentieth centuries would have been recognizable to eighteenth-century women: Anne de Courcy, *Circe: The Life of Edith, Marchioness of Londonderry* (London, 1992).

[15] Martin Gilbert, *Churchill: The Man behind the Legend* (London, 1998), 40, 42–3, 45, 49, 53, 56; Roy Jenkins, *Churchill* (London, 2001), 28, 38.

[16] Public Record Office (hereafter PRO), 30/29/4/2/64, fols. 242–4^{v}, Lady Rockingham to Lady Susan Stewart, n. pl., July [1765]; ibid. 65, fol. 246^{r-v}, Lady Rockingham to Lady Susan Stewart, Peterborough House, 6 Aug. [1765].

her exhaustive efforts on behalf of the New Interest Whigs in Oxfordshire in the 1750s serve as a case in point.[17]

I would like instead to situate my research as a response to Patrick Collinson's call for a new political history that is 'social history with the politics put back in', an examination of political processes which includes rather than ignores its social dimensions.[18] By focusing on politics and eighteenth-century governance through the interrelated political arenas of social politics, patronage, and electoral politics, it aims to perform the dual historical tasks of recovering women as political figures and reintegrating them to form a more comprehensive picture of the political culture of the eighteenth-century political elite. Doing so delineates the workings of a politically charged society, where the personal could be public; the political, social; and the social, political. For the political elite, politics was inextricably interwoven into the very fabric of life, and women were no exception. While political awareness was not necessarily synonymous with interest or involvement, and I make no attempt to argue that *all* elite women were politically active—indeed, some women used the pervasive societal rhetoric against women's involvement in politics to limit their involvement, while others used arguments of familial duty to validate theirs[19]—the majority of women from politically active families appear to have been involved in politics in some way at some point in their lives. The nature, extent, and duration of their activities varied widely, as did the enthusiasm with which they approached them. Exceptional women did exist, as did exceptional men, but most politically active women were not exceptions: they were simply the products of their society and time, and their political activities need to be seen in this context.

The society that takes shape is one full of contradictions and unresolved tensions about women's political involvement. In order to understand them, it is essential to remember that it was a society where the

[17] See my '"My Lord Lady Sue": Lady Susan Keck and the Great Oxfordshire Election of 1754' (in press).

[18] Patrick Collinson, *De Republica Anglorum: or, History with the Politics Put Back* (Cambridge, 1990), 14, 15. While Collinson cast his argument in terms of class, it is equally applicable to gender. His advice echoes comments made by Paul Monod, 'The Politics of Matrimony: Jacobitism and Marriage in Eighteenth-Century England', in E. Cruickshanks and J. Black (eds.), *The Jacobite Challenge* (Edinburgh, 1988), 24.

[19] For examples of these differences among the Lennox sisters, especially between Caroline, who used conventional arguments against women's political involvement as an excuse to limit hers, and Emily, who used beliefs about a wife's duty to advance her husband and family's best interests to forward her own involvement, see British Library, Additional Manuscripts (hereafter BL, Add. MSS) 51,415–16, 51,426; also Tillyard, *Aristocrats*.

polity was resolutely imagined to be male. In theory, politics was men's business, and gendered beliefs about women's nature defined them as politically unqualified and incompetent.[20] In practice, it was a society that accepted women in every role, from political confidante through to political partner. Women were political hostesses and socio-political 'fixers'; in the patronage system, they were clients, brokers, and patrons; and, electorally, they were anything from fashionable accessories to men at elections, through to exceptionally effective canvassers and formidable managers of election campaigns or family interests. It was a society that could cast political women as the personification of Liberty or Corruption—at the same time and for the same activities.[21] It was a society that accepted women as political actors as long as their participation did not threaten the fiction of a male polity on the one hand or that of female inferiority and natural subordination on the other. This had important ramifications. As long as women's actions could be interpreted in light of traditional female roles, familial duty, or the supportive ideal of a female helpmeet, they were welcomed and taken for granted. When women were perceived to step out of this character and become politicians in their own rights, however, especially when they proved to be more effective politicians than their male competitors, they posed a serious threat to the polity and, on a much more fundamental level, to the place of women in regard to men—thus, to one of the key building-blocks of eighteenth-century society.

[20] Susan Kingsley Kent suggests that women's increasing political involvement in the second half of the eighteenth century caused particular anxiety because it occurred at the same time that men of the middling and lower sorts began to demand more political say. She argues that two solutions were employed to remove the threat to the polity posed by women: assumed gendered differences between men and women were exaggerated and used to reinforce the idea that women were unfit for politics by nature; and the polity was reimagined in yet more 'aggressively masculine' terms by reformers of the middling sort who equated feminine influence with effeminacy and corruption and sought to remove all traces of it from the political arena: Kent, *Gender and Power in Britain, 1640–1990* (London, 1999), 117–19. For other recent explorations of the gendered nature of the polity, see Hilda L. Smith, 'Women, Intellect, and Politics: Their Intersection in Seventeenth-Century England', in id. (ed.), *Women Writers and the Early Modern British Political Tradition*, 1–21; Weil, *Political Passions*; Wilson, 'Citizenship, Empire, and Modernity in the English Provinces'; Kathryn Gleadle and Sarah Richardson, 'Introduction: The Petticoat in Politics: Women and Authority', in Gleadle and Richardson (eds.), *Women in British Politics*, 1–18; 'Introduction', in Guest, *Small Change*, 4–18; Amanda Vickery, 'Introduction', in Vickery (ed.), *Women, Privilege and Power*, 1–55.

[21] Contrast the electioneering prints of the duchess of Devonshire during the 1784 election, e.g. *The Apotheosis of the Dutchess* (1784), where she is lifted above Scandal by the Virtues, with Thomas Rowlandson's *Two Patriotic Duchess's on their Canvass* (3 Apr. 1784), where she is kissing a butcher while simultaneously slipping a purse into his pocket.

When this occurred, women's political involvement was labelled suspect at best and inherently corrupt and corrupting at worst. Slander—particularly sexual slander which tarnished a woman's reputation—was the weapon of choice for critics and reformers who wanted to ensure that women stayed within the accepted boundaries of female political involvement. It was an apt choice. For contemporaries, corruption was about undue influence, and, when it came to elite women, this fitted neatly into other beliefs about sexuality and class. At its most basic, women's political influence was assumed to stem from the power of female sexuality; hence its effectiveness and its potential for corruption. Non-elite men in particular were assumed to be unable to resist this combination of sexuality and class. Bribery and other traditional forms of male influence might be countered, but no man could counter the power of female sexuality.

The degree to which concerns about sex, politics, and corruption may have been valid is impossible to determine, as there is little in the sources that survive to suggest that women were either more or less corrupt than their male counterparts, or that they were more likely to use their sexuality to achieve their goals. Indeed, given the distance that most women tried to maintain between themselves and those of lesser rank, and the reluctance with which they approached such customary physical practices as the electoral kiss, it seems unlikely that they made much overt use of their sexuality in their dealings with voters.[22] Where sexuality may have played more of a political part was in women's dealings with men who were their social equals—but even here it leaves only the faintest imprint in the sources. It would be surprising if a pretty face, a charming manner, and a flirtatious conversation over a dinner table or at a drawing-room, assembly, or ball had not been used to effect, but, while sources record the results of these encounters, they say very little about how the women managed them or about their manner with men. It is only when something was remarkable enough to provoke comment that it has survived. Thus, it is only courtesy of some catty comments from self-righteous Pittite women that we learn that Lady Elizabeth Foster used the duke of Richmond's infatuation with her (during a brief romantic interlude in the middle of her long-standing affair with the duke of Devonshire) to secure an ambassadorship for her spendthrift brother.[23] But such examples are rare. Even the vicious press campaign waged

[22] See my 'Kisses for Votes: The Kiss and Corruption in Eighteenth-Century English Elections', in Karen Harvey (ed.), *The Kiss in History* (Manchester, 2005).

[23] 'Duchess of Devonshire to Lady Spencer, n. pl., 26 July 1787', in *Georgiana: Extracts from the Correspondence of Georgiana, Duchess of Devonshire*, ed. Bessborough (London,

against the duchess of Devonshire for her supposed exchange of kisses for votes in the 1784 Westminster election was more about political opportunism, and the power of the press in picking up on underlying societal fears about women, sex, and politics, than it was about the actual event—if it occurred at all—or about the true nature of elite women's political activities.

So what was it, then, that inspired women to take an active part in political life? The auspices for involvement were not great. Gendered beliefs precluded women from full citizenship and made them legally, economically, and socially dependent upon men. Most of the 'spoils' of patronage were unavailable to them, and they were always more prone to criticism for their political involvement than men. What becomes apparent is that, while gender shaped women's political involvement, it did not fundamentally change their motivations or methods. These were not all that different from those of their male counterparts. Like men, women became involved in politics for a combination of personal, familial, or factional reasons. Given their limitations, it is not surprising that they were more likely than men to become involved in politics in order to advance family interests or out of a sense of duty, either to family members or clients they deemed deserving. Even this was not entirely altruistic: women could benefit from successful political involvement. They benefited personally if their families' social or economic circumstances improved. They also benefited more directly politically, if they were able to demonstrate that they had good connexions and political influence, or were competent managers of family interests, thus setting themselves up as figures of note on the local or national political stages. And, like men, women were also motivated by personal interest, sheer ambition, the excitement of being part of a great event or a grand game—and occasionally by strong beliefs.

Politics in the eighteenth century took place on multiple political stages—local, regional, and national—and, while parliament and the clubs were male venues, there was no shortage of other spaces and events where men and women mixed. These ranged from the home, through public venues like gardens, assembly rooms, the theatre, and the opera, to community events such as race-meets or the assizes, or formal society events such as the drawing-rooms at Court. Any social encounter might be politicized. When face-to-face interaction was impossible, both men

1955), 123; PRO, 30/29/4/6/65, fol. 1078^{r-v}, [Lady Augusta Murray] to Lady Stafford, n. pl. [6 Sept. 1787]; see also Foreman, *Georgiana: Duchess of Devonshire*, 197–8.

and women worked through intermediaries gleaned from their networks and/or by letter. This was especially true of their involvement in patronage. While women made far fewer requests for patronage than men—they made about 10 per cent of all the requests that the duke of Newcastle received when first lord of the Treasury between 1754 and 1762, for example—there were always some women involved in any of a number of patronage networks. Here, class and connexion rather than gender seem to have been more significant in shaping participation and results: like men, women made their requests directly to patrons or indirectly through brokers, by letter, and in person. They structured their requests in the same way, asked for similar things, and justified their supplications with similar references to family, rank, lineage, honour, loyalty, and service. They had no guarantee of success, yet they could and did succeed.

This is important to remember: at first glance the eighteenth-century political world looks inimical to women, yet the personal and familial nature of politics, the importance attached to influence, interest, and patronage, and the interpenetration of the social and political arenas provided them with points of access and reasons for becoming involved. These factors also gave them ways to reach their goals. Politically active women were always a minority in the eighteenth century. Some came to politics out of interest; others out of duty. Some were propelled into political activity through widowhood. Some made brief forays into politics under duress—the demands of circumstance of some sort, be it a contested election, a specific patronage goal, or some form of political or personal crisis—and retreated as soon as possible; others got a taste for politics and, once active, remained so. The most dynamic political women found in politics a means of self-expression and a way of demonstrating their loyalty to family, faction, or nation, as well as a way of securing appointments, pardons, and places—and winning votes.

The chapters that follow place women's involvement in political life in context, politically, personally, and socially. Chapter 1 addresses fundamental questions about women's relationship to formal politics, and concludes that women's involvement in political life was, even if examined only in terms of electoral privilege and practice, more complicated and more amorphous than has frequently been assumed. While custom prevented women from voting or serving in parliament, other factors, including variations in franchises, differences in local customs and practices, and the tendency to view politics in familial terms, provided them with an assortment of opportunities and reasons for involvement. Moreover, it calls attention to women's electoral privileges in burgage and freeman boroughs, revealing not only that contemporaries recognized that women could have political influence and treated with them accordingly, but also that influence was not exclusive to exceptional or elite women.

Chapter 2 situates women personally in political life by focusing on their overall political roles as confidantes, advisers, agents, and partners. In revealing a political culture where the boundaries between the social and the political were blurred, and where some degree of female political involvement was often accepted and even expected, it maintains that most women's roles were rooted in the traditional female roles of wife/widow, mother, sister, and daughter. It presents women's political roles as fluid and flexible, varying according to personality, family circumstances, and the demands of particular political situations. Highly political women who operated as partners alongside men in political understakings were, like highly political men themselves, always a small group, an elite within the political elite. Whatever the societal rhetoric against women's political involvement, the actuality of eighteenth-century political life included women in a variety of roles and levels of involvement. As long as their activities could be interpreted in light of arguments of duty to individual, family, or faction, and as long as they did not emerge as more competent or charismatic politicians in their own right than the men for whom they were ostensibly campaigning, then their involvement could be acknowledged or even praised.

Chapter 3 concentrates on women's involvement in the social aspects of eighteenth-century political life. It calls attention to the interconnexion of politics and society, and to the importance that contemporaries attached to the management of people and social situations for political ends. It suggests that women played a vital part in the construction and maintenance of a highly politicized society. For women from politically active families, politicization often began at home; moreover, society itself, especially in London, was permeated by politics. As guests or hostesses, women used social occasions and their socializing with men and women knowingly and politically. Their correspondence networks could be put to similar purposes through the importance that was attached to the gathering and dissemination of socio-political fact and rumour that was deemed 'News'. When political issues dominated society, they affected women as well as men. Manifestations of popular politics demanded ritualized responses from women, and could be potentially dangerous. It was, however, when elite society became politically inflamed and divided, as it did during the Regency Crisis, that women took a leading part. Then everything, from their clothing to their participation in highly politicized social events at private homes and public venues, might be politicized—and this, like other aspects of their political involvement, could generate a mixed and sometimes hypocritical response from contemporaries.

Chapter 4 examines women's involvement in patronage. It explores the nature of patronage as a system and its place in eighteenth-century politics, and suggests that patronage was well suited to women. Not only was it socio-political and non-institutional, but it also had multiple points of access and a range of levels of involvement, thus allowing the involvement of women from a significant cross-section of eighteenth-century society. A brief examination of women's requests to the duke of Newcastle while he was first lord of the Treasury reveals that they formed at least 10 per cent of his total requests, and demonstrates that women used the system in much the same way and for many of the same reasons as men. Their requests can be categorized into the same five 'Ps'—place, pension, preferment, parliament, and peerage—and seem to have achieved similar results. The subsequent examination of women's involvement as clients, patrons, and brokers over the course of the second half of the century reveals, once again, that women's involvement was not perceived to be innovatory or radical; it was, instead, accepted and justified on familial as well as political grounds. Most women were clients, but women who had useful political connexions or political influence were frequently brokers, and those who had their own political interests or managed family interests were patrons. This led not only to women making requests of men, but also to female patronage networks operating within larger male networks, and to men making requests of women. Gender was a factor in patronage, but its impact, here as elsewhere, was complicated by other considerations, such as social status and connexion.

Chapter 5 shifts the focus to women's involvement in the electoral process. It opens with a study of Lady Irwin's extended and successful struggle for control over her borough of Horsham against the duke of Norfolk in the last quarter of the eighteenth century, and suggests that her motivations for electoral involvement, and those of other women like her, were personal, familial, and ideological—not unlike those of their male counterparts. By highlighting the electoral activities of a number of aristocratic widows, it serves to remind us that we need to look beyond the stereotype of the sexually alluring young female canvasser if we wish to obtain a more rounded understanding of women's electoral involvement. Eighteenth-century electoral politics was an ongoing process that incorporated social politics and patronage, and women from politically active families were frequently expected to take part in at least its social side. While women's electioneering was always potentially risky, as being too forward, too sexual, or too casual opened women to criticism, if not outright slander, the nature of eighteenth-century electioneering provided some loosening of social sanctions, and, as long as women took care to preserve class distinctions as much as modesty, their involvement raised few concerns.

Chapter 6 goes on to discuss women's contributions to family interests by exploring the nature of familial politics and the kinds of socio-political activities that women could engage in. It argues that women need to be seen as fully functioning members of successful political family units. They were frequently involved in election-specific socializing (some, like visiting with voters' wives, sex-specific), in formal as well as informal canvassing, in making (or granting) politicized patronage requests, and in administering and managing people and political interests. Personal and family concerns outweighed ideological considerations for most, but not all, women.

Chapter 7 sharpens the focus by examining women's involvement during and after election campaigns. It argues that when election fever hit, it would have been very difficult for women of the political elite to remain unpoliticized. While the female canvasser of contemporary stereotype was a pretty, young, single woman who used her beauty and charm to win votes, the reality was much more varied. Moreover, the experiences of female canvassers demonstrates that the boundary between acceptable and unacceptable electioneering behaviours had a certain amount of flexibility and might vary according to situation. By looking specifically at two outstanding female campaigners, Lady Susan Keck in the Oxfordshire election of 1754, and the duchess of Devonshire in the Westminster election of 1784, both of whose activities attracted much press coverage, it becomes clear that sexual slander was the weapon of choice for attacking women who threatened the status quo by becoming political figures in their own rights. Women who controlled political interests and operated in the same way as their male counterparts, however, went largely unremarked. They were part of the mix that made up an area's political profile. Finally, while women might go on to play a part in scrutinies and petitions, the chapter suggests that women also played a part in restoring harmony and ensuring that normal social interactions were re-established after elections were over.

The conclusion makes a case for women's involvement in political life, arguing that it needs to be understood in context. By no means all women, even at the level of the political elite, were politically active, yet women were an integral part of the political world of the eighteenth century. For many women, involvement in political life was motivated by familial considerations, but the effectiveness of such involvement should not be underestimated; furthermore, while questions about whether women made a 'difference' might be hard to evaluate in national terms, in local or personal politics—in terms of places gained, preferments and promotions secured, votes won, and supporters wooed—there can be little doubt but that they did.

I

Women and Politics

In the gathering tension before the 1784 general election Lady Spencer made one of her periodic but futile attempts to direct the political behaviour of her younger daughter, Lady Duncannon:

never mind what other people say my Dearest Harriet but I intreat you to avoid entering into disputes on that Odious subject [politics]—it is easy to excuse yourself by saying you fear to hurt the cause you wish well to, by trying to support it, or that you are not sufficiently inform'd to talk upon the matter, with fifty other ways you have ingenuity to find out—for connected as you are, I do not wish you to *appear*, or to *be*, uninterested upon it—but in the situation things now are, trust me if you once allow your[self] [to] Argue upon it, you will nine times out of ten say things you will afterwards wish unsaid—[1]

Her admonitions are illuminating because, consciously or unconsciously, she identifies fundamental themes, ambiguities, and inconsistencies around the involvement of the eighteenth-century female political elite in English political life. She reveals that politicization was inescapable for the women of the political elite. As an integral part of the web of personal, familial and/or factional networks, or connexions, that comprised political society, they were expected to be politically aware and involved. One need only look at the political coverage in a publication such as the *Ladies Magazine*, with its detailed reports of speakers at county meetings, lists of bills given royal assent, information on taxes and the Budget, and its roster of new Court appointments, among other political occurrences, to have this confirmed.[2] Nonetheless, there were contending opinions about how women's political interest and allegiance should be expressed. On the one hand was the belief that elite women had influence and that their involvement could affect political outcomes; on the other was the presumption that the polity was male and that politics was men's business.

[1] BL, MS Coll. Althorp, F. 38, fols. 254–5: Lady Spencer to Lady Duncannon, n. pl., 4 Feb. 1784. Unless otherwise specified all references to Lady Spencer are to Georgiana Spencer, née Poyntz, the wife/widow of the 1st Earl Spencer. Her daughter-in-law, Lavinia, is identified as Lavinia, Lady Spencer, throughout.

[2] See e.g. *The Ladies Magazine; or, Entertaining Companion for the Fair Sex* . . . , 15 (1784).

Thus, the ideal female response was informed silence. As Lady Spencer made clear, however, the actuality of political life did not always sit comfortably with contemporary ideals of a passive, apolitical femininity.

This conflict between the ideal and the real constitutes the essential paradox that besets eighteenth-century women's political involvement.[3] There was continuous tension between the pervasive rhetoric of the time, which opposed women's political involvement of any sort, and the reality, which saw significant, if widely varying, female political participation. In actuality, women were accepted as political actors as long as their involvement could be explained so as not to threaten the fundamental belief that the polity was male. While Lady Spencer's comments concentrated on women's political influence, and the importance of that influence should not be underplayed, women's involvement extended well beyond this. Their involvement was more widespread and readily acknowledged by contemporaries than previously imagined. Even when women's place in the polity is looked at narrowly through their electoral status and privileges, these tensions are revealed. Although the ideal polity was wholly male, the real polity could not be: factors ranging from variations in the franchise through accidents of birth and high male mortality ensured that there were always some eighteenth-century women who were undeniably political actors and challenged this fiction. Some women, from the level of freeholders up, had recognized electoral privileges—the right to make their husbands into voters, or even the legal right to vote (and thus the right to choose men to vote in their steads). These privileges were only finally removed with municipal corporation reform in 1835.

While Lady Spencer's attempt to influence Lady Duncannon's political behaviour was typical of her ongoing attempts to control her adult daughters, she was by no means a model of political restraint herself. By 1784 she was a widow with more than twenty years of political experience. Her involvement in politics was familial: she knew what maintaining a family interest entailed, and had never shirked her duties as a political wife. Significantly, her husband had trusted her political judgement and organizational abilities enough to place her in charge of the election campaign for the family borough of St Albans in the past.[4] While her contemporaries knew her to be a political actor, she was always

[3] Hilda Smith has aptly referred to the 'confused realities' of early modern women's political involvement: 'Introduction', in Smith (ed.), *Women Writers and the Early Modern British Political Tradition*, 9–12.

[4] PRO, 30/29/4/6/75, fol. 1102^{v}, Rachel Lloyd to Lady Gower, n. pl. [1780]; ibid. 30/29/4/6/77, fol. 1108^{r-v}, 5 Sept. [1780].

ambivalent, at least on paper, about her political participation. Politics was for her a family duty—and a long-standing love–hate relationship at that. Her alleged distaste seems never to have stopped her from participating: she discussed political developments with friends of both sexes on an ongoing basis, avidly followed certain issues in parliament, and took part in social or electoral politics when and where necessary. Indeed, by saying one thing and doing another, she embodies the ambivalence with which the eighteenth century viewed women and politics. The gap between her rhetoric and her actions becomes even more clear with hindsight, for within six weeks of writing this letter both she and her daughters were electioneering furiously, caught up in one of the most intense general elections of the century. Lady Spencer devoted all her energies to heading the election committee and managing the election in St Albans; she even went so far as to persuade her daughters to leave London and canvass St Albans to secure the vote for the family's candidate. This familial canvassing was viewed positively; it was their canvassing for Charles James Fox in Westminster which gained them notoriety and a place in history. For the Spencer women and other women like them, the 1784 election was one of those situations when the demands of political circumstance superseded personal and/or societal uncertainty about women's political involvement.

In recognizing that some degree of political participation was inevitable for women who were 'connected' in the way that her daughters were, Lady Spencer was acknowledging the importance of 'connexion' in eliciting women's 'interest' and justifying their participation in political life. For contemporaries, connexion operated simultaneously on personal and ideological levels. It extended beyond family and kin relationships, to include friends and associates who were bound together by shared political ideals and aspirations. Connexions formed both the bases of political factions and the vertical and horizontal structures of patronage and clientage which distributed the rewards of political involvement: power, profit, and status. The concept of 'interest' was related to that of connexion and was similarly amorphous. It denoted the degree of political power and influence that an individual, a family, an interest group, or a political connexion could exercise. This could be quantifiable or intangible. Interest played a part in everything from securing patronage and seats in parliament to the development of policy and its implementation.[5]

[5] Eighteenth-century usage indicates that contemporaries were always aware of the political meanings of these terms. The *Oxford English Dictionary* notes that 'connexion'

Lady Spencer's concerns about the dire consequences of mistaken political enthusiasm become more understandable when her daughters' connexions and potential for interest are taken into account. Both Lady Duncannon and the duchess of Devonshire were ardent Whigs who had learned their politics at home. Their father, who had been prevented by the will of his great-grandmother, Sarah, duchess of Marlborough, from accepting any government post or pension,[6] divided his frustrated political energies between the House of Lords and managing his boroughs instead. Through the Marlborough line they were related to the families of the dukes of Manchester and Montagu, and those of Lords Bolingbroke, Pembroke, Cardigan, and Bateman, among others. These kin connexions were augmented significantly when each married into yet another politically active aristocratic family. In marrying Frederick Ponsonby, Lord Duncannon, the heir of the earl of Bessborough, Harriet became part of the Ponsonby family, with its extensive Irish and English connexions. Her marriage also served to strengthen the ties between the Bessborough and the Devonshire families. Georgiana's husband, William Cavendish, 5th duke of Devonshire, was Duncannon's first cousin. As individuals the Cavendish men may have seemed dull and monosyllabic, but as a family the Devonshires had political influence and had played a significant part in Court and parliamentary politics since the Glorious Revolution. Furthermore, Devonshire's sister was married to one of the other leading Whig peers of the second half of the eighteenth century, the duke of Portland.[7] Devonshire was ill-suited to be a politician himself, but he lavished money on the Foxite Whig cause, and, as the Foxites' most outstanding political hostess, Georgiana turned the Devonshires' homes into the faction's unofficial headquarters. By family, background, marriage, and circumstance, therefore, Harriet and Georgiana were firmly enmeshed in the political world. Although they did not have electoral interests of their own, their connexions were extensive and their potential for influence was indisputable, stretching from obscure

was the original English spelling and that the modern variant, 'connection', only began to appear in the second half of the eighteenth century. The earlier spelling has been used here to refer to the eighteenth-century socio-political bond. *OED*, iii. 744–7; vii. 1099.

[6] Frances Harris, *A Passion for Government: The Life of Sarah, Duchess of Marlborough* (Oxford, 1991), 350.

[7] For further information on these families see, Georgina Battiscombe, *The Spencers of Althorp* (London, 1984); John Pearson, *Stags and Serpents: The Story of the House of Cavendish and the Dukes of Devonshire* (London, 1983); and *Lady Bessborough and her Family Circle*, ed. Bessborough and A. Aspinall (London, 1940).

country families through the upper echelons of the aristocracy to the prince of Wales himself.

WOMEN IN A MALE POLITY

Despite the amorphousness of eighteenth-century politics and the lack of a firm party structure, the system worked because the politics of influence and interest throve in a climate that was distinguished by personal relationships, complex networks of connexions, and extensive webs of obligation. Its very fluidity provided women with various points of access and opportunities for involvement. Much of the networking, solicitation, manoeuvring, and negotiation of politics—be it about policy or patronage, factional alliances, or election outcomes—took place in social situations that included women.[8] Moreover, a good deal of what could not be done in person was done by letter—and eighteenth-century women could be tireless and effective correspondents.

It was still predominantly a world of family interests, where parliamentary seats and even some places in government were seen as forms of property to be passed down through generations. As women were prevented by custom from voting, holding most patronage appointments, or sitting in the Lords, even if they were peeresses in their own rights, it is hardly surprising that their interest and involvement in politics were chiefly familial and were based in their traditional roles as sister, wife, mother, and widow/matriarch. Conduct-books encouraged young women to dedicate themselves to lives of family duty and the advancement of family interests. A good wife was repeatedly advised to adapt her personal interests to suit those of her husband and his family, and be prepared to manage his fortune, household, and family interests if he was 'neglectful'.[9] For a widow, especially one who was left to preserve an estate and

[8] Kim Reynolds sees the 'interface' between the social and the political as providing aristocratic women with a role that was especially important in defining the context of nineteenth-century political discourse: Reynolds, *Aristocratic Women and Political Society in Victorian Britain.*

[9] Isabella Howard [Countess Dowager of Carlisle], *Thoughts in the Form of Maxims Addressed to Young Ladies on their first Establishment in the World* (London, 1789), 2, 3; Halifax, 'The Lady's New-Year's-Gift: or, Advice to a Daughter' (1750), in *The Complete Works of George Savile, First Marquess of Halifax*, ed. and intro. Walter Raleigh (Oxford, 1912), 7–19, 20; *The Female Ægis; or, The Duties of Women from Childhood to Old Age, and in most Situations of Life, Exemplified* (1798), 3–4; *Letters Addressed to Two Young Married Ladies, on the Most Interesting Subjects*, 2 vols. (London, 1782), i. 73–4.

family interest for a son who was still a minor, this could become an obligation.

Consequently, there was no neat dividing-line between family and politics, and the step from familial duty to political involvement was often small and readily justified. On occasion this resulted in the kind of high-profile electioneering or politicized socializing that overstepped the bounds of acceptable female political involvement and earned the criticism of contemporary critics, moralists, and satirists alike. Unsurprisingly, it has tended to be these highly visible incidents and their conveniently printed reproaches that have captured historians' attention—the best-known being those published during the manufactured kisses-for-votes scandal of the 1784 Westminster election. However, the involvement of most politically active women was less historically conspicuous. On the whole, women's main concerns were with the bread-and-butter of political life: they dealt with local people and concerns, especially if they remained in the country while their menfolk went to parliament; they handled requests for patronage; and they participated in whatever politicized socializing was suited to their status and their family's political position. Canvassing or other forms of public electoral involvement were an occasional addition to these more everyday political activities.

Thus, despite the fact that the most important fiction which underpinned the English polity in the eighteenth century was that it was *male* and that politics was *men's* business,[10] even extensive female political participation could be rationalized as non-threatening to the polity and conveniently subsumed into male politics if it could be interpreted in the light of women's traditional roles and placed in a familial paradigm. As long as women's political activities could be interpreted as supportive of and/or subordinate to men's (preferably to a family member or members), or carried out in the line of duty to family or the family interest, they were largely taken for granted. Even women who were recognized as political figures in their own localities or by the administration in London could be incorporated into the imagined political order as long as their activities could be interpreted according to the familial model. Politicians' correspondences through the second half of the century, even at the very highest levels, attest to women's familial motivations. Thus, Lady Thompson in 1753 approached the lord chancellor, Lord Hardwicke, on behalf of her nephew, wanting him to overturn her nephew's appoint-

[10] Carlisle, *Thoughts*, 68; *Female Ægis*, 8–9.

ment as sheriff of Essex;[11] Lady Archer in 1775 approached Lord Guilford to secure his vote and that of Lord North, then first lord of the Treasury, against an enclosure bill that she believed would be ruinously expensive to her;[12] and Mrs M. A. Adams in 1791 solicited a place for her husband, without his knowledge, from William Pitt the Younger, on the grounds of wanting to forward her husband's career and provide financial stability for her young family.[13] Lady Courtown provided another variation on the theme: she wrote directly to the king to request a British peerage for her husband. Her past experience as a lady-in-waiting to the queen gave her a personal connexion that could be put to familial advantage.[14]

Problems arose whenever women stepped outside this familial framework (or were deemed to have done so). When a woman came to be seen as a political player in her own right, and especially if she proved herself to be a better politician than the men she was competing against, as did Lady Susan Keck in Oxfordshire in 1754 and the duchess of Devonshire in Westminster in 1784, she became a threat to the status quo. Not only did such women challenge one of the fundamental building-blocks of society—the 'natural' balance of power between men and women—but they also called into question the basis upon which the solely male political order was constituted. Women were, after all, barred from full citizenship on the grounds of entrenched gendered beliefs about their sexuality and emotionality, their 'natural' political incompetence—their passivity and dependence, and their allegedly limited intellectual, moral, and physical capabilities.[15]

Such situations were guaranteed to bring out the moralists and critics of the day. Fearful of change, they were vicious in their attacks on women whom they believed had overstepped the invisible line between acceptable and unacceptable political involvement. The most common approach was to label their political activities trivial (thus, not worthy of notice; not truly political) or unnatural and/or corrupt (thus, illegitimate and dishonourable). While lengthy, Thomas Gisborne's biting satire of 1797 is

[11] BL, Add. MS 35,604, fol. 79, Lady Thompson to Hardwicke, Highgate, 5 Feb. 1753.

[12] Bodleian Library (hereafter Bodl.), MS North d.16/13, fol. 73^v, Lady Archer to Guilford, Hale, 14 Nov. 1775.

[13] PRO, 30/8/107, fols. 125–6, M. A. Adams to William Pitt, Lambeth, 26 May 1791; ibid., fol. 129, 13 Apr. 1792.

[14] 'Lady Courtown to George III, n. pl., 14 June 1790', in *The Later Correspondence of George III*, ed. A. Aspinall, 5 vols. (Cambridge, 1962), i., no. 603, 484.

[15] Kent, *Gender and Power in Britain*, 117.

representative of how elite women's involvement in politics, particularly their participation in social politics and patronage in London, could be trivialized and discouraged:

It is among Peeresses and the wives of Members of Parliament, and those whose husbands discharge the executive functions of Government, or are stationed in some of the subordinate departments of office, that we are to look for the persons whom the rage of politics seizes first. At their houses, and at the houses of their near connexions, they are accustomed to hear questions relating to the national welfare canvassed; they witness a miniature resemblance of the Parliamentary debate of the preceding evening; they become personally acquainted with some of the public characters, whom eloquence and talents have elevated into fame. To listen to the censure and to the applause severally bestowed on individuals in the political world, while it excites and nourishes curiosity, pleases and foments the spirit of party. To be addressed in private circles, though it be only on the state of the weather, by him whom Senates have admired, stimulates while it gratifies ambition. By degrees they catch the passions of the other sex, and are transformed into profess'd partizans; and when the change has once taken place, generally exceed their husbands in violence, and bitterness, and a prying spirit. To worm out a political secret, to extract from the highest authority the earliest tidings of a victory, or a defeat, of a projected dismission from office, of an intended pension or grant of nobility, is an object which calls forth the utmost exertions of their adroitness. When they have attained it, the pride of triumph commences. They hasten from dressing-room to dressing-room, from assembly to assembly, spreading the news as they fly along, exaggerating the truth to heighten astonishment, and confounding their rivals with the blaze of superior intelligence. In the mean time their attention is not blind to more substantial acquisitions. They omit neither address nor importunity towards men in power, when there is a hope that the one or the other may affect the distribution of preferment. To obtain a living, an appointment, a step in naval or in military promotion, for a relation or a dependent, affords them the double delight of conferring an obligation on a person whom they are desirous to serve, and of displaying their interest with the rulers of the state . . . In proportion as the example of ladies in the highest circles affords encouragement to vanity or to hope; it is studied and followed by numbers of their female acquaintance, whose situation gives them an opportunity of treading, though at an humble distance, in the same steps. Even women who have no connexion with the political hemisphere are seen to be inspired by the passion communicated from their superiors; imbibe the quintessence of political attachment and antipathy; and by the ardour with which they copy the only part of their model which they have the means of emulating, shew that it is not through want of ambition that they are left behind in the race.[16]

[16] Thomas Gisborne, *An Enquiry into the Duties of the Female Sex* (London, 1797), 321–5.

For Gisborne and others like him, politics was no place for women; indeed, it was a temptation that women should resist. It catered to a quiverfull of traditional female character-flaws: women's love of consequence and eminence, their thirst for admiration, and their overweening ambition and competitiveness. Politics stimulated the very passions that women were supposed to be striving to subdue, and spurred them on to ever greater extremes of folly, pride, envy, or extravagance.[17]

The most effective weapon wielded by critics of women's political involvement was sexual slander. Given the importance of female reputation at the time, they sought to dissuade women who were perceived to be a threat from future political involvement by charging them with immodesty, dubbing their activities unladylike or, even worse, sexualizing their involvement and calling into question their chastity or comparing them to prostitutes. This sexualization was particularly telling as it was a commonplace at the time that women's political influence rested upon a combination of class and sexuality. It also cemented the link between women and corruption. Eighteenth-century understandings of political corruption revolved around notions of secret and undue influence, and women's political influence was, according to this definition, both unaccountable and unchallengeable. The most dangerous political women were those who were young and beautiful and turned their sexual appeal to political ends, thus corrupting the polity yet further:

> Which is the most genuine description of *Secret Influence?* A Peer of the realm advising his Sovereign in great national concerns, and avowing it openly in the great national assembly, or a P—— e [Prince] obliging his tradesmen by the terrors of dismission, and D——sses [Duchesses] employing all the fascinating attractions of female beauty, to cause them to vote contrary to their judgement, and in opposition to what they conceive to be for the public welfare?[18]

This approach was especially noticeable in the more graphic prints. William Dent's, *The Duchess Canvassing for her Favourite Member*, for instance, published two weeks into the poll in Westminster in 1784, presents the duchess of Devonshire as embracing a bovine-looking butcher prior to kissing him and simultaneously lifting his apron to caress what appears to be an erect penis. The sexual message is reinforced

[17] See e.g. *Female Ægis*, 121–2; for a list of 'errors peculiar to women because of their make-up', see ibid. 12–13.

[18] As cited in J. Hartley *et al.*, *History of the Westminster Election, containing Every Material Occurrence, from its Commencement on the First of April, to the Final Close of the Poll, on the 17th of May* (London, 1784), 230.

visually and textually: the duchess's skirt is tucked up with erect fox's tails, the street sign in the corner of the print indicates that the encounter is taking place on 'Cockspur Street', and the duchess is pointedly made to say, 'I'll leave no Stone unturned to serve the Cause'.[19] Then, to add financial corruption to sexual corruption, and to reinforce the commercial element of the transaction, the duchess's female companion stands behind her extending a purse full of coins.

While concerns about sex, politics, and corruption were not new, the removal of women and their influence (especially aristocratic women) came to be seen as essential to reforming the political order and making it more manly and pure from the 1760s onwards.[20] These claims emerged in conjunction with rising anxieties about aristocratic vice and more general concerns about sexual and political corruption. Socially, they translated into a desire for ever tighter controls over female sexuality and a more strictly domestic role for women; politically, they emerged as demands for a more accountable, respectable form of politics.[21] They were given extra emphasis by the conservative response to the French Revolution and the negative perceptions of French women's part therein. It could be argued that they were enshrined in the Reform Act of 1832, which made it illegal for women to vote.[22] However, the nineteenth century did not put paid to women's political involvement: among at least the upper echelons of the political elite, family-based electoral involvement continued, as did women's engagement in patronage, although the nature of patronage itself changed.[23] Similarly, women continued to use the social arena for political ends.[24] Indeed, even in nineteenth-century fiction we find women who would have been readily recognized by their eighteenth-century forebears: Anthony Trollope's mid-nineteenth-century characters of Lady Laura Kennedy, Lady Glencora Palliser, and Madame Max

[19] William Dent, *The Duchess Canvassing for her Favourite Member* (13 Apr. 1784).

[20] For the Wilkite radicals' desire to purify and masculinize the polity, see also Kent, *Gender and Power in Britain*, 118.

[21] Ibid. 120–4.

[22] Vernon, *Politics and the People*, 39.

[23] See e.g. chapters by Sarah Richardson, Kathryn Gleadle, and Matthew Cragoe in Gleadle and Richardson (eds.), *Women in British Politics*; Reynolds, *Aristocratic Women and Political Society*, 129–52. For the later nineteenth century, see Pat Jalland, *Women, Marriage and Politics, 1860–1914* (Oxford, 1986), 189–249. For patronage, see J. M. Bourne, *Patronage and Society in Nineteenth-Century England* (London, 1986), 15, *passim*.

[24] Richardson, '"Well-Neighboured Houses": The Political Networks of Elite Women', in Gleadle and Richardson (eds.), *Women in British Politics*, 56–73; Reynolds, *Aristocratic Women and Political Society*, 153–87; Jalland, *Women, Marriage and Politics*, 189–94.

Goesler, and Oscar Wilde's late nineteenth-century political women, Lady Chiltern and Lady Cheveley, for instance.[25]

WOMEN AND POLITICS

In order to explore women's involvement in political life, it is necessary to begin at the beginning and answer some of the most basic questions about women and eighteenth-century politics. Of course, there is no denying the fact that women's political participation in the formal political arena was ultimately subject to a ceiling imposed by gender. Even then, however, their formal political position remained somewhat ambiguous. The most elevated position in English politics, that of the monarch, could be held by a woman; and, right at the bottom of the political system, women could vote for and hold minor offices at the parish level, a practice that was confirmed in law by a King's Bench ruling on *Olive* v. *Ingram* in 1738/9.[26] Yet gender prevented peeresses *suo jure* from sitting in the House of Lords and women of the electorate from voting in parliamentary elections—and therefore from contributing directly to policy and governance. These constraints were customary, not legal. Women were only legally disenfranchised in England and Wales (though not Scotland) with the Reform Act of 1832, which specified 'Male Person' as a qualification for the franchise. It was not until the Municipal Corporations Act of 1835 that they lost the last of their electoral privileges.[27]

Women may not have been able to vote, but even this needs to be seen in context: in the eighteenth century the overwhelming majority of the population could not vote. In terms of electoral politics between 1754 and 1790, hereditary peers could not vote, and overall, only 17.2 per cent of adult males, or 4 per cent of the total population of England and Wales,

[25] See Anthony Trollope, *Phineas Finn* (London, 1869); *Phineas Redux* (London, 1873); Oscar Wilde, *An Ideal Husband* (London, 1895).

[26] *The Laws Respecting Women, as they regard their Natural Rights, or their Connexions and Conduct*... (London, 1777), 10; *Olive* v. *Ingram*, Hilary term, George II, 7 Mod. 263, *English Reports*, 87 (Edinburgh, 1932), 1230–7; Hilda L. Smith, 'Women as Sextons and Electors: King's Bench and Precedents for Women's Citizenship', in id. (ed.), *Women Writers and the Early Modern British Political Tradition*, 324–42.

[27] *The Nineteenth-Century Constitution: Documents and Commentary*, ed. H. J. Hanham (Cambridge, 1969), 264–5. Interestingly, the Scottish version of the Representation of the People Act, 1832, refers only to 'Person', not 'Male Person'. See also Derek Hirst, *The Representative of the People? Voters and Voting in England Under the Early Stuarts* (Cambridge, 1975), 19; Vernon, *Politics and the People*, 39.

were enfranchised.[28] Elections were not yet common; contested elections even less so; consequently, suffrage was not yet the kind of issue for eighteenth-century women that it would become for women a hundred years later. They did occasionally express a desire for greater political involvement, but these comments were rare and situation-specific, arising from strong feelings about certain political measures or men. The response of Mrs Trevor, one of the dowager duchess of Newcastle's correspondents, to the fierce battle over the publication of parliamentary debates early in 1771 serves as a case in point. She was so frustrated with what she believed were the corrupt and dishonest actions of the North ministry that she was driven to complain: 'I never wished My Self a Man till now had I been a Man I would have Died free.'[29] Lady Polwarth was somewhat less vehement in her comments in 1775, but then they arose in response to a less controversial issue. When the Rockingham Whigs proposed an amendment to the Militia Bill that she approved, even though she usually supported the administration, as did her families of birth and marriage, she wrote to her mother: 'I suppose a similar one [amendment], will be propos'd in the House of Lords; & if I were in Parliament I should certainly vote for it. I confess I think *we* are letting slip through; the only real Increase of Power that the Crown has offer'd at for many Years.'[30]

Most of the time women seem to have been satisfied with their political status. Certainly their letters indicate that they did not feel alienated. Instead, their correspondence is often peppered with comments indicating their identification with their family interests, a faction, or a particular cause or measure. Phrases such as 'our friends',[31] 'our enimys',[32] 'our Interest',[33] 'our party',[34] 'our Strength',[35] and '*our* Side of

28 O'Gorman, *Voters, Patrons, and Parties*, 179.

29 BL, Add. MS 33,082, fol. 102^{v}, Mrs G. Trevor to dowager duchess of Newcastle, Cirencester, 28 Mar. 1771.

30 Befordshire Record Office, Bedford, Wrest Park (Lucas Papers) (hereafter WP), L30/9/60/69, fol. 2, Lady Polwarth to Marchioness Grey, Wrest Park, 21 Nov. 1775.

31 'Lady Palmerston to Sir Gilbert Elliot, Sheen, 19 June 1790', in *Life and Letters of Sir Gilbert Elliot First Earl of Minto from 1751 to 1806*, ed. Nina, Lady Minto, 3 vols. (London, 1874), i. 363.

32 Exeter College Archives, Bray Papers (hereafter BP), L.IV.7.C/27, Lady Susan Keck to Revd Thomas Bray, 29 Mar. [1754].

33 BL, Add. MS 32,989, fol. 105, Lady Lade to Newcastle, Hanover Square, 9 Mar. 1768.

34 BL, Add. MS 51,426, fol. 129, Lady Kildare to Henry Fox, Kildare House [3 Nov. 1757].

35 Bodl. MS. North, D.9, fol. 19, Sarah Osborn to Guilford, Dublin Castle, 30 Jan. 1762.

the question'[36] abound. Neither was this kind of allegiance limited solely to women who were at the heart of the political world. It is not entirely surprising to find Joseph Yorke writing to his sister, Lady Anson, the wife of the first lord of the Admiralty, for confirmation of naval manoeuvres, because, 'I have so much faith in what you write, especially in Your own Department, that I don't believe any body else'.[37] Similarly, given the centrality of the duchess of Devonshire to the Whig party, it is understandable that she could refer to the leading Foxite Whigs as 'all my tribe'.[38] Women whose connexions were political but were themselves well away from the centre of political power could also be strongly politicized. Agneta Yorke, who as a widow tended to spend most of her time out of London, and was politically as well as personally at odds with her brother-in-law, the 2nd Lord Hardwicke, remained passionately political: 'Surely we of the opposition have but too much [r]eason for our fears and dispondency; and what the Ministry will say to the Houses when they meet, I cannot imagine.'[39]

Despite often being frustrated with politics and politicians, women seldom sought wider political powers for themselves. In part, this was because the structural conditions necessary for the emergence of feminism were not present in the eighteenth century. Most importantly, the critical mass of politicized, disaffected, middle-class women who were to catalyse the nineteenth-century suffrage movement did not yet exist. Instead, it was assumed that the female members of the political elite already had the necessary opportunities and connexions to achieve their political ends: they did not need to vote.[40] Lower down the social scale, of course, it mattered even less, as the vast majority of men were equally disenfranchised. Moreover, all women were included in the fiction of virtual representation. Just as the law deemed that the husband and wife were one person, and that person the husband, so Members of Parliament were assumed to represent not only the disenfranchised lower sorts of both sexes, but also, on a personal level, the women in their own families.

36 'Lady Stafford to Granville Leveson Gower, Whitehall, 29 Jan. [1790?]', in *Lord Granville Leveson Gower (First Earl Granville) Private Correspondence 1781 to 1821*, ed. Castalia, Lady Granville, 2 vols. (London, 1916), i. 20.

37 BL, Add. MS 35,388, fol. 64^{v}, Joseph Yorke to Lady Anson, The Hague, 4 Apr. 1755.

38 Devonshire Papers, Chatsworth House, 5th Duke's Group (hereafter Chatsworth MSS), 608B, duchess of Devonshire to Lady Spencer [20?] Mar. 1784.

39 BL, Add. MS 35,386, fol. 261d: Agneta Yorke to Philip Yorke, Tittenhanger, 15 Sept. [1779].

40 This argument was tenacious and was used consistently by anti-suffragists over the next century: Brian Harrison, *Separate Spheres: The Opposition to Women's Suffrage in Britain* (London, 1978).

When the question of women's suffrage did arise in the eighteenth century, it was almost always raised by men, and usually as part of an ongoing debate over the nature of political representation. As Eliga Gould has pointed out, conservative writers in England during the American Revolution, including John Wesley, Josiah Tucker, and William Paley, all noted the inconsistencies of a strategy for political reform that sought to replace virtual representation with enfranchisement for men—but only men—regardless of property or status.[41] If political representation was a natural right, William Paley argued, such a system would actually be less representative than the one currently in place:

> If this right be natural, no doubt it must be equal, and the right, we may add, of one sex as well as of the other. Whereas every plan of representation, that we have heard of, begins by excluding the votes of women: thus cutting off, at a single stroke, one half of the public from a right which is asserted to be inherent in all, a right too, as some represent it, not only universal, but unalienable and indefeasible.[42]

More radical writers contended that the current system was itself inherently discriminatory. In early 1788 'Calidore' reminded readers of the *Gentleman's Magazine* that there was 'undoubtedly an inconsistency in allowing women to hold the supreme executive power, without any subordinate; to be queens, but not constables; and in denying them the least part of the legislative'.[43] Moreover, he (if indeed the writer was a 'he') maintained that if women's 'natural' sensibility had been allowed political expression, 'the inherent mercy of the female mind' would have been instrumental in preventing the development of some abuses, particularly the most inhumane aspects of the penal system:

> To confound misfortune with fraud; to allow debtors to pine and rot in loathsome gaols, because they are destitute of property; to croud wretches together to breed infectious distempers, and to harden each other in iniquity; to render those desperate whose only fault at worst is indiscretion; and to suffer those tragic scenes . . . to shock our eyes . . . even without the sanction of any positive law, are absurdities truly *masculine*, and which posterity, if meliorated by female sensibility, will view with the same horror as the burning of men for creeds and witchcraft.[44]

[41] Eliga H. Gould, 'American Independence and the Cosmopolitan Foundations of Britain's First Counter-Revolution', *Past & Present*, 153 (Feb. 1997), 135.

[42] William Paley, *The Principles of Moral and Political Philosophy*, 2nd edn., bk. 6 (1785), 489.

[43] *Gentleman's Magazine*, 18, pt. 1 (Feb. 1788), 101.

[44] Ibid.

That women curbed men's 'natural roughness' and acted as a civilizing influence was already a well-accepted belief by the middle of the eighteenth century. The author of *Female Rights Vindicated* had used it to argue for greater political involvement for women in the 1750s, and it would still be used to justify women's suffrage over a hundred years later. It is, however, a mark of the distance that arguments for women's suffrage still had to travel that in 1788 'Calidore' still had to cloak his fundamental claim—that women had 'a *natural* and *equal* right to participate in the management of public affairs'—with satire. If women were allowed to sit in parliament, not only would the 'sprightly sallies of a fair burgess' prevent the House from somnolence, but they would also create a 'younger, an handsomer, and a politer Parliament', less inclined to the 'indecent excesses' of contemporary debate. Moreover, female '*electresses*' would never have let certain unpopular measures pass into law, such as the tax on female servants.[45] His clinching argument was both serious and nationalistic—an argument well known to radicals and proponents of parliamentary reform. He argued that the current political status of Englishwomen was historically 'un-English', and that granting them parliamentary representation would only be freeing them from the effects of the Norman Yoke and reviving their ancient rights:

> it was part of our constitution to admit women to a share of the legislation: let them assert, if they dare, that history makes it evident, that women, when permitted to govern, have been found unequal to the task: and let them deny, if they are hardy enough, that many advantages would accrue by reviving this equitable usage of our ancestors, by which they tempered the stern mind of man with feminine delicacy, and by that means *seasoned justice with mercy*.[46]

ELECTORAL PRIVILEGE AND PRACTICE

Given the idiosyncrasies of regional customs and the diversity of borough practices, it is impossible to conclude categorically that eighteenth-century women *never* voted, but it does seem probable that seventeenth-century precedents which disallowed female votes made it less likely. As Derek Hirst has pointed out, the political position of seventeenth-century women—propertied widows, in particular—was unclear. His research has revealed instances of seventeenth-century women who believed that they had the right to vote, of candidates who tried to poll

[45] Ibid. (Mar., 1788), 222.

[46] Ibid. 223.

them, and of election officials who were ready to accept their votes. Hirst saw these occurrences as symptomatic of the 'primitive state of electoral law and custom' at the time, and implied that women were eventually excluded from voting because it became politically dishonourable for men to depend upon women for electoral success.[47] The fact that his conclusions were drawn from disputed elections, and sometimes from last-minute protests at that, raises the possibility that some female voting may well have taken place without comment in less fraught situations. Still, two trends in the second half of the eighteenth century would have decreased the chance of women voting: growing concerns about female propriety among the middling sort, and the gradual refinement and codification of electoral practices which was slowly removing ambiguities and creating a more compact electorate.

Indeed, it is arguable that women benefited politically from these ambiguities: both from the variety of franchises, and the ways in which they were implemented. At the county level up until 1832, the franchise was set by the Forty Shilling Freeholder Act of 1430.[48] While this ensured that the 40*s*. franchise was uniform, its 'effective devaluation' in the later eighteenth century not only raised concerns among some elements of the political elite about the worthiness of freeholders as a group, but also, as Langford has demonstrated, resulted in various anomalies in its implementation.[49] Complications could arise in determining what forms of property besides land constituted the equivalent of a land-tax qualification and thereby conferred the right to vote.[50] To compound matters, there was no official register of voters or easy way to prove voting qualifications.[51] In practice, therefore, the county franchise varied even for men. Women who met the property criteria were technically qualified to vote.

In the main, the various franchises which operated prior to reform reflected the general belief that the right to vote should be the preserve of the propertied. This in itself did not exclude women, as they were able to own and inherit property. At a time when the vote was seen as a form of personal or familial property, and when, in some instances, it was the direct result of property-ownership, women formed a small but

[47] Hirst, *Representative of the People?*, 18–19.

[48] Edward and Annie G. Porritt, *The Unreformed House of Commons: Parliamentary Representation before 1832*, 2 vols. (London, 1909), i. 20.

[49] Langford, *Public Life and the Propertied Englishman*, 271.

[50] I would like to thank Stephen Taylor for sharing his knowledge of county politics and for his insights into the interplay between electoral law and local practice in the counties.

[51] Porritt and Porritt, *Unreformed House of Commons*, i. 25–8.

undeniable political constituency. Tax records suggest that eighteenth-century women owned approximately 10 per cent of English property.[52] Studies of household formation, although less inclined to tackle the question of property-ownership itself, supply additional if oblique support by suggesting that 9–14 per cent of eighteenth-century English households were headed by women.[53] Moreover, women also benefited from fertility and mortality factors which remained in their favour from 1660 up to at least 1760 (gradually decreasing thereafter), which increased the probability of their becoming heiresses and/or propertied widows.[54] Widows and single women had the most latitude in controlling their political interests.

Married women who brought property and political interests into their marriages retained widely varying amounts of influence. While control over a woman's property passed to her husband upon marriage, formal recognition of her ownership survived politically, with husbands being formally acknowledged as voting 'in right of' their wives.[55] At the very least, married women were instrumental in establishing links between families and shifting the boundaries of local political power. At best they remained political figures in their localities, with their husbands and other politicians publicly recognizing their right to have a say in political decisions. Thus, when George Oxenden was seeking support for Sir Brook Bridges's candidacy in Kent in 1763, he wrote to Lord Guilford to ask for his support and that of Lady Guilford.[56] Lady Guilford, who

[52] Langford, *Polite and Commercial People*, 110.

[53] Historians have called attention to the societal implications of an 'extremely significant' minority of female-headed households across eighteenth century Europe. Olwen Hufton's work on widows and spinsters in eighteenth-century Britain and France supports the conclusions reached in Richard Wall's demographic study of female-headed households in England. Maura Palazzi's work on urban Italy has corroborated these findings by demonstrating that 14% of households in Bologna and 16% in Milan were headed by women in the late eighteenth century. She has also suggested that a similar proportion of female-headed households can be found in other European cities at the same time. See Olwen Hufton, 'Women Without Men: Widows and Spinsters in Britain and France in the Eighteenth Century', *Jl. Family Hist.*, 9 (1984), 355–76; Richard Wall, 'Women Alone in English Society', *Annales de démographie historique*, 141 (1981); and Maura Palazzi, 'Female Solitude and Patrilineage: Unmarried Women and Widows in the Eighteenth and Nineteenth Centuries', *Jl. Family Hist.*, 15 (1990), 443–59.

[54] The most comprehensive demographic examination of English society remains E. A. Wrigley and R. S. Schofield. *The Population History of England, 1541–1871: A Reconstruction* (Cambridge, 1989).

[55] T. B. Oldfield, *The Representative History of Great Britain and Ireland: Being a History of the House of Commons and the Counties, Cities, and Boroughs of the United Kingdom from the Earliest Period* 6 vols. (London, 1816), iii. 570.

[56] Bodl., MS North D.9, fol. 141^{r-v}, Sir George Oxenden to Guilford, n. pl., 16 Oct. 1763.

had married Guilford as his third wife, was the widow of Lord Rockingham and had maintained control over her own property after the marriage. It is impossible to determine to what extent her stated political stance was her own and not Guilford's, but, given the tenor of the time, there would have been little need for Oxenden to ask specifically for her political support, or for a conservative man like Guilford to have made a show of reporting her opinions as well as his own, if the entire exercise had been an elaborate fiction: 'Lady Guilford . . . has been so good as to say she should not like to give her interest in Kent to any person who shall declare himself to disapprove the one [the Peace], or be an enemy to the [o]ther [Lord Halifax].'[57]

In close election contests, patrons, candidates, or agents might even expedite marriages among freeholders in order to make men into voters. Two days before the opening of the poll in the Oxfordshire election of 1754 Lady Susan Keck sent just such a couple to Oxford. As she pointedly reminded the Revd Thomas Bray, he was to ensure that the marriage took place and defray whatever costs it incurred: 'I send you my Bridegroom and Bride I desire you will instantly take out a Licence and Marry them forthwith; you are to pay everything; This makes the Bridegroom a Voter therefore never see my face if they are not married.'[58]

Sir Roger Newdigate's notes on the extended parliamentary deliberations that followed the eventual double return in this contest suggest that the husband's 'right' to vote on his wife's property could be lost if the marriage broke down and the couple separated. Ed Spragg's vote, for instance, was objected to because he had voted on an estate that had been and remained the property of his estranged wife. She had been a widow at the time of their marriage, and the estate was not only assessed in her name, but she also received the rent and profits from it. Moreover, she had turned him out and taken out a bond against him.[59] As the vote was hers, by customary practice it was up to her to decide who would serve as her proxy and vote in her stead: this could be a more distant relative, a neighbour, a friend, or a tenant. Newdigate's notes also suggest that a number of other familial voting combinations also existed at the time. He listed sons voting on their mothers' estates, a son-in-law voting on his

[57] Bodl., MS North D.9, fol. 143^{r-v}, Guilford to Sir George Oxenden, Chesterton, 22 Oct. [1763].

[58] BP, L.IV.7.C/32: Lady Susan Keck to Revd Thomas Bray [recd. 15 Apr. 1754].

[59] Warwickshire County Record Office (hereafter WCRO), CR136 B.2524 B/8, 11 January 1755 VII, no. 320, Parliamentary notes on the Oxfordshire Election of 1754 by Sir Roger Newdigate.

wife's mother's estate, a father voting on his daughter's estate and a nephew voting on his aunt's estate. While these votes were open to challenge, such voting practices were neither innovative nor unique to Oxfordshire. In a less heated election they might well have been accepted without question.[60]

Variations in franchise and local practice were yet more marked at borough level. The 203 boroughs differed widely in size, the characters of their electorates, and the extent of their independence. Some valued their liberty highly, while others were under tight proprietorial or patronal control. Similarly, qualifications for enfranchisement were neither uniform nor clearly gendered—some approached universal male suffrage whereas others had strictly limited electorates, or electorates that were determined solely by property-ownership. Moreover, even among those boroughs which ostensibly had the same franchises, unresolved local disputes about the legal constitution of the electorate or peculiarities in local electoral custom could result in differences in practice which could facilitate or prevent female involvement.

In the eleven potwalloper or householder boroughs (twelve after 1768), the franchise was in all inhabitant householders; only those receiving poor relief or alms were excluded from voting. In the ninety-two freeman boroughs, the right to vote lay in the freemen. It was frequently complicated both by differing local criteria for the creation of freemen and by local variations in the franchise (the vote being in resident freemen only, in freemen paying scot and lot, or in assorted combinations of freemen, freeholders, householders, and burgage-holders, for example). Similar local stipulations could also qualify the electorate in the thirty-seven scot-and-lot boroughs, where the franchise was ostensibly determined by all those inhabitant householders who paid the poor rate. In the twenty-nine burgage boroughs the franchise appeared equally simple: the right to vote was in the ownership of burgages—ancient pieces of property which were customarily assumed to have had the franchise. In actuality, lack of documentation and reliance upon custom and local memory, especially in boroughs where elections were infrequent, meant that what constituted a burgage and what residence requirements (if any) needed to be met in order to qualify to vote upon one were open to debate. The six freeholder boroughs were an offshoot of burgage boroughs, in that the franchise rested in the ownership of property—freeholds, in this case.

60 Ibid., B.2524–9.

As the parliamentary historians Edward and Annie Porritt pointed out at the turn of the twentieth century, while women's involvement in some boroughs, particularly in householder and scot-and-lot boroughs, might be limited to influence and acting as 'the channels between the bribers and the bribed', they did have 'places recognized by custom and by the determination of election committees' in freeman and burgage boroughs (treating the freeholder and burgage boroughs as one). These, they concluded, amounted to official electoral privileges, with those in burgage boroughs being the most direct and valuable.[61]

Considering that the freeman, burgage, and freeholder boroughs as a group comprised 125 boroughs, or 62 per cent of all boroughs, this is in itself a striking conclusion. Not only does it suggest that the potential for recognized female electoral involvement was much higher than historians have usually assumed, but it also raises questions of definition and raises some further questions about the nature of the extra-parliamentary and parliamentary nations in the eighteenth century. If women were operating politically from boroughs in which they had recognized electoral privileges, was their political involvement public or private, direct or indirect, formal or informal? Were women formally or informally involved in politics if they met all of the necessary requirements to vote (except gender)? If they could assign their votes to men of their choice? And if, as a result, they were canvassed in the same way as their male counterparts? The shortcomings of such labels become increasingly apparent as interconnexions become clearer on the ground.

In the ninety-two freeman boroughs the extent of women's electoral privileges and the ways in which they were administered varied somewhat according to local practice, but they followed a general pattern. Women who were the daughters of freemen (or, occasionally, their widows) had the right to make their husbands freemen and voters. In boroughs like Bristol, Grimsby, Ludlow, Maldon, and Wells this process was relatively straightforward; in others it was more complicated. In Hertford the privilege was limited to the eldest daughters of freemen who had no sons, whereas in Dover men retained their freeman status only in their wives' lifetimes.[62] While there is no easy way to measure the effect that this privilege had on levels of women's politicization and activity, it gave them local status and an undeniable platform for wielding influence over

[61] Porritt and Porritt, *Unreformed House of Commons*, i. 39–41.

[62] J. Cowley, *Orders and Resolutions of the House of Commons on Controverted Elections and Returns*, 2nd edn. (London, 1736), 23, 107–8, 159–60; Porritt and Porritt, *Unreformed House of Commons*, i. 78.

their husbands' votes (and perhaps over their husbands). It also had additional personal benefit, as it was an acknowledged, if intangible, supplement to a woman's value in marriage, a fact that was not lost on contemporaries:

I am a Countryman of small Fortune, who accidentally fell in Love with a Freeman's Daughter of your City. The Agreeableness of her person, and the Recommendation of her being a good Manager in her Father's Family, together with the Certainty of my being distinguished by the honourable Title of a *Free-Burgess* of BRISTOL, soon prevailed on my Love, my Industry, and Ambition to determine my Choice.[63]

The contest which took place in Bristol in 1754 saw this electoral privilege take centre-stage. In an attempt to control the outcome of the election, a by-law was passed that attempted to limit the number of non-resident voters. Only the daughters of Bristol freemen who remained inhabitants of the city were to be allowed to make their husbands voters. This resulted in the above election address, aimed directly at 'the Free-women of Bristol'.[64] The address drew upon the traditional political rhetoric of urban independence and placed the women firmly within its remit, reminding them that if they allowed the historical privileges of their 'Sisters' to be illegitimately removed by this product of 'Arbitrary Power', they were accepting the first step in a campaign to remove all female privileges—and thus emasculate the borough by prohibiting their honest and independent freemen husbands from voting.[65] The married 'Free-women' of Bristol were therefore given two charges: to use their interest with their husbands in order to ensure that non-resident women's privileges were restored; and to ensure that their husbands voted for the candidate who represented liberty and honourable independence:

Will your Husbands', Ladies, who addressed the H[onoura]ble House of C[ommo]ns against the *General Naturalization* and *Jew Bills*, suffer this Partiality of Behaviour? And will *you* not rouse them out of their Lethargy? Remember your *Sisters* in the *Country*. Make it a Point for them, the Free-Electors of BRISTOL, to

63 'The Dundry Petition: Or the Countryman's Humble Address to the Free-Women of the City of Bristol', in *The Bristol Contest: Being a Collection of all the Papers Published by Both Parties, on the Election, 1754* (Bristol [1754?]), 54–6. My thanks to Madge Dresser for bringing this to my attention.

64 Ibid.

65 This appeal to urban independence and traditional rights was both part of the rhetoric of urban borough politics and the reality of their expression: Rosemary Sweet, 'Freemen and Independence in English Borough Politics, *c.*1770–1830', *Past & Present*, 161 (Nov. 1998), 84–115.

redress their Wrongs ... Make *This, one Condition* of your Husbands Votes and Interest;[66]

Although it was rare to seek female political support so openly in print, this address reflects two persistent eighteenth-century beliefs about women and politics: that women with political interests retained political influence even after marriage; and that women's influence over men's votes was real. Agents and candidates ignored it at their peril. Lord Townshend, recording the support of voters in Tamworth in 1765, knew only too well that it was necessary to have their womenfolk on side. His annotated poll-book notes that the carpenter, Thomas Healey had promised to be neutral, but 'Wife governs, against us'. Similarly, John Hunter, the mason, 'wish'd us well, but his Wife govern'd—but was not then Engaged'. Even an initial pledge of support could have little meaning if a man's wife was adamantly opposed. Despite two previous canvasses of one unspecified voter, and an initial pledge of support, it was not until the third canvass that Townshend felt secure of the vote, commenting laconically, 'his Wife in better Humour'.[67]

Few candidates appear to have taken women's privileges in freeman boroughs as far as John Huske did in Maldon in 1763. Described by a historian of the borough as 'a tough, unscrupulous adventurer from New Hampshire', Huske was a friend of John Wilkes, who helped him canvass the borough. He conducted a ruthless campaign against the sitting member, Bamber Gascoyne, and won the seat through the support of the Corporation and the creation of freemen, despite having the government interest against him.[68] His reported method of canvassing the freemen was effective, but unconventional. As the *Chelmsford Chronicle* reminded readers when eulogizing him years later, he had focused on the women who had the right to make freemen, rather than on their husbands:

The novelty of this mode raised the curiosity of the ladies, in a company of which, he was one day asked, Why he never solicited the men, as was most customary on such occasions: To which he replied, I have ever, ladies, entertained the highest opinion of your sex, especially in the power and influence you have over us; but, in this respect, I think myself highly justified in asking you, ladies, rather than

[66] 'Dundry Petition', 55.

[67] BL, Add. MS 41,152, fols. 17–18, 25^{v}–6. For the nineteenth century, see Matthew Cragoe, '"Jenny Rules the Roost"'.

[68] John Raymond Smith, 'The Borough of Maldon, 1688–1768', (M.Phil. thesis, University of Leicester, 1981), 150. Even Namier and Brooke described it as a 'brazen and skilful campaign': Sir Lewis Namier and John Brooke, *The House of Commons, 1754-1790*, 3 vols. (London, 1964), i. 280.

your husbands, as it is to you they owe such a privilege, and it is but justice that you should have some influence in the disposal of it.

This anecdote, and the accompanying sexual innuendo that Huske wanted to be the women's 'little member',[69] may be apocryphal, but they would not be out of keeping, either with Huske's character or with other appeals to women's influence. By stripping away the male façade of eighteenth-century politics and bluntly and openly acknowledging the reality of female influence, he would have been playing up to beliefs that were widely held.

Women's electoral privilege in freeman boroughs may have sanctioned the use of female influence, but it was in burgage and freeholder boroughs that women were most visibly and directly involved in electoral politics.[70] There, the right to vote was attached to the ownership of the relevant form of property; consequently, women who inherited or purchased burgages in the twenty-nine English burgage boroughs, or freeholds in the six freeholder boroughs, technically possessed the same right to vote as men.[71] This involved two groups of women directly in local electoral politics: the women of the electorate, who might own or purchase individual burgages; and the women of the political elite, who might own or purchase enough of the burgages to have a significant or controlling interest in the borough.[72]

It was among property-owning women like these that the tension between gender and politics in the eighteenth century was most obvious. While these women's right to vote was recognized, they were still prevented by custom from exercising it. Instead, a practice grew up whereby they were allowed to appoint a man to vote in their stead. Among the latter, women seem to have operated in conjunction with their agents in the same way as men: they acquired boroughs if and when available, and ensured that appropriately minded tenants were installed, complete with any necessary paperwork, in time to meet the borough's residence requirements, if any, prior to an election.

Evidence survives of candidates trying to use the votes of widowed burgage-holders to their advantage in seventeenth-century Knaresborough and Richmond. It was only after the disqualification of widows' votes in Richmond in 1678 that the practice of the 'discreet transfer' of

[69] *Chelmsford Chronicle*, 10 Dec. 1773.

[70] Porritt and Porritt, *Unreformed House of Commons*, i. 41.

[71] Brooke, *House of Commons*, 44; Namier and Brooke, *House of Commons*, i. 31.

[72] The Porritts present a similar breakdown: Porritt and Porritt, *Unreformed House of Commons*, i. 41.

women's right to vote emerged in burgage boroughs.[73] By the second half of the eighteenth century it had become customary. Evidence of men voting on their wives' and mothers' burgages can be found as early as 1699 in Pontefract and Corfe Castle, and the practice continued well into the nineteenth century.[74] Writing in 1816, for example, T. B. Oldfield named the Hon. Charles Anderson Pelham as having the most political influence in the borough of Yarmouth, Isle of Wight, where he held twelve burgages in the right of his wife.[75] The amount of influence that wives retained over the way their husbands voted undoubtedly ranged widely, but marriage certainly curtailed their ability to exercise their electoral privilege to its full extent. Like women in freeman boroughs, they were unable to withdraw the right to vote from their husbands and assign it elsewhere as long as their marriages lasted. This was exactly where unmarried women and widows who were burgage-holders benefited. They were not only expected to appoint men to vote for them—family members, distant relations, tenants, or neighbours—as long as they met local requirements, but they could also change their assignations if they wished.[76]

Limitations imposed by surviving sources and a recognition of constantly changing patterns of landownership in the eighteenth century make attempts at quantifying women's overall burgage- and freehold-ownership difficult, if not impossible. While certainly a minority interest, women could be a significant minority, as revealed by a report from Lord Irwin for the borough of Horsham from 1764. Horsham was a burgage borough with a notoriously complicated variety of votes. At mid-century it had eighty-three votes, nineteen of which were in women.[77] The trend towards elite consolidation of power over these sorts of boroughs in the late eighteenth and early nineteenth centuries undoubtedly had an impact on small owners, male and female alike, but whether this affected women more than men is difficult to determine.

[73] Hirst, *Representative of the People?*, 18–19.

[74] Ibid.

[75] Oldfield, *Representative History of Great Britain and Ireland*, iii. 570.

[76] Porritt and Porritt, *Unreformed House of Commons*, i. 40.

[77] William Albery, *A Parliamentary History of the Ancient Borough of Horsham, 1295–1885, with Some Account of Every Contested Election*, intro. Hillaire Belloc (London, 1927), 93–7. An undated, seemingly eighteenth-century account of the burgages in the borough lists 85 burgages, with the steward who did the survey contending to Lord Irwin: 'I Cannot See where I Could mis any. I hope your Lordship will understand my works I have don the Best a Can with out any help I think any body that knows the town may find the voats.' Horsham Museum, Hills (Irwin) Papers (hereafter HM), MS 798.3, A Survey of Horsham Burgages, [n. d.: mid-1700s?].

Although the right to assign a vote was doubtless a formality for those women who were uninterested in politics or whose boroughs were uncontested, it could be turned to real advantage by women who saw the economic potential of the situation or were politically inclined or particularly astute. The ability to choose voters whose views tallied with their own provided women with a means of expressing their own political opinions, albeit at one remove. The ownership of property, especially burgages, also gave women status in the community. With the approach of elections, if there was even the hint of a contest, this political status could be turned to financial advantage. Like their male counterparts, these women were courted by politicians hoping to make votes, and, depending upon the virulence of the contest, they might command significant sums for their political support. As early as 1747, for instance, the deliberations on the controverted Westbury election reveal a widowed burgage-holder, a Mrs Cockle, being given the vast sum of £100, 'as a consideration' for her 'Assignment'.[78] Not all transactions were so blatant or so lucrative, though. As in other boroughs, 'considerations' might come in the form of debts being paid or written off, favours being proffered, or promises given. And, of course, for those women and men who were willing to trade future political interest for immediate financial gain, there was always the possibility of the ultimate 'consideration' and selling up to the highest bidder. Given that a widow like Mary Sumersett could earn £1,750 for the sale of her '3 messuages, Garden &c' in Horsham in 1788, possibly setting up herself and her family for life, it is perhaps more surprising to note that there always were some women even in hotly contested elections who refused to sell.[79]

At the level of the political elite burgage-ownership was one way of establishing or securing a family's political interest. Some burgages were passed down through women, others were managed by women for underage sons, while yet others were owned and contested by women. In the second half of the century Lady Andover nominated to one of the seats at Castle Rising; when her daughter married, the burgages (and the political interest) formed part of her portion.[80] Similarly, as Sarah Richardson has revealed, Elizabeth Lawrence, the early nineteenth-century proprietor of the borough of Ripon, inherited her controlling political interest from female relatives. Lawrence operated in the same way as a male borough

[78] *Commons Journals*, 25 (1745–50), 577.

[79] HM, MS 3, no. 26, An Account or Rental of the Burgages purchased by His Grace the Duke of Norfolk in the Borough of Horsham, 25 Dec. 1788.

[80] Oldfield, *Representative History of Great Britain and Ireland*, iv. 271.

patron, showing her commitment to the borough through regular displays of charity and benevolence, frequent treating, and continuous involvement in civic politics.[81]

Splitting burgages between co-heirs could be a risky business if the co-heirs (and/or their spouses) were politically ambitious. A rivalry between different branches of a family could upset the balance of power in a borough and set off tremendous and enduring political contests. The conflict over the borough of Downton is a case in point. It began with Lord Feversham's death in 1763, when his estate was divided between Feversham's two daughters and a distant cousin, Thomas Duncombe. Duncombe acquired the settled estate, but one of the daughters, Anne, Lady Radnor, acquired a portion of the burgages at Downton. When an injunction trying to force the sale of these burgages was overturned in Chancery, the struggle for control of the borough began in earnest. It remained an issue even after Duncombe's death, as he had bequeathed his estate in Downton to his daughter, who was married to Robert Shafto. Shafto contested the borough against the other 'family' interest in 1780. As late as 1790 control of the borough was still unsettled.[82]

Of course proprietorship was no guarantee of uninterrupted electoral peace. Women did fight, sometimes fiercely, to maintain or increase interest in burgage boroughs, be it for themselves or their families. In East Grinstead, at the beginning of the nineteenth century, the widowed duchess of Dorset's control extended to ownership of twenty-nine of the thirty-six burgages and the appointment of the borough's returning officer (the bailiff) at her annual court. Still, she had to contend with a challenge from a radical candidate in 1802.[83] Widows with political aspirations for their under-age sons seem to have been especially keen to preserve their sons' inheritance. Even Sir James Lowther, the boroughmonger of the century, owed some of his political interest to his mother's efforts during his minority. The young Sir James had been left sixty-seven burgages in the borough of Appleby, where a established compromise operated to share the representation with the Thanets, the other leading political family. When the Thanets broke the compromise

[81] Ibid. 308. Sarah Richardson, 'The Role of Women in Electoral Politics in Yorkshire During the Eighteen-Thirties', *Northern Hist.*, 32 (1996).

[82] Alexander Luders, *Reports of the Proceedings in Committees of the House of Commons upon Controverted Elections (1785–1790)*, 3 vols. (London, 1825), i. 114; Namier and Brooke, *House of Commons*, i. 32–3.

[83] Oldfield, *Representative History of Great Britain and Ireland*, v. 59; O'Gorman, *Voters, Patrons and Party*, 305.

by having a candidate of their own elected mayor out of turn in 1751, Katherine Lowther acted quickly in order to prevent them from gaining control of the borough. Between 1751 and the contested election of 1754 she purchased another twenty-seven burgages. Although she did not capture the Thanets' seat (it may not have been her intent), she did succeed in holding her own family's seat. She also put enough pressure on the Thanets that they renewed the political compromise.[84]

While women's electoral privileges granted them a certain amount of official recognition and they were often active in various aspects of electioneering,[85] they were also involved formally and informally in the legal processes which were used to challenge and resolve electoral outcomes. Women can be found taking an active part in both post-election scrutinies which took place in the localities, and the deliberations in parliament which followed petitions about controverted elections. It is here that their part in the making of electoral history is most clearly recorded. The women of the political elite can be found securing witnesses (some of whom were women) and forwarding useful, perhaps even crucial, evidence to the men conducting the proceedings. When controverted elections interested them personally or aroused their passions, they could also be found following the parliamentary proceedings eagerly, either by attending the proceedings in the House or by having MPs who were their friends or relations keep them posted by notes from the floor of the House. Indeed, by the 1760s it had become positively fashionable for women from the opposing sides of a cause to attend the deliberations in the Commons and cheer their sides on (metaphorically, if not actually).[86] Lady Mary Coke, for instance, records attending the Commons at least eight times over the Cumberland election in 1768, usually as part of a group of eight or nine women.[87]

And it is important to recognize that women did attend both the Commons and the Lords. According to Grantley Berkeley, who spoke

[84] Brian Bonsall, *Sir James Lowther and Cumberland and Westmorland Elections, 1754–1775* (Manchester, 1960), v. 15–35. Katherine Lowther's involvement in Appleby was not unique; she was also involved in a battle of burgage purchases with Lord Egremont in the borough of Cockermouth in 1756: ibid. 37–42.

[85] See my '"That epidemical Madness": Women and Electoral Politics in the late Eighteenth Century', in Hannah Barker and Elaine Chalus (eds.), *Gender in Eighteenth-Century England: Roles, Representations and Responsibilities* (Harlow, 1997), 151–78.

[86] Lady Caroline Fox deplored the new fashion: see 'Lady Caroline Fox to Lady Emily Kildare, 10 Dec. [1768]', in *Correspondence of Emily, Duchess of Leinster (1731–1814)*, ed. Brian Fitzgerald, 3 vols. (Dublin, 1949–57), i. 556.

[87] See her journal entries for 28 Nov.–15 Dec. 1768: *The Letters and Journals of Lady Mary Coke*, 4 vols. (privately printed, Edinburgh, 1889–96), ii. 416–28.

in favour of the admission of female spectators to the House of Commons in 1835, women had been present in both the gallery and on the floor of the Commons from 1716.[88] They had been in the lobby garnering support for private legislation as early as 1698.[89] That women could have and wield political interest and influence, or, more generally, that political affairs concerned women, was recognized by male politicians, although never uniformly welcomed. There were always some voices advocating the inclusion of women in the political process (even if only as spectators), just as there were always others who wished to exclude them entirely.

The famous exclusion of women from the Strangers' Gallery of the Commons that took place on 2 February 1778 was due more to circumstance and the reactions of the women present at the time than to a clear-cut victory to the exclusionists. Nor, it appears, might women's exclusion have been as thorough and long-lasting as has often been suggested. It took place as the result of a situation that began on 29 January 1778, when Colonel Henry Luttrell moved that the standing order for excluding strangers from the Commons be strictly enforced. Luttrell's annoyance needs to be placed within the context of contemporary concerns about the publication of parliamentary debates. It stemmed from a newspaper report which had (falsely, he maintained) accused him of unparliamentary and disorderly behaviour. His motion reopened debate on the propriety of opening the galleries to the public at all, something upon which MPs were firmly divided. This was not a new topic for Luttrell; he had been defeated in April of the preceding year on a similar motion.[90] The debate that followed saw well-rehearsed arguments aired by both sides. What was new, especially given the situation that was to arise only days later, was that women's presence in the Commons was included in the discussion. Richard Rigby, who would have preferred having the Commons completely closed to the public at all times,[91] argued that exclusion orders should apply equally to both sexes because women, too, could be political: 'not only against gentlemen but ladies; as the latter as well as the

[88] Porritt and Porritt, *Unreformed House of Commons*, i. 580.

[89] Ibid.

[90] *Parliamentary History*, 19, cols. 207–9. He had, on 30 April 1777, proposed a motion to limit the attendance of strangers by establishing a system that would have allowed MPs to introduce one guest each (registered in advance) only after four p.m. daily. The motion was defeated 16 to 83.

[91] Rigby had argued in 1777 that the admittance of strangers was an unnecessary inconvenience for MPs. It subjected them to being pushed about and insulted, placed them at the mercy of unscrupulous newspaper reporters, and made them targets for pickpockets. Ibid., col. 210.

former, might dabble in party disputes, and have their predilections and preferences for one party before another.' An independent country gentleman, Charles Turner, responded that the Commons should be accessible to all: 'if one door was shut to exclude all the men another should be opened to let in all the women.' It was Edmund Burke, however, who provided the most reasoned contribution and persuaded Luttrell to withdraw his motion. In addition to reiterating the conventional justification for open galleries—that they gave constituents the means to follow the progress of concerns that interested them, and that they provided young men, prospective MPs themselves, with a political education—he reminded his audience that it should not underestimate the importance of parliamentary attendance for women: 'as the source of information and amusement to the ladies, it was a matter of very serious concern, and ought not to be done away and sported with at pleasure.'[92]

The crunch came on 2 February, when a 'vast multitude' had gathered in the lobby and around the Commons seeking entry to the gallery for the debate on the American war. Having been refused admission by the doorkeeper, the crowd forced an entry. Colonel Luttrell immediately called for the exclusion of strangers. The men were then asked to leave, but the ladies were not, 'through complaisance', although it was reported that there were 'near 60' of them, including the duchess of Devonshire and the speaker's wife, Lady Norton. This brought complaints from Governor Johnstone, who argued that if the purpose of the clearance was to safeguard the secrets of the nation, then the women should also be excluded as 'he did not think them more capable of keeping secrets than the men'. They were subsequently asked to leave.[93] They appear to have refused, for it reportedly took two hours of 'riot and confusion' before they were eventually removed. When the galleries reopened to the public some days later, women were not readmitted, although no official steps had been taken to ban them. This practice was allegedly maintained by both the subsequent speakers, thus effectively barring women from the Commons.[94]

When this incident is referred to by historians, it is usually cited as evidence of hardening attitudes towards women and politics: as yet another step in the exclusion of women from political life.[95] Seldom are

[92] Ibid., cols. 648–50. Rigby and Burke's statements are repeated in the report of the day's proceedings in the *London Chronicle*, 31 Jan. 1778.

[93] *London Chronicle*, 3 Feb. 1778.

[94] Ibid., 5 Feb. 1778; Porritt and Porritt, *Unreformed House of Commons*, i. 580–1.

[95] See e.g. Gervas Huxley, *Lady Elizabeth and the Grosvenors: Life in a Whig Family, 1822–1839* (London, 1965), 82.

the details of the event itself, its historical context, or its aftermath examined. Indeed, when they are, they present a multilayered version of events. Not only was the question of women's attendance fresh in MPs minds at the time, as it had been raised only days before in the previous debate, but it needs to be seen as part of a larger, fundamental debate about parliamentary accessibility and the nature of governance.[96] Moreover, the immediate historical context needs to be acknowledged, as it undoubtedly played a part in provoking the incident. This was, after all, a period of heightened domestic and international tension. The American War was not going at all well, and debate in the Commons was becoming increasingly vitriolic, as the opposition levelled charges of gross misconduct and misappropriation of funds at Lord North's administration. Concerns about the intentions of the French were also high; within a month France would openly join the Americans and declare war on the English. Thus, news and rumour were eagerly sought and circulated, and all things military, be it men or measures, took on increased importance. The women of the political elite had responded to the situation with an outburst of patriotism. They had accompanied their husbands to camp, lived in tents, socialized with officers, and adopted and reviewed regiments. Female versions of regimental uniforms had become the latest fashion statement. Given this, and the fact that this political situation coincided with the height of the social season when London was at its fullest, it is not surprising that large numbers of women were drawn to the Commons or that little was needed to ignite such a mixture. Finally, it is questionable as to how thoroughly the ban was implemented, at least immediately: the German tourist Carl Philipp Moritz records that there were 'not unfrequently' ladies in the Strangers' Gallery when he attended the Commons in 1782,[97] and Lady Elizabeth Foster records the duchess of Gordon asking her and the duchess of Devonshire to make up a group of four women, two ministerial and two opposition, and seek admittance to the Commons during the debates on the Regency in January 1789.[98] The duchess of Gordon's sister, Lady Wallace, was if anything both more politically radical and more personally daring than her sister: she took every precaution against being ejected when she attended the Commons

[96] Annoyance at women's actions should not be over-emphasized, as Lord Effingham, in a similar debate on the admission of strangers into the Lords on 9 March 1778, argued that women should be allowed into the gallery on the days that the king came to the Lords: *Parliamentary History*, 20, col. 474.

[97] Carl Philipp Moritz, *Travels Through Several Parts of England in 1782*, intro. P. E. Matheson (London, 1924), 59.

[98] BL, 41,579, fols. 21^{v}–22, Lady Elizabeth Foster, Journal, 8 Jan. 1789.

in March 1788, and succeeded, as Sir James Bland Burges remarked to his wife: 'There was a curious phenomenon in our house last night—no less than Lady Wallace sitting in the front row of the gallery, apparelled in a brown scratch wig, coat, waistcoat, breeches, and boots. She came in at a little past eleven yesterday morning, and sat out the whole debate, till she was forced to retire with the others on the division at seven this morning.'[99] Indeed, women's continued interest in attending the Commons may well have been behind the compromise which did eventually remove them entirely from the Strangers' Gallery. At some point after 1779 a seating and viewing area was created specifically for women in the small, hot, uncomfortable room above the ventilator in the middle of the roof of St Stephen's Chapel.[100] Although the space was limited and no more than eight women could be seated at once (they had to obtain a ticket through an MP in order to attend), it did give them a view of the proceedings and remarkably good sound. While this placed new limits on women's parliamentary attendance and, what is perhaps more important, separated them physically and psychologically from the mass of (male) spectators, they were not hermetically sealed in the Ladies Gallery. They could not go down to the floor of the Commons to mix with the MPs, but the MPs could and did come to them.[101]

Women's exclusion from the Commons should not, therefore, be read simplistically as an outright attack on female political privilege. It was, after all, the response to a particular and complicated situation; furthermore, enough importance was attached to women's attendance that alternative arrangements were made to accommodate them. What is more, women continued to attend the Lords, occasionally on their own—thus, George Canning's encounter with the duchess of Gordon, whom he finds under the throne listening avidly to a debate in 1794[102]—but also in such numbers on the benches of the Lords for occasions like

[99] Sir James Bland Burges, *Selections from the Letters and Correspondence of Sir James Bland Burges, Bart.*, ed. James Hutton, (London, 1885), 96–7. The second Mrs Sheridan reputedly did the same thing in June 1804 in order to hear her husband's speech on the Additional Forces Bill: see Walter Sichel, *Sheridan ... including a manuscript diary by Georgiana Duchess of Devonshire*, 2 vols. (London, 1909), i. 135, n. 4; *Life and Letters of Sir Gilbert Elliot*, ed. Minto, iii. 348.

[100] *Life and Letter of Sir Gilbert Elliot*, iii., 581.

[101] See Lady Shelley's vivid description of her first trip to the Commons in 1818, courtesy of Lord Brougham: 'April 19', in *The Diary of Frances Lady Shelley, 1818–1873*, ed. Richard Edgcumbe, 2 vols.(London, 1913), ii. 7–10.

[102] '21 January 1794', in *The Letter Journal of George Canning, 1793–1795*, ed. Peter Jupp, Camden Society, 4th ser., 41 (London, 1991), 47.

the King's Speech that, as Lord Ailesbury complained in June 1787, it could be difficult for the Lords themselves to find seats.[103]

While there was a group of men in parliament who believed that women had no place whatsoever in political life—just as there was in society at large—both were, if anything, increasingly on the defensive in the second half of the eighteenth century. Not only were women a part of eighteenth-century political life in the localities, courtesy of the nature of eighteenth-century politics and through their more narrowly defined electoral privileges, but it is also arguable that they were becoming more politically aware and involved in national politics as well—albeit in support of particular politicians or specific issues. Both Charles James Fox and William Pitt the Younger had their supporters among women, as did, surprisingly enough, John Wilkes. Moreover, women took sides on political issues raised by Wilkes or the Regency Crisis, for instance, and from the 1760s onwards along humanitarian and commercial lines over slavery. The exclusionists' victory was never complete.

[103] '1 June 1787', in 'Diary of Thomas, Earl of Ailesbury, 2 vols, i', in *HMC 43*, Fifteenth Report, Appendix, pt. vii (London, 1898), 285.

2

Women's Political Roles

As Lord Rockingham's sister, Lady Charlotte Wentworth could hardly have been closer to the centre of the political world. She was politically astute, and her advice on men and measures was usually well thought out and valued by both Rockingham and Lady Rockingham. She did not, however, always agree with her brother over politics. At times these disagreements overflowed into Rockingham's correspondence to his wife. In one such case, Lady Rockingham was prompted to remark that she had at first attributed Rockingham's 'tart stile as if you [was] in a Tiff at something . . . to the quantity & quality of the Oranges you had eat'. As soon as she realized that it was 'a political puzzle', courtesy of Lady Charlotte, she wisely resolved to stay out of it. Since Lady Charlotte had put him into the puzzle, she could also put him out of it again.[1]

Lady Charlotte's worth as a political adviser was far too high for Rockingham to be annoyed with her for long. In April 1777 Rockingham, who was a notoriously reluctant parliamentary speaker, was preparing to lead the Rockingham Whigs back into parliament after the previous November's secession in order to oppose the bill for payment of the King's Civil List debts.[2] He planned to speak in the debate, and it was his sister who pointed him in the direction of the text for the speech that he gave on 16 April 1777:[3]

If you should attend on Wednesday & mean to speak, I have a notion you wd: find a passage in Blackstone which you wd not dislike to introduce—it is in his 1st Vol: speaking of the excellency of the Constitution as settled at the Revolution—he says something to this purpose 'That notwithstanding all the precautions taken the Crown is every day gaining an accession of power; which is the more dangerous as it is less observed—'[.] The Stern Voice of *Prerogative* indeed is

[1] Sheffield City Libraries, Wentworth Woodhouse Muniments (hereafter WWM), R168-102, Lady Rockingham to Rockingham [1777].

[2] Geoffrey Holmes and Daniel Szechi, *The Age of Oligarchy: Pre-Industrial Britain, 1722–1783* (London, 1993), 247.

[3] I would like to thank Stephen Farrell for drawing my attention to this.

not longer heard but the milder power of Influence pervades the whole—I spoil it, but it is worth your looking at—.[4]

While few women, even from politically active families, appear to have rivalled Lady Charlotte's command of Blackstone, few were political ciphers either. The policy of informed silence on politics advocated by people like Lady Spencer may have been followed by those women who acted solely as men's political confidantes, but for those who filled the progressively more demanding and important roles of adviser, agent, and partner this was not the case.[5] Some were diffident; others took a high moral tone and spoke out with confidence; however, even the most active and involved of political women—those who acted as partners in familial or factional political undertakings—could be accepted politically as long as they did not threaten to outstrip men politically and become political actors in their own rights.

Examining women's political involvement in terms of these roles is admittedly artificial, not only because the women themselves would not have categorized it in this way, but also because these roles are not mutually exclusive or even sharply divided. They are a rough categorization of women's participation, but as such they provide a useful framework for thinking about varying degrees of female political participation and a sense of the shape and nature of women's political involvement. Indeed, each subsequent role builds on those beneath it. Some women may have filled only one role, but the sources indicate that they were more likely to combine several roles or to shift back and forth among them depending upon the people they were dealing with and/or the circumstances they were in. Pyramid-like, women's political participation rises from a base of women whose political involvement was the most limited, passive, and private—those women who acted as confidantes—up to an apex of highly political women whose participation was the most extensive, active, and public—those women who served as partners. The higher up the pyramid, the more political knowledge, social adroitness, and self-confidence the women had. In this schema, the division between advisers and agents is perhaps the most significant, as it often marked a shift from women's indirect to direct participation, from acting as counsellors to becoming themselves involved. Agents and, especially, partners

[4] See WWM, R169-129, Lady Charlotte Wentworth to Lord Rockingham, 14 Apr. 1777. See also S. M. Farrell, 'Wentworth, Mary Watson-marchioness of Rockingham (*bap.* 1735, *d.* 1804)', *Oxford Dictionary of National Biography* (Oxford, 2004): http://www.oxforddnb.com/view/article/68349.

[5] Pat Jalland has suggested that Victorian and Edwardian political wives had three very general political roles: mistresses of households and political hostesses, confidantes, and election campaign workers. Jalland, *Women, Marriage and Politics*, 189–220.

tended to be the most independent, direct, and openly political of all women; unsurprisingly, given this, their relationships with political men reflected the greatest trust and intimacy.

CONFIDANTE

Contemporary letters suggest that most women who were closely connected to active politicians acted as confidantes. While some men believed that politicians should not take their wives into their confidence, because they believed women were unable to keep secrets[6] or for other reasons, this had more to do with individual men's beliefs about women's nature than it did specifically about politics. Men who were on good terms with women and respected their intelligence and insights regularly shared political opinions, news, and speculations with select female friends and family members. Letters from MPs in London to wives who remained in the country are most likely to reflect this. They frequently combine personal accounts of parliamentary occurrences with concerns about the implications of rumoured changes or developments, as well as assorted snippets of social and political gossip. Sir Gilbert Elliot even went so far in 1756, during the crisis caused by the duke of Newcastle's resignation, as to arrange a code with his wife. This allowed him to keep her abreast of the ongoing political manoeuvrings, particularly the composition of the new administration and his chance of gaining office.[7] He knew that he had an ally in her, and she, in turn, was interested enough in his political news and aware enough of contemporary political nuances to annotate some of his letters with her own political commentaries.[8] Not long after Sir Gilbert became a lord of the Admiralty in November 1756 she joined him in London, where her friends included such highly political women as Lady Dalkeith and Mrs George Grenville. Given these factors, it seems unlikely that her political involvement was limited to the role of confidante.

As recipients of confidences, women were given insights into the workings of the political world but required to do little in return. Few

[6] 'Marchmont to Alexander Hume Campbell, n. pl., 21 Oct. 1755', in *HMC Polwarth*, ed. Revd Henry Paton (London, 1961), v. 306.

[7] Hon. George F. S. Elliot, *The Border Elliots and the Family of Minto* (Edinburgh, 1897), 352.

[8] See Lady Elliot Murray's memo on the back of Sir Gilbert's letter to her recounting his first important speech in the Commons in 1751: ibid. 341.

women, however, appear to have acted solely as confidantes. Not only does the tendency to proffer advice in return seem to have been nearly insuperable, but also the reality of women's participation in social politics would have made it very difficult to remain passive or even consistently politically aloof. Thus, 'confidante' shades into 'adviser'. Despite this, it is worth retaining the separation between the two, if only because of the one-sidedness of some correspondences.

As confidantes, women's connexion to the political world and their participation in it was dependent upon men and primarily directed by male concerns. The apparent asymmetry could, however, mask women's ability to encourage and elicit confidences. For a young wife, becoming a confidante may have been a way of showing her husband that she shared his interests, as well as a way of winning his trust. For a woman who was interested in politics, it could also serve as the first step in developing a more important political role. This certainly seems to have been the case among some young couples. In July 1767 the 3rd duchess of Portland, who had been married less than a year, encouraged her husband to keep her informed of political developments that involved him: 'I shall not be a little impatient to know how these affairs are settled, for tho' I am not a great Politician yet I have not a desire of remaining quite Ignorant.'[9] Nearly twenty years later another young wife of only a few months, Lavinia, Lady Spencer, elaborated upon the same theme: 'I long for the account you will send me (or have sent) of the debate in the House of C: last Tuesday—I never was a politician before but I confess I feel myself at present a little agitated & anxious about public affairs—At so important a juncture if one did not—all pretentions to any more feeling than there is in a block of Marble must be laid aside—'.[10] Whereas the duchess went on to maintain her political interest and become increasingly involved in politics over time, Lady Spencer soon reverted to type. In making her dislike of politics apparent and making a point of not participating in politicized socializing or electioneering, she used conventional attitudes against female political involvement as a way to express her disapproval (and, seemingly, her jealousy) of her glamorous and politically active sisters-in-law.

Success as a confidante seems to have depended upon two factors: a modicum of interest (real or simulated) on the part of the women; and varying but potentially significant amounts of trust from their male

[9] Univ. of Nottingham, Portland Papers, PwG 37, duchess of Portland to Portland, 11 July 1767.

[10] BL, MS Coll. Althorp, G. 289, Lavinia, Lady Spencer to Spencer, 29 Nov. 1781.

counterparts. Women who were confidantes were essentially listeners: they provided the men in their lives with shoulders to cry on, or ears to bend. They acted as outlets for the men's needs. This was especially true in the literary catharsis of correspondence, which made confidences doubly safe through the intimacy of the relationship and the distancing (both real and psychological) of the medium. Men who had female confidantes expected them to be interested, sympathetic, and understanding. Contemporary correspondence indicates that they were.

In 1766, during her first lengthy separation from the duke, the duchess of Portland's correspondence with him was made up largely of love letters and political confidences. Portland, who was in London, was facing the most difficult decision of his political career. Despite being encouraged by his friends and male relations not to resign with the rest of the first Rockingham administration, he was agonizing over his decision. He depended upon the duchess, whose pregnancy kept her in the country, to provide him with a sympathetic hearing and give him a safe outlet for the frustrations and fears that he could not express in London:

> I have ten thousand things to say to you ... I never was so perplexed about any part I was to take; I never as yet acted contrary to my own inclinations without being convinced, & now dread that I am upon the brink of that precipice & that I shall be exposed to reproach & censure: which I shall almost be inclined to think I deserve. They all tell me, nay even Lord John, that I ought not to quit. So that in short I am quietly patiently tamely to see my friends abused & insulted, am to appear as if I separated myself from them, & for what reason, why, upon account of some few enthusiastick ravenous followers of a man [William Pitt] of whom I never had or can have any opinion, & upon a pretence of preserving the Whig Cause. Thus much I could not help troubling you with.[11]

Political confidences were part of ongoing relationships based on mutual trust and respect. Sons who had been raised by political mothers—especially those whose mothers had been widowed while the young men were still minors—often took their mother's role as confidante for granted. In December 1783, when the Fox–North coalition was forced to resign, George, Lord Spencer, was quick to pass this information on to his mother. He reported the rumours he had heard about an upcoming dissolution of parliament and expanded at length on his ideas for the elections. This type of political sharing was a regular and valued part of their relationship: 'I thought you would like to hear my ideas on most of these subjects & for the rest I am really so accustomed to talk to you

[11] PwF 10,527, Portland to duchess of Portland, 29 July 1766.

unreservedly upon them, that it is quite grown into a natural habit to me.'[12]

Sisters and daughters also acted as confidantes, especially if their brothers were unmarried or their fathers widowed. Men who were caught up in the middle of political developments, as J. H. Addington was in 1782, tended to expect that their sisters would be interested: 'I assure you I had fix'd upon to-day as a day of special Indulgence to you for almost this Week past, that I might give you an Account of the Event of our Election.—"Nevill for ever"—is in every Mouth; they will soon teach the babbling Gossip of the Air to cry out "Nevill." You can have no Idea of the universal Exultation which his Success has occasion'd . . . '[13] For some men, this presumption may have been derived from a mistaken belief that anything that interested them had to be fascinating to the women in their lives, but in the majority of cases their expectations appear to have been valid and the interest was reciprocated.

Fathers who confided in their unmarried daughters may have also had an additional purpose in mind. Lord Granville (Carteret) regularly sent his 15-year-old daughter his opinions on the political developments of the day as part of her education. Whether or not he was consciously grooming her for marriage into a political family is debatable, but she subsequently married Lord Shelburne, and her involvement in political life as an adult implies that her early lessons were well learned.[14]

In general, then, women acted as confidantes for a mixture of personal, political, and social reasons. For some women participation had less to do with an interest in politics than with a personal and emotional investment in the men themselves (although initial lack of interest, especially early in a marriage, seems to have often been short-lived). Involvement could also stem from a strong sense of duty, which might suggest that women internalized at least a certain amount of contemporary prescriptive literature's emphasis on adopting and sharing men's—especially husbands'—interests. In addition, for members of the political elite the social and political arenas were closely intertwined, and being a confidante meant vicarious involvement in a world dominated by colourful characters (heroes or villains, according to the onlooker's ideological bent), competing story-lines, gossip, and scandal. However, confidantes not only followed politics in the way that they read novels, they were also

[12] BL, MS Coll. Althorp, F. 14, Spencer to Lady Spencer, Brookes's [19 Dec. 1783].

[13] Gloucester Record Office, Bragge Bathurst Papers, D421 C8, J. H. Addington to Charlotte Addington, Feb. 1782.

[14] Bodl., MS. Lyell, Empt. 35. See e.g. his letters to her in 1759–60.

able to put the knowledge that they gained to social ends. It could be a weapon in the carefully orchestrated battles of social one-upsmanship that occurred among eighteenth-century women. In the larger political arena, knowledge could also give the possessor status by suggesting her proximity to the 'fountainhead' of power, thus intimating potential political influence. Inside information was especially useful during elections or periods of political tension or crisis, when current political developments came to dominate conversation, social gatherings, and society itself.

ADVISER

Advisers extended the range of involvement manifested by confidantes. Correspondence suggests that most of the women who acted as confidantes also acted as advisers. All advisers performed similar tasks. Primarily, they provided political men with a discreet (or not-so-discreet) combination of support, criticism, direction, and strategy, either through correspondence or in person. They also acted as sources of political information by gathering news from the public arena, screening it, and then relaying it. A similar combination of public and private informed their actions as intermediaries among various family connexions or political groups. The primary difference in terms of advisers' political involvement was one of degree, both in terms of politicization and the extent to which they attempted to influence or direct political decisions. The most detailed and specific advice usually came from intelligent, assertive women who tended to form an elite within the political elite. Contemporaries recognized that advisers could possess significant—if, in hindsight, unquantifiable—political influence. In spite of this, even the most active advisers' involvement still took place through men, and their influence was dependent upon their abilities to persuade or manipulate.

While much of what advisers did entailed reacting to men's confidences and providing them with feedback, they were more autonomous than confidantes, supplying men who were absent from their localities, the capital, or the country with 'News'. Among the political elite, 'News' was often first political, then social. Women who were at the centre of political action by being in London during the parliamentary season or in the country during periods of intense local politics were in the best position to act as advisors. Then, even politically uninterested women like Hester, Lady Newdigate, would reluctantly became involved.

When she was in London during the early 1780s and her country-gentleman-cum-MP husband, Sir Roger, was not, her letters to him regularly included electoral as well as parliamentary information.[15] She advised him of political developments as she heard of them, not because she was personally interested, but because it was expected of her.

Women who were interested in political developments made far more exciting correspondents. Lady Temple, who was in London during the commotion over the Massacre of the Pelhamite Innocents, was representative in the breathless way that she wove politics and gossip together:

> there have been this day several coming in & turning out 3 have kiss'd hands & the places are all to be fill'd in a moment it is believed & given out that even to a hund[red]. cousin of those that have not behaved well are to march out of the most trifling places, it [will be] well if your two window peepers won't be call'd upon. Mr. Ellis is secretary at War. Mr. Rigby treasurer of Ireland Lord Charles Spencer is out ranger of Windsor forest with something else that comes to 12 hundred pd. pr. Annum my Lord & Lady Vere mighty uppish some sarcasms thrown at my head & Mr. Brand came in for a snub pretty often because he did not entirely agree with them my Lord Vere thinks it perfectly right that they shou'd take away the smallest place & make a thorough cleaning for it was always done in all ministrys Lord George & Mr. Brand deny'd it & said it was impolitick & foolish to go so far as those trifling places it wou'd raise them a flame for nothing, Lord Vere said the Duke of Newcastle did it, they both answer'd it was no such thing.[16]

Whether advisers were based in London or in the country, their prerequisites were the same: they had to be sensitive to their correspondents' political interests, able to gauge the depth of political feeling in the locality, and aware of the latest political developments. Sometimes women's participation emerged in response to men's spoken or unspoken demands; at other times it was part of an ongoing, transactional process—part of the flow of the relationship itself—which operated at differing levels of mutual understanding and interest.

The amount to which advisers annotated the news they sent varied greatly. As levels of women's politicization and interest rose, so did their personal involvement. Advisers who were highly aware and keenly interested frequently provided their correspondents with significantly more analysis and direction than information. When Lady Betty Waldegrave sent her brother Lord Gower news of the duke of Newcastle's negoti-

[15] Warwick Record Office, Newdigate Papers, CR136B.2705–2858.
[16] BL, Add. MS 57,806, fols. 119–20, Lady Temple to Temple, 17 Dec. [1762].

ations with William Pitt and Henry Fox in 1756, she summed up the situation, then went on to discuss Newcastle's probable reaction:

> then what is to be done next? rather than give up, wch. is the advice of his sincerest friends: his Grace will attempt to govern without either; & in spight of all their oratory will flatter himself with numbers, there are people & not fools neither; they think he may succeed in this, if he has resolution enough to stand it. I do not think this new scheme can last, above one Sessions; perhaps that, it may.[17]

Highly politicized advisers tended both to give their own opinions and try to influence men's decisions. This was particularly noticeable among women who united political families through marriage, or political groups. As an intermediary between two prominent political leaders, her brother Gower, and her brother-in-law the duke of Bedford, Lady Betty Waldegrave helped to maintain their political connexions by relaying political information between them. At one point during the aforementioned negotiations she wrote to tell Gower that he should expect to receive a summons to town from Bedford. Her frustration with his political indolence overcame her, though, and she ended by giving him a piece of her mind: 'I shall not enter into any particulars, with regard to politicks: but only say in general that I believe never were such times, nor such rogues; as now, you will be surprised & from your own good heart, will I dare say, be a Dydemus. but for Godsake come up & hear & judge for yr-self, for I will not say one word more upon these subjects.'[18] Lady Betty's annoyance was symptomatic of the fundamental limitations placed on women by their position as intermediary. It presented them with the unenviable task of facilitating understandings and negotiating compromises, but chiefly by means of persuasion or manipulation. Final decision-making power remained firmly under male control.

Where Lady Betty used a variety of tactics to try and motivate her brother, Lady Emily Kildare depended predominantly upon manipulation when advising her husband. Her ability to manoeuvre her way around the pompous and mule-headed Lord Kildare was remarkable. By judiciously demanding the benefit of Kildare's 'superior' judgement in insignificant matters, she freed herself to speak her mind on political affairs. By the age of 23 (in 1755) Lady Emily had already settled on the method of combining political analysis with advice and flattery that was

[17] PRO, 30/29/1/17/965, Lady Betty Waldegrave to Gower [1756].
[18] PRO, 30/29/1/17/967, Lady Betty Waldegrave to Gower [1756].

to become her hallmark. Her comments about Irish political affairs are revealing:

I am glad to hear you say *our affairs look well*. I hope you mean by that the heads of our party are likely to be reasonable, which is all you can judge of as yet, and what I own I had my doubts about. Don't let them work you up to expect too many concessions from these people. Nobody cou'd be more inclined to peaceable measures than you were, and I hope you will continue so; tho' rather than be dirty or do any thing that had the appearance of being bought off I wou'd renounce all expectations and oppose as violently as ever. My dear Jemmy has always used me to talk to him upon this subject and tell my mind freely, so I hope he don't think I have said too much.[19]

She was careful to couch what she said in such a way as to cushion Kildare's ego, but her advice was definite—and she clearly expected her views to be taken seriously.

As the sister of the duke of Richmond and the sister-in-law of Henry Fox, Lady Emily's family background provided her with a set of connexions and an understanding of politics that spanned the social and political worlds in both Ireland and England. She had two ambitions and she used her role as adviser to advance both: her long-term goal was to obtain a dukedom for Kildare—and he was created duke of Leinster in 1766;[20] her short-term goal was to acquire for him some lucrative place and the possibilities of 'future emoluments' to help support their rapidly expanding family and allow them to proceed with their 'schemes for improvements'.[21] When Kildare became disillusioned with politics in 1759 and considered resigning a post worth £1,500 per annum, thus threatening their future prospects, her advice dropped its subordinate posturing:

Indeed, my dear Lord K., I am more of that opinion than ever; because I hear all your enemies here triumph so much in it, and are so much delighted at the thoughts of you giving up so good a thing as this in a huff. If 'tis done when you receive this you will hate me for telling you this, but I will run the risk of that in

[19] Lady Kildare to Kildare, 12 May [1755], in *Correspondence of Emily, Duchess of Leinster*, ed Fitzgerald, i. 14. As a woman who played all of the political roles with consummate skill, it is worth noting that Lady Emily's political involvement took place in spite of almost constant pregnancies. Married at 15, she bore no fewer than seventeen children in twenty-six years; nevertheless, maternity seems to have been less appealing to her than politics, for her ever-expanding family played a decidedly secondary role in her correspondence.

[20] Lady Kildare to Lord Kildare, 2 June [1757], ibid., i. 40.

[21] Lady Kildare to Lord Kildare, 22 May [1759], ibid., i. 92; Lady Kildare to Lord Kildare, ibid., 23 [Dec. 1762], i. 161–4.

the hopes that if you are inclined to keep the employment it may strengthen you in any such intention.[22]

Political mothers, or women who were filling a mother's place, also acted as advisers. Familiar as they were with giving personal and moral guidance, the step to political guidance was relatively small, especially for widows who had been involved in maintaining the family political interest while their sons were minors. Political mothers seem to have been particularly concerned to provide sons at university or on the Grand Tour with the political information and direction necessary to make wise political judgements upon reaching their majorities. Lady Elizabeth Pembroke maintained just such a steady correspondence with her son Lord Herbert while he was away on the continent. Not only did she discuss current political developments with him, such as the court martial of Admiral Keppel and the ministry's handling of the American War, but she also gave him subtle political guidance, either through her analysis of political situations or by expressing her own political opinions and commenting on the political actions of others. For instance, as a strong believer in morally guided political independence she felt that politicians were correct in occasionally opposing the administration, but she drew the line at a determined opposition. When her husband moved into open opposition in 1780 after the loss of his Lord-Lieutenancy, her advice was only just veiled:

I hope & believe he will go on very properly in his Political line, he seems to see that this is his first appearance in that way, & that it is of consequence; I wish him to oppose what he dissaproves with coolness, firmness, & *avoid all* pitifull, frothy abuse, by which means he will raise the dignity of his character, & make himself of more consequence. I assure you, you was much mistaken in thinking me Ministerial, I am quite the contrary, but my head is not yet enough turn'd by *Party* not to see reason now & then, that's all.[23]

Later the same year she dropped the veil entirely when she drew on her own knowledge of Court politics to give Herbert explicit directions about how to forward his application for a position in the prince of Wales's household:

to be sure you must not attend the Address, whatever may happen afterwards, as the Queen at least is so good & the K. too as to be really I believe taking *your affair* into consideration, & trying to twist it about so as not to seem to partial in the eyes

[22] Lady Kildare to Lord Kildare, 22 May [1759], ibid., i. 92.

[23] Lady Pembroke to Herbert, 23 Feb. [1780], in *Henry, Elizabeth and George, 1734–80*, ed. Herbert (London, 1939), 416.

of others; I do not think we are likely to succeed, but they are at least civil in not taking the heart to say no at once, as was certainly natural in our situation.[24]

Similarly, the widowed Agneta Yorke did her best to protect the political interest of her stepson Philip (later 3rd earl of Hardwicke) while he was a minor. She took pains over his political education and was determined that he should understand the importance of social politics. After having given an election dinner in his name (in the lead-up to the 1780 election), she was quick to make a political lesson out of the event:

The feast which was given in your name at Hamels did a great deal more good than I expected, Mr Wolfe wrote me word that it had a great share in the success of the Day; above four hundred People partook of the Crums which fell from your Table eight Hogsheads of Ale were emptied, and I rejoice they were made so good a use of, for you will find the benifit of such a conduct when you are of age nothing obtains popularity sooner than a free and generous use of the goods of fortune, & as you come after an old gentleman who lived in that style of Hospitality People will see that his fortune is well bestowed.[25]

Her uncomfortable relationship with the rest of the Hardwicke family seems to have prompted her to be especially clear in her political advice. After a difference of political opinion with Hardwicke, who was supporting the administration, she encouraged Philip to base his future political conduct around honourable independence:

indeed Philip I did not think I should have lived to have seen such an alteration in the Political principles of your Family—It is true they have laid themselves under obligations to the crown & therefore I suppose think themselves bound to support the measures it adopts, whether right or wrong—. What a blessing is independancy! and who would forfeit it that has enough to live on comfortably. you my dear Yorke may enjoy that blessing, & I hope will never forfeit the freedom your large Fortune will give you.[26]

Like many other political mothers, she ostensibly retreated from involvement once Philip came of age: 'my important Part is entirely over.—Yet tho I am no longer the watchful Guardian, I shall ever be the anxious Friend.'[27] Not surprisingly, she continued to provide him with advice whenever she felt he was in danger of making a political misstep.[28]

[24] Lady Pembroke to Lord Herbert, 24 Oct. [1780], in *Pembroke Papers (1780–1794)*, ed. Herbert (London, 1950), 54.

[25] BL, Add. MSS 35,386, fol. 60^{v}, Agneta Yorke to Philip Yorke, 6 Mar. [1780?].

[26] Ibid., fol. 68^{v}, Agneta Yorke to Philip Yorke, 5 Dec. [1780?].

[27] Ibid., fols. 256–7, Agneta Yorke to Philip Yorke, 5 Sept. 1779.

[28] Ibid., fols. 281^{v}–2, Agneta Yorke to Philip Yorke, 28 Apr. [1780].

Lady Denbigh, who had taken a motherly interest in Edward Miller Mundy after he was orphaned in 1767, was decidedly less restrained in her political advice when he came of age in 1771. Her animosity towards electoral politics speaks strongly of disillusionment stemming from previous involvement—she had, after all, reputedly secured men to head mobs in Sir George's Vandeput's favour during the 1749 Westminster election, one of the most violent contests of the first half of the century.[29] According to Lady Denbigh, Mundy should stay away from electoral politics, as electioneering was 'a Branch of Expence almost as dangerous as Gaming & perhaps more immoral from the Perjury, Drunkenness, & other Vices which usually attend it':

> The Honor which a Seat so obtain'd can confer is certainly not worth the Purchase. The Man who has no farther aim in hurting his Fortune than to be a Member of Parliament is a Fool. He who means to repair it again by selling his Vote—is a Knave; and considering the little Dependance to be plac'd on Ministerial Promises & Fluctuations which for several Years past have attended Ministerial Power, probably will find himself in the End a Fool also . . . [30]

While mothers and matriarchs had the benefit of age and experience in giving political advice, a well-placed, intelligent, and politically aware sister could also fill the role of adviser admirably. Sir Joseph Yorke's correspondence with his sister Elizabeth, Lady Anson, echoes with his thanks for her 'inimitable letters' that 'contain so clear an account of our Confusion, that I have as compleat an Idea of it as if I was within the Circle myself.'[31] As a diplomatist stationed at the Hague, Sir Joseph depended upon 'my dear Emissary Westminster'[32] to provide him with parliamentary news, details of the political schemes and intrigues of the moment, and analyses of the state of the English political world. Lady Anson could do this with ease. As the daughter of the lord chancellor, she had grown up in a family that was as political as it was literary. Her marriage to Lord Admiral George Anson, commander-in-chief of the Channel Fleet during the Seven Years War, made the Admiralty her home—and she flourished there. It gave her unrivalled access to people

[29] BL, Add Ms 57,806, fol. 106, Lady Temple to Temple, n. pl. [1754?].This election, and Lady Denbigh's involvement in it, bears further exploration: Nicholas Roger, *Whigs and Cities*, 168–96.

[30] 'Lady Denbigh to Edward Miller Mundy, 1771', in *The Cheverels of Cheverel Manor*, ed. Lady Newdigate-Newdegate (London, 1898), 56.

[31] BL, Add. MSS 35,388, fol. 101, Sir Joseph Yorke to Lady Elizabeth Anson, 30 Sept. 1755.

[32] Ibid., fol. 185, 13 July 1756.

and politicians, and political news of all sorts. Although Sir Joseph was in continuous contact with the administration through his correspondence with his father and the duke of Newcastle, his sister provided him with valuable additional insights and information. He frequently repeated his appreciation for her news and advice: 'I cannot sufficiently express how sensible I am of your friendship to me, & how anxious you are to inform me, of everything that is going forward in these troublesome times';[33] or, 'Your accounts are so exact & so curious, that you must forgive my repeating to you a thousand times over, how much I am flatter'd with your attention to me'.[34]

Lady Anson also served as an adviser to her other brothers. She carried on detailed political correspondences with them, her father, and her sister-in-law, Marchioness Grey. In her relationship with her husband, however, she was a partner, not just an adviser. She had won both her husband and her family's approval for her political ability soon after her marriage, when she played a vital part in achieving an electoral 'treaty' with Lord Gower that secured one seat at Lichfield for the Anson family. Later she came to act as her shy husband's political secretary, taking over a portion of his correspondence as he found the demands of letter-writing onerous. Her family respected her facility with words, and it was put to public political use at least once. When the Admiralty was under attack over the invasion of Minorca in 1756, she took the lead, writing a defence of the Admiralty, passing it on to her eldest brother, Lord Royston, for comment, and then having him arrange to have it copied into an unknown hand and submitted for publication. It appeared under a Roman (male) pseudonym in the *Public Advertiser* on Friday, 27 August 1756.[35]

Advisers were well-known figures in eighteenth-century politics. The stock character of the 'favourite' was an adviser whose power and lack of accountability inspired at best envy, and at worst, fear of undue influence and corruption. Female as well as male advisers could be thought to possess overweening power, as indicated by contemporary assumptions

33 BL, Add. MSS 35, 388, fol. 9: Sir Joseph Yorke to Lady Elizabeth Anson, 19 Mar. 1754.

34 Ibid., fol. 11: Sir Joseph Yorke to Lady Elizabeth Anson, 22 Mar. 1754.

35 For references to Lady Anson's electoral participation, see ibid., fol. 3^{v}, Sir Joseph Yorke to Lady Elizabeth Anson, 8 Feb. 1754; fol. 6^{r-v}, 5 Mar. 1754; fols. 57–8, 21 Mar. 1755; fols. 61–2, 1 Apr. 1755. For Sir Joseph's comments on her publication on the invasion of Minorca, see ibid., fol. 135, 17 Feb. 1756; for her collaboration with Lord Royston on this publication, see BL, Add. MS 35,376, fols. 132–3, Lady Elizabeth Anson to Royston [8Aug.? 1756].

about wives' political influence over their husbands. The duchess of Bedford was frequently cast in this role by contemporaries who believed her to be one of the primary political forces behind the Bedford faction.[36] There is no question that she was a valued adviser: in 1762, when Bedford was involved in peace negotiations in France, she was entrusted with political details that the ministers felt were too sensitive to put into writing.[37] By 1765 Lord Ilchester classed her and Richard Rigby as Bedford's most influential advisers: 'I hear it is with much difficulty that Rigby & the Duchess have prevaild with the Duke of Bedford not to resign his employment *now*.'[38] This view was shared by many, not least by George Grenville, who always kept a close eye on the duchess when gauging his reception by the duke.[39] The strongest assertion of her influence, and a useful insight into her methods, can be found in Lord Charlemont's damning indictment. The duchess, for him, was dangerous because, in the end, political power rested ultimately with her and not the duke:

> The duke, a man of excellent parts, though deficient in common sense, was in the highest degree passionate, but perfectly good-natured. By thwarting his temper, her wily grace was wont to provoke him, which was not difficult, to hasty, rude, and even savage expressions of anger, well knowing that his subsiding passion would give way to unbounded penitence; and in those moments of contrition her powers were without limits. Of this lady (the most artful and dangerous of women) I am almost afraid to speak.[40]

Like Lady Anson, the duchess of Bedford was by no means confined to the role of adviser, but for many women such a role may have been ideal. A valued political adviser was given access to the political world and her input was generally acknowledged and respected by political men. The role legitimated women's political awareness and interest, provided them with an acceptable way of expressing political opinions, and allowed them to affect political decisions with little risk to reputation. As advisers, they could have significant political influence, but since their participation remained indirect and was usually carried out privately and in person, others could only guess at the extent of their power; furthermore, they could not be held publicly accountable for political decisions.

[36] John Brooke, *The Chatham Administration, 1766–1768* (London, 1956), 30–2.

[37] Richard Rigby to Bedford, 30 Sept. 1762, in *Correspondence of John, Fourth Duke of Bedford: Selected from the Originals at Woburn Abbey*, ed. Lord John Russell, 3 vols. (London, 1842), ii. 131–2.

[38] BL, Add. MSS 51,421, fol. 98, Ilchester to Holland [31 May] 1765.

[39] BL, Add. MSS 42,083, fols. 172^{v}–3, 237.

[40] *HMC, 12th Report, Appendix, Part X*, 10.

AGENT

The role of agent incorporated and extended the roles of confidante and adviser through increasingly public, direct, and autonomous political involvement. As agents, women were the acknowledged delegates of their families, friends, or political connexions. They could hold positions of trust and responsibility. Their activities extended across the political spectrum, from the social politics of race-meets, assemblies, and balls, through the non-institutional politics of patronage, to direct electoral involvement. For some women, especially the wives of active politicians, being an agent could also mean actively participating in factional politics.

Agents operated under varying degrees of supervision; nevertheless, they took an open part in the political world. At their most involved they were in leadership positions over men and made political decisions. Women filled the role of agent in a variety of ways: by acting as secretaries for their menfolk (with varying amounts of individual input), and managing their correspondences if they were ill, absent, or otherwise occupied; by standing in for men who were unable to represent their own best interests because they were away from home (particularly in election-related social politics or the patronage system); or by serving as the connecting link among families, representing the interests of each side to the other. When Lord Exeter knew that he would be away prior to the 1761 election, he left no doubt as to who would act in his place should 'any change happen in the borough of Stamford... Lady Exeter will make the offer to Mr. Noel of bringing in either Lord Carbery or Mr. Edwards, as Lady Exeter has undertaken the management of my affairs'.[41] Even that most uninspiring of all political wives, Lady Chatham, was forced to play this part during Chatham's extended illness. She became his 'borrowed hand' and took over his correspondence; she also acted as his personal representative and link to the political world.[42]

There were always some women who acted as personal political representatives for their families and were recognized as such. Their involvement could range from representing their families at politicized

[41] J. M. Lee, 'Stamford and the Cecils, 1700–1885: A Study in Political Control', B.Litt. thesis, University of Oxford (1957), 68.

[42] BL, Add. MSS 43,771, fols. 45–6, Lady Chatham to John Calcraft, 10 Apr. 1770. For a good example of the latter, see Lady Chatham's dealings with the duke of Grafton during the Chatham Administration: Augustus Henry Fitzroy, *Autobiography and Political Correspondence of Augustus Henry Third Duke of Grafton*, ed. Sir William R. Anson, Bt. (London, 1898); Brooke, *Chatham Administration*.

social events like the local race-meets, taking part in election processions and canvassing votes either by letter or in person, or running elections in family boroughs. Thus, when Lady Stafford's unmarried son, Granville, was steward of Lichfield races in 1791, she knew that her presence as family representative would take on increased political importance. Shirking her duties would be out of the question: she would have to be 'more proper than I ever have been—for I must go to every thing that is to be done during the Races'.[43] Similarly, the sisterly canvass of St Albans in 1784 saw the duchess of Devonshire and Lady Duncannon canvassing for their brother against Lady Salisbury, who was canvassing for her brother. While Lady Spencer's movements were temporarily curtailed by a knee ailment during this election, she nevertheless managed the St Albans election from her home. Never one to value other people's abilities highly, she took charge of the election committee herself and directed the men under her as necessary. This, as she explained to her friend Mrs. Howe, took both time and energy: 'I have for some time got up invariably at 6.—& the two or three busiest day's of the Election my Committee & I met at a little after five.'[44] Moreover, she was good at what she did, as H. C. F. Lansberry noted in his examination of the politics and government of St Albans: 'Undoubtedly, the best agent the 2nd Earl Spencer had in St Albans was his mother.'[45]

The demands placed upon agents did not necessarily require them to be more politically aware than advisers, but rather to be more openly involved if the opportunity arose. Although it is impossible to quantify the number of women who acted as agents, the sources suggest that fewer women acted as agents than as confidantes or advisers. They tended to be women who were closely connected to men who were important in local or national politics—themselves a relatively small proportion of the political nation. The wives or widows of politically active aristocrats or MPs, and occasionally their mothers, sisters, and daughters, were the most likely to be agents. Their political involvement, like that of their male counterparts, was not continuous, but varied both with the time of the year and the state of political nation.

43 Birmingham University Library, Special Collections, Stafford Letters (hereafter BUL), MSS 14/v, no. 42, Lady Stafford to Lady Worcester, Trentham, 1 Sept. [1791].

44 BL, MS Coll. Althorp Papers. F. 53, Lady Spencer to Mrs Howe, 5 Apr. 1784. Lady Spencer's correspondence on her involvement in the 1784 St Albans election runs through F. 14, F. 53, F. 109, F. 114–15, F. 119–21, F. 123, F. 130–1, G. 276, G. 287, and G. 289.

45 H. C. F. Lansberry, 'Politics and Government in St. Albans, 1685–1835', Ph.D. thesis, University of London (1964), 161.

PARTNER

The dividing-line between agents and partners was often difficult to pinpoint, as the principal difference was one of degree. Partners were the most highly politicized, directly involved, and independent of all political women. They acted in conjunction with men—usually, but not always, their husbands and close male relatives—but they often made political decisions independently. Their political judgement was trusted and their influence recognized, even sometimes feared. As long as their involvement could still be explained so as not to threaten the existence of the male polity, they were praised, not criticized. Just as the most active male politicians formed a small select group at the top of the political world, so too did the women who acted as partners in familial or factional political enterprises. The majority of partners were the wives, widows, or mothers of politically active men, which is not surprising given the predominance of familial politics in the eighteenth century. There were, however, also some women whose claim to political involvement was based in ideology or on the irrefutable eighteenth-century grounds of control over property, including political interests and patronage.

Partnership was highly individual. Women who acted as partners combined intelligence, confidence, and assertiveness with sensitivity to social and political nuance, and highly developed personal skills. They were accomplished operators who used their comprehensive knowledge of people and politics to advantage. They shared not only the concerns but also many of the fatigues of male politicians. Of course, not all women, even those from highly political families, could—or wanted to—fill this role. Character and ability made the difference. Lady Emily Kildare and Lady Caroline Fox, both daughters of the 2nd duke of Richmond, illustrate the differences. Both married politicians and both went on to raise politically active sons, yet Lady Caroline's peevishness and chronic insecurity hardened into a distaste for politics that never allowed her to become more than her husband's adviser. Lady Emily, on the other hand, found politics a natural outlet for her intellect and vivacity, and made good use of her ability to manipulate both people and situations. She became her husband's partner within a short time of their marriage.

Women who acted as partners were likely to be involved directly and publicly in political life. Some controlled family interests or took leading roles in political connexions. On the whole, though, they were more independent and more likely to make political decisions than other groups of women. To cite only one example, Urania, Lady Portsmouth, was faced with the difficult decision of deciding whether her son should stand for parliament when he returned from the Grand Tour in time for the 1790 general election. The family political interest had been carefully maintained for him and, if all had gone well, this would have been a matter of course. Things, however, had not gone well, and Lady Portsmouth was forced to recognize that even time on the continent had done nothing to cure her son's mental deficiencies. She consulted with male relatives about what to do, but as she told Sir John Griffin Griffin, the decision and the responsibility for it rested with her:

> every flattering hope of his supporting a public Station with Credit is almost entirely vanish'd. With this melancholly Knowledge can we consistently with our Duty towards him Place him in a Station which will continually expose his Imbecillity to the World? On the other hand can we with justice deprive him untried of that which I cannot help considering as a part of his Birth-Right? Or how can we possibly justify ourselves for setting him aside without being Ourselves the Proclaimers of his Misfortunes? Here my Lord, is our Distress—here is the Difficulty which we have to encounter—a difficulty which presses the more hardly upon me—because *I* must determine, *I* must bear the blame or Praise of the Determination, and what adds not a little to my Affliction is, let me, determine or Act which way I will, I am almost certain to incur the Censure of the world, which must in a great Measure be ignorant of the Reasons or Motives of my Conduct.[46]

Partners were potentially the most powerful political women in the eighteenth century. They filled a variety of political positions: secretary, unofficial whip, manager, co-ordinator, negotiator, canvasser, broker—even patron. Male and female contemporaries acknowledged them as political actors with influence and/or interest, and approached them accordingly. They existed at all levels of the political elite.

Lady Rockingham was well known by contemporaries to fill this role in relation to her husband and the Rockingham Whigs. She identified closely with her husband's political concerns and appears to have found politics genuinely intriguing, stimulating, and fulfilling; moreover, she was in many ways the ideal political partner, as she never threatened to overstep the bounds: her participation was always firmly based in the familial paradigm. To what degree she had been politicized prior to marriage is uncertain, but she made a concerted effort to become a

[46] Essex Record Office, Audley End Papers (hereafter ERO), D/DBy C9/53, Urania, Lady Portsmouth, to Sir John Griffin Griffin, Lymington, 30 June 1789.

member of her husband's most intimate political circles very soon after their marriage. In the 1750s, while she was still consolidating her position, she made a point of reassuring him that she preferred politics to the social whirl.[47] By the 1760s their partnership was well established and she had become an accomplished political actor. The fact that she remained childless may also have contributed to her political activity; it certainly meant that she did not have the demands on her time that other women had. She could, therefore, take on time-consuming political tasks and serve as her husband's political helpmeet in a way that women who were preoccupied with bearing and raising children might well have found more difficult. There is no question of the esteem in which she was held by her husband and other members of the Rockinghams for her political abilities, and it is possible that this went some way to substitute for the status she would have had, had she provided the family with an heir.

Lady Rockingham operated politically both separately and in conjunction with her husband. Her services as a secretary and copyist were often much in demand. Two notes to the duke of Portland on 28 June 1767 give some sense of her involvement. The first is dated 'past three o'clock',[48] the second, 'past twelve o'clock', thus, actually the morning of 29 June. In it, she makes it clear that it has been a long day: 'My Lord is a little better to Night & I trust will be able to sleep after this tedious fatigue that he has gone through all day, & which is only just ended, occasion'd from this Protest, taking so much finishing—I shall conclude with My *Protest* that I am tired to death with sitting all day watching the Nod of my Sovereign & writing Notes for him . . . '[49] When Rockingham was too busy or away on business, she acted as his personal representative, by extension the faction's representative, and took over his correspondence. An old friend, Sir George Savile, was very familiar with this division of labour and accordingly addressed his correspondence directly to her during the lead-up to the 1774 general election:

> Lady Rockingham knows that I have long plac'd her near the head of my list of Politicians, & therefore altho' the letter beginning *Dear Sr George* & written in the Hand of the Lady is sign'd by the Gentleman, I yet shall write my answer to Wentworth. I gather indeed from the Servant as well as from Lady Rockingham's Postscript that Ld Rockingham does not return to Wentworth between the Northallerton Business & York Races.[50]

[47] WWM, R168-21-1, Lady Rockingham to Rockingham, n. d.
[48] PwF 9161, Lady Rockingham to Portland, 28 June 1767. [49] Ibid., PwF 9162.
[50] WWM, R1-1498, Sir George Savile to Lady Rockingham, 10 Aug. 1774. See also PP, PwF 10744, duchess of Portland to Portland, 4 Oct. 1780.

While her administrative abilities were important and valued, it was perhaps her excellent interpersonal skills and her ability to use the social arena for political ends, either to conduct business or to secure supporters, that was even more significant. She entertained politically in London and Yorkshire; she used her visits to Bath for political ends (as the next chapter will demonstrate); and she whipped in members and solicited votes as necessary.[51] She also joined her sister-in-law Charlotte in providing Rockingham with solid political advice.

When the duke of Cumberland died in 1765 Lady Rockingham was in Bath for her health; however, this did not stop her from telling Rockingham at length, without excuses or apologies, what she felt he should do to capitalize on the temporary political instability and gain for the Rockinghams more political security. Her comments are worth considering in full for what they tell us of her understanding of people, psychology, and politics:

Was I you I would take the first opportunity of speaking to the K—g upon the subject of this Melancholy Event, & I would speak boldly & openly for I think all Political success will greatly turn upon the Channel his Confidence now falls into, & therefore I would hasten as much as possible to draw his mind to *a right* decision & determination at this time—in short I would tell him this, that the juncture was now more critical than *ever*, that every real Friend to his M——y must deeply lament the Loss he sustains in his Uncle, whose abilities & judgmt: were of so superior a sort as to be irreparable, that the only attempt to any degree of equivalent must be the superadded assiduity of his Administration to endeavour to make his M——y & the publick suffer as little from the blow as the nature of such a sad Event can admit, & that his Ministers can only be enabled so to do by the concurrence of his Majesty's firm & unreserved Confidence, that therefore you humbly presumed to submit it to his consideration whether he was so far satisfied with the Conduct of his present Ministers as to think they merit the continuance of that full & *undevided* Confidence they Must expect to enjoy, in order to serve him well, if so you could answer for yourself that yr: endeavours to carry on his business should be indefatigable; that on the other hand, you should be ready with the greatest submission to resign the Trust to his better choice, if any other plan should be more to his inclination or interests, for the same motive would influence you on, every occasion, & does so at this present instant of beseeching his Majesty that his Confidence & his Ministers may ever be undevided of whomsoever his administration is composed; as no other method can secure permanent benefit nor any set of Ministers could either in conscience or prudence venture, to build without that head corner Stone the complete

[51] PwF 9172, Lady Rockingham to Portland, 6 May 1772; WWM, R156-12, Rockingham to Lady Rockingham, Grosvenor Square, 9 April 1767.

Confidence of their Sovereign. Something to this effect, in yr: words, I mean, & would have said at first, to show him that the confidence he placed in the Duke must now it its full scope be transferr'd to *All* of you; & instantly, for I think now wd: be the time for *certain past Influences*, to try to revive in case they find themselves *too much down*, & this also wd: be the period most likely for it to succeed in some degree, for when the mind is again on flat for a repositary it is the more liable to sink back into old habits; You are all in a manner Strangers to the King, my Politicks are to fix him now, or give him up for ever—.[52]

Given the depth of political knowledge and perspicacity that this and other of her letters reflect, it is no wonder that Rockingham relied on her judgement, lamenting the loss of '*my Minerva* at my Elbow' whenever they were apart.[53] Moreover, her political contribution was well known to contemporaries. That fact that it was preserved for posterity can be attributed to Edmund Burke, who advised her after Rockingham's death to preserve her correspondence alongside that of her husband:

Pray therefore let them be returned to keep company with the rest and to remain with the family as documents of the constant support and assistance you have uniformly given to your excellent Lord in the Course of that Conduct which will make this age a pattern of Virtue to the next, and to many more succeeding, notwithstanding its having its full share of evil examples. Your Names indeed ought to go down together; for it is no mean part you have had in the great services which that great and good man has done to his Country.[54]

[52] WWM, R168-177-1–2, Lady Rockingham to Rockingham [Nov. 1765].

[53] WWM, R156-9, Rockingham to Lady Rockingham, 31 Mar. 1767.

[54] Edmund Burke to Lady Rockingham, Beaconsfield, 20 Nov. 1782, *The Correspondence of Edmund Burke*, ed. Holden Furber and P. J. Marshall (Cambridge, 1965), v. 45–7.

3

Women and Social Politics

In late November 1765 both Lady Rockingham and William Pitt were in Bath. There, society was less politically charged than in London and the social circle was sufficiently small to facilitate socializing across political divides. As her letters to her husband demonstrate, Lady Rockingham made this into a political advantage. The death of the duke of Cumberland at the end of October had left the Rockingham Whigs lacking public credibility and believing that confidence in the ministry would be restored if they could obtain some mark of support from William Pitt.[1] In early November the Cabinet had decided to approach Pitt formally, but, since the king's disapproval had prevented further action,[2] any overture had to be handled very carefully indeed. It would need to be made informally and in such a way that the ministry would not be compromised if nothing came of it in the end. Given this, and the fact that Pitt's unpredictability made dealing with him difficult at the best of times, Rockingham put the matter into a safe pair of hands: his wife's. He trusted her political acumen; she was socially adept and used to socializing for political ends. What is more, she knew the innermost workings of the ministry without being an official part of it.

Ostensibly, Lady Rockingham approached Pitt because she wanted to buy a pair of his coach-horses. The horses were actually a convenient cover for carefully choreographed socio-political action. They gave her the excuse she needed to establish contact, first by note and then later in person through reciprocal visits. The process whereby she secured a visit from Pitt and, in return, paid a visit to the Pitts is a model of exquisite politeness and flattery.[3] These exchanges gave her the opportunity to

[1] BL, Add. MS 32, 971, fol. 290, Newcastle to Grafton, 6 Nov. 1765; BL, Add. MS 32,972, fols. 78–9, Newcastle to Featherstonhaugh, 30 Nov. 1765. For an earlier interpretation of this episode, see Paul Langford, *The First Rockingham Administration, 1765–1766* (Oxford, 1973), 104–5.

[2] BL, Add. MS 32,971, fol. 287, Rockingham to Newcastle, 6 Nov. 1765; 'George III to Bute [10 Jan. 1766]', in *Letters from George III to Lord Bute, 1765–1766*, ed. Romney Sedgwick (London, 1939), 241–6.

[3] WWM, R156-6, Rockingham to Lady Rockingham, Grosvenor Square, 28 Nov. 1765; WWM, R151-1, Pitt to Lady Rockingham [Bath, Nov.–Dec. 1765]; PRO, 30/8/54, fols. 230–1, 232–3, Lady Rockingham to William Pitt [Bath, Dec. 1765].

gauge Pitt's political stance and allowed her to transmit a Treasury minute from Rockingham. As such, she served as a safe intermediary through whom Rockingham and Pitt could communicate.[4] By securing Pitt's approval of the minute, she laid the groundwork for future negotiations. While nothing further ensued, because Pitt was unwilling to play a part in any ministry of which he was not the head, she had fulfilled her remit. She had bought the horses,[5] opened a line of communication with Pitt, and obtained his approval of the minute. And she ensured that both sides emerged without losing face.

At the same time that she was courting Pitt, Lady Rockingham was also working to establish links with the Camdens, key supporters of Pitt, who were also in Bath at the time. Once again she made use of the social arena, but, as she reminded Rockingham, social politics took time—it could not be rushed:

> I will say all you desire to Ld: Camden the first time I see him, in regard to the dining it must be as it happens, I told you he was quite free & easy to me, & we talk'd much of my removal to this house with many fine speeches from him of losing me from the other, which made me say I should hope to see him in this, therefore I think if it falls in my way I may perhaps ask them to drink tea, which I believe will seem less premeditated than the form of a dinner, & I fancy you will agree with me—I din'd to day with Mr: Murray & Ly Kath: they had besides, General Stewart, & Mr: Hunt who is here, the latter I must tell you was invited in the political way, Ly: Kath: thinking that as he was a good Minority Man he would be pleased to be asked of the Party with me, he lives in the same house with them—Ly: Kath: ought to be the Ministers Wife, I assure you—.[6]

This tea-first, dinner-later strategy was eminently sensible. Both were activities in which women commonly took leading roles, and neither was likely to be politically embarrassing if handled correctly. By beginning with a meeting over tea, she could initiate contact with the Camdens in a relatively informal, superficially social situation. This played down her political purpose and obviated the need for any kind of commitment on either side. Given her position as the 'Ministers Wife', this was important. Dinner invitations had to come later. They suggested a degree of intimacy and connexion that was more than social, especially coming from someone in her political position. Lady Katherine Murray's dinner serves as an immediate case in point. By inviting a man with known Whig sympathies

[4] PRO, 30/8/54, fols. 230–1, Lady Rockingham to William Pitt [Bath, Dec. 1765]. See also their correspondence in WWM, R151-1–4.

[5] PRO, 30/8/54, fols. 234–5, Lady Rockingham to William Pitt [Bath, Dec. 1765].

[6] WWM, R168-180, Lady Rockingham to Rockingham [Bath, 1765].

to a dinner where Lady Rockingham was the guest of honour, she was acknowledging Lady Rockingham as a political figure and using the dinner to flatter the guest's self-importance and reinforce his allegiance.

These anecdotes bear examination for what they show about women's involvement in the social aspects of political life. On one level, they reveal an ongoing dialogue about politics—indeed, a working political partnership—between Lady Rockingham and her husband. On another level, Lady Rockingham's matter-of-fact tone in recounting them suggests that both she and Lady Katherine Murray saw themselves, and were seen by the men in their circles, as functioning members of a political world where social situations were frequently used for political ends.

SOCIAL POLITICS

Political historians have always accepted that there was some interweaving of society and politics in eighteenth-century England; most would also accept that this involved some elite women. Like other historical commonplaces, however, these assumptions have been accepted largely at face value. Little serious attention has been paid to the social aspects of politics, the construction and operation of politicized society in the eighteenth century, or the part that women played in that society. There are historiographical and evidential reasons for this. Although social politics is concerned with the politics of the ruling elite—the very stuff of traditional Whig and Namierite political history—it focuses neither on high politics nor on men. Indeed, for some historians it will be replete with half-forgotten memories of 'old corruption', concerned as it is with both the disenfranchised female half of the political elite and the operation of a highly personal, influenced-based form of politics that took place outside of parliament in social situations. It does not fit easily into studies of popular politics either, where it is disqualified by class as well as gender. Moreover, as a subject it remains amorphous and anecdotal. It lacks clear boundaries and specific sources; it is stubbornly unquantifiable and impervious to neat correlations with policy decisions.

Eighteenth-century women were social beings and, at a time when politics permeated elite society and men as well as women used the social arena politically, this fusion of society and politics ensured politicization. Politics gave the political elite a common language, common concerns, and, to a larger extent than previously assumed, a shared experience. It also served as a determinant of status. For the political elite as a whole, society became an extra-parliamentary stage upon which both small and large political dramas could be enacted. While some venues did exclude women, many did not. The social arena gave women opportunities for political discussions and debate, ways of making political statements through their clothes or actions, and the chance to forward specific cases or causes. For them, social politics—the management of people and social situations for political ends—was often a fact of life. While it was often fashionably deplored and could lead to serious criticism of women's politics as the politics of trivia or corruption, particularly if women overstepped the bounds during periods of high political excitement and came to be seen as fostering or perpetuating the politicization of society for their own reasons, we ignore it at our peril.

Taking social politics seriously means realizing that the social arena *was* a valid political venue in the eighteenth century. Our understanding of women and politics has suffered from an understanding of politics that has placed parliament at the top of a hierarchy of political venues and tacitly equated 'real' politics with high politics. In order to be 'real', therefore, actions and venues had to have some direct impact on high politics and policy decisions. In the main, this interpretative framework has led historians on a quest to discover how women made a 'difference', usually in relation to the operation of electoral or parliamentary politics.[7] While useful, this limits what is considered worth studying and devalues those aspects of women's political involvement which are not immediately direct or quantifiable. While there can be little question that, institutionally, eighteenth-century government and acts of governance were male, the structures and processes which underpinned them were not so rigid. Thus, there was always some scope for political involvement for those men who did not possess the necessary prerequisites, and for women.

Politics is, however, not always quantifiable or direct. It is, in fact, a very messy, nebulous business, where outcomes can be shaped by such intangible elements as personality, appearance, and influence, and by the creation and manipulation of belief and atmosphere. It is an art as well as a science—and it is with this in mind that we need to approach social politics and evaluate women's socio-political activities. Their part in the

[7] See, e.g. the literature around the best-known of all eighteenth-century political women, Georgiana, duchess of Devonshire. Until recently academic interest in the duchess focused on her electoral activities during the Westminster election of 1784. Even Amanda Foreman's admirable biography of the duchess, while clearly demonstrating the full range of her political activities, still implicitly privileges this hierarchical notion of politics: Foreman, *Georgiana*.

creation and maintenance of a politicized society is in itself a highly valuable political contribution and should be recognized as such. If and when it is possible to demonstrate that individuals or groups of women were able to directly affect policy through their socio-political endeavours, this should be done, but it should not be the primary goal.

A POLITICIZED SOCIETY

Undoubtedly, the extent to which society was politicized in the second half of the eighteenth century owes a great deal to the historical moment and to the institution of parliament. At this time parliamentary service was becoming more prestigious, more and more legislation was being passed, and the nation as a whole was becoming more politicized. The parliamentary political world, however, remained the prerogative of a relatively small elite. Still, by making what was, in contemporary European terms, such a sizeable group of men into political actors, politics became a feature in the lives of a similar number of women. This laid the foundation for more extensive female political involvement than Court-based politics had ever provided.

Whenever parliament was sitting, it excited a persistent buzz of curiosity, capturing the imagination of the nation in a way that is difficult for us now to comprehend. Parliamentary affairs were debated and dissected in person, by letter, and in the press, not only because they were the issues of the moment, but also because they involved the most important—and frequently the most colourful—figures of the day. Family involvement in parliamentary politics often demanded some degree of participation from women, especially in maintaining family interests at the local level, but just having an MP or a politically active peer in the family had an impact on women's lives. It could determine how and where women lived, how much time they spent with their husbands, who they socialized with, what kinds of social events they attended, and, occasionally, even what they wore. Parliament took MPs and peers to London for between three and nine months every year, and by the second half of the century more women (and children) appear to have joined in the annual migration as parliamentary sessions lengthened and the accompanying social season became increasingly important. The lone MP in lodgings, still a familiar figure in the 1750s, was increasingly replaced by the political family living on a fashionable street in the West End by the last quarter of the century.

Parliament brought the political elite to London, but not all political manoeuvring went on in the Houses of Parliament. The Commons, in particular, was notoriously cramped, uncomfortable, and inconvenient. A wide assortment of exclusively male clubs, taverns, and coffee-houses partially filled politicians' need to socialize, but the significance of other, mixed-sex venues should not be underestimated either.

In London, more consistently than anywhere else in the country, 'society' itself was charged with politics. A political current ran through events at the Court, the theatre, the opera, balls, and assemblies; even everyday encounters in the streets, parks, or public gardens could be politicized; so too were activities like visiting, dinners, and cards. A late debate or a division could take enough men out of circulation to spoil the best-laid plans of any society hostess: dinners were delayed; routs, drums, and assemblies were blighted; balls suffered from a shortage of partners; and the crowds at the theatre and the opera were noticeably thinner. Interest in politics was such that the first man to arrive from the House of Commons after an important division could bring a loo party to a halt, as Colonel Montgomery did at Lady George Sackville's after a vote on the land tax in 1767,[8] or Lord Edgcumbe did at Princess Amelia's on the occasion of the debate on the King's Speech in 1774.[9] Social evenings could be interrupted so that controversial new publications, such as Wilkes's address to the freeholders of Middlesex, could be read aloud;[10] and important decisions, such as the prince of Wales being voted out of the Queen's Council during the Regency Crisis, could flash through a theatre, completely diverting the audience's attention away from the stage.[11] During particularly tense moments women postponed meals and stayed up, sometimes all night, in order to follow the latest political developments through notes delivered by messengers.[12] During the marathon debate of 17–18 February 1783, the dowager Lady Spencer's network of male family members, friends, and political supporters kept her very well informed. She received a stream of notes from parliament detailing the latest developments in the debate. They came in turn—first from her son, then from Lords Jersey, John Cavendish, and Lucan, then

[8] 'Journal, London, 27 Feb. 1767', in Coke, *Letters and Journals of Lady Mary Coke*, i. 158–9.

[9] '30 Nov. 1774', ibid., iv. 437.

[10] '6 Feb. 1769', ibid., iii. 19.

[11] 'Hon. Mrs Martha Harcourt to Lady Harcourt [London], 16 Jan. 1789', in *The Harcourt Papers*, ed. E.W. Harcourt, 14 vols. (Oxford, 1876–1905), vol. iv, pt. 1, p. 178.

[12] Journal, London, 26 May 1767, in *Letters and Journals of Lady Mary Coke*, ii. 6; duchess of Devonshire to Lady Spencer [London, 19 Dec, 1788], Chatsworth MSS 934.

from Henry Minchin, followed by another from her son, and finally by one from Richard Rigby—at 8 p.m., 10 p.m., 10.30 p.m., 'past 12 o'clock', 3 a.m., 8 a.m., and 8.05 a.m., respectively.[13]

Just being members of this society ensured a degree of female politicization. Political excitement and interest periodically swept through society, affecting everything and everyone in their wake. When this happened it was impossible not to be affected by what contemporaries often referred to as a contagion: the 'rage of politics'.[14] Nor was this a new development. Writing during the first uncertain months of the Broad Bottom administration in 1744, Lady Hervey had explained to a correspondent that, 'if one does not know how to use the words *war*, *invasion*, *treaty*, *minister*, *patriot*, *rogue*, and *rascal*, with all the rest of the political jargon, one must not pretend to correspond or converse with any human creature, either in town or country'.[15] Similarly, writing from London nearly thirty years later, Lady Spencer would concentrate on 'those three material articles the Peace the Debates in Parliament & the Opera'.[16] During times like these, even women who were well away from London were likely to remark that there was suddenly 'no Subject of conversation but Politics'.[17]

THE CHAT OF THE TOWN

And conversation there was in abundance. Politics was something that the members of the political elite had in common, and talking about politics served a number of purposes. The quest for the latest 'News' was unending. As a careful distillation of the most up-to-date information about people, places, and political developments, News referred to information that was political or social, or a mixture thereof. It was most likely to be political gossip. News was found anywhere that members of the political elite met. It could be provincial or metropolitan, but it was most likely to be centred on, and generated by, London and Westminster. For

[13] See BL, MS Coll. (Althorp Papers), F. 120.

[14] 'Lady Spencer to Nuneham, Rome, 13 Apr. 1764', in *Harcourt Papers*, ed. Harcourt, viii. 75.

[15] 'Lady Hervey to [Mr Morris], Ickworth, 7 Apr. 1744', in *Letters, with a Memoir and Illustrative Notes* (London, 1821), no. 15, p. 57.

[16] Chatsworth MSS 472, Lady Spencer to the duchess of Devonshire [London], 8 Dec. 1782.

[17] BL, Add. MS 35,386, fol. 435^v, Agneta Yorke to Philip Yorke, Sydney Farm [18 Jan. 1789].

contemporaries, it was simply 'the Chat of the Town'.[18] Those who needed more information than they could gather in person, or lacked the necessary personal contacts, often supplemented their store of News with that found in a growing number of printed publications, particularly pamphlets and newspapers.

Once gathered, News was pondered and analysed. It was then disseminated, either in person or by letter. On one level it served as little more than padding: social chit-chat. As such, it fulfilled all of the functions of gossip: it narrated, interpreted, and judged; it fostered a sense of inclusivity; and it acted as a means of social control.[19] At another level it served a political purpose. For the socially ambitious—men and women—knowledge of men and measures suggested proximity to power and was marker of insider status worth having for those who were jockeying for position in elite society. For politically ambitious women it was the very essence of interest and influence. Being the first to know the latest developments (and pass them on or not) could be decisive, personally or electorally. Personally, News mattered because of the importance that rumour, gossip, and speed of action could play in securing elections or obtaining patronage. Forecasting the downfall of an administration or calculating the timing of a dissolution—and disseminating that information to the right people as quickly as possible—could make the difference in the outcome of an election or even decide whether an election would take place at all. The eagerness with which contemporaries sought to ascertain who was likely to live or die, or who was 'in' or 'out' with the minister or the king, was part of a dynamic that can appear morbid or inordinately self-seeking to modern sensibilities. It was, however, only logical at a time when an individual's career, a family's social status, or its economic situation could depend upon the swift receipt and judicious use of just such information. It is no wonder that social interactions among the political elite often had an air of self-interested political alertness that barely masked a sharp competitive edge.

For socially active women, or women whose homes were political meeting-places, collecting News was not difficult. Although Lady Grey excused her tardiness in sending electoral information to her husband in 1760 by saying, 'News is not apt to Walk into ones Dressing-room to one',[20] she was not entirely correct. Apt or not, it occasionally did. For

[18] BL, MS Coll. Althorp, F. 119, General Cunningham to Lady Spencer, St James's Place, 17 Nov. 1772.

[19] See Patricia Meyer Spacks, *Gossip* (New York, 1985), esp. 3–23.

[20] BL, Add. MS 35,376, fol. 40^{v}, Lady Grey to Royston [Wrest Park, Jan. 1760].

fashionable women in London, dressing-rooms could be meeting-places and the source of all sorts of information.[21] In general, News entered the home via family members, friends, and visitors (male and female), and was shared as a matter of course during visits, over cards, or with food and drink. The type of information that women gathered reflected the circles in which they moved. Once gathered, news was passed on. Comments about parliamentary men and measures appear—unsurprisingly—most consistently in the letters of women who had close parliamentary connexions. Mothers with an eye to their children's political education or careers frequently included chronicles of political events in their letters. Mrs Harris, the mother of the future Lord Malmesbury, was typical when, in 1763, she recounted the day's developments in parliament to her adolescent son: 'Your father returned from the House at two this morning: great debating. Lord North moved . . .'[22] Daughters from politically active families were likely to do the same. Writing to her father, Lord Guilford, in 1775, Louisa Verney reported all that she had learned about who would get the new Cabinet appointments. She also enclosed the preceding Tuesday's minutes of the House of Lords.[23] From the opposing Foxite camp, the duchess of Devonshire regularly sent what she learned to her mother: 'All our uncles din'd here today. The dissolution is not credited in the city.'[24] For Lady Spencer, who needed to begin campaigning in St Albans as soon as parliament was dissolved, this sort of information was vital. News of national import was also certain to be passed on and discussed. The victorious battle of the Saints in April 1782 elicited a sardonically patriotic response from Anne Brompton: 'Mr A[ddington]—is all exultation upon this important victory & is writing at a great rate on the subject—we females may be allowed I hope to participate in the general satisfaction it has occasioned amongst the other Sex—for my one part I feel much interrested tho' no great *Politician*, & truly wish the French, Dutch, Spaniards & all a *total* defeat—'.[25]

[21] Chatsworth MSS 610, duchess of Devonshire to Lady Spencer, London, 24 Mar. 1784.

[22] 'Mrs Harris to James Harris, Whitehall, 15 Nov. 1763', in *A Series of Letters of the First Earl of Malmesbury, his Family and Friends from 1745 to 1820*, ed. Malmesbury, 2 vols. (London, 1870), i. 99. Lady Stafford's political grooming of her son, Granville Leveson Gower, began yet earlier. By the time that he was 12 (in 1787) she had already set up William Pitt as his model politician and was regularly including an assortment of political information in her letters to him: *Letters of Lord Granville Leveson Gower*, ed. Granville, i. 5, *passim*.

[23] Bodl., MS North d.16, fols. 61–2, Louisa Verney to Guilford, London, 8 Nov. 1775.

[24] 'Duchess of Devonshire to Lady Spencer [London], 17 Mar. 1784', in *Georgiana*, ed. Bessborough, 77.

[25] Gloucestershire Record Office, D421 C8A, A. Brompton to Charlotte Addington, n. pl., May 1782.

POLITICS IN THE HOME

Although the commercialization of leisure that was taking place during the eighteenth century meant that there were more opportunities and places for men and women to mix, the home remained one of the main venues. The importance of personal connexions in politics and patronage, and the relatively amateur and informal approach to politics itself, meant that people from across the political elite met, mingled, and plotted in each other's homes. Much of the politicking that would take place in public or in institutionalized settings later in the nineteenth century was still firmly based in the home in the eighteenth century.

The extent to which social activities in the home were politicized depended upon the political importance of the host family and those on the guest-list. Timing and location could also be important. Activities in London during the parliamentary season were the most consistently politicized, but so too could be the visits, dinners, house parties, and Public Days that were part of maintaining a political interest in the country. As elections approached they were increasingly likely to become openly political.

Visits and dinners served the widest range of political ends. By the second half of the eighteenth century visiting was a ritualized activity, which ranged from the ceremonial to the purely personal.[26] In some households, guest-lists were predetermined by the hostess's or the family's political affiliation, but most politically active families attracted a wide assortment of visitors. Social events were largely considered to be women's prerogative. Contemporary men's and women's sources are rife with references to visiting 'Mrs This' or dining at the home of 'Lady That'. In his pocket diary for 1754 the solid Tory squire, Sir Roger Newdigate, noted the majority of his dinner engagements by hostess rather than host.[27] James Boswell, as a young man about town in 1762, did the same: 'I had Erskine with me at breakfast, after which he and I went to Lady Frances Erskine's, and then I went to Lady Northumberland's.'[28] More than thirty years later Sir Gilbert Elliot also regularly followed this pattern. His account of one such dinner is particularly revealing, as it emphasizes what could happen when women controlled

[26] For a careful examination of the ritual of visiting at the turn of the eighteenth century, see Whyman, *Sociability and Power*.

[27] WCRO, CR 136 A(585).

[28] 'Journal, 30 Dec. 1762', in *Boswell's London Journal, 1762–1763*, ed. Frederick A. Pottle (London, 1950), 111.

the family's socializing but held different political views than their husbands:

I dined on Sunday at Mrs Legge's in Grosvenor Square, with Windham, Pelham, Douglas, Cholmondeley, and Elliot. Legge is a violent Tory, or, if you please, in his heart strongly against all our party. This is occasioned by his connexion with Lord Bagot and his family, who have, I know not why, a perfect dominion over him. He is so quiet a little man, that I never suspected this till lately; but as Mrs Legge and all her friends are of another sort, I fear Mr. Legge suffers much internal mortification, for he never sees at his own house any company of his own way of thing; and as *we* are pretty strong, and sufficiently violent in our conversation, he must undergo it all in solitary silence and dudgeon.[29]

For young women, this sort of politicized socializing in the home often formed an important part of their informal political education.[30] A young guest of Mrs Delany's in 1783, for instance, was left to contemplate the *realpolitik* of allegiance, ambition, and power after sitting in on a discussion which revealed that Lord Stormont's family had switched political allegiances:

My uncle Frederick came and staid near 2 hours. Lady *Stormont* came; they talk'd of ye politicks of ye day; Lady S[tormont] was more animated and open upon the subject than usual. The K[ing] was blamed for his want of *openess*, in short ye language of ye S[tormont] family was totally different to what I *had ever* heard it. Ye P[rince]'s conduct was praised. Mr. F[ox] was *no longer* an obnoxious person. I will make no further mem., for it is painfull to dwell on the *power of interest* over ye human mind and heart![31]

The homes of those politicians who were 'in business' were often awash with information. Members of these families were expected to keep their friends and correspondents informed. When the fleet returned to port for a refit in 1778, Lady Mount Edgcumbe was thrilled to her patriotic core to have her home become the '*rendez-vous*' for 'Admirals, Captains, & Secretaries . . & A. Keppel his lodging'. This gave her unrivalled access to naval news, and as she informed Lady Harcourt,

[29] 'Sir Gilbert to Lady Elliot, Pall Mall Court, 20 Jan. 1789', in *Life and Letters of Sir Gilbert Elliot*, ed. Minto, i. 267.

[30] See e.g. Elizabeth Appleton, *Private Education: or, A Practical Plan for the Studies of Young Ladies: With an Address to Parents, Private Governesses and Young Ladies*, 2nd edn. (London, 1816), 292–3.

[31] 'Miss Hamilton, Diary, Clarges Street, 22 Dec. 1783', in *The Autobiography and Correspondence of Mary Granville, Mrs. Delany: With Interesting Reminiscences of King George the Third and Queen Charlotte*, ed. Lady Llanover, 3 vols., 2nd ser. (London, 1862), iii. 187.

'you may depend upon it that I know the truth, & you may depend upon it that I tell it'.[32]

Men and women who were in London during the parliamentary year were expected to be sources of news, no matter what their personal preference. For those who disliked politics, this was a burden. One of William Shenstone's male correspondents fell into this category: 'Now for News—I am in *London*; for which Reason, I suppose I must not be excused; tho' I hate it, remember very little, and am most likely to blunder in the Recital of that little. The House of Commons have addressed the King . . . '[33] Lady Frances Scott, who both disliked politics and made fashionable ennui a way of life, strove to find ways to confound her correspondents' expectations. As her stepfather was Charles Townshend, the chancellor of the Exchequer, and the family lived in Downing Street, she could not plead ignorance. Instead, writing to the duchess of Portland, she turned the argument around neatly: 'I suppose you do not expect news from me, as I daresay you know, much more at Welbeck, than I do in the *Chancellor of the Exchequers* House, for there one hears too much either to remember or believe anything; for which reason I shall not tire your Patience with a tedious list of all those who either do, or are Expected to fill the vacant offices.'[34] For those who were interested in politics, this task was not as onerous. A steady stream of visitors to the Admiralty kept Lady Anson supplied with information. She put what she learned to good use in what she light-heartedly termed her 'Office' as '*News-Writer* to ones freinds'.[35] In her case, the 'freinds' were primarily the members of her family who were not in London.

Information gained in this way was valuable coin in the currency of social exchange, but it could also have direct political purpose. When, in November 1783, a morning visitor of Louisa Macdonald's confirmed rumours about the Fox–North administration's plans for action on India at the beginning of the upcoming parliamentary session, she immediately sent the news to her stepmother, Lady Gower. She knew that it would give Lady Gower ammunition to press the ever-reluctant Gower, then in opposition, to attend:

[32] Lady Mount Edgcumbe to Lady Harcourt, Mount-Edgcumbe, 2 Aug. 1778, in *Harcourt Papers*, ed. Harcourt, viii. 274–5.

[33] Mr Whistler to William Shenstone [London], 13 Apr. [n. d.], in Frances Seymour, *Select letters between the late duchess of Somerset . . . and others*, 2 vols. (London, 1778), ii. 31.

[34] PP, PwG 169, Lady Frances Scott to duchess of Portland, Downing Street, Dec. [1766–7?].

[35] WP, L30/9/3/83, Lady Anson to Lady Grey, Admiralty, 24 Oct. [1758].

I hear the Ministers intend to bring forward & carry through as much Business as possible before Christmas as many People whom they think likely to oppose them are not come up. An adherent of theirs told me so yesterday morning. The first that will come upon the Tapis will be the subject of India, where I understand the administration are to strike a bold stroke & recal Mr. Hastings sending in his Place his avowed Enemy Mr. F[rancis]. The former has so strong a Party in this Country that I own I did not think they would have ventured it & scarcely know how to believe it yet, but it is not intended to bring it on as a direct Question lest in that Form it should not be carried, but to institute a Board who are to report to the Crown their advice respecting all Measures & the Crown to be invested with a power of acting. All this is however only the Town Talk but it is much credited.[36]

Although her information was gleaned from a social call, some visits were motivated more—or entirely—by political concerns. Political visits sought to persuade or pressure, seek or dispense advice, or declare or discern allegiances. All could lead to women visiting and being visited with political intent. In the country, requests for pardons and patronage were frequently made of women who were the representatives of leading families and/or had useful connexions of their own. Anne Boothby Skrymsher was both a member of a leading county family in Leicestershire and a friend of Charles Jenkinson. As a result, her interest was eagerly sought. In 1763, after having been 'worryd continualy' to obtain a reprieve for a man who was believed to have been unjustly convicted, she took up the case with Jenkinson: 'I Shall thank You as long as I live for upon my honor hear is one of the aldermen of Leicester has come running Seven mile on foot in a heavey rain to desire me to write to you again.'[37]

For women from politically active families, and especially for women who were known to be politically active themselves, these sorts of visits were a matter of course. They were encouraged by prevailing beliefs about influence as inherent in intimate, personal relationships: women who were close to political men were assumed to have at least the potential for matchless political influence. At times, both men and women appear to have self-consciously, even cynically, exploited this belief and other negative stereotypes about women and politics. Assumptions about women's 'natural' inclination to meddle or their lust for power could be used to trivialize or dismiss their involvement in politics,

[36] PRO, 30/29/4/5/47, fols. 719^{v}–20, Louisa Macdonald to Lady Gower, Adelphi (London), 14 Nov. [1783].

[37] BL, Add. MS 38,201, fol. 91, Anne Boothby Skrymsher to Charles Jenkinson, Tooly Park, 20 Sept. 1763.

but they could also be used to provide a convenient cover for action. Thus, women could act as principals or intermediaries in political manoeuvres which might prove difficult or compromising if handled directly by men. If the women were successful, the affair could then become official; if they failed, it could be dropped discreetly.

At times, therefore, the purpose of visits was implied rather than stated. When the duchess of Portland received a visit from William Burke prior to the opening of parliament in 1774, she was left slightly puzzled: 'I think his visit to me was chiefly to desire me to press you all in my power to come to town some time before the Parliament meets.'[38] Similar examples can be found in the correspondences of politically active families, great and small, throughout the period. When George Grenville became first lord of the Treasury, Gilbert Elliot paid a special visit to Elizabeth Grenville. In part, the visit was to reiterate his personal support for Grenville. More importantly, he came to tell her that he had been authorized to relay Lord Bute's support: 'that he wished every friend of his to give their thorough assistance.'[39] As Bute's representative, he passed the message on to her as Grenville's representative: it was then up to her to decide whether she wanted to pass this information on to Grenville himself and complete the transaction.

That women also turned their visits to political ends underlines both the interconnexions between society and politics at the time and the way that familial politics integrated women into political life. During election years candidates' and patrons' wives were expected to exchange visits with the womenfolk of the leading voters; between elections these visits, while less frequent, aimed at maintaining or consolidating the family's political interest. Similar visits also took place on a grander scale in London. Women as politically and personally diverse as the duchess of Northumberland and Lady Rockingham can be found socializing with the lord mayor and lady mayoress of London when their factions were in need of political support.[40] As it was *de rigueur* for the elite to view the lady mayoress as the epitome of vulgarity, the onset of these visits invariably generated sarcastic comments from the supporters of other

[38] PP, PwF 10,661, duchess of Portland to Portland, Burlington House, 14 Nov. 1774.

[39] 'Mrs Grenville's Narrative of Events from November 1763–January 1764', in *The Grenville Papers: Being the Correspondence of Richard Grenville, Earl Temple, K.G., and the Right Hon. George Grenville, Their Friends and Contemporaries*, ed. William James Smith, 4 vols. (London, 1852–3), ii. 243.

[40] PRO, 30/29/4/2/32, fol. 170^{v}, Lady Irwin to Lady Gower, Templenewsam, 2 Mar. 1770.

factions. The fact that Lady Rockingham's visits coincided with the duke of Grafton's resignation did not go unremarked by Lady Irwin, a partisan of the new North administration: 'the Gentle Marchioness I hear has been twice to visit the Lady Mayoress what a regard they must have for each other! such Patriotesses.'[41]

The resumption of visiting between women who had been divided by politics was also remarked, as it served to indicate the restoration of social harmony. Although such visits might mean little more than the resumption of ordinary social relations, they also bore watching. Depending upon people and circumstances, they could also be a sign of an impending political reconciliation. For the women who were involved, these sorts of visits required tact. The duchess of Devonshire, re-establishing contacts in Derbyshire after the vitriolic 1784 election, knew this well: 'I went to Mrs Gisborne & found [her] vastly fearful of any offence being taken about Election disagreements & you may be sure I was very very civil.'[42]

When political divisions were familial, the situation was yet more delicate. The complicated, on-again-off-again relationships of the Grenville cousinhood are a case in point. Whenever the men were not speaking, their wives handled the necessary business between the families through letters and visits. When reconciliation became a possibility, it too was mooted through the women. In 1764, when relations between Lord Temple and George Grenville were at an all-time low, a family situation arose that allowed Grenville to make the first step towards re-establishing contact and political connexion. As Elizabeth Grenville's journal indicates, the women dealt with the situation smoothly:

Tuesday Feb: 12. Mr Grenville recd. a letter from Mr H. Grenville from Constantinople dated Jan: 3d. stating to him the uneasiness of his situation there & his earnest wish to be recall'd. Mrs Grenville went to Lady Temple Wednesday 13 to communicate this to her & to acquaint her with the proposition Mr Grenville intended to make to Mr Henry of the office of one of the Comis-s[ioners] of the Customs then vacant wch. as it would oblige him to vacate his seat in parliament would exempt him from involving himself in the unhappy differences in his own family. Lady Temple seem'd pleas'd with the kindness of this scheme towards Mr Henry & said she would take an occasion to apprize Ld.

[41] PRO, 30/29/4/2/33, fol. 173, Lady Irwin to Lady Gower, Templenewsam, 2 Apr. 1770.

[42] Chatsworth MSS, 639A, Duchess of Devonshire to Lady Spencer [Chatsworth], 16 Aug. 1784.

Temple of it. Mrs Grenville told her she was at liberty to do it if she pleas'd but that she brought no message from Mr Grenville to Ld Temple.[43]

Visits could also be put to factional ends. When the duke of Gloucester married without the king's approval, the opposition took his side while the administration supported the king. This division was pointedly underlined in women's visits to the new duchess. Almost without exception, only the wives of opposition MPs called upon her.[44] A similar situation arose when the duke and duchess of Bedford's house had been attacked by a mob of weavers in 1765. Sympathizers from across the political spectrum had called to express their support. There was, however, one notable absence: the Butes. Animosity between the Bedfords and the Butes had been fuelled by Bedford, who had tactlessly insisted to the king that Bute had instigated the riot. Although the Northumberlands, representing Bute's following, paid a token visit, the duchess of Bedford took the view (correctly) that Lady Bute's non-appearance was a political as well as a social slight:

Ld & Ly Northd. made a visit at Bedford House while Mr Grenville was there, Ld Northd. had a very cold reception & the language wch. pass'd before him could not be very pleasing. The Dutchess of Bedford [said] that the only persons who on this occasion had neither sent nor come to her was Lady Bute & Mrs Anne Pitt & that she was very glad of it as it put an end to all difficulties of situation between her & Lady Bute.[45]

Grenville's evaluation of Northumberland's reception as a way of measuring the political temperature between the Bedfords and the Butes, reinforced as it was by his wife's recording of the duchess's comments, reflects the ways in which politically active eighteenth-century men and women 'read' visits in light of larger political situations. For a woman whose political antennae were well tuned, as were those of Elizabeth Montagu, even a game of cards might have political meaning in certain circumstances:

The night before I was at an assembly at Mrs. Pitt's, where I found Sir John Mordaunt playing at cards with Lady Hester Pitt; this might be accident, but among political folks one is apt to look deeper perhaps than the truth lies, but this

[43] BL, Add. MS 42,083, fol. 116^{r-v}, Political diary of George Grenville, 1761–8 (by Elizabeth Grenville).

[44] BL, MS Coll. Althorp, F.43, Mrs Howe to Lady Spencer, Grafton Street, 22 Feb. [1773]. A similar use of visiting by opposition women as a statement of political support can be found during the Queen Caroline affair in 1820. See E. A. Smith, *A Queen on Trial: The Affair of Queen Caroline* (Stroud, 1993).

[45] BL, Add. MS 42,083, fols. 172^{v}–3, Grenville Diary, 20 May 1765.

and General Conway being received into grace and sent to Le Cas to settle the cartel for exchange of prisoners, makes me suspect some coalition may be designed between the folks at Leicester House and the D(uke) . . .[46]

As this example demonstrates, by no means was all of the socializing that took place in the home intimate mixing among friends. While women from politically active aristocratic families hosted Public Days when in the country during the summer, the most politically and/or socially important women often opened their homes in London on designated days or evenings during the parliamentary season. These 'days' saw guests come and go, exchanging polite conversation, society gossip, and political affairs. Cards, refreshments, music, or even an impromptu hop might be included. In December 1760, when the big houses were just starting to open up for the winter, Anne Brudenell informed Lord Guilford that the 'Duts: of Norfolk is very soon to open her house every Wednesday, the Duts: of Bedford has begun Thursday'.[47] And, in 1762, Boswell was thrilled to receive an invitation to the duchess of Northumberland's select Fridays.[48] While the balance between the social and political components of these events varied, the political allegiances of the hostesses and their families, and the political loyalties and/or ambitions of the guests, could be reflected in who attended. The duchess of Norfolk, although a member of the Catholic aristocracy, identified with the Old Corps Whigs; the duchess of Bedford was a central figure in the Bedford faction; and the duchess of Northumberland was both a member of the Court and related through marriage to Lord Bute.

As hostesses, women were well placed to be political facilitators. Those who had menfolk 'in business', or who had social or political aspirations themselves (or whose families did), worked to achieve the right blend of society and politics. In 1780, after William Eden's political ambitions were boosted by his appointment as private secretary to Lord Carlisle, the new lord-lieutenant of Ireland, his wife opened their house so regularly that contemporaries spoke of her 'constant Supper'. Although she never succeeded in becoming one of London's leading hostesses, her home did become a minor political venue much frequented by the members of the *bon ton* and the clientele of Brookes's club.[49]

[46] 'Elizabeth Montagu to [her husband?], [London], 4 Jan. 1759', in *Elizabeth Montagu: Queen of the Bluestockings*, ed. Emily J. Climenson, 2 vols. (London, 1906), ii. 158.

[47] Bodl., MS North d.8, fol. 28^v, Anne Brudenell to Guilford, London, 4 Dec. 1760.

[48] 'Journal, 10 Dec. 1762', in *Boswell's London Journal*, ed. Pottle, 73.

[49] PRO, 30/29/5/2/55 fol. 205, Lady Waldegrave to Lady Gower, Whitehall, 30 Oct. 1780.

The outstanding political hostesses of the period were mistresses of social politics. Placed at the centre of the political world by birth or marriage, they made a 'career' of politicized socializing, using their skills more for factional than family ends. Most of what is known about eighteenth-century political hostesses still centres on the semi-legendary activities of the foremost opposition hostesses of the last quarter of the century. They did not hold the field alone, however. More work needs to be done to uncover the activities of their administration counterparts. Lady Salisbury, for example, loved spectacle and splendour and seems to have channelled her inexhaustible energy into her activities as a hostess with the same verve that she put into fox-hunting. Her most impressive socio-political coup came with entertaining George III and Queen Charlotte at Hatfield House in 1800, when they came to review the local militia in the park.[50] In her memoirs, Lady Hester Stanhope, William Pitt's last hostess, included Lady Salisbury as one of the few outstanding hostesses of the late eighteenth century. She grouped her together with the Ladies Liverpool and Mansfield, the marchioness of Stafford, and the duchesses of Rutland and Gordon. Each had her own style. Given Lady Hester's own hoydenish predilections as a young woman, it is not surprising that she preferred the duchess of Gordon's flamboyance and informality to the duchess of Rutland's elegance and restraint. She recalled the duchess of Rutland's entertainments as 'so heavy—a great deal of high breeding and *bon ton*; but there was, somehow, nothing to enliven you', whereas at the duchess of Gordon's, 'there were people of the same fashion, and the crowd was just as great; but then she was so lively, and everybody was so animated, and seemed to know so well what they were about—quite another thing'.[51] Intriguingly, it was for Lady Liverpool, a woman whose skills as a political hostess have gone unremarked, that Lady Hester reserved her highest praise: she rated her as a more skilled all-around hostess than the famed duchess of Devonshire:

I have seen Lady Liverpool come into a room full of people; and she would bow to this one, speak to that one, and, when you thought she must tread on the toes of a third, turn round like a tetotum, and utter a few words so amiable, that everybody

[50] Tracing the activities of the administration hostesses is difficult because they have left fewer caches of relevant documents. See David Cecil, *The Cecils of Hatfield House: A Portrait of an English Ruling Family* (London, 1975), 188–91.

[51] *Memoirs of the Lady Hester Stanhope, as Related by Herself in Conversations with her Physician*, ed. Charles Meryon, 3 vols. (London, 1845), ii. 52–3. The duchess of Gordon's flair for entertaining seems to have been passed on to at least some of her daughters. The ball hosted by her daughter, the duchess of Richmond, on the eve of the battle of Waterloo has become legendary.

was charmed with her. As for the Duchess of D[evonshire], it was all a 'fu, fu, fuh', and 'what shall I do? Oh, dear me! I am quite in a fright!'—and so much affectation, that it could not be called high breeding; although she knew very well how to lay her traps for some young man, whom she wanted to inveigle into her parties, and all that.[52]

The ability of political hostesses to 'inveigle' potential supporters was crucial to the opposition during their years in the political wilderness in the late eighteenth century. Lacking the administration's built-in ability to use power, place, and patronage to attract followers, the opposition had to make membership desirable if they wished to maintain a credible political following. How better to do it than to invest it with social cachet? Fortunately for the fate of the late eighteenth-century opposition, the charisma of Charles James Fox was equalled by that of its leading political hostess, the duchess of Devonshire. She and Lady Melbourne, in particular, were both leaders of the *ton* and dedicated to the opposition cause. They were renowned for keeping their houses 'perpetually open' and attracting a glittering, if fast, cross-section of elite society. According to a disapproving Lady Harcourt, all of the prince of Wales's subsequent—and in her view, wrong-headed—political actions could be traced to them. While it was understandable that the young prince had been attracted to the homes of 'two young, handsome, and agreeable women' who were fond of amusement, it was in their homes and through their doing that 'Mr. Fox, Mr. Burke, and Mr. Sheridan had first free access to him'.[53] The political dividends that the Foxite Whigs reaped as a result of their hostesses' efforts were obvious to contemporaries. Lady Hester Stanhope was not alone in recognizing the special part played by duchess of Devonshire; her efforts even won the grudging admiration of a much sterner critic, Lady Mary Coke. She conceded: 'She really is a very good Politician. As soon as ever any young man comes from abroad he is immediately invited to Devonshire House and to Chatsworth—and by that means he is to be of the Opposition.'[54]

This combination of good company, preferably supplemented by good food and drink, was a staple of eighteenth-century politics. Meals of all sorts, but especially dinners, proved ideal for political gossip, discussion,

[52] Ibid. 105–6.

[53] Elizabeth, Lady Harcourt, 'Memoirs of the Years 1788–89', in *Harcourt Papers*, ed. Harcourt, vol. iv, pt. 1, p. 41.

[54] Scottish National Register of Archives, Douglas-Home MSS D95/54: diary of Lady Mary Coke, 12 Sept. 1787, as quoted in Foreman, *Georgiana*, 174. My thanks to Amanda Foreman for making me aware of this.

or debate. They were also well suited to seeking favours or support, openly or through the exercise of charm, flattery, and solicitation. Women's presence at dinners seems to have been increasingly taken for granted. At the very least, by the second half of the century the woman of the house was expected to do the honours. It is not uncommon to find references to dinners where men outnumbered women,[55] but a dinner that had no women at all—a 'Man dinner'[56]—seems to have come to occasion comment and even some complaint by the last quarter of the century. Henry Mackenzie, writing in 1792, complained about just such a dinner with friends in London. The food and the wine had been excellent, but he had 'an objection to the entertainment': 'It was a *male* party, Mr. Hom[e's wife] not being with us.' She had, he reveals, gone to the theatre to see Mrs Siddons perform.[57]

Attending or hosting dinners with overt or covert political purposes was expected of women from politically active families. In the country, dining with the squire and his family, with the local aldermen (with or without their wives), or even with groups of freeholders (most likely during election years) was a familial political duty, hardly an option. In London, where the need to entertain across social divides in order to maintain a political interest was minimized, dinners might dwindle into social gatherings of friends. On the other hand, as Lady Katherine Murray's dinner with Lady Rockingham indicated, they might also be politicized to advance personal or factional interests. In such cases, it was important that the company include a number of hand-picked guests who could be relied upon to flatter the guest of honour's sense of self-importance or put him at his ease.[58]

Eighteenth-century politicians sometimes used private visits and dinners *en famille* as marks of favour.[59] For women this could be an imposition, but it was an inescapable one. Usually husbands and wives

[55] This practice did not disappear in the nineteenth century. Lady Shelley records being the only woman present at a dinner of politicians at Robert Peel's on 23 Nov. 1819: 'Of course politics were much discussed, though we are all on the same side—against the Radicals', in *Diary of Frances Lady Shelley*, ed. Edgcumbe, ii. 90.

[56] When Therese Parker's MP husband held 'a Man dinner which she did not like', she simply went and dined with her sister: BL, Add. MS 48,218, fol. 37^{v}, Anne Robinson to Frederick Robinson, Whitehall, 1 Mar. 1773.

[57] 'Henry Mackenzie to [unknown], London, 26 Mar. 1792', in *HMC Home* (1902), 137–8.

[58] See Lady Shelley's efforts to ensure that the duke of Wellington's first visit to her home in Sussex was a success: '10 Oct. 1819', *Diary of Frances, Lady Shelley*, ed. Edgcumbe, ii. 66–8.

[59] See Newcastle's use of an invitation to dine with his wife: BL, Add. MS 32,933, fol. 269, Newcastle to Henry Bilson Legge, Newcastle House, 13 Jan. 1762.

worked together to ensure that a few select guests were present to ease the burden of entertaining. Occasionally, however, even a woman as committed to playing the part of 'La femme d'un Ministre' as Lady Emily Kildare could find herself in an awkward situation, if a guest arrived completely unexpectedly:[60] 'My Sister says she don't understand the Adjutant Generals dining with me *en famille* that as you may imagine was by chance Lord K[ildare] had invited him as he does all Officers & people in employment now he is in the Government and he happened to come one Day when we were quite alone that's to say *en famille* the Girls, Lady Dowager and ourselves.'[61] Indeed, such a predicament would have been difficult for Lady Kildare's sister, Lady Caroline Fox, who was uncomfortable in social situations. Lavinia, Lady Spencer, was another political wife who kept her socio-political activities to a bare minimum, but in her case it was because she disliked having to mix with persons of lower rank. When her husband was at the Admiralty during the French Revolutionary Wars, it was customary to invite all returning sea captains to dinner. She accepted the men but refused to invite their wives, thus pre-empting any need to maintain their acquaintance later.[62]

Politically astute or ambitious women not only accepted the necessity of these sorts of meals, but also even initiated them. An invitation to dine with Lady Rockingham was known to be as political as it was social. Whether she was persuading chance guests to stay for dinner and discussion at Wentworth Woodhouse,[63] or issuing invitations as part of her political armoury in Bath or London, she frequently acted on her own. Like the duchess of Devonshire after her, she turned her London home into the Whigs' headquarters. She was particularly noted for using her dinners to secure Rockinghamites who were wavering in their loyalties. That she would have 'influence' was simply assumed: 'Mr Arskine & Gilbert Elliot came to see me ... I told him of Lady Rockingham having invitd Mr Townshend to supp with her, & that she had done the same by Mr Conway when he was supposed to be cool towards the Ministers; that a fine Lady wd always have influence, & I wish'd they wou'd not accept of her invitations.'[64] While being a 'fine

[60] BL, Add. MS 51,426, fol. 119^{v}, Lady Kildare to Henry Fox, Kildare House, 5 Mar. 1757.

[61] Ibid., fols. 76^{v}–7, Lady Kildare to Henry Fox [Carton?], 19 Aug. [1756?].

[62] *Diary of Frances Lady Shelley*, ed. Edgcumbe, i. 78.

[63] See e.g. Bodl., MS North d.11, fols. 68–9, Dartmouth to Guilford, Sandal, 7 Oct. 1767.

[64] 'Journal, London, 16 Mar. 1767', in *Letters and Journals of Lady Mary Coke*, i. 178.

Lady' in all its senses was surely a factor in a political hostess's success, the best hostesses had other characteristics as well. They were charming, good at handling people, sensitive to social nuance, and possessed a thorough understanding of the workings of the political world. These were skills that were honed with age and practice. According to Lady Holland, who spoke from experience, being a political hostess was ideally suited to 'all women of a certain age and in a situation to achieve it'.[65]

Of the older women who were political hostesses in the second half of the eighteenth century, Lady Hervey was the most renowned. Cultured and intelligent, her wit and beauty as a young woman had been celebrated in the writings of Pope, Gay, and Voltaire. As a maid of honour to Queen Caroline, and later as the wife of the famous courtier Lord Hervey, she had been at the heart of the political world for most of her adult life. By the accession of George III she was in her sixties, and had been connected with the Court for nearly half a century. This put her in a strong position as an experienced hostess and political advisor at the start of George III's reign. She was known for her daily dinners during the parliamentary season, at which there would be no more than six guests, 'all chosen esprits' (male and female).[66] A lifelong Francophile, she self-consciously patterned her entertaining along French lines, but her political instincts were distinctly English. She provided her guests with an excellent table and, if contemporary comments are to be believed, encouraged them to exchange 'News' and discuss politics. They, in turn, seem to have found their evenings profitable as well as enjoyable. Thus, when Lord Ilchester relayed the latest Wilkite gossip to his brother in 1763, he noted: 'All that I have wrote I heard this evening at Lady Hervey's.'[67] Similarly, when Sir William Musgrave sent a report to Lord Carlisle regarding his prospects for a seat at Morpeth, the information he had gathered at Lady Hervey's was included: 'The duke [Grafton] has hopes that Mr. Black may be induced to quit Sudbury and engage on your interest, but I have just been dining with Lady Hervey, where I saw Lady Sar[ah] B[unbury], and she thinks that Mr. Bl[ake] is too far engaged.'[68]

[65] 'Lady Bessborough to Granville Leveson Gower, [?] Feb. 1811', in *Letters of Lord Granville Leveson Gower*, ed. Granville, ii. 381.

[66] Hester Chapone to [unnamed], Chelsea, 28 July 1768, in *The Works of Hester Chapone*, 4 vols. (London, 1807), ii. 166.

[67] BL, Add. MS 51,421, fol. 42, Ilchester to Holland [London, 3 May 1763].

[68] 'Sir William Musgrave to Lord Carlisle, London, 29 Oct. 1767', in *HMC Carlisle*, 218.

Lady Hervey's regular guests included established politicians[69] interleaved with interesting and/or beautiful young women, some of whom, like Lady Sarah Bunbury, were also political. Promising young men were also included. Securing the support and favour of a political hostess could ease a young man's entry into political society and influence his future 'connexions' by introducing him to 'appropriate' politicians in a social setting. Henry Fox recorded just such a meeting in 1758: 'On Thursday at Ly Hervey's to meet a very amiable young Man, of great Merit,—Lord Charlemont.'[70] Several years later, when Charlemont was working frantically to avert a political crisis over the superficially trivial issue of the Irish peeresses' right to walk in the procession at George III's wedding, he turned to Lady Hervey for advice. In his memoirs he reflected with pride on his acquaintance with her: 'as all the celebrated men of rank and talents in London or Paris then were.'[71]

Of course, mixed-sex dining was by no means a guarantee of dinner-table politics, or breakfast or tea-table politics for that matter. There were undoubtedly many instances when stereotypes ran true and politics entered the dining-room with the port, after the ladies had retired. Contemporary sources suggest, however, that among the political elite this was not the norm. Instead, the political content of meals seems to have been as varied (and as variable) as the guest-list. Some people were simply expected to be sources of political information: 'Dinner—Mrs Crewe came but no News', noted Edmund Burke ruefully in 1787.[72] Others were political sponges. When Lady Mary Coke was not debating political issues over the dinner tables she frequented, she seems to have been soaking up political gossip. Her journal entries and letters to her sisters record many dinners and much News. Whether Lady Mary regularly 'worked' the dinners she attended for her own ends is hard to say, but there is no doubt that she did so at times. Personal and political agendas were often bound together, and a captive audience over a dinner table was too good an opportunity to pass up. If nothing else, the conversation could be turned so as to broach a subject and gauge reaction; if well received, it could be followed up later through other channels.

69 See, BL, Add. MS 51,416, fols. 19, 57, 67, 90.

70 BL, Add. MS 51,416, fol. 57, Henry Fox to Lady Caroline Fox, Pay Office, 28 Nov. 1758.

71 *HMC Charlemont*, i. 15–17; *Memoirs of the Political and Private Life of James Caulfield, Earl of Charlemont*, ed. Francis Hardy (London, 1810), 64.

72 'Edmund Burke to Richard Burke Jr, n. pl., 19 June 1787', in *Correspondence of Edmund Burke*, ed. Copeland *et al.*, v. 340.

POLITICS AND SOCIETY

Just as eighteenth-century politics was by no means restricted to high politics, women's exposure to or involvement in politics was not limited to the home. Remaining politically aloof or unaware would have been almost impossible for women whenever a political situation came to dominate society. At the end of the Seven Years War, when popular animosity against Lord Bute was at its height, Elizabeth Montagu's sister, Mrs Scott, described the situation in England to her brother in Italy:

> The lowest artificer thinks now of nothing but the constitution of the government . . . The English always seemed born politicians, but were never so universally mad on the subject as at present. If you order a mason to build an oven, he immediately inquires about the progress of the peace, and descants on the preliminaries. A carpenter, instead of putting up a shelf to a cupboard, talks of the Princess Dowager, of Lord Treasarre, and of secretaries of state. Neglected lie the trowel and the chisel, the mortar dries and the glue hardens while the persons who should use them are busied with dissertations on the government.[73]

Whenever this reign of politics swept out into the streets, as it did in the form of crowd action, it affected women as well as men. Only a particularly brave or foolhardy woman chanced attracting the ire of the crowd. Something of both, Lady Mary Coke put herself at risk during the Middlesex election of 1768 by neglecting to ensure that her servants were properly primed: 'I mett with a Woman in Piccadilly that was rather uncivil. As I came by, She was crying out, "Wilkes & liberty", & my servants making no answer, She gave such a blow to my Chair that She had very near over set it.'[74] Her situation could have been much worse. Horace Walpole, writing at the same time, described the mobs blocking Piccadilly; they were busily tearing apart the coaches of Wilkes's opposition, scratching and spoiling other carriages with graffiti, and breaking their windows.[75]

Windows, in general, were a favourite target of crowd action. Residents who did not illuminate their houses or accede to other crowd demands were fortunate if broken glass was the only damage they

[73] 'Mrs Scott to Mr. Robinson, n. pl., Sept. 1762', in *A Lady of the Last Century*, ed. John Doran (London, 1873), 125–6.

[74] 'Journal, London, 29 Mar. 1768', in *Letters and Journals of Lady Mary Coke*, ii. 226.

[75] 'Horace Walpole to Sir Horace Mann, Arlington Street, 31 Mar.–1 Apr., 1768', in *The Yale Edition of Horace Walpole's Correspondence*, ed. W. S. Lewis, 48 vols. (London, 1937–83), xxiii. 6.

suffered. With a hostile crowd even these regular precautions might not prevent vandalism. Given the potential danger to people and property that crowd action could pose, refusing to comply with a mob's demands was a political statement in itself. It took as determined a woman as the duchess of Hamilton to refuse to compromise her political beliefs in the face of a Wilkesite mob:

> The day was very quiet, but at night they [the mob] rose again, and obliged almost every house in town to be lighted up, even the Duke of Cumberland's and Princess Amelie's. About one o'clock they marched to the Duchess of Hamilton's in Argyle Buildings (Lord Lorne being in Scotland). She was obstinate and would not illuminate, though with child and as they hope of an heir to the family, and with the Duke her son and the rest of her children in the house. There is a small court and parapet-wall before the house: they brought iron crows, tore down the gates, pulled up the pavement, and battered the house for three hours. They could not find the key of the back door, nor send for any assistance.[76]

This kind of popular political action was most likely to occur when particular issues divided society into political camps. But the social activities of the political elite—far from immune to 'the baneful effects of politicks'[77]—could become specifically, sometimes surprisingly aggressively, politicized by events that did not involve the masses. Balls and assemblies seem to have been the most regularly affected. Held simultaneously by the hostesses of opposing factions, or sponsored by contending candidates or clubs, they raised political awareness, polarized political feelings, and forced the members of the political elite to declare their allegiances publicly through their attendance and, at times, by their dress.

Like other aspects of their involvement in political life, women's participation in highly politicized social events elicited a double-edged response. They were expected to take part, but they were also criticized for doing so. Conservatives, moralists, and individuals who found it politically convenient to condemn the activities of an opposing faction might all complain of women' activities. If nothing else, traditional notions about women's love of meddling still had some purchase, and blame for the periodic bouts of political frenzy that swept through society could be laid at their feet. While there is little evidence that women fostered dissension out of spite or some inborn desire to unleash the forces of chaos, it is true that they were often actively engaged in elevating

[76] Ibid. 6–7.

[77] BL, MS Coll. Althorp, F. 53, Mrs Howe to Lady Spencer, n. pl., 17 Apr. [1784].

the political temperature and politicizing elite society itself. Personal loyalty, political belief, and a desire for social or political importance were all motivating factors. So, too, was the sheer excitement of the game.

THE REGENCY CRISIS

It was with the Regency Crisis of 1788 that this interweaving of politics and society reached its eighteenth-century apogee. Historians have tended to focus on the constitutional aspects of the Crisis and the machinations of the various politicians and doctors, but they have paid little attention to the fact the Crisis was also an intensely divisive socio-political event, one in which women took a leading role.[78] Not only did women play factional parts in the Regency Crisis, but their social activities also came to take on symbolic importance for the political community at large.

George III fell ill at the beginning of November 1788, a time of year when few politicians were in London. By the time that it became apparent that a Regency would be necessary and the political elite had gathered in London, it was the beginning of December.[79] From then on the political temperature rose rapidly. By the end of December the Regency had become the dominant and divisive issue in society. This had dire consequences for social harmony. Lord Jersey complained to his old friend, Lady Spencer, 'one subject only occupies the minds & consequently no other discourse can prevail—I have been witness to very few unpleasant scenes, but I have heard that many, almost too serious, have occurred when accidental opposite opinions have met in private houses'.[80] Women from the opposing political camps became actively—even avidly—partisan. It was not long before conservative men like Lord Sydney were attributing the enmity to women's political enthusiasm:

[78] John Derry's high-political monograph on the Regency Crisis remains unrivalled: John W. Derry, *The Regency Crisis and the Whigs, 1788–88* (Cambridge, 1963). Most recently, Amanda Foreman has touched on the socio-political aspects of the Crisis in exploring the involvement of the duchess of Devonshire. She also reveals the rivalry between the women of the opposing factions and marks the triumph of the administration political hostess, the duchess Gordon, at the end of the Crisis. See Foreman, *Georgiana*, ch. 13.

[79] e.g. the duke and duchess of Devonshire and Elizabeth Foster were still at Chatsworth when the king became ill. They left for London on 18 November, arriving at Devonshire House at 5 a.m. on 20 November. Charles James Fox undoubtedly had the longest and most exhausting trip, tearing across Italy and France to arrive in London on 24 November. See BL, Add. MS 41,579, Elizabeth Foster, 'Journal of events of my own times, 1788'; Derry, *Regency Crisis and the Whigs*.

[80] BL, MS Coll. Althorp, F. 112, Jersey to Lady Spencer, London [31 Dec. 1788].

We have seen no times when it has been so necessary to separate parties in private company. The acrimony is beyond anything you can conceive. The ladies are as usual at the head of all animosity, and are distinguished by caps, ribands, and other such ensigns of party. They have driven old Queensberry out of England by calling him a Rat for deserting his master to hobble after a young Prince.[81]

The Crisis generated such antagonism between the opposing groups that even the façade of carefully constructed politeness that marked late eighteenth-century society was breached. While finding the highly political and equally eloquent duchess of Gordon at the opera 'surrounded by men talking politics as fast and as loud as possible' would not have been unusual at any time,[82] an assembly where the women of one faction greeted the entrance of those from the other with distinctly unladylike hooting and groaning definitely was.[83] Similarly, the behaviour that Martha Harcourt encountered at another assembly would have made conduct-book writers despair: 'there was a great assembly; the Regency Caps nodding at each other all over the room, and boasting against those who were without them, and against those who wore the Constitutional Coats, which were also very numerous. You may be sure the Dss of Rutland did not wear the cap.'[84] Another supporter of the Court remarked with satisfaction on a comparable situation at one of the duchess

[81] 'Sydney to Cornwallis, London, 21 Feb. 1789', in *Correspondence of Charles, First Marquis Cornwallis*, ed. Charles Ross, 3 vols. (London, 1835), ii. 406.

[82] 'Miss Sayer to Madame Huber, Audley Street, 27 Jan. [1789]', in *The Journal and Correspondence of William, Lord Auckland*, ed. Robert J. Eden, Bishop of Bath and Wells, 2 vols. (London, 1861), ii. 281.

[83] 'Journal, London, 2–3 Mar. [1789]', in *Betsy Sheridan's Journal*, ed. William Lefanu (Oxford, 1986), 153. I would like to thank Susan Skedd for this reference.

[84] 'Hon. Mrs Martha Harcourt to Lady Harcourt [London], 16 Jan. 1789', in *Harcourt Papers*, ed. Harcourt, vol. iv, pt. 1, p. 180. The reference to Constitutional Coats is to the 'Constitutional uniform' adopted by the members of the Constitutional Club. These men who supported the king used fashion in the same way that the supporters of the prince used blue and buff. Their uniform, as described proudly by James Bland Burges, would have been striking: 'a dark blue frock, with a broad orange velvet cape and large yellow buttons round each of which is the inscription, "Constitutional Club". The waistcoat is white kerseymere, with yellow buttons bordered round with orange-coloured silk. The breeches are white kerseymere with yellow buttons. In point of taste we certainly beat the Blue and Buff of our opponents.' Moreover, as Sir James makes clear in a letter of 11 Jan. 1789, they wore the 'uniform' in the Commons as well as at social events: 'Our uniform goes well. Several people told me they will put it on. To-day in the House we were a pretty knot of orange capes, Pitt, Lord Mornington, Lord Bayham, Lord Belgrave, Villiers, Addington, and myself. I never saw Mr. Lamb so pleased with anything as with this dress, which he says is a wise and manly thing. I have been endeavouring to make Hasting's party assume it, and I believe I shall be successful, for two have promised to do so.' As quoted in *Letters and Correspondence of Sir James Bland Burges, Bart.*, ed. Hutton, 126.

of Gordon's balls: 'The Prince ask'd the Dutchess of Gordon to wear such a Cap; she said she would sooner be hang'd. He made the same Request to the Dutchess of Rutland, who refused, tho' in politer Terms'.[85]

This use of fashion to declare political allegiance was a long-established eighteenth-century practice by the time of the Regency Crisis.[86] It was especially common during elections, when women and men both sported cockades, and women ornamented their dresses (often in 'party' colours) and themselves with ribbons, bandeaux, and other political symbols. True to form, the practice engendered both criticism and encouragement—usually simultaneously—from opposing political camps. The adoption of the Regency Cap by the female supporters of the prince of Wales during the Regency Crisis is probably the best-recorded instance of the politics of fashion. The cap itself was an impressive creation: 'mountains of tumbled gauze, with three large feathers in front, tied together with a knot of ribbon, on which was printed in gold letters, "Honi soit qui mal y pense, de la Regence".' It was also expensive, costing at least seven-and-a-half guineas.[87] While this alone must have ensured that it remained fashionably exclusive, enough acerbic comments survive to suggest that it was worn by women other than those of the innermost Whig circle. Above all, it was most decidedly a political purchase and was worn deliberately. Regency Caps appeared at an assortment of social functions, where they served their purpose well: they attracted attention and made a forceful, visual, political statement.

When the king recovered, the country celebrated. The celebratory Drawing-Room of 26 March 1789 was a testimony to the importance still attached to the monarchy. It saw such numbers of the political elite in

[85] Lady Stafford to Granville Leveson Gower [London], 12 Feb. 1789, in *Letters of Lord Granville Leveson Gower*, ed. Granville, i. 14–15.

[86] During the brouhaha prior to the repeal of the Jewish Naturalization Act, opposing political factions appear to have vied to 'out-Christian' each other. *The Connoisseur* satirized women's use of Christian symbols, especially the cross, to decorate their clothing and themselves: 'I observed the other Night at the Assembly, that the Ladies seemed to vie with each other in Hanging out the Ensigns of their Faith in orthodox Ribands, bearing the Inscription on NO JEWS, CHRISTIANITY FOR EVER. They likewise wore little Crosses at their Breasts; their *Pompons* were formed into Crucifixes, their Knots disposed in the same Angles, and so many Parts of their Habits moulded into that Shape, that the whole Assembly looked like the Court on St. *Andrew's* Day': *The Connoisseur*, no. 13 (25 Apr. 1754), i. 77. Interestingly, this piece was quoted in *Jackson's Oxford Journal*, where the battle to spearhead the repeal was most heated: *Jackson's Oxford Journal*, 18 May 1754.

[87] 'Harcourt to Lady Harcourt, London, 25 Jan. 1789', in *Harcourt Papers*, vol. iv, pt. 1, p. 200. Madame Huber claims that the caps cost at least 7 guineas: Madame Huber to Mrs Eden [London], 21 Feb. [1789]', in *Journal and Correspondence of Lord Auckland*, ed. Eden, ii. 292.

attendance that there was an excessive crush. Supporters of the king came to reiterate their loyalty, those who had supported the prince to reinvent it. Lady Louisa Stuart (Lord Bute's daughter) informed her sister of her experience:

The King is recovered, and everyone else is gone mad! Oh, what a winter we have passed! The Drawing-room on Thursday was crowded many degrees beyond any Birthday I ever saw, and really made a frightful scene—many people crying and fainting, and going into screaming fits. I was so squeezed and demolished myself, I was near crying too, and trembled so when I was thrown against the Queen, I did not know what she said to me. Lady Macartney was in violent hysterics after she came home.[88]

Lord Jersey echoed this, but looked at the situation more pragmatically. The problems, he informed Lady Spencer, arose from bad planning of crowd movement past the queen, combined with people's desire to be the first to proffer their congratulations: 'the consequences were natural; faintings away, screaming, loss of Caps, bags, shoes, & I suppose almost every part of the dress that was not quite attached strongly to the Person of the wearer.' There was also a certain triumphalism among the king's female supporters that manifested itself in their dress: 'A very great majority of the Ladies wore a bandeau with God save the King upon it, & had pictures, Medals & a variety of extraordinary & curious modes of expressing & marking the same sentiment—the Dss. of Portland, Ly Fitz[william] & others of the same opinion [the women of the prince's camp] did not wear any such symptoms of loyalty.'[89] Lady Louisa Stuart's more detailed description makes it clear that refusing to wear some token of loyalty would have been immediately noticeable, as even the queen and the princesses had done so:

Almost everybody at Court had some motto or other in their cap. '*God Save the King*' '*Long life to the King*.' '*Vive le Roi, Dieu nous l'a rendu*.' The Queen had a *bandeau* of '*God Save the King*' in diamonds, the Princesses the uniform cap with gold spangles, but two or three ladies had stuck up a huge print on sattin as big as one's two hands, in a frame, Britannia kneeling to return thanks, which was a *new touch*, indeed.[90]

[88] 'Lady Louisa Stuart to Lady Portarlington, South Audley Street [post-26 Mar.] 1789', in *A Prime Minister and his Son*, ed. E. Stuart Wortley (London, 1925), 217.

[89] BL. MS Coll. Althorp, F. 112, Jersey to Lady Spencer [London, 27 Mar. 1789].

[90] 'Lady Louisa Stuart to Lady Portarlington [London], 30 Mar. 1789', in Lady Louisa Stuart, *Gleanings from an Old Portfolio*, ed. Mrs. Godfrey Clark, 3 vols. (Edinburgh, 1895–8), ii. 119.

Balls also heralded the king's recovery. Balls were one of the most consistent vehicles of faction for the political elite, and this event proved to be no exception. The political divisions between the members of White's and Brookes's clubs carried over into the subscription balls they held at the Pantheon and the Opera-house, respectively.[91] White's triumphal ball took place first and appears to have been the most splendid, presumably reflecting both the ten guineas that each of the organizers subscribed and their sense of self-conscious, political theatre. To emphasize their loyalty to the king's cause (and their success), they specified that all the women appear dressed in an elaborate costume: 'a very pretty white Uniform with gold lapels',[92] to be worn with a medallion around the neck and loyal versions of the Regency Cap. Young and fashionable women were to wear caps with ' "*God Save the King*" upon it in gold spangles, and four very high feathers on the other side'; a less showy variation without feathers was designed for chaperones.[93] As Lady Louisa Stuart pointedly remarked, 'Loyalty is a most expensive virtue at present'. According to her sums, the costume for White's ball cost between twenty-three and twenty-four pounds, the medallion five guineas, and the caps another six guineas. While some women would have been able to cut costs by using their own dressmakers, others would have had to turn to one of the three milliners who had been appointed to make the costume by the arbiters of fashion for the night, Lady Chatham and the duchesses of Rutland and Gordon.[94] One (probably intended) consequence of the dress requirements was to ensure that the vast majority of opposition women refused to attend:

> The Opposition ladies . . . decline coming to the ball; but there probably will be some exceptions. Mrs Sawbridge had ordered her dress, but upon finding that the Duchess of Devonshire was not to go to the ball, she thought it would be improper in her, and therefore countermanded her dress. I know the Queen had a wish, with the Princesses, to see the ball; but it was given by subscription, and was evidently a party ball. The idea was laid aside, and they are not to come.[95]

[91] 'A. Storer to William Eden, London, 21 Apr. 1789', in *Journal and Correspondence of Lord Auckland*, ed. Eden, ii. 315.

[92] Margaret Grenville to Lady Camelford [London, ?3 Apr. 1789], BL, Add. MS 69,292 [unfoliated].

[93] Lady Louisa Stuart to Lady Portarlington [London], 30 Mar. 1789, in her *Gleanings from an Old Portfolio*, ed. Clark, ii. 119. Lady Louisa's detailed description of the 'uniform' itself in this letter emphasizes its splendour. The visual impact in the ballroom must have been dazzling.

[94] Ibid.

[95] 'Lt.-Gen. Grant to Lord Cornwallis, London, 18 Mar. 1789', in *Correspondence of Cornwallis*, ii. 434–5.

With an entrance fee of three-and-a-half guineas per person, Brookes's ball was also meant to be exclusive. However, it was not the cost, but whether the women who had supported the Court would attend that made it the talk of the town. Even Gilbert Elliot, who was anything but enamoured with what he termed 'petticoat politics', informed his wife that it was rumoured that the women of the Court faction would attend, 'by way of censuring ours for staying away from White's'.[96] On the day of the ball itself it was still a matter of speculation. People believed that the Court women would not attend after all, wrote Anthony Storer, 'as the ladies in opposition would not honour the Pantheon with their appearance, so (it is said) the ladies who support Government will not deign to attend to-night the ball at the Opera-house'.[97] It was because the women were a politically identifiable group—'the ladies who support Government'—that their attendance was at issue. As the vanguard of the victors, what they did bore the scrutiny of the political world at large. Not only did their actions reveal the depth of the social divisions caused by the Crisis and the willingness (or lack of it) of the winners to show magnanimity and begin the healing process, but they were also important politically, as a foreshadowing of the nature of political dealings between the administration and the prince's supporters in the immediate future.

96 'Sir Gilbert to Lady Elliot, London, 2 Apr. 1789', *Life and Letters of Sir Gilbert Elliot*, ed. Minto, i. 294.

97 'A. Storer to William Eden, London, 21 Apr. 1789', in *Journal and Correspondence of Lord Auckland*, ed. Eden, ii. 315.

4

Women and Patronage

In January 1759 Lady Henry Beauclerk first addressed the duke of Newcastle in his role as first lord of the Treasury, in what was to become an extended campaign for patronage:

> As your Grace possobly may not give me an opertunety of Speaking to you before you See the King, I beg leave to tell you: I have wrote to His Majesty to beg an addition to My Pension. I have no reason to doubt of His Majestys good Intention towards me: but cannot hope to Succeed So well as by your Graces assistance. Therefore My Lord Duke flatter Myself you will on this occasion, recollect the many pretentions I have to the Royal Favour. I Shou'd not prehaps have wanted this Instance of It had not my Father risqued with the Late Lord Lincoln & others all His fortune in Supporting the Succession of the House of Hanover: I Value myself on the Honour of My family, who ventured, & was ruin'd. In So glorious a Cause but let not me & mine, be the only unprovided of that Sett. I dare not name a Sum: your Grace will find me now Stand, I believe the Lowest on the List. but I will hope Through your favour to receive from the Kings Bounty, a proper Maintainance, for Lord Lovelaces Daughter, a Servant of the late Queen's; and the Wife of Lord Henry Beauclerk.[1]

Lady Beauclerk's appeal is representative of patronage requests made by many eighteenth-century women and men: she appealed first for herself (to have her pension augmented) and then for her children; she made her requests both directly to patrons and indirectly through brokers, by letter, and in person; and she was firm in her belief that she was owed patronage on personal and familial grounds. She based her arguments on a combination of factors, including rank, lineage, honour, loyalty, and service. Like most supplicants, she had no guarantee of success—immediate, or even eventual. Her arguments carried weight, however, and her determination and sheer dogged obstinacy finally produced results.

[1] BL, Add. MS 32,887, fols. 442–3, Lady Beauclerk to Newcastle, n. pl., 31 Jan. 1759.

THE PATRONAGE SYSTEM

It is a historical commonplace that patronage was central to eighteenth-century English politics. The expansion of the state and the growing importance of parliament saw a significant rise in the amount of patronage available and in its importance as a tool of political management. In a political society where modern notions of professional, meritocratic public service had yet to make any significant impact, and where access to the trinity of power, place, and profit remained personal and idiosyncratic, patronage operated through linked networks of individuals by means of interest and influence. Political patronage was only one manifestation of a universal phenomenon. As a means of recruitment and advancement, patronage also pervaded the eighteenth-century domestic, cultural, social, and economic domains. It was still, as Linda Levy Peck has noted for the seventeenth century, simultaneously 'symbiotic and symbolic', comprised of 'private, dependent, deferential alliances' that benefited both client and patron, and was expressed in a 'theory of mutual, indeed, social benefits, and the practice of gift-giving'.[2] The political affiliations which formed the basis of many eighteenth-century client–patron relationships were still formed through personal contacts—largely through mutual friends, relatives, or people in the community who were acknowledged as middlemen or brokers.

Historians who have studied patronage in the eighteenth century have tended to treat it as a male stronghold. In part, women's invisibility stems from the assumption that contemporary social and legal constraints effectively precluded them from involvement by preventing them from fulfilling the transactional requirements of patronage. Little attention has been paid to mitigating factors. Women had a demographic advantage for at least the first half of the century, which increased the possibility of their inheriting property, political interests, and patronage themselves or having to manage it for under-age sons. Similarly, wars took men away from home, which left women managing their husbands' or families' interests. Furthermore, there were always some women who brought property, political interests, and patronage into marriage and who retained influence over its bestowal, either informally because of their relationships with their husbands, or formally because of the nature of their marriage settlements. These factors combined to ensure that not all

[2] Linda Levy Peck, *Court Patronage and Corruption in Early Stuart England* (London, 1990), 3.

women were clients: there were always some who had significant influence as brokers and others who were patrons in their own rights, or in the right of their sons or husbands. Finally, while patronage was about reciprocity and women might not in themselves be able to reciprocate in the way that men could, the importance of the gender difference can be overstated: in the eighteenth century patronage was frequently bestowed upon individuals as representatives of families for services already rendered; even when patronage was encumbered with future expectations that women could not fulfil personally (for instance, for support in parliament), these demands might readily be met by male family members.

Despite its importance, however, eighteenth-century political patronage has frequently attracted more polemic than analysis. For many nineteenth- and early twentieth-century historians, especially those grounded in reforming or Whig traditions, it was simply something to be reacted against: a symbol of the old corruption of pre-reform, pre-modern politics. Mary Bateson, for instance, writing in 1892, was representative in describing the 'appetite for promotion' found in the duke of Newcastle's papers (and in eighteenth-century political correspondence in general) as both a 'vice' and an 'evil'. Nor was she alone in smugly believing that it had been expunged by the forces of progress over the course of the nineteenth century.[3] This equation of patronage with corruption was effectively undermined by Lewis Namier in the 1920s. In revealing the limitations on eighteenth-century patronage, he demonstrated not only that the Crown and Treasury had less control over patronage than had often been assumed, but also that patronage was generally used to reward past service or relieve current need: it was not a guarantee of future political support.[4]

The mid-twentieth-century rise of social history and the subsequent move away from high politics, compounded perhaps by a modern distaste for the self-seeking sycophancy of client–patron relationships, shifted historians' attention away from patronage.[5] J. M. Bourne, writing in 1986, returned to the subject to argue for the continued importance of

[3] Mary Bateson, 'Clerical Preferment under Newcastle', *Eng. Hist. Review*, 7 (1892), 685–96.

[4] Namier, *Structure of Politics*; Harold Perkin, *Origins of Modern English Society* (London, 1991); J. H. Plumb, *The Growth of Political Stability in England, 1675–1725* (London, 1967); also his *The First Four Georges* (London, 1987), 78.

[5] See e.g. Richard Middleton, 'Newcastle and the Conduct of Patronage During the Seven Years' War', *Brit. Jl. Eighteenth-Century Studies*, 7 (1989), 175–86; James J. Sack, 'The House of Lords and Parliamentary Patronage in Great Britain, 1802–1832', *Hist. Jl.*, 23 (1980), 913–38; M. W. McCahill, 'Peers, Patronage and the Industrial Revolution, 1760–

patronage long after parliamentary reform in 1832. While initiatives from the late eighteenth century onwards gradually removed rotten boroughs and the most obvious forms of Crown and Treasury patronage, other opportunities for patronage actually increased in the nineteenth century. The growth of local and national government (especially the proliferation of boards, commissions, and committees), the creation of the civil service, the growing importance of empire (particularly India), the development of the honours system, and so on all provided new possibilities for patrons and clients alike.[6] To what extent women were included or excluded by these developments requires a study that is more specifically attuned to women's involvement than Bourne's account; however, anecdotal examples reveal nineteenth-century women operating as their eighteenth-century grandmothers had. Moreover, Bourne highlights two important points of continuity which suggest that women of the political elite could well have retained the motivation and the opportunity for continued involvement: first, that family remained 'at the centre of the world which the pursuit of patronage reveals', and that forwarding the interests of the family was 'a duty, an opportunity and an aspiration'; and secondly, that private, domestic patronage, centred on the country house, remained 'a socially significant phenomenon until the certainties of English upper-class life were overwhelmed in the aftermath of the Great War'. Patronage may have lost some of the 'peculiar intensity and importance' that it had held in the eighteenth century, but it was far from a spent force.[7]

Bourne's conclusions echo those of social scientists, who have concluded that patronage adapts instead of disappearing with modernization.[8] Indeed, most of the recent research into patronage arises from social scientists' interest in the nature and operation of patronage as a

1800', *Jl. Brit. Studies*, 16 (1976), 84–107. The preponderance of contemporary work on patronage has focused on the early modern period: Linda Levy Peck, 'Benefits, Brokers and Beneficiaries: The Culture of Exchange in Seventeenth-Century England', in B. Y. Kunze and D. D. Brautigam (eds.), *Court, Country and Culture: Essays in Early Modern British History in Honor of Perez Zagorin* (Rochester, 1992), 109–27; also her *Court Patronage and Corruption in Early Stuart England*; Barbara J. Harris, 'Women and Politics in Early Tudor England', *Hist. Jl.*, 33 (1990), 259–81; Kevin Sharpe, 'Faction at the Early Stuart Court', *Hist. Today*, 33 (1983), 39–46; Simon Adams, 'Faction, Clientage, and Party: English Politics, 1550–1603', ibid. 32 (1982), 33–9; David Starkey, 'From Feud to Faction: English Politics Circa 1450–1550', ibid. 16–21.

[6] Bourne, *Patronage and Society in Nineteenth-Century England*.

[7] Ibid. 97, 64, 29.

[8] Jeremy Boissevain, *Friend of Friends: Networks, Manipulators and Coalitions* (Oxford, 1974); S. N. Eisenstadt, 'Preface', in Verena Burkolter, *The Patronage System: Some Theoretical Remarks* (Basel, 1976), p. vii.

system of transactions, relationships, and power. They see patronage as a system particularly well suited for apportioning resources in stratified societies, based as it is upon 'a certain logic of social exchange', structured around transactions which are unequal and open-ended, but mutually beneficial.[9] Their insights are useful to keep in mind when considering patronage in the eighteenth century. As Naomi Tadmor has demonstrated, political patronage operated in the localities, not just at the level of the political elite, but also extended downwards to include the disenfranchised: thus, patronage was central to the 'dense network of political "*friendship*"' in which non-voting shopkeepers such as Thomas Turner were embedded. Client–patron relations in Turner's village of East Hoathly extended down from the local magnate, the duke of Newcastle, through his agent and the agent's daughter, who was married to the local rector. Consequently, even such everyday business decisions—whether he would buy the agent's wool at the price demanded or whether he would sell the rector's wife raisins at cost price—had political dimensions.[10]

Patronage arrangements are made through networks of individuals, with clients approaching patrons directly or through brokers. The brokers' value is strategic, depending upon the size of their networks, their access to information, and their proximity to (and influence over) patrons.[11] All of the parties enter into and end patronage relationships voluntarily, usually preferring to keep them indeterminate and long-term. A sense of debt and credit provides leverage for future transactions, and allows the balance of power to shift with circumstances.[12] The gains offered by patronage may be tangible—jobs, money, position, and votes—or intangible—good-will, reputation, honour, promises of support, reciprocity, and loyalty. The vertical connexions created by patronage may predicate against the formation of strong horizontal ties, but the system as a whole encourages a sense of inclusivity or cohesion that might not otherwise be present in the society.[13] Paradoxically informal yet

[9] Luis Roniger, 'The Comparative Study of Clientelism and the Changing Nature of Civil Society in the Contemporary World', in id. and Ayse Günes-Ayata (eds.), *Democracy, Clientelism, and Civil Society* (London, 1994), 3.

[10] Naomi Tadmor, *Family and Friends in Eighteenth-Century England*, 225, 223.

[11] Boissevain, *Friend of Friends*, 154–63.

[12] S. N. Eisenstadt and Luis Roniger, *Patrons, Clients and Friends: Interpersonal Relations and the Structure of Trust in Society* (Cambridge, 1984), 48.

[13] Ayse Günes-Ayata, 'Clientelism: Premodern, Modern, Postmodern', in Roniger and Günes-Ayata (eds.), *Democracy, Clientelism, and Civil Society*, 24.

binding, patronage is at best quasi-institutional. It is also simultaneously public and private. Deals forged in private are displayed in public;[14] patron–client relations depend upon the public and the private arenas being interwoven.[15]

Eighteenth-century women's involvement in patronage, other than cultural patronage, has received little attention from historians. Still, some important work on early modern women and patronage has been done which demonstrates that eighteenth-century women's involvement had strong historical precedents. Publications by Barbara Harris and Linda Levy Peckboth reveal that early modern English women used their positions as members of political families to seek cultural, ecclesiastical, or political patronage for themselves, their kin, or their clients.[16] They reveal that women sought patronage through a multiplicity of connexions and networks, in much the same way as their male counterparts. According to Peck, early modern women made the transition from magnate-centred to Court-centred patronage by capitalizing on societal acceptance of their earlier activities and quietly extending their activities into the new arena. A similar shift may well explain women's subsequent transition to parliamentary patronage in the early eighteenth century.[17] Furthermore, the institutional powerlessness of women could mask significant patronage power—a conclusion reached by both Harris and Peck, and echoed by Sharon Kettering in her study of the patronage power of early modern French noblewomen.[18]

PATRONAGE AND POLITICS

The patronage system was, in a number of ways, eminently suited to women, especially women of the political elite. As a unique, intermediate area of political involvement, patronage linked together social and electoral politics, providing women with an important way of participating in political life. It throve in the grey areas between formal and informal

[14] Ibid.

[15] Ibid. 215.

[16] Harris, 'Women and Politics in Early Tudor England'; Peck, 'Benefits, Brokers and Beneficiaries'; also her *Court Patronage and Corruption*.

[17] Peck, *Court Patronage and Corruption*, 48, 68.

[18] Sharon Kettering, 'The Patronage Power of Early Modern French Noblewomen', *Hist. Jl.*, 32 (1989), 817–41; also her 'Gift-Giving and Patronage in Early Modern France', *French Hist.*, 2 (1988), 131–51; 'The Historical Development of Political Clientelism', *Jl. Interdisciplinary Hist.*, 18 (1988), 419–47; *Patrons, Brokers, and Clients in Seventeenth-Century France* (New York, 1986).

political involvement, public and private life, and the political and social arenas. Moreover, it also worked primarily through personal contact, connexion, and persuasion. It functioned as readily face-to-face in the dining-room and ballroom as it did at politicians' levees, in the lobbies of Westminster, or at Court. It was in this very personal, socio-political world that women were likely to move most comfortably and be most active.

The flexibility of the patronage system, with its multiplicity of points of access and degrees of involvement, could facilitate women's participation, allowing them to shape their actions to suit their inclinations or circumstances. Unfortunately for historians, the most informal and/or personal patronage requests were made face to face; consequently, they appear only tantalizingly and anecdotally in surviving sources, usually as a result of follow-up letters to confirm or formalize what had been said, or more elusively, they are mentioned in passing in letters to other correspondents. Thus, it is necessary to concentrate on the more formal aspects of patronage, particularly women's written requests preserved in political correspondences, to explore women's involvement. While the results are necessarily impressionistic, women's written patronage requests do provide insight into the kinds of requests they made, as well as their motivations and methods. They also demonstrate that women from well outside the inner political circles took part in patronage.

Fortunately, women's patronage requests survive—many from women who have left no other historical records—in the correspondences of politically active or important local families, and of politicians great and small. The more patronage that a politician controlled, the better his connexions, greater his influence, or wider his networks, the more likely he was to be solicited by men and women alike. A rich and powerful aristocrat serving as first lord, with direct access to the king and the rich pickings of Crown patronage, was certain to be inundated with requests. Among eighteenth-century first lords, the duke of Newcastle was the unrivalled master of the patronage system and has left the most extensive record of his involvement.[19] Only Robert Walpole might have had a better understanding of the importance of political patronage, but even he had relied upon Newcastle's expertise in Church and Court patronage. By 1754, when Newcastle became first lord, he had nearly fifty years of

[19] Thomas Pelham-Holles (1693–1768) was created duke of Newcastle in 1715 by George I. He was one of the few eighteenth-century politicians who did not profit personally from his lifelong involvement in Whig politics. Instead, he encumbered his vast estates and overspent an enormous rent roll in the Whig cause.

experience of borough control and electoral management, as well as thirty years of dealing with the demands of patronage that were required of a secretary of state.[20] Subsequent first lords approached patronage with varying degrees of ability or enthusiasm, but all recognized its importance, even William Pitt the Younger, whose dislike for it was such that it made him 'bilious'.[21]

WOMEN'S REQUESTS TO THE DUKE OF NEWCASTLE

Women's patronage requests in the Newcastle Papers during Newcastle's time as first lord (1754–62) are illuminating in sketching out the nature of women's involvement throughout the period. Newcastle's correspondence reveals that a small but diverse group of women took an active part in patronage, even at the highest political levels. Between 3 May 1754 and Newcastle's resignation on 26 May 1762, the Papers include 377 letters from 144 women. Of these letters, 73.2 per cent are for patronage and protection (occasionally with multiple requests per letter); 15.4 per cent are social or personal; 10.9 per cent are solely political; and a minute 0.5 per cent deal with business or legal affairs. These are only the requests that are made by women themselves; they do not include those that are made by women but appear in Newcastle's correspondence only through the medium of men's letters.

These requests suggest that women took part in patronage for many of the same reasons, in much the same way, and often with similar results, as their male counterparts. Women, like men, sought the five Ps of patronage: place, pension, preferment, parliament, and peerage. All had one of three goals in mind: to obtain something for themselves; something for their family members (usually, but not always, male); or something for others who were close or important to them (usually friends, relatives, clients, or retainers). Operating as they did in a political world where women frequently participated in politics for familial reasons or justified their involvement with familial arguments, it is understandable that the women who wrote to Newcastle often had recourse to roles as wives/widows, mothers, sisters, and daughters when making their claims. As

[20] Norman Sykes, 'Newcastle as Ecclesiastical Minister', *Eng. Hist. Review*, 57 (1942), 59–84; Reed Browning, *Newcastle* (London, 1975), 25–6; BL, Add. MS 32,927, fols. 48–9, List of Queen's Officers [7–8 Sept. 1761]; BL, Add. MS 32,925 fol. 237, Newcastle to Francis Reynolds, 21 July 1761.

[21] John Ehrman, *Younger Pitt*, 234.

might be expected, most of the women who wrote to Newcastle were clients seeking patronage—but not all. His letters also reveal women acting as brokers and, occasionally, as patrons in their own right. The avidity with which men and women appear to have sought these women out testifies to a practical acceptance of them as political actors and, by implication, to their ability to secure results.

In order to make effective requests, women had to know what patronage was available, what they could ask for, and to whom they should address their requests. This required significant political acuteness. They had to be knowledgeable enough to know which relatives, friends, or acquaintances—male or female—had influence with which patron, and who could be depended upon to lend support or act as a broker. They also had to be alert to changes in the political climate that might prejudice their chances of success by threatening a patron's access to favour or power.

While any attempt at quantifying the extent of women's overall participation in patronage is fraught with difficulties, Newcastle's surviving patronage requests for his years as first lord reveal that approximately 10 per cent of his total requests came from women. This is a small proportion, but it is not insignificant. Moreover, it also considerably under-represents women's overall involvement. Not only does it omit entirely that portion of patronage that was negotiated face to face in predominantly social situations, but it is also an incomplete record of women's written requests. As extensive as the Newcastle Papers are, anecdotal references in other politicians' correspondences indicate that a variety of women's requests to him have gone astray over time. In addition, the papers of local political families, backbench country gentlemen MPs, and politicians who were in charge of other, more specialized forms of patronage (Lord Hardwicke, Lord Holdernesse, and Henry Fox, to name only a few), all reveal additional requests. Some of these come from women who also wrote to Newcastle and were simply trying to elicit extra official support to bolster their cases, but many are from women who are not represented in the Newcastle Papers. This is due in part to different networks of acquaintances and political affiliations, but it also a reflection of the decentred nature of power and patronage at the time and of women's ability to make applications knowingly and selectively.

The demand for patronage in eighteenth-century England always outstripped supply. Considering that women's ability to benefit directly from patronage was circumscribed by their inability to hold most government appointments or places, serve in the Church, or sit in parliament, it is perhaps remarkable to find them participating at all. Yet they did, and although there are variations of degree, their requests fall into the same general categories as men's. They asked for patronage for themselves, their family members (especially sons), or for more distant relations, clients, or retainers. Their letters use the same kind of political language as men's; they were structured in the same ways; and—what is worth emphasizing—they did obtain results. The most persistent claimants even modified their arguments, their requests, or even their patrons depending upon political circumstances. It is a telling point, both about the nature of the political world and about the relationship between class and gender in the eighteenth century, that rank and relations (kin and connexions) appear to have mattered more in shaping requests and expectations, and in determining responses and outcomes, than whether the individuals making the requests were male or female. A politically knowledgeable and experienced woman of rank with a history of familial and/or factional service and loyalty, and a genuine request, was hard to ignore; she was yet harder to ignore if she also had some political interest and a link to the broker or patron.

The pattern of women's requests between 1754 and 1762 indicates that they understood the larger political context in which patronage operated. The number of requests rose when Newcastle was in a strong political position after the 1754 election, plummeted when he resigned and was briefly out of office in 1756–7, and then rose again when he returned to power. Women's involvement peaked during the 1758–9 parliamentary season. As this was both the high point of the Seven Years War and the year before a general election, military and electoral patronage requests dominated. After George II died, in October 1760, Newcastle's political position became increasingly tenuous. He continued in office under George III, but did so in the face of open hostility from the king and Lord Bute. His ability to deliver patronage was greatly diminished, and this was reflected a sharp drop in the number of patronage requests he received from men and women. Supplicants instead turned their attention to people who were in favour or had direct access to the king and Lord Bute, such as Charles Jenkinson and the duke and duchess of Northumberland.[22]

This suggests a significant level of female awareness and involvement. In terms of structure, motivation, and supporting arguments, women's patronage requests to Newcastle and other politicians conform to the

[22] See BL, Add. MS 32,928, fol. 48; BL, M/297, Reel 18, vol. 35, fol. 11^{v}.

same basic formula as men's. There is little regard to gender. They open with a brief apology for troubling the reader, followed by a passage setting out the writer's parentage and any pre-existing connexions with socially or politically important people (especially the reader). Special care is then taken to establish the claimant's worthiness: particular emphasis is paid to records of personal or familial political allegiance and service. Only then is the case in question presented, complete with whatever extenuating circumstances make it particularly unique, worthy, or distressing. More apologies—rhetorical or otherwise—then ensue. The letters usually end in a flourish of expressions of thanks and subtle or not-so-subtle attempts to flatter the reader into action, usually by praising his or her reputation and public character.

If a 'sphere' did exist with regard to patronage, it was one defined first and foremost by status and connexion, not gender: the less acquainted or lower in rank the clients, the more formal, self-deprecatory, or flattering their application. Thus, without the information that reveals that the second of the two following excerpts comes from a woman, it would be difficult to distinguish between them:

> It may appear great presumption in me, at so distant a situation to your Grace to take this Liberty. but when I consider Your Graces high Quality, and most Honorable employments have not extinguish'd the most Noble, and Generous sentiments so eminently conspicuous in [your] Graces whole Conduct, I must hope to find Pardon.[23]

> The great Character your Grace bears with all the world for Humanity and benevolence, has emboldened a woman, who once saw better days as may be Conjectured, to ask the honor of your Graces name . . .[24]

Nor did the language of clientage change if the broker or patron was a woman, as is evidenced by the following two excerpts from very different letters to the duchess of Newcastle:

> Your Grace's known goodness & Charitable Disposition makes us Humbly Hope, that You will Compassionate our unhappy Case, & be our Advocate with His Grace, since you cannot imploy those Noble Qualities upon Objects who stand more in need of Your Powerful Protection, then my Sister & My Self.[25]

[23] BL, Add. MS 32,908, fol. 229, Mr Perkins to Newcastle, n. pl., 12 July 1760.

[24] BL, Add. MS 32,909, fol. 276, Catherine Jemmat to Newcastle, n. pl., 14 July 1760.

[25] BL, Add. MS 32,735, fol. 534^{r-v}, Anne Jackson to duchess of Newcastle, Arlington Street, 21 June 1754.

I can make no apology for the very great trouble I presume to wish Your Grace to give yourself, as it is solely upon my own account that I venture to request it, & feel but too conscious of my own unworthiness to imagine that I deserve so much favor at Your Graces hands.[26]

The humility of the first excerpt is understandable once the reader is aware that the client was a woman, much lower in rank, and not at all well known to the duchess. The second is more intriguing, as the writer was a man who equalled the duchess in rank and knew her well. The deferential tone of the young duke of Portland can, however, be attributed to a combination of factors: the disparity in age between them; the duke's respect for the duchess personally and as the widow of his first political leader; and finally, to a political situation which put a premium on securing the three votes that she directed in the House of Lords.

For the most part, self-confident and assertive patronage requests increased with close connexion or similar social status. Among individuals of equal rank, male or female, letters were often brief to the point of brusqueness. Aristocratic women might even dispense with salutations and most social niceties when petitioning old acquaintances. When the duchess of Norfolk realized that Newcastle had some doubts about the character of a man whose suit she was supporting, she chastised him and defended her choice by linking it to her honour: 'I am sure you will doe me the Justice to be assured that I am incapable of becoming a Sollicitor in a Cause that appear'd to me doubtful.'[27] Few requests and reminders equal the stark brevity of many sent by Newcastle's widowed sister-in-law, Lady Katherine Pelham, however. Personality differences ensured that their relationship was often stormy, and varying levels of impatience with the duke are mirrored in her correspondence. Curt and to the point, Lady Katherine's reminders were designed to elicit action from a notoriously busy and dilatory politician: 'Ly Kath: Pelham was orderd by ye D: of Newcastle to remember him to provide for John Heath as soon as possible: She therefore acquaints his Grace, that there is likely to be a vacancy in the Stamp Office, one of the Stampers being thought adying; and it is the D: of Newcastles turn to put me in.'[28]

[26] BL, Add. MS 33,082, fol. 97, Portland to duchess of Newcastle, Berkeley Square, 14 Feb. 1770.

[27] BL, Add. MS 32,879, fol. 122, duchess of Norfolk to Newcastle, Chelsea, 9 Apr. 1758.

[28] BL, Add. MS 32,873, fol. 319, Lady Katherine Pelham to Newcastle, Greenwich House, 27 Aug. 1757.

While it might be assumed that the female members of the aristocracy would be this politically aware, they were by no means the only women who wrote to Newcastle for patronage. Newcastle's supplicants constitute a cross-section of English political society: of the letters that Newcastle received from women requesting patronage between 1754 and 1762, just over half (53 per cent) come from titled women (knights' wives upwards); the remainder (47 per cent) come from women who were untitled, ranging from members of the upper gentry down into the artisanate. They also appear to have been demographically representative: given the importance of marriage for women in eighteenth-century England, it is not unexpected to find that married women and widows, roughly equally represented, make up nine-tenths of his correspondents.

Arguments for patronage varied, but women often put great store (real or fabricated) on family membership and background—be it the family of their birth, or that into which they had married.[29] Lord Rodney's sister, Maria Constantia Nethercott, stressed her membership of the Rodney family with its tradition of loyalty and service when she sought either a renewal of her pension or a place for her husband: 'my Family for many Generations past of both sides have been Servants of the Crown, the Rodneys always in the Navy & Army, & my Grandfather Sir Henry Newton was twenty one Years Minister at Genoa & Florence.'[30] Lady Forbes, however, had no need to refer to her family of birth when petitioning for a pension to replace one that had been stopped after her husband's death: her position as the widow of an important man and the head of their family sufficed. She began by reminding Newcastle of the details of her case. A pension had been granted to her husband as 'a Personal Honnour' and had remained in place even after his death, until it was peremptorily terminated by a signed warrant from the lords justices some time later. What she wanted was to have it reinstated, partially on economic grounds, but more so for familial reasons. As she pointed out, she and everyone else knew that pensions were not normally recalled unless the receivers had forfeited them through bad behaviour. As the head of her family, she was particularly concerned about the impression that the loss of the pension created: 'being treated, on a foot, with those who do not entertain, Greatfull, and Loyal Sentiments for our Royal

[29] For women as repositories of family knowledge, see D. Woolf, 'A Feminist Past? Gender, Genre and Historical Knowledge in England, 1500–1800', *American Hist. Review*, 102 (1997), 645–79.

[30] BL, Add. MS 32,936, fol. 157^{r-v}, Maria Constantia Nethercott to Newcastle, Tynemouth, 26 Mar. 1762.

Benefactor.'[31] Such treatment could only cast aspersions on her family's reputation.

Those requests which can be clearly identified as coming from unmarried women also tended to use familial arguments (mainly their positions as members of deserving families) to identify themselves and justify their claims. Charlotte Rich's approach is representative. She wrote to Newcastle in 1759 after the death of her father, the earl of Warwick. She sought the continuation of his pension on the grounds that it would publicly recognize her status as the last surviving direct descendant 'of so Antient a Family'.[32] While this was true, her financial concerns were at least equally pressing: she and her mother had been left in dire circumstances. Whether she downplayed this fact because it was personally distasteful or because she knew that familial arguments had more political purchase is impossible to gauge. But she was successful in her claim.

Occasionally, women based their requests on other claims. Lady Cecilia Isabella Finch (or Lady Bell, as she was known) could easily have used familial arguments to support her solicitations; she chose instead to rely on the twin foundations of personal connexion and past promises. A member of an eminent legal family, with long-standing connexions to the Court through both the male and female lines, she was the daughter of the Tory-turned-Whig politician, the earl of Nottingham and Winchilsea. Claims of rank and family service were at her service. As Princess Amelia's woman of business, however, she had a recognized position and was a respected and well-established member of the Court herself.[33] She was at the centre of the political world in her own right and had her own networks of political contacts upon which to draw. She also had a degree of political influence—both with the princess, whose sharp tongue and long history of political intrigue ensured that she remained a political force to be reckoned with as long as her father was alive, and more directly, over Sir Brooke Bridges and his vote in parliament.[34] Spirited, witty, and highly independent, not only was she one of a

[31] BL, Add. MS 32,859, fol. 42, Lady Forbes to Newcastle, New Bond Street, 9 Sept. 1755.

[32] BL, Add. MS 32,895, fol. 355, Lady Charlotte Rich to Newcastle, n. pl., 11 Sept. 1759.

[33] 'Her RHss. places an intire confidence in me as to what relates to her Finances': BL, Add. MS 32,919, fol. 122, Lady Cecilia Isabella (Bell) Finch to Newcastle, Berkeley Square, 19 Feb. 1761.

[34] In the attempt to get support over General Warrants, Newcastle sought Lady Bell's influence with Sir Brooke Bridges. Not only was she successful, but she also took the opportunity to chide Newcastle for his political short-sightedness when Sir Brooke sided

small group of women who were members of the Court at any point in time, but she was also characteristic of a certain group of assured aristocratic women whose status was unquestioned and whose expectations were high.

When in 1756 Lady Bell decided to seek the living of Fobbing for a deserving clergyman, John Ryley, she had been friends with Newcastle and his wife for thirty years. Her request to him combined her personal and professional connexions to him. Capitalizing on the common assumption that politicians used their positions to serve their friends, she opened her campaign in typical eighteenth-century fashion by casting it as an obligation upon Newcastle: she reminded him that she had never been granted the slightest favour during their long acquaintance, and pointed out that she had even given up an earlier patronage appointment in order to help Newcastle's brother, the late Henry Pelham, out of a tight spot. In case he had forgotten, she spelled it out for him. A place had already been granted to a man of her choosing, but she had ceded it upon Pelham's request so that it could be given instead to someone recommended by Lady Yarmouth, the king's mistress. Not granting her request now would mean that Newcastle was ignoring his brother's final intentions, for, as she pointed out, the last time that Pelham had been at her house before his death he had specifically promised her 'yt he would give me as good a Thing in any Shape I pleas'd'.[35] Lady Bell was persistent, and over the course of the next four years she badgered the duke about the appointment. She also enlisted the help of the duchess, who was very interested in ecclesiastical appointments in general and supportive of Lady Bell's request in particular. Newcastle's papers for November 1760 indicated that he intended it to be one of the first appointments made by the new king, George III. Unfortunately for Lady Bell and her client, however, George III's implacable hostility to Newcastle was demonstrated in his refusal to grant patronage requests.[36]

with the majority over the Cider Act: 'you've forgot Kents a Hop Country. wch was his motive as Representatives of Counties must a little humour their Constituents really the Minority Seem to me in general asleep': BL, Add. MS 32,955, fols. 56–7, Newcastle to Lady Bell Finch, Claremont, 4 Jan. 1764; ibid., fols. 450–1, Lady Bell Finch to Newcastle [Berkeley Square, 12 Feb. 1764]; Alan Hardy, 'The Duke of Newcastle and his Friends in Opposition, 1762–1765', MA thesis, University of Manchester (1956), 182.

35 BL, Add. MS 32,862, fol. 494^{r-v}, Lady Bell Finch to Newcastle [Berkeley Square], 14 Feb. 1756.

36 BL, Add. MS 32,999, fol. 96^{v}, Memorandum, 20 November 1760; also BL, Add. MS 32,919, fol. 122^{v}: Lady Bell Finch to Newcastle, Berkeley Square, 19 Feb. 1761; fol. 145, Newcastle to Holdernesse (draft), Newcastle House, 20 Feb. 1761.

Women would not have submitted as many requests as they did, or phrased them as commandingly, if they had not stood a chance of achieving their goals. Of the fifty-one responses that survive for women's requests to Newcastle between 1754 and 1762, 57 per cent were successful and a further 24 per cent were potentially successful (that is, promises were given that they would be filled as soon as possible). This is a small sample and, as Lady Bell's request indicates, not all of the promises would be filled, but it does confirm that women's applications were taken seriously, even at the highest political levels. There was enough chance of being successful to justify women's involvement.

WOMEN AS CLIENTS

Most women who were involved in patronage over the second half of the eighteenth century were clients: like Newcastle's correspondents, they sought patronage for themselves, the members of their nuclear (and sometimes their extended) families, and for a variety of retainers or dependants for whom they felt some degree of responsibility. Like men, they became involved in patronage for a variety of reasons: self-interest, duty, necessity, greed, and social or political aspirations all played their parts. Some women's requests were tentative, obsequious, and overly apologetic, but so too were some men's. Exceptional circumstances could demand extra deference, even from people of equal rank, but not all clients were humble. Older and experienced women, and women of rank or fortune, were often the most confident. On the whole, the most assertive and knowledgeable patronage requests came from men and women who were members of politically active families and who knew the brokers or patrons they were approaching personally, or were connected to them through family or politics. Most of these women had extensive and useful personal networks which provided them with valuable information and contacts. They were usually socially active and based in or around London during the parliamentary season. By background and experience, they were political insiders. They knew how the political world worked, what patronage was available, and how best to apply for it. They used their knowledge and connexions to get what they wanted.

Women's requests for themselves tended to be solicitations for pensions or annuities, demands for larger sums or for payment of arrears, or, less often, requests for places or peerages. Their motivation varied, but their arguments were usually made on financial and socio-political grounds. The growing use of strict settlements undoubtedly helped to give women some financial security, but they were not infallible.[37] Women's claims of poverty are difficult to evaluate, however, for they are both highly personal and relative to social situation; still, there can be no doubt that there were women requesting patronage who were in genuine financial distress. For others, these requests were less about money than about prestige or politics.[38] Women who felt that their circumstances justified state support, claimed it. Some secured brokers to take their requests up the political ladder; others handled their own claims without aid of any sort; still others submitted their own requests but enlisted influential friends to act as character references and provide additional support (or pressure).

The way that plaintiffs marshalled their facts and presented their cases is particularly useful in revealing women's identification with familial political units and their use of familial arguments. When the widow, Cat Stephens, sought a 'small subsistance' out of her late son's place as a landwaiter (a customs official) in 1756, she began by drawing Newcastle's attention to the fact that her son had received his place from Sir Robert Walpole and that Sir Edward Walpole had been his lifelong patron. Her late husband had served in the army for forty years, at one point in the same regiment as his brother, Henry Pelham, and he had been ranger of Richmond Park. After assembling this formidable record of past service, she solicited Newcastle's support in ensuring that the grant be made to her in regard for her husband's faithful service, 'as It is usually done'.[39]

An admiral's widow, Ann Clinton, played on similar themes when she sought a pension through naval channels by applying to Lord Anson and the duke of York in 1761. She sought Newcastle's personal support

[37] Just how much women benefited from the development of strict settlement is still a matter of some debate. For the positive argument, see Lawrence Stone, *The Family, Sex and Marriage in England, 1500–1800*, abridged edn. (London, 1979); John Habakkuk, *Marriage, Debt and the Estates System: English Landownership, 1650–1950* (Oxford, 1994); Eileen Spring paints a more negative picture in *Law, Land, and Family: Aristocratic Inheritance in England, 1300–1800* (London, 1993). Hunt, *Middling Sort*, makes a valid point when she notes that while marriage settlements helped to protect women's interests, they were not infallible, and that women could still be 'kissed' or 'kicked' into turning over their assets to rapacious husbands.

[38] See e.g. Lady Schaub's requests for renewal: BL, Add. MS 32,878, fols. 67–8, 183–4, Lady Schaub to Newcastle, n. pl., 28 Feb. 1758; 11 Mar. 1758; or Sophia Georgina Cresset's claim for payment: BL, Add. MS 32,861, fols. 473–4, Sophia Georgina Cresset to Newcastle, Somerset House, 26 Dec. 1755.

[39] BL, Add. MS 32,865, fol. 470, Cat Stephens to Newcastle, n. pl., 28 Oct. 1756.

because he was kin by marriage and because of his political influence—factors which would, she asserted, markedly improve her chances. She endeavoured to allay any concerns he might have about setting precedents as well, arguing instead that 'most of the Admirals Widows have been consider'd'—a theme that she also reiterated in her memorial. This elaborate patronage request marshalled a number of factors upon which she based her claim. They included: her financial situation; her husband's fifty years of constant naval service; his lack of opportunity to enrich himself or his family with prizes or emoluments; the limited financial recognition he had received from the state, which left him barely able to support 'the Dignity of the Character he bore'; and finally, pointedly, his family background—noble, loyal, and zealously pro-Hanoverian.[40]

Similar arguments can be found in other political correspondences as well. Thus, in 1783 an unnamed but informed correspondent sought Lord North's support in addressing her request for a pension before parliament descended into seasonal inertia: 'The Time being so short to April, after which I apprehend, it will be more difficult to obtain anything from Government.'[41] After reminding him of the promise he had already given her, she bolstered her case by supporting it with specific reference to her brother's service to the Crown. In 1799 Mrs Adams approached William Pitt for a small pension that 'wou'd make me the happiest Old Woman in the world'. She proffered supporting arguments that were interchangeable with those used in Newcastle's day: 'for I am not a common beggar, My Maternal Uncle was in the House of Peers, My Paternal Uncle in the House of Commons, my Fortune was nearly twenty thousand pounds & my late Husband was a General officer.'[42] The well-established pattern of submitting a memorial to the king through one politician while simultaneously writing to the first lord to get his personal backing also continued. In 1788, for instance, Lady Camilla Robinson's memorial ended with panache, bringing to mind once again Lady Beauclerk's summation of her credentials: 'this small annuity [£200 p.a.] You will naturally perceive insufficient to maintain myself & Son of eight years old, keeping the honor of my birth in view, as Daughter, & Sister, to a Peer, of Great Britain.'[43]

[40] BL, Add. MS 32,930, fols. 66–7, Ann Clinton to Newcastle, London, 26 Oct. 1761; ibid., fols. 68–9: Memorial of the Hon. Ann Clinton to the Rt. Hon. Ld. Anson [Oct. 1761].

[41] BL, Add. MS 61,868, fol. 35, [unknown] to Lord North, 17 Mar. 1783.

[42] PRO, 30/8/107, fol. 123, Mrs M. Adams to William Pitt, Westminster, 24 Oct. [1799].

[43] PRO, 30/8/172, fol. 91, Camilla Robinson to William Pitt, Holborn, 12 July 1788.

Women's claims for themselves also extended to places and peerages. Admittedly, some were refused on the grounds of gender, but in general politicians seem to have considered their requests seriously and responded to them individually. Of course, it could be argued that the women who made requests were unlikely to ask for positions that custom would have prevented them from filling. There always were some appointments at Court and some places—like that of housekeeper to the Treasury or Excise—that were solely or usually female. Mrs Fountaine, for instance, wrote to the earl of Guilford in 1769 to get him to forward her request for the place of housekeeper to the Treasury to his son, Lord North. She had heard that the housekeeper was dying and she wanted the place as a form of insurance: 'I should not have askd this great favour, of Your Lordship, if a large Family, an Extravagant Younger Son, & great Losses had not prevented Mr: Fountaine's making a provision to make me live Comfortably in Case of my Surviving him.'[44] She drew upon her own connexion with the Guilford family to strengthen her case: Guilford had been taught by her father, and her own family had had 'first' care of both Lord North and his younger brother. Thirty years later, when William Pitt received a request for the same place from Elizabeth Alms, little had changed: she maintained that the combination of her personal situation as an unsupported widow with a large family, and her credentials—her late husband's upstanding character, his military career and rank as an officer, and her own character references—would more than justify her demand and testify to her suitability.[45]

In others appointments precedent and convention jostled up against gender in determining appointments. Rangerships, in particular, had traditions of female incumbents. The ranger, keeper, and constable of the Forest of Dean, and the rangerships of Greenwich Park and Bushy Park, were all held by women at various points in the century.[46] When Lady Berkeley requested the Forest of Dean appointment for herself in 1755, she did so because she wanted it for political rather than social reasons. As someone who had been recently widowed and left with an

[44] Bodl., MS North d.12, fol. 182^{r-v}, I. Fountaine to Guilford [1769].

[45] PRO, 30/8/107, fols. 259–61, Elizabath Alms to William Pitt, Chichester, 1 July 1799.

[46] Sarah, duchess of Marlborough had held the former; Lady Katherine Pelham was still Ranger of Greenwich Park in 1770; Lady North held the latter until her death: BL, Add. MS 32,852, fol. 244, Lady Berkeley to Newcastle, 24 Jan. 1755; *Annual Register ... 1770* (London, 1770), 76; 'Clarence to Thomas Coutts, 22 Jan. 1797', in *Mrs Jordan and Her Family, Being the Unpublished Correspondence of Mrs Jordan and the Duke of Clarence, Later William IV*, ed. A. Aspinall (London, 1951), 37. My thanks to Kimberly Crouch for drawing my attention to this last.

under-age heir in an area with a strong political rivalry, she knew that someone had to hold the post for her son until he came of age if she was to protect her family's political interest and standing in the community: 'I find by ye presidents of the Dutchess of Marlboroughs and some others that they Can be held by a woman, and I have it Confirmed by Sr George Lee, opinion that I am capable of takeing and holding a Grant from ye Crown, of the Offices of the Constable, of the Castle of St. Brevials, and Keeper of the forest of Dean.'[47] When the king agreed to grant it instead to a deputy of her choosing, she was satisfied.[48]

There were also always a few women who sought patronage in order to obtain other marks of distinction or peerages for themselves. When Philip Yorke succeeded as the 3rd earl of Hardwicke, his half-sister wrote almost immediately to ask him to support her claim for Papers of Precedence. She made her argument cunningly, playing on his commitment to his family and on his desire to appear well with the prime minister in the eyes of the world: 'I own it would hurt me very much to be pass'd over, & have it said either that you did not think it worth while, or had not Interest enough to obtain it . . . the success of my Petition depends solely on your kindness for me, & Mr Pitts readiness to oblige *you*.'[49]

Women who wanted to obtain or revive peerages for themselves did so for familial reasons: to raise family prestige and, almost universally, so that they could then pass the titles on to their sons. A request from Lady Bingley in 1754 for a peerage for her daughter is highly unusual.[50] Prior to Pitt's additions to the nobility at the end of the century, Hanoverian monarchs had been remarkably stingy with peerages; thus, new creations or revivals of titles that had fallen into abeyance were unquestionable marks of royal and political esteem, and were highly valued. As a result, campaigns for peerages were frequently long, frustrating, and often unsuccessful. The women who competed for peerages did so against men and on the same grounds. They employed batteries of arguments about lineage and status, paraded family histories of service and loyalty to the Crown, and occasionally brought in electoral arguments as well. Thus, when Elizabeth Perry, heiress to the Sidneys, earls of Leicester, wanted to revive the barony of Lisle for her son, she made a point of

47 BL, Add. MS 32,852, fol. 244, Lady Berkeley to Newcastle, 24 Jan. 1755.

48 Ibid., fols. 307–8, Lady Berkeley to Newcastle, Knightsbridge, 30 Jan. 1755.

49 BL, Add. MS 35,395, fol. 26^v, Caroline Yorke to Philip Yorke, n. pl. [May 1790].

50 BL, Add. MS 32,995, fol. 260, List of Persons who have made Applications for peerages [Spring 1754]. Lady Bingley's is the only female request out of the seventeen listed; two others, however, are noted as 'promised'.

emphasizing that he would have considerable estate and political interest when he came of age, and more to the point, that she was a political figure in her own right whose electoral support should not be discounted:[51] 'my interest in Kent alone the last election gave Mr. Watson near three Hundred votes, which Circumstances I should not take the Liberty to mention to Your Grace, but in regard to my Son, who is the last of the Sidney family.'[52] In the 'do me here, do you there; interest of both sides ... done & done' reciprocity of patronage, being female was not necessarily a disqualification.[53]

Reviving a famous title was especially desirable. As the sole heiress and last direct descendant (through her mother) of Lord Chancellor Clarendon, Lady Charlotte Hyde's attempt to revive the earldom of Clarendon and Rochester for herself and her posterity was a goal that she and her husband worked for together. The fact that her request was not granted until 1776, during Lord North's administration, after more than twenty years of lobbying, is illustrative of the long-term nature of some patronage requests and of one of the difficulties posed in trying to determine their success or failure.[54] She had initially broached the subject in person with Henry Pelham, who had urged caution, suggesting that she begin by reviving her uncle's lapsed barony and holding it jointly with her husband. This she did. She then started working towards the earldom in 1754. Through her husband and via Newcastle, she submitted a memorial to the king. After Newcastle fell from power she resubmitted her claim to George Grenville. And so on. While her husband may have been involved in directing her or formulating her claims, she wrote without apologies or histrionics; her right to make a request and hold the title was simply assumed. She made it clear that the title, if gained, would be passed down to her son: it was her *duty* to uphold the dignity of her birth:

I feel neither vanity, ambition, or an improper impatience, but reverence to my ancestors, justice to my situation and posterity, and a grateful conformity to the late Lord Hyde's testamentary disposition [making her legally his heiress] ... I being lineally from that Chancellor, and being the first representative of his family who has not been higher in rank than I am, and who has not been favoured

[51] BL, Add. MS 32,879, fol. 54, Arthur Collins to Newcastle, n. pl., 4 Apr. 1758; ibid., fol. 298, Elizabeth Perry to Newcastle, Leicester Street, 25 Apr. 1758.

[52] BL, Add. MS 32,906, fol. 24, Elizabeth Perry to Newcastle, Leicester Street, 12 May 1760.

[53] Oliver Goldsmith, *The Good Natur'd Man* (London, 1768), 41.

[54] See BL, Add. MS 32,734, fols. 352–3, Thomas Villiers to Newcastle, Admiralty, 25 Mar. 1754; 'Lady Hyde to George Grenville, The Grove, 14 May 1764', in *Grenville Papers*, ed. Smith, ii. 317–20.

with emoluments . . . Without saying more, I can but flatter myself that the title of Clarendon, so considered by the Crown, so dear to the Constitution, so known and respected in history, may be delivered down, as others have been, through the same blood to later posterity.[55]

When women were not making requests for themselves, they were making requests for family members or others in their networks. They solicited places and pensions for daughters, and the full range of patronage possibilities for husbands and sons. Thus, we find Lady Katherine Pelham asking for the place of housekeeper to the Custom House for her daughter Frances in 1754, and sweetening the request by emphasizing that Frances would share the income from the post with a deputy, her eldest sister's former retainer, who would perform the actual work of the post. One appointment would therefore supply two women with a livelihood. The duchess of Hamilton and Argyll, on the other hand, writing to William Pitt in 1790 to request a pension for her daughter Augusta, simply based her claim on her years of service to the Crown as a member of the queen's household.[56]

The interchangeability of claims and family members reinforces the notion that patronage was understood to benefit families as a whole. In 1756 Mary, Lady Vandeput, reminded Newcastle that he had promised Lady Yarmouth, Lord Rochford, and Lord Brooke that he would grant 'a small Place or Pention' for herself and her husband.[57] In 1761 Mabell Russell requested some provision that would give her two grown daughters 'some little Independance' in a 'naughty Age', or an employment for her husband, a long-time JP and ardent Whig.[58] And in 1787 Lady Rothes solicited William Pitt to have her husband, the successful doctor Sir Lucas Pepys, appointed physician to his Majesty. He did after all, she insinuated, have something coming to him, for it was only because of his prosperity that she had not needed the pension that she could otherwise have claimed on familial grounds.[59]

While women were likely to benefit from patronage for male family members, the requests themselves could mask specific female agendas. When Lord Hardwicke granted the living of Newington to a young man

55 *Grenville Papers*, ii. 317–20.

56 BL, Add. MS 32,736, fols. 109–10, Lady Katherine Pelham to Newcastle, Tunbridge Wells, 25 July [1754]; PRO, 30/8/108, fol. 223, duchess of Hamilton and Argyll to William Pitt, Ealing Grove, 4 Sept. 1790.

57 BL, Add. MS 32,865, fol. 302, Lady Vandeput to Newcastle, 28 July 1756.

58 BL, Add. MS 32,927, fol. 61^{v}, Mabell Russell to Newcastle, Basing, 16 Aug. 1761.

59 PRO, 30/8/172, fols. 39–40, Lady Jane Leslie to William Pitt, London, 3 July 1787.

who was still up at Oxford in January 1754, his widowed mother thanked Hardwicke in his stead.[60] On the surface this appears to have been simply a matter of a mother doing her best to secure her son's future, but by returning to her original request for patronage in 1753 an additional argument emerges. At that time Elizabeth Billingsley had feared that her husband, who held the living of Newington, was dying—and if he died, that she would be forced to move. Thus, she wanted her son to be given the living, because it 'will be of the greatest consequence to me as it will save me a great deal of trouble, as I am come to that time of Life & feel those Infirmitys which render removeing & Incumbrance very disagreable'.[61] When it became clear that Hardwicke was considering Newington as one of two options for the young man, she wrote again to make her preference clear. In Newington she had a good neighbour and peaceful parishioners: 'Happyness's not often to be met with.'[62] To what extent she influenced Hardwicke's final decision cannot be ascertained, but her son did obtain the living and, in guaranteeing his future, she also secured her own comfort.

Perhaps the best example of a woman who made use of patronage in this double-edged fashion is Lady Scarborough. A daughter of the earl of Orkney, she had married a man who made his way into the peerage through his service to the state, first as an ambassador and then as treasurer of the household to Frederick, prince of Wales. This may explain her desire, as a widow, to do everything she could to maintain her family's hard-won status.[63] Between 1754 and 1760 she bombarded Newcastle, whom she would undoubtedly have known personally, if not well, through her link to the Court, with requests for an Irish earldom for her son-in-law Peter Ludlow, an untitled Irishman.[64] Time and again she deployed arguments of loyalty, service to the Crown (that of her own family and of her husband), and political interest. Ludlow's proven political loyalty, demonstrated by his willingness to use his own fortune to support the government in a recent contested election, received particular attention. Underlying her request was a pressing need to retrieve

[60] BL, Add. MS 35,359, fol. 272, Elizabeth Billingsley to Hardwicke, Newington, 21 Jan. 1754.

[61] Ibid., fol. 268, 7 Dec. 1753.

[62] Ibid., fol. 270, 8 Jan. 1754.

[63] See T.W. Beastall, *A North Country Estate: The Lumleys and Saundersons as Landowners, 1600–1900* (London, 1975).

[64] See also Langford, *Public Life and the Propertied Englishman*, 518.

her daughter's rank and reinforce her family's prestige, both of which she felt had suffered as result of the Ludlow marriage.[65]

Her campaign is interesting because of what it reveals about family and status. When, in 1755, Ludlow accepted an Irish barony as the first step towards future elevation, she was mortified. She would have preferred to have him remain untitled than to have her daughter suffer such a loss in status.[66] Three years later it still vexed her, especially when Princess Amelia, with her usual forthright tactlessness, asked her publicly 'why I would let her loose her Rank'.[67] She recounted the incident to Newcastle as a way of underlining her embarrassment when she repeated her request. She returned to the same theme again months later, after having finally succeeded in cornering Newcastle at a Drawing-Room and obtaining his promise to speak to the then lord-lieutenant, the duke of Bedford: 'You may believe it is A Most disagreable Sircumstance to Me, & them; that My daughter who did take Place as Youngest Viscountess, Now has only ye Rank of Allmost one of the Youngest Baronesses of Ireland.'[68] It took her until 1760, but her hurt pride was finally assuaged when her request for Ludlow was granted.[69] His elevation not only served to retrieve her daughter's status but, by extension, also contributed to the status of the family as a whole. In this case at least, an outwardly male patronage appointment served a plurality of purposes.

In a society where married women's status was always affected by, although not always predicated upon, that of their husbands, women identified closely with their husbands' careers and ambitious women frequently used the patronage system to forward them. They were especially likely to act for their husbands if they had better (or sometimes the only) chances of success. Kinship was an 'in' that could always be exploited. Thus, when Lord North received a request from a Mrs Beydell

[65] BL, Add. MS 32,735, fol. 605, Lady Scarborough to Newcastle, Midgham, 29 June 1754.

[66] Ibid., fol. 376, Lady Scarborough to Newcastle, Grosvenor Street, 19 Mar. 1755.

[67] BL, Add. MS 32,877, fol. 233, Lady Scarborough to Newcastle, Grosvenor Street, 25 Jan. 1758.

[68] BL, Add. MS 32,882, fol. 75, Lady Scarborough to Newcastle, Grosvenor Street, 26 July 1758.

[69] BL, Add. MS 32,908, fol. 110, Lady Scarborough to Newcastle, Grosvenor Street, 5 July 1760; ibid., fols. 389–90, 20 July 1760. Lady Scarborough continued to forward Ludlow's cause even after this. In 1767 she sought and obtained Newcastle's support for Ludlow in his candidacy for a seat at Boroughbridge: BL, Add. MS 32,987, fols. 163–4, Lady Scarborough to Newcastle, n. pl., 3 Dec. 1767; ibid., Newcastle to Lady Scarborough, fols. 178–9: 5 Dec. 1767.

for a place for her husband, he asked John Robinson to see what could be done for her: '[she] is my near relation, & I should wish to oblige her. Her husband . . . though not her equal in birth, was, I believe, her equal in fortune; The circumstances of both were, &, I am afraid, are still very moderate.'[70]

Aristocratic women were no less keen to use similar avenues, especially if they had married below themselves in any way. No matter how close the relationship, though, success was never assured. Lady Sarah Lennox, who married into the military-mad but poor Napier family, regularly enlisted her politically active relatives in her ongoing attempts to obtain suitably elevated military positions for her husband, his brothers, and later her sons. During the Shelburne administration and the Fox–North coalition she should have had as good a chance as any to get her husband the company of Guards that he coveted, as it saw a number of relatives or close connexions in important posts: her brother Richmond as master of the Ordnance; her sister-in-law's second husband, General Henry Seymour Conway, as commander-in-chief; and her cousin, Charles James Fox, as both foreign secretary and, later, as the leading figure in the Fox–North coalition.[71] In December 1782 she sent an initial request to Lady Ailesbury (Conway's wife). Then, having laid in in the meantime, followed it up in March 1783 with a direct approach to Conway.[72] Richmond and Fox both added their support. Despite this formidable array, she achieved limited success. As she told her cousin, Lady Susan O'Brien, who was also seeking patronage for her husband: 'Mr Conway has at *my request* (not my Brothers) given Mr N. a Captains Commission in the 100th Regt. It is a *Step* but if it dont lead to something better soon It will by no means answer my intention in asking it.'[73] She pressed on. Ironically, her cause may have suffered as a result of her kinship with Fox. Fox may have been in place, but his lack of influence over patronage reflected just how little he was in power. However, his unpopularity with the king was not the only reason when she was unsuccessful. Fox proved unwilling to promote the claims of family over those of friendship:

[70] BL, MS Facs. 340(2), Rotographs from the Robinson Papers at Bridge Castle, fols. 257–8, North to John Robinson, Waldershare, 1 Oct. 1781.

[71] Holmes and Szechi, *Age of Oligarchy*, 359; Charles Grant Robertson, *England Under the Hanoverians* (London, 1958), 283.

[72] BL, Add. MS 49,090, fols. 8–9, Lady Sarah Napier to [Lady Ailesbury], n. pl., 21 Dec. [1782]; ibid., fols. 13–14, Lady Sarah Napier to General Conway, n. pl., 15 Mar. 1783.

[73] BL, Add. MS 52,354, fol. 160^{v}, Lady Sarah Napier to Lady Susan O'Brien, n. pl., 25 Mar. 1783.

he [Fox] knows that a Company in the Guards is the utmost of our ambition & particularly suited to Mr N. ... Charles also knows, that Mr N. is not unreasonable & is so averse to an improper promotion that he would be happy to be assured of a Compy. in 3 or 4 years; Well! Charles knowing all this, Complains that he cannot make Genl. Conway do what he wishes ... & in the midst of this Complaint, Charles gets Mr Stanhope rewarded for the loss of Tobago, by a Company in the Guards & the very next week he gets him the 2d best place in the Ordnance, sans soufler un Mot to us.— ... I had a great Mind to be in a *Rage* but I have overcome my anger ... I have no right to expect from him an attention which no one relations of his ever yet acquired ...[74]

The care that wives took over their husbands' careers is clear in patronage requests, especially for men who could not or would not make claims for themselves. Rumours always prompted action. In 1788, hearing that one of the chaplains of the Presidency of Bengal was very ill, Charlotte Loftie dashed off a letter to Charles Jenkinson (by then Lord Hawkesbury), requesting the post for her husband.[75] Wars similarly encouraged military and naval wives to make patronage requests, especially for husbands who were on active service. Jenkinson's letterbooks, when secretary at war, testify to this, as do those of Henry Dundas when he held the same post at the turn of the century.[76] For Lady Band, it was the prospect of a regiment for the defence of Jamaica; for Mrs Gordon, that of a new corps in Scotland; and for Mrs Anderson Gisborne, the post of adjutant of the Woolwich Division's (Marines) acting quartermaster.[77] While there were many simple requests for promotions or transfers, competition for the best regiments or the most prestigious posts was always intense. As a group, military wives seem to have been the most eager to supplicate for their husbands, but, as might be expected, it was the women near the top who had the most to gain. They made the most effort to know exactly what was available (or likely to become so), who stood in line for what promotions, and what it was that they specifically wanted. It is difficult to determine the degree to which they were deputized or instructed by their husbands, but the sources suggest that they acted both autonomously and in conjunction with them.

74 Ibid., fols. 170^v–171^v, 10 Nov. 1783.

75 BL, Add. MS 32,223, fol. 105, Charlotte Loftie to Hawkesbury, Canterbury, 9 July 1788.

76 See Jenkinson's letterbook, 21 July 1779–2 Sept. 1780: BL, Add. MS 38,307; see also Melville Papers, MS Eng 699, Lists of Applications and Appointments.

77 BL, Add. MS 38,307, fol. 97^v, Lady Band to Charles Jenkinson, London, 11 Dec. 1779; ibid., fol. 22^v, Mrs Gordon to Jenkinson, London, 24 Aug. 1779; Melville Papers, MS Eng 699, 26^v, 27 Oct. 1807.

Women also took control of patronage requests if their husbands were too reticent or too proud to act for themselves. In some cases they acted with their husbands' knowledge, but not always. When Newcastle's niece, Lady Poole, felt that 'the precarious state of our affairs' had become too worrisome in 1757, she wrote to Newcastle without consulting her husband: 'I can't help being fearful that thro' his great dislike to the slightest appearance of being troublesome, that our real circumstances have never been truly represented.'[78] Similarly, Lady Deskfoord wrote to Newcastle frankly in 1758, informing him that Lord Kintore was dying and asking that her husband be granted Kintore's pension of £400 per annum and his office of 'Knight Marischal', which would provide an additional £400 per annum: 'I wou'd have had my Lord write your Lop. himself but he won't write about any thing he himself may possibly be concern'd in.'[79] She obtained useful additional support from Lord Kinnoull, who acted the part of an honest broker. Kinnoull not only agreed that her claim was valid and should be supported, but also pointed out to Newcastle that granting her request would be cost-effective, giving him 'an Oppertunity of terminating an Affair which has given you so much Trouble, to the Satisfaction of the Person's concerned, without any Additional Charge to the King's Revenue'.[80]

If women used patronage for their husbands, who could, on the whole, make requests for themselves, then it is understandable that they were even more likely to do so for sons, particularly those who were just at the outset of their careers and may have lacked the necessary connexions and self-confidence to plead their own cases effectively. While widows seem to have been the most active overall, mothers' requests for their sons cover the entire range of patronage opportunities. Women who had political ambitions used the system to ensure that their young men received a proper political start. Occasionally they acted in conjunction with their husbands. When the Croftes wanted to launch their son into parliament in 1761, Mr Croftes made the initial contacts. Money was not an issue, so Mrs Croftes assumed that the details would be quickly concluded; unfortunately Croftes was overawed by Newcastle and returned to the country with the matter still unsettled. In frustration

[78] BL, Add. MS 32,870, fol. 165^{r-v}, Lady Poole to Newcastle, Lewes, 8 Feb. 1757.

[79] BL, Add. MS 32,884, fol. 297, Lady Deskfoord to Newcastle, Banff Castle, 9 Oct. 1758.

[80] BL, Add. MS 32,885, Kinnoull to Newcastle, Bradsworth, 28 Oct. 1758.

she then took charge of the affair: 'Mr. Croftes, some where, with great expence', appears upon a memorandum within two days of her letter.[81]

Anne Boothby Skrymsher's attempt to get her son Charles (better known later as 'Prince' Boothby, one of the closest friends of the prince of Wales) into parliament provides one of the most detailed examples of a mother's quest for electoral patronage. An active political woman herself, she was determined that Charles should enter parliament as soon as possible. Beginning when he was still on the Grand Tour in 1760, she had the duke of Rutland suggest him to Newcastle as a potential candidate for Leicestershire (at his own expense). Once this initial contact had been made, she took over. She assured Newcastle of Charles's character and loyalty, referring him to Rutland and Lord Granby for character references. She also added two other details that were certain to appeal to the over-solicited (and flattery-prone) duke. The young man had, she assured him, 'no relations to Sollicit favors for, or any veiws, further than an opinion that parliamentary busness is a proper employment for the mind of a young man at his first entrance into Life'.[82]

By 1762 she was able to inform Newcastle that she had succeeded in having Charles chosen as a candidate for the county. He quickly sent his approval. Unwilling to sit quietly in the background, she seems to have taken a leading part in managing the campaign; certainly, it was she who approached Newcastle for electoral support.[83] He was more than obliging: 'If Mr Boothby knows of any Persons, who would have a regard for my Inclinations upon this Occasion, upon the least Notice from you of their Names, I will immediately make the proper Application to them; I most sincerely wish your Son Success.'[84] She took him at his word. Although in the end Charles withdrew from the contest after an unfavourable canvass—and seems not to have ever served in parliament, thus leading to the distinct possibility that this campaign was entirely the result of his mother's political aspirations and not his own—her own political involvement continued unabated

That women believed they had a right to be involved in patronage is best demonstrated in their requests for members of their families (blood

[81] BL, Add MS 32,919 fols. 19–20, Mary Croftes to Newcastle, Jermyn Street, 15 Feb. 1761; ibid., fol. 58^{v}, Memo to Lord Kinnoull, 17 Feb. [1761].

[82] BL, Add. MS 32,902, fol. 141, Anne Boothby Skrymsher to Newcastle [Tooly Park?] [1760].

[83] BL, Add. MS 32,935, fols. 200–1, Anne Boothby Skrymsher to Newcastle, Upper Grosvenor Street, 5 Mar. 1762.

[84] Ibid., fol. 285, Newcastle to Anne Boothby Skrymsher, Newcastle House, 9 Mar. 1762.

or extended), and for their friends, retainers, and clients. Numerous claims survive, motivated by a mixture of genuine concern, duty, and loyalty—and undoubtedly, in some cases, by guilt. The common eighteenth-century assumption that connexions were there to be used applied to women as well as men, and it would have been difficult, if not impossible, for women whose situations, families, or marriages gave them access to patronage to refuse to make requests on behalf of those who did not. As Lady Diana Bolingbroke complained to her mother, the duchess of Marlborough, she wanted to be able to do at least as much for her husband as her sister Elizabeth had done for hers: 'it wou'd be, I must own, a most real mortification to me, that his being my husband, shou'd not be of as much service & help to him in the world, as Ld. Pem: [Pembroke] being married to Sis: Betty, has been to him.'[85] In particular, she wanted her brother to get for Bolingbroke 'a Place of real value', equivalent to that of the master of the foxhounds, or a pension of about the same amount (£2,000 p.a.) on the Irish establishment.

At times, ambition and aspiration were replaced by much more serious concerns, as in 1788, when Lady Macclesfield solicited Lord Hawkesbury, a personal and political acquaintance of over thirty year's standing, for a place or pension for her brother. She was afraid that without something to ease his situation he might be driven to suicide. His personal circumstances were depressing in themselves—he was nearly blind and very deaf—but he had been pushed to the point of extremity by financial disasters which his stubborn refusal to seek help had only exacerbated.[86]

Although the context of women's requests is not always so detailed, these examples demonstrate that women participated in a variety of patronage networks for any number of reasons. Their desire to serve their 'friends' comes through repeatedly. This ill-defined group included members of extended families, companions, social or political acquaintances, and an assortment of worthy clients or faithful retainers.[87] Examples abound: in 1758 the widowed duchess of Marlborough obtained an academic post for a favoured ex-tutor by approaching Newcastle

[85] BL, Add. MS 61,668, fol. 131^{r-v}, Lady Diana Bolingbroke to duchess of Marlborough, n. pl. [7 Oct. 1761].

[86] BL, Add. MS 38,223, fols. 153–4, Lady Macclesfield to Hawkesbury, Shirburn Castle, 26 Aug. 1788; ibid., fols. 161–2, 31 Aug. 1788. Lady Macclesfield's acquaintance with Jenkinson dated back at least to the Oxfordshire election of 1754.

[87] See Tadmor, *Family and Friends in Eighteenth-Century England*, for a detailed examination of the concept of 'friends'.

through his wife; in 1767 Lady Brandon sought the duke of Northumberland's help, and through him Lord Bute's, after having made repeated appeals to numerous lord-lieutenants of Ireland for an Irish peerage for her only brother; in 1771 Lady Tyrconnel succeeded in persuading Lady Cust to give the living of Fauldingworth to her nephew; in 1780 Mrs Soame requested that Charles Jenkinson promote Capt.-Lieut. Stevenson out of regard for the memory a dead friend; in 1790 Mary Rebow sought William Pitt's support for naval preferment for an unspecified relative of her late husband's. The list could be extended indefinitely.[88]

Although many supplicants were well-known, frequently titled women, requests also survive from otherwise unrecorded women who felt impelled to seek patronage for people they felt were deserving: Katherine Barrett, who sought for a tide waitership or a clerkship in the Secretary's Office at the Custom House for a worthy young man; Miss Reade and Mrs Walkinshaw who separately recommended a Mr Beaton to be collector of Montrose. Elite women's preponderance owes largely to the fact that they had more 'friends' to serve, more chances to know what was available, wider spheres of influence, and stronger arguments to deploy. The duchess of Dorset, for instance, called upon her service to Queen Caroline and that of her husband as lord-lieutenant of Ireland to strengthen her argument for a pension for a female friend;[89] likewise, the duchess of Hamilton's 'regard & esteem' for an acquaintance led her to seek a vacant stall in Windsor for him, arguing for the preferment with 'all my Weight & interest'.[90]

WOMEN AS BROKERS

As these examples demonstrate, the position of 'client' shifted towards that of intermediary, or 'broker', with requests that were made for others. Most women—and most men— took part in patronage as clients. Some,

[88] BL, Add. MS 32,885, fol. 344, Newcastle to Marlborough, Newcastle House, 15 Nov. 1758; BL, M/297, reel 18, fols. 40–1^{v}, Lady Brandon to Northumberland, n. pl., 15 July 1763; Bodl. MS North c.4/1, fols. 101–2, Lady Tyrconnel to Lady Cust, April, 1771, as cited in Elizabeth, Lady Cust *et al., Records of the Cust Family*, 3 vols. (London, 1898–1927), ii. 298; North to Guilford, Pay Office, 14 Oct. 1767; BL, Add. MS 38,307, fol. 121, Charles Jenkinson to Mrs Soame, War Office, 20 Jan. 1780; PRO, 30/8/170, fol. 217, Mary Rebow to William Pitt, Colchester, 2 Aug. 1790.

[89] BL, Add. MS 32,854, fols. 230–1, duchess of Dorset to Newcastle, n. pl., 22 Mar. 1755.

[90] BL, Add. MS 32,899, fol. 209–10, Ann, duchess of Hamilton to Newcastle, Bury, 30 Nov. 1759.

however, were brokers; a few were patrons. Although the category of 'broker' is a creation of modern social scientists, it identifies the intermediary position in eighteenth-century patronage. Brokers inhabit an amorphous place in the middle of any patronage system. Their power is nebulous and strategic, for, while they do not have the resources to grant requests, they are an important channel to patronage and have the ability to refuse to support requests. Their power is founded upon access to information and individuals, sound personal and political judgement, and a reputation for getting results.[91] Brokers are, however, always in a somewhat precarious position. The very personal nature of their power, the methods that they use to attain their goals, and the extent to which they profit personally from their involvement lays them open to accusations of corruption.

In the eighteenth century the alleged corruption of the patronage system provided opposition politicians with a convenient platform from which to attack other politicians, the current administration, or even the monarch. When women were involved, historical precedents (real or mythical) could be dredged up to give examples of influential women—specifically kings' mistresses—who had sold, or were presumed to have sold, places, or had secured patronage for favourites through illegitimate sexual influence. These sorts of accusations were usually little more than political ploys which evaporated once they had served their immediate political purpose, but their existence reflects widespread political concerns about 'undue' influence and lack of political accountability. In the second half of the century increasingly vocal demands for reform were accompanied by hardening attitudes towards corruption, and the patronage system became symbolic of all that was wrong with the unreformed political system.[92] Reform was envisaged as purification, and purifying the polity meant making it more honest, manly, and meritocratic. Where women were concerned, anxieties about the venality and opacity of the patronage system, and its lack of accountability, were compounded by eighteenth-century concerns about women and women's natures. In particular, they cannot be disentangled from traditional gendered concerns about female venality, rapacity, and ambition, and perhaps yet more importantly, with long-standing fears about the political implications of women's sexual power over men.

[91] See Boissevain, *Friend of Friends*, 154–64.

[92] See e.g. John Wade, *The Black Book; or, Corruption Unmasked* (London, 1820).

Early in the eighteenth century accusations of corruption had repeatedly been levelled at the two leading female brokers at Court, George I's mistress, the duchess of Kendal, and his half-sister, the countess of Darlington.[93] Much later, two highly publicized legal cases brought the issue to the fore again. The first, in 1773, saw Lord Sandwich's mistress, Martha Ray, charged with corruption as part of an opposition attempt to discredit him. The charges could not be substantiated and the case failed miserably.[94] The second, in 1809, which took place in the midst of the conservative reaction to the French Revolution and its accompanying concerns about female political involvement, was more damaging. It saw opposition politicians succeed in discrediting the duke of York and forcing him to resign by revealing that his ex-mistress, Mary Anne Clarke, had taken money for influence.[95] The Wardle affair, as it came to be known, was a gift for reformers. Eventually it led to the passage of the Sales of Offices Prevention Act, which made seeking money for offices a penal offence. For women, the Wardle affair was particularly unfortunate, as it reinforced negative stereotypes about connexions between women, politics, and corruption.

Undoubtedly some degree of venality did exist among brokers of both sexes in the eighteenth century. However appealing, though, the connexion of female brokers with rapacity, illicit sexuality, and corruption is conspicuous by its absence in the sources. What went on in person behind closed doors is lost to us, but the very absence of rumour and scandal in as tightly knit and highly competitive—and gossipy—a society as that of the eighteenth-century political elite suggests that the patronage activities of female brokers were largely unremarkable. This certainly applies to the most active female brokers around the various first lords across the second half of the century, most of whom were middle-aged wives or widows from politically active families. Indeed, their participation appears to have been taken for granted by both clients and patrons alike. Their backing was often enthusiastically sought and their aid was openly acknowledged. On the whole, they appear to have shared a common belief

[93] Ragnild Hatton, 'George I as an English and a European Figure', in Paul Fritz and David Williams (eds.), *The Triumph of Culture: 18th Century Perspectives* (Toronto, 1972), 192–98.

[94] *The Evidence ... in the Trial wherein the Rt. Hon. John, Earl of Sandwich, was Plaintiff, and J. Miller, Defendant* (London, 1773); N. A. M. Rodger, *The Insatiable Earl: A Life of John Montagu, 4th Earl of Sandwich* (London, 1993), 167, 188.

[95] For the duke of York and Mary Anne Clarke (the Wardle affair), see I. R. Christie, *Wars and Revolutions: Britain, 1760–1815* (Cambridge, Mass., 1982), 302; Robertson, *England Under the Hanoverians*, 440, 442.

that it was their duty to use their family membership or their social or political positions to secure patronage for deserving candidates. Theirs was a calculated altruism, though, when it was altruism at all. Their choices and the timing of their requests were often carefully made and had personal or familial implications. Acting occasionally for clients of low social status or no political interest may have given the broker little more than personal satisfaction, but it was also sure to add to her reputation and create a fund of good-will for the future. Backing the applications of clients who were higher in rank, or who were actual or potential political supporters, was often more purposeful. It helped to establish networks of obligation that might later be turned to personal or political advantage. Thus, attempts to secure patronage for voters were especially common in advance of elections.

A client who did not have direct access to the necessary patron, or who felt that his or her application would not be weighty enough to convince the patron without support, often began by securing the support of a broker, someone who was perceived to have a personal connexion with the patron, as well social and/or political influence. The goal was to obtain the broker's support or 'patronage'—thus the difficulty in some sources of differentiating between brokers and patrons—in bringing the request to the notice of whoever actually had the desired appointment in his or her gift. Take, for instance, the example of one of Lady North's correspondents when lamenting the death of Lady Drake in 1782: 'The heartfelt Gratitude & Esteem which I have hitherto entertained of the high Favor confired on me by her Ladyship's Patronage, will cause me to revere her Memory to the latest Period of my Life.'[96] From this, it is impossible to ascertain whether Lady Drake really was a broker or a patron in her own right; what is important, however, is the value that was attached to her activities.

Women became brokers by dint of birth, marriage, and connexions—or a combination of all three. They were understood to possess influence; hence, their 'patronage' was solicited. Women who were close to political men, particularly through blood or marriage, were expected to act as brokers. Many did. The more important a man was politically, the more access he had to patronage, especially lucrative and/or prestigious patronage; consequently, the more likely the women in his immediate circle were to be solicited. When Lord Buckinghamshire went to Ireland as lord-lieutenant in 1776, both Lady Louisa Conolly and her sister the

[96] BL, Add. MS 61,874, fol. 119: B. Symes to Lady North, Musbury, 17 June 1782.

duchess of Leinster assumed—correctly—that Louisa, who was resident in Ireland and whose husband was Lady Buckinghamshire's brother (and himself a leading Irish country gentleman, albeit in opposition), would be inundated with patronage requests:[97]

I have . . . kept perpetually employed . . . in writing very disagreeable letters, which are those of denial, to the millions of applications that are coming to me in consequence of Lord Buckinghamshire's coming to Ireland. I wonder when they will have done, and was considering t'other day the impossibility of obliging everybody. For if I had had the appointing of Lord Buckinghamshire's family, and the naming of all his tradesmen, I could not satisfy one half of the requests made to me.[98]

A full year later the requests were still flowing in. As a conscientious and religious woman, Lady Louisa found the limitations of her position painful at times:

You say you are sure I have hundreds of applications. In truth I cannot number them, the most distressing of all are the poor wretches condemned to death, who all apply to me, so that I quite dread the sight of a petition, and have suffered so much from those I took in, that (as I cannot assist them) I have been obliged to make the servants enquire the nature of every petition before they bring them to me.[99]

A broker's 'gift' rested in her right to refuse and in the improved chances of success that her elevated status or proximity to patrons or power was assumed to supply. In general, applications fell into two groups: a few came from people who were genuinely unsure about the merits of their requests and wanted to have them vetted by someone who understood the system before being forwarded; the majority, however, came from people who saw the broker as someone the patron in question took seriously, someone whose support would ensure that their requests had a better hearing than they would otherwise have obtained. For Joseph Yorke, who frequently used his sister's brokerage to promote military and naval appointments during the Seven Years War, it was exactly this combination of intimacy and inside knowledge that made her such an important broker and made him solicit her aid repeatedly. For him, she was variously the 'Protectress of the new American Regiment', the

[97] Her involvement in Irish politics at this period is passed over entirely in Tillyard's *Aristocrats*.

[98] 'Lady Louisa Conolly to duchess of Leinster, Castletown, 21 Dec. 1776', in *Correspondence of Emily, Duchess of Leinster*, ed. Fitzgerald, iii. 243.

[99] 'Lady Louisa Conolly to duchess of Leinster, Castletown, 5 Dec. 1777', ibid. 262.

'Protectrice' of the Swiss Guards, and the 'friend & Protectress' of the navy.[100]

Most of the women who acted as brokers were members of politically active families. Their involvement was characteristically pragmatic and businesslike, carried on in person and/or by letter. Usually the kinds of requests that brokers received were determined by their personal connexions: thus, naval wives like Lady Rodney tended to be solicited for naval appointments. The larger a woman's network of useful political contacts and the better her reputation as a broker, the more likely she was to receive an assortment of requests. Some female brokers tended to specialize in certain types of patronage. While the duchess of Newcastle always received some requests for places and pensions, she was personally interested in and primarily involved with matters of ecclesiastical patronage. Her correspondence with Newcastle is laced with references to men whose preferment she was supporting. Moreover, like other female brokers, she received requests from women as well as men. Her requests reveal a female patronage network that functioned within the larger, official (male) system of patronage.[101] Other female brokers were less focused. Lady Stafford's correspondence, for instance, reveals her being regularly solicited for various military appointments, places, preferments, and promotions. Newcastle's sister-in-law, Lady Katherine Pelham, was much solicited in the same way. She prioritized her selections and chastised Newcastle roundly if she thought that there was a chance he might not pay a request the attention that she felt it deserved: 'If what I am going to ask, you will call one of Ly Kath:'s Jobb's to some of your intimates, whom I never desire to make mine; I beg to drop my request: but if you will receive it as I wish.'[102] The support of a politician's wife (or, in the case of Pitt the Younger, of his mother) could be crucial to success. As the duchess of Hamilton and Argyll explained when making a request of Lady North, 'when ever one finds out the way to Succeed with a Minister it is natural to take the Same Method'.[103] As Lord North's list of recommendations to the (English) Customs and Excise demonstrate, Lady North made use of her ability to recommend to places: so too did a

[100] See BL., Add. MS 35,388, fols. 120, 138, 204: Joseph Yorke to Lady Anson, The Hague, 12 Dec., 24 Feb., 3 Oct. 1756.

[101] For the duchess as an intermediary in ecclesiastical appointments, see BL, Add. MS 33,075, fols. 72–3: Newcastle to duchess of Newcastle, Kensington [Mar.–May 1756].

[102] BL, Add. MS 32, 906, fol. 474: Lady Katherine Pelham to Newcastle, Whitehall, 3 June 1760.

[103] BL, Add. MS 61,868, fol. 15: duchess of Hamilton and Argyll to Lady North, Argyll House, 6 Aug. 1779.

number of other women from other political families, including the duchesses of Queensberry and Marlborough, and the dowager Lady Wynne.[104]

Female brokers were neither necessarily aristocratic nor associated only with leading politicians. Mary Gollop, whose brother, John Tucker, was at the Pay Office, was approached in the same way as her aristocratic counterparts. Like other brokers, she had to decide which requests were the most important, worthy, or urgent and then forward them with appropriate personal recommendations. Tucker may not have had access to patronage on the scale of more important political men, but her letters show that her support was nevertheless regularly in demand: 'Tis with Regret I give you so much trouble as I do about other Peoples affairs, & was I to give way to all the Sollicitations, that are made me, for your favr. I might justly be deemed, very Impertinant.'[105]

The support of women who were the acknowledged heads or representatives of political families in the localities was also seen to be important. Local concerns or the need to keep voters happy led them to exploit their political connexions. Sometimes the issues were more significant than the usual run-of-the-mill search for pardons and places. In February of 1765, for example, Anne Boothby Skrymsher sent one of her periodic requests to Charles Jenkinson, then senior secretary to the Treasury, this time to obtain his support for the local Turnpike Bill. Given that he was also one of the 'King's Friends', a group notoriously averse to party politics, she structured her request for maximum appeal. She placed great emphasis, first on the community's need to relieve a chronic shortage of corn, and then on the bill as a matter of political consensus:

> all the peopel that have lent mony upon the Harborough road have signed the petition for this road and will be ready to advance mony upon this new one the whole mony wanted will not exceed 1500 pound and one person has already told me he will answer for £700 = it comes over Several Gentlemens Estates who all consent . . . they See the necessity of it as does all the other Gentlemen and freeholders over whoes property it passes . . . and you may assure your self it is not a party jobb = all the opposition that can be given will be from a few that have inns upon the Harborough road for their own private intrest for Gentlemen and freeholders of all opinions except the self intrested are agreed this is a publick Benifit . . . indeed you may assure yr self it is no party jobb . . . [106]

[104] Bodl., MS North C.68, fols. 5–6: Recommendations (Customs and Excise) England.

[105] Bodl., MS Don. b.19, fol. 207: Mary Gollop to John Tucker, Burton, 4 July 1757.

[106] BL, Add. MS 38,204, fols. 76–7: Anne Boothby Skrymsher to Charles Jenkinson [Tooly Park?], 16 Feb. 1765. For Charles James Fox's involvement in a similar turnpike

Sometimes all that the supplicant wanted was the broker's stamp of approval. When Mr Jones, the comptroller-general of the Customs in Scotland, wanted the Treasury to refer his memorial to the commissioners of the Customs at Edinburgh in 1763, he approached his friend Lady Herbert for help. He assured her that she need only take 'the trouble of writing a few lines to Mr. Jenkinson'.[107] Her forwarding letter was a one-sentence model of brevity: 'Mr Jones who is my very good friend, has requested of me to writ to you, & at the same time has agreed to be the bearer of it himself, because he is much better able, to explain the favour he desires of you then I am able to do.'[108] Petitioners who took a broker's approval for granted, though, or misrepresented her by using her name without leave, invited swift reprisals. When the dowager Lady Gower found out that a chairman, whose application for patronage she had refused, had persisted in using her name in his requests to Guilford, she wrote firmly to Guilford asking him to withdraw whatever 'Charitable Intentions' he had in mind for the man. She then went on to chide him for taking the man's word without her verification: 'Had Ly G: given into his making this Request to Lord Guilford, she shd: have done it by her own Hand.'[109]

The existence of female patronage networks allowed women to solicit other women for patronage. Some women seem to have made their female acquaintances their first points of contact as a matter of course. When Lady Germaine wanted to secure something for a tenant of hers, she applied to Newcastle, apologizing that she would normally have sent her request to the duchess first, but the duchess was not in town.[110] Other women used their female and male patronage networks tactically, or simultaneously, for maximum impact. Lady Bell Finch's aforementioned campaign for Mr Ryley provides just such a case in point. She not only wrote to both Newcastle and duchess, and obtained the duchess's support and advocacy, but was advised by Newcastle to use her female network as

situation for Lady Ilchester, see BL, Add. MS 51,467, fol. 20^{v}: Charles James Fox to [William O'Brien], London, 15 Dec. 1777.

[107] BL, Add. MS 38,200, fol. 338: Mr. Jones to Lady Herbert [1763].

[108] BL, Add. MS 38,200, fol. 336: Lady Herbert to Charles Jenkinson, Grosvenor Street [17 May 1763].

[109] Bodl., MS North, D.20, fol. 165: Dowager Lady Gower to Guilford, Pall Mall, 8 Mar. [n. d., 1752–85].

[110] BL, Add. MS 32,736, fol. 1: Lady Elizabeth Germaine to Newcastle, Knolle, 1 July 1754.

well: 'Write to your Friend My Lady Holdernesse to speak to My Lord.'[111]

Although politicians might get some respite from patronage requests during parliamentary recesses, their arrival in the country or their presence at a friendly gathering at a country house could be a gift to a determined broker. In 1780 Lady Brudenell took advantage of her Christmas visit to Bushey Park to solicit Lord North for a place for a client of hers.[112] When he quibbled, she enlisted the assistance of Lady North and the North family: 'Lady Brudenell attacked Lady North at the same time. She said that the matter was not as yet settled, but believed it would do; there was some hitch in the way which deferred it, but [she] did not know what it was. *Voici! où nous en sommes.* The whole family promise that he shall not eat his breakfast in quiet till it is done'.[113]

Some households were particularly political and some women thrived upon the machinations of patronage. The Staffords were just such a family. It was often difficult to spur Lord Stafford into political action, but he was an eminent political figure with significant influence even when he was not 'in business' himself; moreover, Lady Stafford sought patronage appointments with the eagerness that some women reserved for cards and scandal.[114] It was well known that she would make patronage requests of politicians who were staying with the family at their country house if she felt a case was worthy of support. When an old acquaintance, Rachel Lloyd, wanted to secure a preferment for a rather unusual reason, she asked for Lady Gower's help in securing the appointment from the lord chancellor:

is my Lord Chancellor now at Trentham? if he is will you present my Compts and the following petition to him, that he would be pleased to bestow the Living of Killuchdyn now vacant in Wales upon my Cousin Mr David Scurlock who writes to tell me that the members both of Town and County and also my Lady Dinivir are willing to apply for it for him, but he does not chuse to be oblig'd to them for he knows the Chancellor does much regard the recommendations of Members of Parliament. but he will be oblig'd to me if I will do it, now as I want this Cousin of mine to do a civil thing by me, (which is to give me all my Lady Trevors Letters

[111] BL, Add. MS 32,881, fols. 39–40, Newcastle to Lady Bell Finch, Claremont, 24 June 1758.

[112] 'Anthony Storer to Lord Carlisle, London, 5 Feb. 1781', *HMC Carlisle*, 453–5.

[113] Ibid., 14 Feb. 1781, 459–60. Storer succeeds by the beginning of the next year: ibid., 7 Jan. 1782, 564–5.

[114] PRO, 30/29/1–8; 5/1–3; *Letters of Lord Granville Leveson Gower*, ed. Granville.

which he, as her Heir at law is in possession of and a vast quantity there are) I am afraid to refuse him.[115]

Just how much—if at all—women's overall involvement in patronage at the highest political levels was affected by the lack of a female presence during the long administrations of William Pitt and Lord Liverpool cannot be judged. Pitt's chilly persona and well-known dislike of patronage may have discouraged some requests, but it does not seem to have deterred those women, like the duchesses of Rutland and Gordon and Ladies Salisbury and Stafford, among others, who were staunch supporters of his administration and knew him personally.[116]

A successful broker often had to be determined, persevering, even stubborn in pursuing her goals. Lady Katherine Pelham's sustained support of John Roberts's claim for a parliamentary seat at Harwich in the 1750s illustrates this, just as it also demonstrates the ultimate frustration of being a broker and not a patron. If birth, connexions, and character were the main contributory factors in the make-up of a politically active eighteenth-century woman, Lady Katherine had them all in abundance. The majority of the applications that she forwarded were for places or preferments; her influence was solicited regularly and, while she only chose to forward those that she felt were deserving, she was Newcastle's most active female broker.[117]

John Roberts had been Henry Pelham's assistant in the management of government boroughs, and been particularly involved in Harwich, a government borough that was torn by animosities between the Treasury and the Post Office. He had stayed on under Newcastle and, in good eighteenth-century fashion, had taken advantage of his position over the years to build up his own interest in the borough.[118] Pelham had suggested that he stand for parliament in 1754, but he had not yet been ready; by 1758 he was. The opening came when Lord Duncannon succeeded his father in July 1758 and vacated his seat at Harwich. Lady Katherine quickly sent one of her terse notes to Newcastle, recommending that

115 PRO, 30/29/4/6/82, fol. 1116^{r-v}, Rachel Lloyd to Lady Gower, 19 [1782?].

116 See PRO, 30/8/175, fol. 78, Lady Salisbury to William Pitt, n. pl. [Feb. 1790]; PRO, 30/8/180/1, fol. 108, Lady Stafford to William Pitt, Whitehall, 13 Feb. 1787; PRO, 30/8/139, fol. 47^{r-v}, Lady Charlotte Gordon to William Pitt, Edinburgh, 15 Nov. 1785 (this request was written for Jane, duchess of Gordon, by her daughter, as the duchess would not delay sending it even though she had just lain in). For the duchess of Rutland, see below.

117 BL, Add. MS 32,887, fol. 121, Lady Katherine Pelham to Newcastle, Whitehall, 12 Jan. 1759.

118 Namier, *Structure of Politics*, 358–89.

Roberts be chosen in his place.[119] Roberts also wrote, explaining how his sinecures could be managed in order to allow him to sit. In December 1759, after much local wrangling and rivalry, Newcastle agreed. Problems arose, however, with the accession of George III. The king wanted his own candidate, Charles Townshend, to get Harwich. As Namier so succinctly expressed it, this put Newcastle in a distinctly uncomfortable situation, 'between the upper and nether millstone, the King and Lady Katherine Pelham, and he hardly knew which was the more formidable'.[120] By February 1761 Newcastle was squirming: 'I disputed it, combated it, and oppos'd it, as much as I could; I did not prevail; But yet I don't despair, but I shall at last be able to get Mr Roberts in at Harwich. But if I can't, It is not my Fault.'[121] Lady Katherine would have none of his excuses. She wanted Roberts to have the seat at Harwich and the first vacancy at the Board of Trade—and immediately: 'I am really sorry for the distresses you are in, and shall always wish to diminish, not increase them; but you must give me leave to say, that you bring them chiefly on your self.'[122] In the end Newcastle found a compromise which placated both the king and Lady Katherine: he installed Roberts and Townshend at Harwich and moved the sitting members elsewhere.

Lady Katherine's frustration at having to work through Newcastle is apparent here and in many of her other requests. This was in part personal, arising from fundamental differences in temperament with her brother-in-law, but it was also inherent in the role of broker. Claims of kinship or obligation, and promises of reciprocity or political service, liberally supported by sheer determination and perseverance, could result in success; yet, in the end, the right to dispense patronage lay with the patron. While some male brokers might have had stronger claims to support or have been able to offer more politically influential arguments than female brokers, the decision-making process was so complicated by a whole range of concerns, including petty rivalries and political expediency, and so dependent upon circumstances, that it was never simply gendered.

[119] BL, Add. MS 32,881, fol. 319, Lady Katherine Pelham to Newcastle, n. pl., 14 July 1758; Namier, *Structure of Politics*, 370–3.

[120] Namier, *Structure of Politics*, 372.

[121] BL, Add. MS 32,918, fol. 279^{v}, Newcastle to Lady Katherine Pelham, Newcastle House, 5 Feb. 1761.

[122] Ibid., fols. 471^{v}–2, Lady Katherine Pelham to Newcastle, London, 12 Feb. [1761].

WOMEN AS PATRONS

Lady Katherine would undoubtedly have been much happier if she had been a patron in her own right. Women were patrons of art, architecture, music, literature, and drama in the eighteenth century, but we still know little about their roles as ecclesiastical or political patrons. While the customary constraints which prevented women from holding official political positions (Lord-Lieutenancies, ministerial posts, and the like) meant that they could not distribute patronage that was in the gift of the Crown or in specific ministers of state, the majority of eighteenth-century patronage remained in private hands. Indeed, women may even have benefited from the prevailing understanding of patronage as private property, thus jealously guarded and passed down carefully through families. The vagaries of birth and infant mortality ensured the existence of female patrons in the eighteenth century, and while there were undoubtedly fewer female patrons than female brokers or clients, they were not anomalies. Jane Austen did not have to invent the female patron when she created Lady Catherine de Burgh in *Pride and Prejudice*; she was drawing on a female type that would have been well known to contemporaries.[123] Nor were female patrons confined solely to the upper strata of the political elite. There were always a few women who were patrons by right of appointment, calculation, or purchase, but there were more who were patrons through inheritance (including widowhood). There were also always some women, usually widows with under-age sons, who were patrons by proxy.

Female patronage ranged from women who, as co-heirs, took turns in presenting to a local living, to women who controlled seats in the Commons and were recognized as electoral patrons by first lords and their men of business.[124] John Ecton's *Thesaurus Rerum Ecclesiasticarum* (1754) lists numerous women who either shared ecclesiastical patronage or controlled it outright, a reality that was underlined by the specific attention paid to the legal niceties of female ecclesiastical patronage in *The Laws Respecting Women, as they regard their Natural Rights, or their*

[123] In *Pride and Prejudice*, written in 1796–7, Austen makes it clear that Mr Collins's sycophancy is due in part to the fact that he owes his living to his patron, Lady Catherine. Given Lady Catherine's rank and character, it would seem unlikely that her use of patronage would have stopped there: in life she would also have had political interest—and used it. Jane Austen, *Pride and Prejudice* (London, 1813).

[124] Namier, *Structure of Politics*, 17.

Connexions and Conduct (1777).[125] In the diocese of Gloucester alone, Ecton identified a number of women in a variety of patronage situations: two women, the daughters and heirs of Mr Perrot, presented to the rectory of Barnsley, St Mary; a Mrs Wade and Mr Hayle, presumably a brother and sister, presented in turns to the rectory of Bleysdon, St Michael; and an unspecified number of sisters, the heirs of William Bayly, presented to the rectory of Fretherne, St Mary. Another six women held curacies or rectories in their sole gift. Moreover, by casting forwards two years to 1756 and the deaths of the heads of the two most powerful families in the county, Lord Berkeley and the duke of Beaufort, and the active parts taken by their widows, it could be argued that significantly more patronage in the diocese came into female hands. Of course, there were always some women whose husbands or male relatives controlled their patronage for them, just as there must always have been a few who paid so little attention to their patronage appointments that they lost their turns to make appointments. A Miss Dobel, for instance, lost her turn to appoint to the living of Streete in Sussex, by not making the appointment within six months.[126] Most female patrons seem to have guarded their power jealously, however.

It is probable, given the amount of ecclesiastical patronage that lay in private hands, that more female patrons existed in this area than in any other. Occasionally women became ecclesiastical patrons by proxy, as did Mrs North and Lady Gower in 1775. Brownlow North, bishop of Worcester, had promised his wife that she would have the right to appoint to the first living that became vacant after his preferment, but when the friend that she had intended for the position declined, 'not wanting so small a thing', she passed it on to Lady Gower. She, in turn, would have been expected to return the favour at some point in the future.[127] There seems to have been no difference in the way that male and female ecclesiastical patrons operated on the whole. Both were approached by men and women alike, both made their appointments according to their own criteria, and they then followed up their appointments, or not, according to personal

[125] For the diocese of Gloucester, see John Ecton, *Thesaurus Rerum Ecclesiasticarum: Being an Account of the Valuations of all the Ecclesiastical Benefices in the Several Dioceses of England and Wales*, updated by Browne Willis, 2nd edn. (London, 1754), 135–51; *Laws Respecting Women*, 123–4.

[126] BL, Add. MS 32,908, fol. 231, bishop of Chichester to Newcastle, Broomham, 12 July 1760.

[127] Bodl., MS North d.25, fol. 67^{v}, bishop of Worcester to Guilford [London], 13 Nov. 1775.

preferences. In some cases, an initial appointment was only the beginning of a larger quest for the clergyman in question. Thus, dowager Lady Gower, having appointed Mr Bliss to her living of Ashford, soon began to take steps to increase his stipend.[128]

Private ecclesiastical patronage could be solely religious in intent, but it frequently coincided with the patron's political sentiments. When the patronage lay in the hands of someone with a strong evangelical agenda, such as Lady Huntingdon, the religious and political agendas could overlap. Other sorts of patronage could also be politicized. It is likely that someone like Lady North, who appointed to 'a Bounty in your Ladyship's own power', garnered mainly requests for charity,[129] but even this sort of 'favour' could have a political dimension. The person being awarded the bounty might have been genuinely in need, but the choice of one needy person over another could have been influenced by who made or brokered the request, and any political circumstances that might make it useful to create or sustain a sense of obligation in particular quarters.

The political aspect of patronage appointments, as well as female patrons' ability to protect their rights, is perhaps best displayed by the Newcastle's encounter with Lady Portsmouth over the appointment of the Mastership of Magdalene College in 1760. As one of the three co-heirs of the earl of Suffolk (d. 1745), Elizabeth Grey (née Griffin—she married John, earl of Portsmouth, as her second husband soon after Suffolk's death) had gained a share of his estate, including 'a joyn'd right to the nomination' of the Mastership of Magdalene College.[130] Her correspondence demonstrates that she was already seeking to become the sole patron as early as 1746, when she directed an agent to search the statutes of the college and determine the details of the nomination. Once she knew that the patronage was attached to the manor of Brooks Walden and the house Audley End, she took steps to buy out the other owner, Lord Effingham. The negotiations were protracted because Effingham demanded a high price (£15,000 at one stage in 1751), but she was confident of her ability to hold her own in estate dealings, and her letters show that she had a good understanding of prices and what the property was worth. By 8 March 1752 she had completed the purchase and acquired the patronage.[131]

[128] 'Dowager Lady Gower to Dartmouth, 11 May 1774', *HMC Dartmouth*, i. 352.

[129] BL, Add. MS 61,868, fols. 13–14, Louisa Perfect to Lady North, n. pl., 14 July 1779.

[130] ERO, D/Dby C42/5, W. Vachell to Lady Portsmouth, Abbington, 16 Sept. 1746.

[131] Ibid. See also D/DBy C42/6, W. Vachell to Lady Portsmouth, Abbington, 2 Sept. 1746. Her correspondence with Vachell, July–August 1751 (letter nos. 11, 12, 12 +) charts

As chancellor of the University of Cambridge, Newcastle was particularly aware of the importance of placing politically accommodating people in key university posts. He was also aware that Lady Portsmouth was an important patron who had to be approached carefully. When the Mastership of Magdalene College fell open in 1760, he became her client, sending her one of his most obsequious letters. Like any other client, he set out his credentials before requesting that she appoint the man that he had in mind:

> being an old Friend, and Humble Servant, to My Lord Portsmouth, & My Particular Relation to the University of Cambridge, as having the Honor to be their Chancellor, will, I hope be my Excuse, for giving your Ladyship this trouble, most earnestly to beg the Favor of You, to Suspend determining anything upon the vacancy of the Mastership of Magdalen College If (as I understand,) the Appointment is in your Ladyship, 'till I have the Honor to lay before you the Wishes, and Inclinations, of the principal Members of the University . . . If I ask too much, I heartily beg your Ladyships' Pardon; But, as I know Your Ladyship's Zeal for the King, and His Interest, And as I have no View but His Majesty's Service, & that of the University, I flatter Myself you will excuse me.[132]

This exquisite politeness was wasted on Lady Portsmouth, as she had already made up her mind.[133] She had chosen an Oxford man and, given Oxford's reputation as a haven for Tories and ex-Jacobites, Newcastle was left fretting about the political sentiments of the new appointee.[134] Fortunately, she had chosen well. Her choice, Dr Sandby, was soon given a letter of introduction from Lord Portsmouth that described him as 'the Gentleman that my wife has appoynted head of the Magdalen College', and sent to meet Newcastle. He won Newcastle over by showing himself to be a hearty Old Corps Whig, and within two weeks Newcastle was writing back to Lord Portsmouth expressing his satisfaction: 'As My Lady Portsmouth did not take one of our own Body, I am persuaded, Her Ladyship could not have made a better Choice, than that of Mr. Sanby.'[135]

her negotiations with Lord Effingham for the purchase of the house, parklands, and presentation. By 8 March 1752 (letter no. 20) the sale seems to have been agreed.

[132] BL, Add. MS 32,907, fols. 137–8, Newcastle to Lady Portsmouth, Newcastle House, 10 June 1760.

[133] Ibid., fols. 160–1, Lady Portsmouth to Newcastle, Hurstbourne, 11 June 1760.

[134] Ibid., fols. 184–5, 351–2, Newcastle to dean of Lincoln, Newcastle House, 12, 25 June 1760.

[135] Ibid., fol. 417, Portsmouth to Newcastle, Hurstbourne, 27 June 1760; BL, Add. MS 32,908, fol. 152, Newcastle to Portsmouth, Claremont, 9 July 1760.

Newcastle communicated with Lord Portsmouth, but he appears to have been acting as his wife's secretary. Her correspondence suggests that she made the necessary decisions herself; to what extent he played a part in influencing her cannot be ascertained. What is important to note is that while Newcastle was worried about who Lady Portsmouth might appoint, he never questioned her right to choose. She was the legitimate patron; gender did not come into the question.

The nature of the eighteenth-century political system ensured that there were always some women who were outright political patrons, managing and controlling boroughs and votes. Matriarchs, especially aristocratic ones, could be powerful political figures, with enough influence over the men in their extended families to be treated as patrons, even if they were not—strictly speaking. As a widow, the duchess of Newcastle played just such a part in the larger Pelham family, even though she and Newcastle had had no children of their own. In 1770, when the duke of Portland was in the midst of his struggle with Sir James Lowther for control of Cumberland, and was canvassing for support in the Lords that would resolve the issue in his favour, he approached the duchess of Newcastle for her support. Couching his request in the deferential language of a client to a patron, he outlined what had happened as well as the current state of affairs. What he wanted to ensure, he told her, was that he had enough support in the Lords; her influence over votes would be of infinite use to him:

> It must be almost unnecessary for me to point out to Your Grace the importance it is & to me to have these hopes [Lowther's plans] disappointed, as you must see that by their failing in the attempt, the security of the property of my friends is established, my own interest in Cumberland confirmed, & the ambitions & malicious views of Sr: James Lowther in a great measure defeated. & therefore my request is that Your Grace would be so good as to express yourself to The Bp of Salisbury Ld Godolphin & Ld Pelham in a manner that might prevail upon them to support The Bill when it comes into The House of Lords.[136]

LADY BEAUCLERK

A closer examination of the twists and turns of Lady Henry Beauclerk's request for patronage, with which this chapter opened, serves as a useful

[136] BL, Add. MS 33,082, fol. 97^{v}, Portland to duchess of Newcastle, Berkeley Square, 14 Feb. 1770.

closure, as it throws additional light on why and how politically astute eighteenth-century women might get involved in the patronage system. Born the Hon. Martha Lovelace, Lady Beauclerk was the only daughter the 4th Lord Lovelace, who had been governor of New York at the time of his death in 1709. She inherited family pride but little more than that as the heir of her brother, the 6th and last Lord Lovelace in 1736. Courtesy of two other bequests—from her aunt, Baroness Wentworth (*suo jure*) and another Wentworth connexion, Mrs Cresswell—she inherited the manors of Leckhampstead and Heyborne-fields in Buckinghamshire. These gave her some local political influence and the right to appoint to the rectory of Leckhampstead.

Her personal involvement in patronage began in 1732 when she benefited from the system, having been appointed maid of honour to Queen Caroline. As a member of the Court, young women were usually expected to do two things: use their positions to build personal and political networks that would enable them secure patronage for family members, and/or make brilliant marriages. Thus, she was undoubtedly involved in some way in having her brother, Lord Lovelace, appointed gentleman of the bedchamber in 1735.

In 1739 she married for love. As the fourth of the eight sons of the 1st duke of St Albans, Lord Henry Beauclerk's rank was outstanding but, like his bride, his birth far outstripped his fortune. As a Volunteer at the siege of Gibraltar in 1727, however, he had attracted George II's notice and had consequently secured both patronage appointments and promotions. His prospects looked good. By 1745 he was an established Whig MP (Thetford) and colonel of the 31st Regiment of Foot Guards; in 1752 he was appointed ranger of New Lodge Walk. Unfortunately, however, a family of seven children—one son and six plain and portionless daughters—required more resources than even these appointments could supply. Lady Beauclerk turned to the patronage system to supplement the family income: in 1749 she secured the reversion of her mother's pension of £200 per annum; in 1756 she obtained the place of housekeeper of Windsor Castle. This gradual improvement in family circumstances came to an abrupt end during the Seven Years War. Lord Henry rashly quit his regiment in a fit of pique when it was posted to Minorca for three years, claiming that he had not been given enough time to settle his affairs. This incurred George II's lasting displeasure. Lord Henry was stripped of his military rank and the king resolutely refused thereafter to consider any of his subsequent requests for military reappointment or other forms of patronage.

The Beauclerks were consequently in a difficult position in 1759. Lord Henry's health was failing, and his limited income left him unable to make satisfactory provision for his growing family, especially his daughters. The only hope that the family had of securing patronage was through Lady Beauclerk. Thus, her requests emphasized *her* claim to patronage through her own and her family's service to the Crown. She seldom mentioned her husband.

When Lady Beauclerk learned that the king had refused her initial request, supposedly because he feared it would set a precedent and result in a flood of claims, she swiftly recast it. Within three days she wrote again, shifting attention away from herself and asking for a pension in the children's names or for a place for her husband. She drew upon a rhetoric of responsible motherhood and laid the blame for her situation at Newcastle's feet:

your Grace might propose Some thing in my Children's Name which wou'd be of the Same Service. My Son will be no troble to the Crown, nor wou'd my Daughters had Lord Hen: Beauclerk had the Common Chances, his Rank demanded: but unless your Grace can find Some employment he is worthy of. I fear I must Still be troblesome for myself & Girls. for you may believe, my Lord I must Suffer, whilst They are unprovided, and If I Suffer must apply for redress, To whom can I apply but to the King. & Through your Grace—.[137]

A little more than two weeks later she wrote again, promising to allay Newcastle's fears of setting precedents if he allowed her to wait upon him in person.[138] As Newcastle explained, this was unnecessary as the king was aware of her case. He promised, however, that he would support her request if she wrote directly to the king and he proved amenable.[139] She did more than this. Between March 1759 and June 1760 she applied to have Lord Henry made lieutenant of the Tower, and twice asked that her eldest daughter be appointed orchard keeper. She also resubmitted her original request for an increased pension and sent a personal memorial to the king.[140]

[137] BL, Add. MS 32,887, fols. 489–90, Lady Beauclerk to Newcastle, n. pl., 3 Feb. [1759].

[138] BL, Add. MS 32,888, fol. 200, Lady Beauclerk to Newcastle, n. pl., 20 Feb. 1759.

[139] Ibid., fol. 208, Newcastle to Lady Beauclerk, Newcastle House, 21 Feb. 1759.

[140] BL, Add. MS 32,889, fol. 167, Lady Beauclerk to Newcastle, n. pl., 20 Mar. 1759; also BL, Add. MS 32,904, fols. 135, 137–8, 396–7, Lady Beauclerk to Newcastle, n. pl., 31 Mar. 1760, Lady Beauclerk's Memorial to George II [Mar.–Apr. 1760], and Lady Beauclerk to Newcastle, n. pl., 14 Apr, 1760. The missing letter requesting the Lieutenancy of the Tower was probably written in October 1759, for a letter from Lord Henry seeking

By 1760 she had become frustrated with what she interpreted as Newcastle's inaction. To persuade Newcastle that she was serious, she threatened to embarrass him at his own levee—traditionally a male event—if he continued to ignore her 'pretentions': '[I] beg you will reflect How little Honour my Attendence at your Levee will do You: for There I must Come. However, disagreble to me, & However unused to Such attendence.'[141] Newcastle must have believed that there was some chance that she would do this, for he immediately sought to pre-empt her: 'If Your Ladyship has any Commands for me, which cannot be explained by Letter, I will, with great Pleasure, do Myself the Honor to wait upon Your Ladyship at Your own House.' Adopting an injured tone, he promised that he would, if she was adamant, bring the matter up with the king yet again. But, he argued, he had little chance of success. The king 'did Absolutely refuse to comply with it. And, that being the case, It is not possible for me to alter His Majesty's Resolution.'[142] She continued to insist that her case was unique:[143] 'you can find no other person so Slenderly provided whose family has been So great Sufferers for The Crown.'[144] In setting out her case for the king, she returned to this argument, reminding him that he had thought highly enough of her family to award her mother the pension from which she still received £200 per annum (although she hastened to add that it was only worth around £100 p.a. after taxes). Providing her family with more money would also serve a patriotic purpose, she maintained: it would 'enable us to bring up a Family by Nature attach't to your Majesty and by example most faithfull Subjects'.[145]

While no further correspondence survives between Lady Beauclerk and Newcastle, she did not give up. By November 1760, with George III on the throne, new patronage opportunities had emerged for young women. There was a royal wedding in the offing and the places in the

William Pitt's support, and another from Lady Henry to Hester Pitt asking her to act as a broker to her husband, survive in the Chatham Papers: PRO, 30/8/19, fols. 6–7, Lord Henry Beauclerk to William Pitt, n. pl., 13 Oct. 1759; ibid., fols. 10–11, Lady Beauclerk to Hester Pitt, Somerset House, n. d.. See also BL, Add. MS 32,904, fol. 135, Lady Beauclerk to Newcastle, n. pl., 31 Mar. 1760.

141 BL, Add. MS 32,904, fol. 135, Lady Beauclerk to Newcastle, n. pl., 31 Mar. 1760.

142 Ibid., fol. 157, Newcastle to Lady Beauclerk, Newcastle House, 1 Apr. 1760. Newcastle did more than just reassure her. In a memorandum for the king, written on the same date, he mentions her by name (ibid., fol. 145).

143 See her subsequent letters to Newcastle of 15 Apr., 11 May, and 10 June: BL, Add. MS 32,904, fols. 396–7; BL, Add. MS 32,906, fols. 54–5; BL, Add. MS 32,907, fols. 133–4.

144 BL, Add. MS 32,907, fol. 133, Lady Beauclerk to Newcastle, n. pl., 10 June 1760.

145 BL, Add. MS 32,992, fols. 154–5, Lady Beauclerk to Newcastle, n. pl., n. d.

new queen's household to fill. She persuaded a relative, the young duke of Grafton, to approach Newcastle about having her eldest daughter serve as a maid of honour at the wedding and be appointed to the household. Grafton performed his part conscientiously: he made a very early application, writing shortly after George III came to the throne. In his letter he stressed both the young woman's rank and family history, reminding Newcastle that she had been educated 'in the best manner', notwithstanding the financial difficulties posed by a large family and her father's limited fortune.[146] Unfortunately his efforts were fruitless, as Newcastle's influence over patronage was spent. He received only six applications for the highly desirable places in the new queen's household—and none of his candidates were successful.[147] Never one to limit her patronage requests to one politician even at the height of Newcastle's power—the good offices of both Lord Bute and William Pitt had been enlisted in the past—Lady Beauclerk transferred her requests accordingly to a more viable patron.

As a result, she finally achieved her goals in 1761. Both Lord Henry and George II were dead, and Lord Bute, an old acquaintance of Lord Henry's, was at the height of his power.[148] Not only was her eldest daughter, Diana, appointed maid of honour to Queen Charlotte,[149] but also, more importantly, Lady Beauclerk was awarded a pension of £400 per annum on the Irish establishment in trust for her daughters.[150] The outcome seems to have satisfied her. Only towards the end of her life, in 1783–4, did she once again become briefly re-engaged in patronage—this time, seemingly, unsuccessfully, as she tried to obtain further ecclesiastical preferment for her son Henry (d. 1817). Having appointed him

[146] BL, Add. Ms., 32,915, fol. 43, Grafton to Newcastle, Euston, 24 Nov. 1760.

[147] BL, Add. MS 32,925, 20 July 1761, fols. 211–12; BL, Add. MS 32,928, fols. 48–9, List of Queen's Officers [7–8 Sept. 1761]. Newcastle was very aware of this loss of confidence: BL, Add. MS 32,926, fol. 192, Newcastle to Devonshire, Most Secret, Newcastle House, 5 Apr. 1761.

[148] Bute had been appealed to in the past, along with Lords Ligonier and Barrington, as the Beauclerks worked together to secure Pitt's support: PRO, 30/8/19, fols. 6–7, 10–11, Lord Henry Beauclerk to William Pitt, n. pl., n. d.; Lady Beauclerk to Hester Pitt, Somerset House [Nov. 1754–Dec. 1761].

[149] BL, Add. MS 32,928, fols. 48–9, List of Queen's Officers [7–8 Sept. 1761]. Miss Beauclerk was still a maid of honour in 1768: 'Journal, Feb. 8, 1768', in *Letters and Journals of Lady Mary Coke*, ii. 185. See also Donald Adamson and Peter Beauclerk Dewar, *The House of Nell Gwyn: The Fortunes of the Beauclerk Family, 1670–1974* (London, 1974), 222–3.

[150] BL, M/297, Syon MSS, reel 18, fol. 11^{v}, George R. An Establishment of List Containing all Payments to be made for the Civil List Affairs of our Kingdom of Ireland ... Accounted Payable from the 25th day of October, last inclusive 1760 [1763].

already to her own living of Leckhampstead, she turned once again to Hester Pitt, by then Lady Chatham and the mother of the first lord, to ask her to act as a broker to Pitt and to lend her support to securing Henry's preferment.[151]

CONCLUSION

Lady Beauclerk's involvement in patronage reinforces the notion that patronage operated in a familial political world, and that political women could and did employ a variety of strategies and arguments—political, familial, or gendered arguments, as appropriate—in making patronage requests to achieve familial ends. Her interactions with Newcastle reveal a woman with a sophisticated understanding of the workings of the patronage system, a long personal history of using it to advantage, and the necessary knowledge to make calculated requests. Moreover, they testify to the fact that contemporary male politicians accepted women's involvement in patronage—and that gender was not, in itself, a bar to success.

The value attached to patronage in the eighteenth century had important implications for women's involvement in political life. Patronage supplied women with a variety of means of approach in an assortment of milieus. It was intrinsically flexible, non institutional, and decentralized, interweaving the political with the social and operating in the marchlands between the public and the private domains. This was a boon to women, as it allowed them the freedom to deal with public affairs from the comfort of their own homes, or private affairs through personal contacts in public venues: there were many combinations possible. It also enabled women to control the type and degree of their involvement, and to shape it, at least to some extent, to fit their lives. Even those women who were unable or unwilling to take part personally in patronage, or felt that they lacked the influence necessary for success, might make the system work at one remove, through male, female, or mixed-sex networks of friends and connexions.

As a group, the women who took part in patronage reflected the structure of eighteenth-century society and the political world: they were predominantly married rather than single, and fractionally more likely to be titled than untitled. Their patronage requests were

[151] PRO, 30/8/19, fols. 13–14, 16–17, 19–20, Lady Beauclerk to Lady Chatham, 6 Feb. 1783, 25 May 1784, 1 June 1784.

remarkably similar to men's in terms of motivations, methods, or demands, and politicians' papers show that they were dealt with seriously. Factors such as property and financial and/or political power, class and connexion, and intelligence and force of character seem to have been predominant in influencing both women's involvement in patronage and their success.

Although the sources do not allow for exact quantification of women's involvement, records reveal them to have been regular participants in a variety of patronage networks throughout the second half of the eighteenth century. Even in the most political and public of correspondence networks, as revealed in the Newcastle Papers while he was first lord, they made roughly 10 per cent of the total patronage requests. This figure, while small, is significant; moreover, the diversity of patronage networks at the time and the amount of patronage that would have been conducted in person suggest that it may well underestimate women's overall involvement.

5

Women and the Electoral Process

When Frances, Lady Irwin, died in 1807, the 11th duke of Norfolk—the notoriously hard-drinking 'Jockey'—finally achieved a goal that had eluded him for twenty years: he gained control over the borough of Horsham in East Sussex. He had contended, overtly and covertly, against Lady Irwin's interest in the borough from shortly after his accession to the title in 1786. The struggle had cost him dearly. William Albery, in his history of the borough, estimated that Norfolk paid out over £70,000 in burgage purchases, repeated contested elections, and petitions to parliament. But success was to prove dearer still. Despite all of his efforts, Norfolk only gained control over the borough after Lady Irwin's death—and, ironically, not long before the Commons once again overturned the election of his candidates and seated her candidates in their place. Moreover, in the end, his extensive investment in the borough counted for little. He was forced to buy the political interest in the borough outright from Lady Irwin's heirs—for the record sum of £91,475.[1]

'HORSHAM IS LADY IRWIN'S BOROUGH'

Lady Irwin's electoral battle with Norfolk was remarkable in terms of its length and cost, but, as an aristocratic widow striving to preserve her family's political interest, she was not unique. What made her different from many other politically active aristocratic widows was that she was not safeguarding the family interest until a son or grandson came of age, but preserving it in order to bequeath it, as a valuable form of property, to her daughter. Lady Irwin inherited a life interest in the estate at Horsham on her husband's death in 1778, and while trustees had been appointed to oversee her affairs, they seem to have existed in name only. As the young attorney, Thomas Charles Medwin, who served as Norfolk's steward and *eminence grise* at Horsham discovered to his chagrin when he was trying to find ways to disqualify Lady Irwin's votes in Horsham, the trustees took

[1] Albery, *Parliamentary History of... Horsham*, 253.

no part at all in running the political interest. This was left entirely in Lady Irwin's capable hands.

Horsham was a burgage borough, where whoever owned the most burgages controlled the borough—as long, that is, as all of the voters were included on the burgage roll and admitted at a Court Baron.[2] Lady Irwin's control over the borough was theoretically straightforward. Ascertaining voting qualifications was particularly difficult in Horsham, however. The burgages were diverse and poorly recorded: houses, barns, stables, fields, and an unverifiable assortment of small plots of land all possessed votes.[3] In 1764, when Lord Irwin's agent had conducted a survey of the borough, he had found a total of eighty-three votes, nineteen of which were in women, all of whom would have appointed proxies to vote for them. Between 1774 and 1787 Lady Irwin and her agents secured an additional thirty-six burgesses. This would have consolidated her control over the borough had there been a Court Baron during that period. As there was not—the Court Baron was under the control of the duke of Norfolk anyway, and thus open to manipulation—these votes remained unrecorded and overall control of the borough remained unsettled.[4]

A Court Baron was finally held under the new duke, in September 1787. Then, and at subsequent Court Barons in 1788 and 1789, it was controlled by Medwin, who hand-picked a Homage Jury of Norfolk supporters and ensured that Lady Irwin's new votes were not included on the burgage roll.[5] By 1787 Norfolk was contemplating expanding his political interest in Sussex, and Medwin, who had already achieved a

[2] Medwin adopted the following strict definition of a burgage: 'The definition of a Burgage as adopted and strictly adhered to by the Committee's, is this, "one undivided and indivisible Tenement, clearly described, neither created, nor capable of being created, within time of memory, which has immemorially given a right of voting".' Horsham Museum Archive (hereafter HMA), MS 3.21, Thomas Charles Medwin to Norfolk, Horsham, 12 Sept. 1788.

[3] O'Gorman, *Voters, Patrons, and Party*, 35. Namier sees the erosion of the Irwin interest resulting from Lord Irwin's death, compounded by Norfolk's conversion to Anglicanism and his desire for political involvement from 1780. The extent of the struggle between Lady Irwin, who had placed both seats at the disposal of the administration in 1780 and 1784, and Norfolk, who was a supporter of the opposition, as well as the eventual outcome of this rivalry, mitigate against a simple causal link between the lack of a male head of family and the destruction of a political interest. Albery, *Parliamentary History of... Horsham*, 75, 114–253; Namier, *Structure of Politics*, 135; Namier and Brooke, *House of Commons*, i. 393.

[4] HMA, MS 3.3, List of Lady Irwin's Burgesses not Admitted and List of Free Burgesses not Admitted, 8 Sept. 1787.

[5] Ibid., MS 3.5, Medwin to Norfolk, Horsham, 30 Sept. 1787; MS 3.19, Medwin to Norfolk, n. pl., 29 Aug. 1788.

certain reputation as a specialist in manorial law, had realized that with a certain amount of sharp dealing it might be possible to overturn Lady Irwin's interest in the borough. He was more than ready to exploit alternative interpretations of the franchise, to take whatever steps were necessary to win over the thirty independent burgesses, and to work quietly behind the scenes to buy up enough of the remaining burgages to give Norfolk the controlling interest. He advised Norfolk to 'look into the State of the Boro' when you have Leisure'.[6] Norfolk was soon persuaded into contesting it in the upcoming 1790 election. The plan to wrest control of the borough away from Lady Irwin was formalized and committed to paper in May 1788, when Medwin met with Norfolk at Deepdene. This secret 'Deepdene Memorandum', as Albery later named it, records the agreement between Norfolk and Medwin. Norfolk would put up two candidates, Timothy Shelley (Medwin was married to Shelley's second cousin)[7] and another unspecified gentleman. Medwin and a legal colleague of his, Robert Hurst, also of Horsham, would devote themselves to 'purchasing Freehold Burgages, for the Duke of Norfolk, for the purposes of securing a future Interest in the Borough'. Norfolk, in turn, agreed to secure Hurst's services with a payment of 300 guineas 'untill the Time of the Election, as a professional Compensation; he having Engaged to devote his time, Skill, and Interest, to prepare and direct the Loyal measures, and other Means, requisite to Attain the Object'.[8]

Lady Irwin would, however, prove a far more formidable opponent than either Medwin or Norfolk expected. By 1788 she was a woman in her fifties, with a lifetime of political experience. Through her networks of friends and acquaintances, she had her own connexions with leading politicians. While she does not appear to have been particularly political in the early years of her marriage, she, like her long-term friend Lady Susan Stewart (later Lady Gower/marchioness of Stafford), became increasingly so as she got older.[9] In so doing, she followed a progression

[6] MS 3.19, Medwin to Norfolk, n. pl., 30 Sept. 1787.

[7] See *The Letters of Bysshe and Timothy Shelley, and other Documents*, ed. Susan Cabell Djabri and Jeremy Knight (Horsham, 2000).

[8] HMA, MS 3.11, Memo of a plan for providing the election of Mr Timothy Shelly and Another Gentleman prepared by Thomas Charles Medwin for the duke of Norfolk, Dorking [24 May 1788]. The memorandum is signed by Medwin.

[9] PRO, 30/29/4/2/2, fols. 109–11, Lady Ingram to Lady Susan Stewart, Templenewsam, 16 Mar. [1761]. By 1766 she was discussing the repeal of the Stamp Act, the problems of the Rockingham administration—'Strange fermentations in the political World'—and her esteem for William Pitt: PRO, 30/29/4/2/19, fols. 142–3, Lady Ingram [Irwin] to Lady Susan

shared by many other women who married into politically active families with traditions of politically active women. Both of these criteria applied to the Irwins: the family was regularly active in Yorkshire and Sussex politics through their estates, and the eighteenth-century had already seen a number of politically active matriarchs in the Irwin family. Indeed, the Irwin interest in Horsham rested on cash advanced to Irwin's grandfather, *c.*1723, for the purchase of twenty burgages by his great-grandmother Isabella, another formidable political widow.[10]

Lady Irwin emerged as a political figure in her own right soon after her husband's death. By August 1779 her name can be found on a list of leading landowners—alongside the duke of Rutland, Lords Scarborough and Bristol, and Sir Gilbert Heathcote—in attendance at a meeting in support of a Mr Monson's candidature for Lincoln.[11] By 1780 she was not only politically active but also knew that she was known to be so. This meant that any letters she sent during the 1780 election might well be opened in the post. This consideration left her chuckling at the end of one long, chatty letter to Lady Gower, especially as it was largely concerned with her time at Newmarket and her housemaids' attempts to attract the attention of male passers-by by repeatedly washing their hands in front of the windows: 'I am laughing ready to die at the thoughts of this letters being read at the office & all about the HouseMaid, taken for some Ministerial treason: I hope it will cost them hours to decypher.'[12]

The 1780 election saw her conduct her first campaign in Horsham. As she informed Lady Gower, she was pleased with the results:

> my little Horsham business went on *flourishingly*, & my vanity is flatter'd at the idea of being *personally well* with the Burgesses. a dreadful opposition broke out against Mr Lascelles who had been so effectually undermined that he thinks it prudent to withdraw himself, & the County [Yorks.] is now deliver'd up to Associators & Oliverians, all the little Interest I had was at Mr Lascelles's Command for I hate the Association.[13]

Stewart, Templenewsam, 24 Mar. 1766; PRO, 30/29/4/2/21, fols. 146–7, Lady Irwin to Lady Susan Stewart, Templenewsam, 26 July 1766.

[10] See Albery, *Parliamentary History of... Horsham*, 75, 114–253; A. F. Hughes and J. Knight, *Hills: Horsham's Lost Stately Home and Garden* (Horsham, 1999), 17–32.

[11] See Nottingham Record Office, Foljambe of Osberton Papers, XI. B. 180–1, John Turner to John Hewett, Caistor (Lincs.), 22 Aug. 1779.

[12] PRO, 30/29/4/2/61, fol. 253^{v}, Lady Irwin to Lady Gower, Templenewsam, 21 Oct. [1780].

[13] PRO, 30/29/4/2/51, fols. 209^{v}–10, Lady Irwin to Lady Gower, Templenewsam [Sept–Oct.?] 1780.

An ardent monarchist, she was a lifelong supporter of the king's ministers. As a middle-aged widow, she had dedicated her influence and the seats at her command first to Lord North's administration and then to William Pitt's. Her control over Horsham was acknowledged and deemed worthy of administration support. John Robinson, in his list of boroughs and borough patrons compiled prior to the 1784 election, noted that Horsham was Lady Irwin's borough, but also recognized that it might need 'a little more management' than before, and allocated her £7,000 accordingly.[14] That it was still commonly assumed to be in her gift in 1790 is reflected in a letter from Alexander Williams to Medwin, who was by this time feverishly campaigning against her. Williams, in good eighteenth-century fashion, was trying to help a friend get into parliament on the cheap, and clearly presumed that Horsham would be uncontested and that Medwin would be working with, rather than against, Lady Irwin: 'The General Election being so near at Hand and Friend of mine wishing to purchase a Seat in the next Parliament, I wish very much to know whether there is any Possibility of obtaining a *quiet* Seat by the Means of *Lady Irwin*—If You will do me the favor to make enquiry on this subject and let me know the Result You will oblige, Dr Sir.'[15]

The battle for control of Horsham began in earnest in 1788. By July, only two months after the Deepdene Memorandum, Medwin and Shelley had already begun to purchase burgages, conveying the new acquisitions to themselves in an effort to avoid attracting suspicion to Norfolk.[16] This often entailed significant manoeuvring. In the case of the miller and baker John Champion, Medwin and Hurst had to compensate him with a plot of land on Horsham Common, where there was a windmill and a rent of £10 per annum.[17] And this was still before the beginning of the all-out purchasing war between Lady Irwin and Norfolk. With Lady Irwin arriving at Hills for a three-week stay and Sir Henry Fletcher conveying his nine burgages to tenants, thus making faggot votes for Norfolk, Medwin knew that 'an Alarm must be taken if it has not Already'. In order not to give the game away completely, he advised Norfolk to find a running-mate for Shelley who would appeal to the independent burgesses.[18]

[14] *The Parliamentary Papers of John Robinson, 1774–1784*, ed. William Thomas Laprade, Camden Soc., 3rd ser., 33 (London, 1922), 91.

[15] HMA, MS 3.36, Alex. Williams to Medwin, Chichester, 5 Mar 1790.

[16] HMA, MS 3.13, Medwin to Norfolk, Horsham, 22 July 1788.

[17] Ibid.

[18] Ibid. Norfolk eventually chose Wilson Bradyll of Lancashire to be Shelley's running-mate.

Indeed, Lady Irwin had been tipped off by Shelley's purchase of Mary Somersett's three messuages and garden for the exceptionally large sum of £1,750 (rental value £69. 9*s*. 0*d*.).[19] Despite Medwin's sending a special messenger off to Kent to negotiate the purchase, and having Hurst write the contract out in Shelley's name in order to prevent knowledge of it 'falling Into the Enemy's Hands',[20] this marked the beginning of the election campaign in earnest. Lady Irwin doubled the length of her stay at Hills: three weeks became six, and she devoted her energies while there to countering Medwin and spurring her agents into action.

In true eighteenth-century electioneering fashion, she immediately began to canvass the independent burgesses herself. She also began to treat—in this case, she held a venison feast at the public house in her interest, the King's Head.[21] Shelley, in turn, responded to Lady Irwin's canvass with one of his own,[22] and Norfolk even emerged from the shadows to sponsor an opposition feast at the public house in his interest, the Anchor Inn.[23] As Lady Irwin explained to one of the most influential independent burgesses, Peter Du Cane, when she requested his support, she was fully aware that there was an attempt under way to take control of the borough away from her. While her appeal to Du Cane was unsuccessful, as he had decided to support Shelley's candidature 'on Constitutional grounds', claiming that he was a long-time supporter of parliamentary reform,[24] she knew that defeating Norfolk would rest on maintaining and/or obtaining control over the poorer burgesses. By 8 September, therefore, the *Sussex Advertiser* was already reporting on the purchasing war that was taking place in Horsham:

> The 'free' Burgesses of Horsham, we hear, are determined at the next General Election to try their strength on behalf of Mr Timothy Shelley Esq. against the interests of Lady Irwin, who has heretofore had the disposal of that Borough in Consequences of which houses that have votes have increased hear a thousand per cent in their value.[25]

[19] HMA, MS 3.16, Medwin to Norfolk [Horsham], 10 Aug. 1788; MS 3.26, An Account of Rental of the Burgages purchased by His Grace the Duke of Norfolk in the Borough of Horsham, 25 December 1788. Mary Somersett's is the most expensive purchase of all the burgages listed; only William White's for £1,000 approaches it.

[20] Ibid.

[21] HMA, MS 3.16, Medwin to Norfolk [Horsham], 10 Aug. 1788.

[22] Ibid.

[23] HMA, MS 3.19, Medwin to Norfolk, Horsham, 29 Aug. 1788.

[24] West Sussex Record Office (hereafter WSRO), Add. MS 5,190, Peter Du Cane to Lady Irwin, Horsham, 23 Aug. 1788.

[25] *Sussex Advertiser*, 8 Sept. 1788, as quoted in Albery, *Parliamentary History of . . . Horsham*, 130.

These sorts of inflated sums must have been especially appealing to widows; however, not all sold. Despite Medwin's best efforts, for instance, he was unable to obtain Elizabeth Bridger's burgage. Her determination to maintain her independence and her political interest echoes that of Lady Irwin herself. Widow Bridger had, through strict settlement, inherited had a life interest in three burgages and, like her aristocratic counterpart, maintained these intact so that she could pass them on to her daughter.[26]

Medwin was kept busy trying to counter Lady Irwin and the efforts of her agents, William Ellis and Mr Wallis, while also striving to allay Norfolk's fears. A letter from Lady Irwin to Sir Henry Fletcher in early September, complaining of Medwin's tactics in Horsham, left Norfolk worrying that she would be protesting directly to him next.[27] Rather optimistically, Medwin informed him that 'the purchase of four or five more Burgages, would seal the Fate of the Borough'. He also tried to reassure Norfolk by telling him that adhering to a very strict interpretation of the legal definition of a burgage would ensure that all but twenty of Lady Irwin's burgages would be disallowed.[28] At about this time Norfolk's cause benefited from the defection of William White. White's father had been steward to Lord Irwin and he controlled the appointment of the town clerk. By 'purchasing' this office from him, Medwin gained for Norfolk control over the Court Leet as well as the Court Baron. There may have been several reasons behind White's desertion of Lady Irwin, but the fact that his sister was married to John Shelley and his niece was to marry Timothy Shelley in 1791 may well have played a part. Family connexions, predominantly through marriage, played a significant role in linking the local Norfolk supporters: for example, Peter Du Cane was married to Hurst's second cousin; Charles and William Smith were Hurst's brothers-in-law; John Smith was the uncle of Hurst's wife; James Waller was Hurst's cousin on his mother's side; Dr Hutchinson was Waller's brother-in-law; John Pilford was Medwin's father-in-law; and Medwin's wife was Timothy Shelley's second cousin.[29]

Whether the Quo Warranto action that Lady Irwin had her steward bring against Timothy Shelley in early 1789 was a direct response to losing control over the Court Leet is hard to say, but recourse to the law was clearly something that did not frighten her. She was unwilling to be

[26] HMA, MS 3.19, Medwin to Norfolk, Horsham, 29 Aug. 1788.
[27] Horsham, MS 3.20, Norfolk to Medwin, n. pl., 8 Sept. 1788.
[28] Horsham, MS 3.21, Medwin to Norfolk, Horsham, 12 Sept. 1788.
[29] *Letters of Bysshe and Timothy Shelley*, ed. Djabri and Knight, 31, 38.

outbid or outmanoeuvred and, like male landowners with political interests, she had good lawyers and was ready to use them. While Shelley ultimately won this first case, the courtroom would provide Lady Irwin with yet another front in her battle against Norfolk. The irregularities of the 1790 election would result in nine separate actions at law, the last of which would only be settled in 1802.[30]

It is a testimony to Lady Irwin's tenacity and success that by the time of the contested election in 1790 Norfolk's only chance of defeating her candidates rested upon his ability to persuade his chosen bailiffs at a packed Court Baron to poll only those voters 'such as were on the Court Rolls of Burgesses, admitted on presentment of the Sworn Homage': that is, to disallow any of the new Irwin votes.[31] Lady Irwin realized that Medwin's deviousness would ensure that her candidates—her son-in-law, Lord William Gordon, and James Baillie, a West India merchant—would lose the election. Consequently, she had her agents concentrate on ensuring that the forty-two faggot voters, which she knew Medwin would try to disallow, would meet the stipulations laid out in the Last Determination of the borough in 1715.[32] While she could have conceded and saved the trouble and expense of an election, or she could have fought the election and then accepted defeat, her efforts in ensuring that her voters would stand up under parliamentary examination suggests that she had decided from the outset that she would, if necessary, pursue the outcome right up to parliament.

Medwin ran true to form. He scheduled the Court Baron for two hours before the election. He arrived half-an-hour late, wasted time by adjourning the court to the Anchor Inn (Norfolk's public house), and then proceeded to allow Hurst to begin with long speech proposing a Norfolk voter. When Ellis, Lady Irwin's agent, successfully objected to this voter, he then proceeded to spend the rest of the time before the election looking out the window, ignoring everyone, including Ellis.[33] His actions ensured that none of Lady Irwin's new voters were admitted or inscribed on the Rolls of Burgesses before voting started. Consequently, her candidates were narrowly defeated. Her son-in-law, Lord William Gordon, and James Baillie, a West India merchant, achieved twenty and nineteen votes respectively against Norfolk's candidates, Timothy

[30] Albery, *Parliamentary History of... Horsham*, 142.

[31] WSRO, Add. MS 5,192, Memm. of What passed on the Election of two Members for Horsham on Saturday 19 June 1790 [unfoliated], 2.

[32] Albery, *Parliamentary History of... Horsham*, 136.

[33] Hughes and Knight, *Hills*, 34.

Shelley and Wilson Braddyll, who secured twenty-five and twenty-four votes each. The ensuing scrutiny led to a petition to parliament. There, Medwin's sharp dealings were quickly exposed, Lady Irwin's attention to detail triumphed, and Norfolk's candidates were promptly unseated.[34]

While it can be argued that Lady Irwin's electoral battle against Norfolk may have been unequal, given Norfolk's status and the depth of his purse, neither of these factors, nor the fact that Lady Irwin was a widow engaging in electoral politics, seems to have been a significant factor either in the struggle itself or its final outcome. Instead, party considerations, self-interest, greed, and a general desire for change were the most influential factors making burgage-owners sell up or switch allegiance. Lady Irwin herself proved to be easily a match for Norfolk, both in her knowledge of electioneering and her determination to make the system work for her.[35] She not only maintained her hold on the borough after the fiery 1790 election, but also fought another contest against Norfolk in 1806, once again defeating him on petition. One can only assume that she would have thoroughly enjoyed knowing that, thanks to her efforts, her daughter's inheritance was increased by nearly £100,000 when Norfolk finally purchased the interest outright in 1807.[36]

WOMEN AND ELECTORAL POLITICS

Lady Irwin's electoral involvement bears recounting for a number of reasons, not least because it reveals her to have been a competent and effective eighteenth-century politician and, like her male counterparts, someone whose motivations for electoral involvement were similarly personal, familial, and ideological. As the head of a family, a landowner, and an electoral patron, she differed little from the men around her, and both her methods and her results echo theirs. She had an intimate understanding of the way that local politics worked on the ground, and an ability to use the system to her advantage. Her letters reveal that she dealt competently and assuredly with both peers and gentlemen, and that she readily assumed authority over men of lower status. She canvassed men of her own rank and, like Norfolk, employed competent agents to handle the mechanics of burgage purchases, treating, and soliciting votes from those of lower rank. While there is no denying that the political

[34] See *Commons Journals*, xlvi, 28–9, *passim*.

[35] Albery, *Parliamentary History of . . . Horsham*, 242. [36] Ibid. 253.

world which she inhabited was ostensibly male, and that a pervasive societal rhetoric existed at the time that denigrated female political involvement, Lady Irwin's participation, based as it was primarily on the twin arguments of land and family, validated her activity and placed her well within the acceptable familial paradigm.

Lady Irwin is representative of a type of political woman who has as yet attracted little concentrated historical attention. Forthright, intelligent, authoritative, and politically knowledgeable, she is a far cry from the enduring stereotype of the eighteenth-century electioneering woman, cast as it was by the critics and satirists of the day in the model of the duchess of Devonshire and that bevy of young, alluring, female canvassers who took to the streets in Westminster in 1784—women whose combination of charming condescension and mild titillation were assumed to be their principal political attributes.[37] Lady Irwin's participation was, however, neither male-directed nor carried out in support of a man; it was instead direct and simultaneously personal and familial. She owed her influence and success, not to youth and beauty (although she had been a beauty in her day), nor to the skilful deployment of female sexuality, but to such everyday factors as family, rank, position in the local community, wealth—and, of course, good lawyers.

As a politically active aristocratic widow controlling a family interest, she was not an anomaly. As John Cannon has shown, 70 per cent of eighteenth-century peerage families went through at least one minority, and one-third of all successions were by minors.[38] Few families suffered the four minorities of the earls of Plymouth, but extended guardianships were not unusual. Over the course of the century the dukes of Bedford were minors for a total of thirty-three and a half years, those of Beaufort for a total of twenty-eight years. The dukes of Hamilton had two consecutive minorities at mid-century for a total of nineteen years.

While some widows had sole control over their children, estates, and family interests, others shared the tasks with male guardians, usually kin connexions. Relations between mothers and trustees varied, but even those widows who had no legal control might be expected to play their

[37] For Grego, writing in 1886, it was 'the seductive wiles of female charms and persuasions' that won votes; writing a century later, Frank O'Gorman still saw the female canvasser's role as little more than 'the public flaunting of fairly innocent sexual and sartorial behaviour': J. Grego, *History of Parliamentary Elections and Electioneering in the Old Days* (London, 1886), 292; O'Gorman, *Voters, Patrons and Parties*, 93.

[38] John Cannon, *Aristocratic Century: The Peerage of Eighteenth-Century England* (Cambridge, 1987), 137.

part in safeguarding the family property and political interest. Lady Anne Fitzwilliam, who was widowed in 1756 when her son was twelve, worked together with Sir Matthew Lambe, her son's guardian, to secure the family's seat at Peterborough. On Lambe's death in 1768 she maintained the family's control over the seat by supporting the (successful) candidature of Lord Belasyse. She then extended and consolidated the family's interest in the borough by spending £2,500 on property.[39] The duchess of Beaufort, widowed in 1756, was left the legal guardian of her eight-year-old son; her brother Lord Botetourt was made principal trustee of the estate. Between them, they not only succeeded in maintaining the family interest of five seats, but they also discovered and greatly reduced a previously unknown debt.[40]

The duchess of Bedford was one of the period's most politically experienced widows. Criticized frequently by discontented or malicious contemporaries for her influence over her husband's political decisions and, by implication, over the politics of the Bedford faction during more than thirty years of marriage, she was widowed in 1771 and left to manage the large Bedford interest of eight seats for her grandson.[41] As such, she was approached for her interest when elections loomed. In 1779 Edmund Burke went through her nephew, Lord Upper Ossory, to seek her support for a candidate standing in Buckinghamshire. Charles James Fox, then an aspiring young politician standing for a seat in Westminster, also contacted Ossory, but he waited on her himself as well. This personal touch may have been doubly important because of the factional differences between the Bedfords and Fox's father, which had led to a breakdown in relations in the 1760s. Fox was confident that as long the duchess could be persuaded not to speak out openly against him, he would be able to secure the votes.[42]

Of course, not all aristocratic widows were well suited or well prepared for political involvement. If either the widows, the trustees, or the agents were inept, a widowhood could provide other local political families with the perfect opportunity to challenge for control of a borough. Since a

39 E. A. Smith, *Whig Principles and Party Politics: Earl Fitzwilliam and the Whig Party 1748–1833* (Manchester, 1975), 14–16.

40 Cannon, *Aristocratic Century*, 107.

41 Namier, *Structure of Politics*, 144.

42 'Edmund Burke to Ossory, Hampden House, 30 Sept. 1779', in *Correspondence of Edmund Burke*, ed. Copeland, *et al.*, iv. 139; BL, Add. MS 47,580, fo. 63^{v}, C. J. Fox to R. Fitzpatrick, Bridgewater, 1 Sept. 1780; 'C. J. Fox to Ossory, London, Sept. 1780', in *Memorials and Correspondence of Charles James Fox*, ed. Lord John Russell, 4 vols. (London, 1853), i. 257.

minority could result in the ruin of a family's political interest, and given the importance of maintaining a viable political interest to a family's status and standing in the community, it is not surprising that most aristocratic widows took steps to pass the family interest on to their heirs intact. For some, like the young duchess of Hamilton, who had not been especially politicized prior to being widowed, this entailed a quick education in political management and electioneering from the other guardians, trustees, and the family's political agents. For others, like the duchess of Beaufort, her daughter the duchess of Rutland, or Lady Irwin, all of whom had been politically active during their marriages, widowhood only extended the scope of their political activities. Some widows retired from active political involvement once sons or heirs came of age, but others seem to have acquired a taste for politics—or at least a lasting commitment to the family's political interest—and remained active long afterwards. An experienced and knowledgeable mother who lived primarily in the country on one of the family's estates could be an invaluable and experienced unpaid partner in running a family's political interest. The dowager Lady Spencer, who knew the people and politics of St Albans intimately and who lived at nearby Holywell, is a case in point.

This is not to suggest that all widows—or all women—from politically active families took part in electoral politics, or that those who did were equally involved. While it was undoubtedly easier for women who did not want to be involved in electoral politics to avoid it by playing up to assumptions about politics as being no place for women, it must be pointed out that not all of the men of the political elite were politically active or enthusiastic either. In part, this is due to the electoral circumstances of the time. While, despite politicians' best efforts, the number of contested elections rose in the second half of the century, there were still boroughs where elections were rarities.[43] In the seven general elections between 1754 and 1790, only between a quarter and a third of elections went all the way to the polls. This is not to suggest, however, that elections were necessarily one-way events directed by an elite consensus at the top.[44] Much money, energy, and activity was expended on contests that were begun but settled prior to the election. The 1780 general election, for instance, shows only two county contests, but there were

[43] This trend continued up to the Reform Bill. The statistics upon which the following paragraph is based are gleaned from O'Gorman, *Voters, Patrons, and Parties*, 107–12.

[44] Frank O'Gorman, 'The Unreformed Electorate of Hanoverian England: The Mid-18th Century to 1832', *Social Hist.*, 11: 1 (1986), 33–52.

also four other campaigns that ended before the poll; similarly, in 1784 seven counties polled, but there were fifteen incomplete contests. If we take Frank O'Gorman's advice and assume that up to 75 per cent of all elections were contested to some degree, the all-consuming 'madness' that elections often generated throughout the political elite becomes more easily understandable, even if we also accept that the most active electoral involvement in any election would still have represented only a relatively small number of men and women. Nevertheless, by including partial contests, the potential for women's politicization and involvement is dramatically increased.

There must have been as many degrees of electoral involvement for women as a whole as there were women. The extent to which they became involved depended upon a complicated interplay of factors: their characters, abilities, and experiences; the strength of their political beliefs; their family traditions and expectations of women's political involvement (or not); and their specific election circumstances. Contemporary sources suggest that women's involvement varied with the demands of the election—political expediency was a great incentive to action. Uncontested elections in small, submissive boroughs required minimal political effort from men or women; conversely, large electorates, intractable freeholders, self-willed corporations, or intense personal rivalries could result in contests that politicized every aspect of life and demanded extensive—and, in the eyes of some contemporaries, excessive—political involvement over a long period of time. In elections such as these, women might either be principles in the contest—that is, at the heart of the planning and organization from the outset, as Lady Irwin was—or reserve troops who emerged to add extra panache and canvassing power to a flagging campaign, as the Foxite Whig women were in 1784.

In either case, it appears that contested elections brought a temporary extension of the everyday boundaries of 'respectable' female political behaviour. Although women always had less latitude in their electioneering behaviour and activities than men—Lady Chatterley-like concerns about gender, sexuality, and class, stemming from the indiscriminate mixing of elite women and lower-class men, were only just below the surface—they were also expected to participate in the social inversion that was intrinsic to eighteenth-century elections. The boundary between acceptable and unacceptable female electioneering was not clearly marked at any time; what might be acceptable in one set of election circumstances or one location might not be in another. In addition, how women's electioneering was viewed depended upon the perspective of the viewer:

the same electioneering behaviours could generate praise or vitriol depending upon which side of the contest the commentator was on. That said, however, women's electioneering seems to have met with little comment as long as it preserved a modicum of dignity and modesty—women needed to be especially careful not to de-class themselves by becoming overly familiar with the lower orders—and as long as it could be rationalized as being dutiful, carried out in support of a family member, a male relative, or a man representing a family interest. Woe betide the woman whose activities overstepped the mark, however, either by making too blatant a use of her sexuality to secure votes, or by descending to any of the other eighteenth-century voting ploys that could lead to charges of corruption and bribery. This only played up to the most negative stereotypes of women and politics. The fiercest attacks on women were aimed at those few women whose popularity and charisma, and whose importance to the outcome of an election, genuinely threatened the notion of the supportive, subordinate, familial female. Their electioneering success demonstrated that women could be powerfully effective politicians in their own rights, even that they could, at time, outdo men at their own game; thus calling into question women's political incompetence, and by implication casting doubts on the 'natural' patriarchal hierarchy of eighteenth-century society.

CONCLUSION

Women who were active in electoral politics in the second half of the eighteenth century came from the same social and political strata as politically active men. While women's electoral involvement was always potentially problematic, women from politically active families were expected to take part in at least the social side of electoral politics. Families were political units and while this may have meant little more for women than appearing at the right social functions and charming the right people, it could also entail significantly more involvement. Fewer women seem to have canvassed, either in writing or in person, but canvassing was still common enough to be largely taken for granted by contemporaries. In addition, there was always a small group of women who were extensively involved in electioneering for personal, familial, or factional reasons. They were most likely to take demanding, managerial roles, to direct campaigns, or to control political interests. They were involved at each stage of the electoral process, where they both worked with, and could be in positions of authority over, men. Their involvement was openly political and was accepted as such: not because they were viewed as honorary men—although this may have been the case in some situations—but out of a combination of respect for their own political capabilities and characters, and deference for their positions within families and/or factions. Those women who controlled seats and family interests were predominantly widows and matriarchs; they held, at least in theory, women's most powerful political positions; however, they, like the peers, were ultimately limited to directing votes without having the ability to vote themselves.

6

Maintaining the Family Interest

Considerations of women's involvement in electoral politics have, not surprisingly, focused on the most colourful and visible manifestations of their activities, mainly their participation in canvassing. While there is no doubt that a successful outcome depended upon thorough and perspicacious canvassing, and that canvassing allowed women to take a direct and easily recognizable part in electoral politics, it was not the sum total of their participation. Elections were undeniably the most intense and climactic part of the electoral process, but managing a family interest well and securing an electorate before or after an election was also vitally important and entailed significant, if periodic, effort. For women from parliamentary families, this last could mean anything from ordinary socializing through to pointedly political manoeuvring carried on in the social arena. In either case, the social niceties had to be adhered to, hospitality offered, philanthropy bestowed, patronage secured, potential defectors charmed, channels of communication with political supporters kept open, and local socio-political events, especially those around the assizes and the annual race-meets, attended. In the immediate lead-up to an election all of these activities took on much more intense political hues. Mundane or intimate socializing over tea or cards, and even the classic social performance of visiting, could become openly politicized. As elections neared, women would be called on to attend election breakfasts and/or balls. Widows with political interests would be expected to host and/or attend special dinners or entertainments, perhaps for the local aldermen and other worthy voters, or even for freeholders and their wives. Depending upon the family and the heat of the election, political wives or daughters might be expected to do the same.

FAMILIAL POLITICS

While historians often pay lip-service to the importance of 'family' in eighteenth-century politics, and regularly speak of 'family' interests, they usually interpret this to mean male kin connexions.[1] Such a narrow definition obscures the contributions that women made to what were truly *family* interests. Politically active families were working units, which included women who were expected to contribute to the maintenance of political interests. Their personal involvement complemented and echoed that of their menfolk. Like successful eighteenth-century male politicians, political women, especially political wives, had to show commitment (real or assumed) to the local community. This was achieved primarily by attending or supporting local events and through personal displays of hospitality, civility, and generosity. Acts of charity, pardons for the unjustly accused, and patronage for the deserving all contributed to a family's political credit. In Lady Orford's Cornish borough of Callington, even the sponsorship of local education was brought to bear, as she provided a school for the children of those freeholders who agreed to vote for her candidate.[2]

Visibility in the community was of vital importance, and between elections women were expected to attend, host, or 'do the honours' at local social events.[3] Keeping up a political interest between elections also meant being 'mighty civil' to neighbours in the country. Some activities were sex-specific—women's reciprocal visiting or men's drinking parties, for instance—but others saw men and women entertaining mixed-sex groups. The country gentry were notoriously prickly about status and quick to take offence, which meant that aristocratic political families had to take extra care when dealing with them. Nor was the potential for social tension lessened significantly if the leading political families in the area were part of the country gentry themselves. In either case, there were difficulties inherent in handling what were essentially power relationships in social situations. The need for sensitivity was multiplied when the interactions were intimate. Dinners were a political civility that could be particularly uncomfortable. Many women would have agreed with Lady Dalkeith, who felt that dining with the squire and his wife was a 'Tax imposed upon us all in the Country'.[4] A successful political wife had to be able to enjoy herself, or at least give the impression of enjoying herself, in this and other social situations. A young, vivacious, and sociable political woman like Lady Sarah Bunbury was the ideal partner for an aspiring

[1] See e.g. Namier, *Structure of Politics*; Wiggin, *Faction of Cousins*.

[2] A. de C. Glubb, *When Cornwall had 44 MPs* (Truro, 1934), 37–8.

[3] J. V. Beckett, *The Aristocracy in England, 1660–1914* (Oxford, 1989), 356.

[4] PRO, 30/29/4/1/52, fol. 99, Lady Caroline Dalkeith to Lady Susan Stewart, Adderbury, 20 [?] 1764.

county politician. She threw herself into her role with enthusiasm, leaving her politically disillusioned sister, Lady Holland, marvelling: 'she was engaged to no less than eight turtle feasts in the town of Bury last time I heard from her.'[5]

PUBLIC DAYS

For politically active aristocratic families, one of the socio-political duties that accompanied residence in the country during the summer was the hosting of Public Days. These 'Days' gathered the local elite together over food and drink, and entertained them with musical performances, cards, and balls. They were used to show off new political connexions, maintain contacts with well-established supporters, and pay special attention to those whose political allegiance was questionable. Wobbly supporters could be wooed, perhaps even encouraged to stay the night and be part of a more select crowd the following day. During the hunting season local gentlemen and ladies might well set off the following morning with their hounds for a 'grand coursing'.[6] They appear to have usually taken place once a week. When the Northumberlands decided to hold two Public Days a week in 1770, they were discussed with something akin to awe by contemporaries.[7] It is unclear whose decision this was, but given the duchess's tendency to grandeur and her love of show, it seems likely that she flourished under a regime that would have left others crying out for more informality and ease.

Public Days provided political families with an opportunity to show themselves off as *families*. They were jointly hosted by husbands and wives, and might include exquisitely dressed—and, ideally, well-behaved—children to complete the family picture. Adolescents or young adults were expected to show off their manners and social graces

[5] 'Lady Holland to Lady Louisa Conolly, Kingsgate, 8 Aug. 1762', in *Correspondence of Emily, Duchess of Leinster*, ed. Fitzgerald, i. 337.

[6] Chatsworth MSS, fol. 549, duchess of Devonshire to Lady Spencer [Chatsworth, 21 Oct. 1783]. Some eighteenth-century women followed the hunts in carriages; others rode to hounds. The English passion for fox-hunting seems to have bemused the young French nobleman François de la Rochefoucauld, who was travelling in England in 1783. He found Englishwomen's participation in hunts decidedly disconcerting: 'plenty of ladies . . . regularly ride to hounds. There is danger in this and it gives me no pleasure to see it, but they jump like the men and are always the first over.' François de la Rochefoucauld, *A Frenchman in England: 1784*, trans. S. C. Roberts (Cambridge, 1933), 53.

[7] 'Revd Theophilus Lindsey to Huntingon, Catterick, 4 Sept. 1770', in *HMC Hastings*, iii. 150.

while taking on a share of the entertaining.[8] Convivial company could make Public Days enjoyable, but they were both costly and demanding. Making a good impression was essential, and everything had to be of the highest standard. The family also had to *look* and *be* grand: this was the time to parade the most splendid and fashionable clothes, and to impress the neighbours with the family's important connexions. The presence of tame poets and writers, or fashionable artists, actors, or musicians, made a statement about the family's cultural standing, while that of leading society figures or politicians underlined the family's wider importance. For women, Public Days were a duty. A model political wife like Lady Marchmont played her part without grumbling, even though, as her daughter-in-law knew, she would have preferred a quieter existence:

> I fancy Ldy. Marchmont in her own Heart would like a public Day, & fewer Dining Visits as well, but it would not do here, & she is a true Pattern of *Accommodableness*. Indeed I think as I did from the first, that there cannot be a better-natur'd, better temper'd Woman, always chearful, easy & complaisant, & not minding her own Trouble, so she can make other People happy.[9]

Her 'Trouble' would have included drawing up guest-lists, issuing invitations, organizing the household and servants, consulting or planning meals and entertainments, and, on the day itself, playing the part of 'a *great* Lady in the Country',[10] to show due respect to her company's self-importance. This ceremonial display of dress and jewellery had to be balanced, however, by a natural and approachable manner and an alert, yet unobtrusive, management of people and events. Egos had to be stroked.

While Public Days were never relaxing, they prompted few complaints if the weather was good, the company enjoyable, and everything went smoothly. It was another story entirely when things went awry or the parochial insularity of the company was suffocating. Even the duchess of Devonshire, who was renowned for her easy manners and ability to get along with people, occasionally found herself stretched beyond endurance. A particularly wearing Public Day in 1784 drove her to grumble in poetry:

[8] Chatsworth MSS, fol. 640, duchess of Devonshire to Lady Spencer [Chatsworth], 19–23 Aug. 1784.

[9] WP, L30/9/60/3, Lady Polwarth to Marchioness Grey, n. pl., 3 Sept. 1772.

[10] 'Mrs Burgoyne to duchess of Argyll, Kensington Palace, 7 Oct. 1773', in *Intimate Society Letters of the Eighteenth Century*, ed. Argyll, 2 vols. (London, 1910), i. 175.

If out of sorts & out of Fancy
When All things seem to turn astray
A toil no mortal ever can see
So irksome as a public day.

Sir Harry Hunloker half grown doating
A worthy antiquated prig.
From pedigree's and small talk quoting
With long flapt coat & poking wig.

My Lounging Lady ogling prating
With scraps of French & scraps of verse
Whilst her fond spouse, her parts o'er rating
Begs her, her riddles to rehearse.

The Captains Squires & Clergy drinking
While toasts & noise their powers display
Are all united, to my thinking
The horrors of a Public day.[11]

POLITICIZED SOCIALIZING

Maintaining good relations with the leading families and institutions in the locality was important to keeping up a political interest. Women were hostesses in their own homes, but they could also serve as hostesses or family representatives at community social events. Some socializing was as political as it was social—or more so if there was an election in the offing. Elegance and affability were sure to win local approval. After the 1784 election in Maldon, the new member and his wife, Lord and Lady Waltham, made use of the following race-meet to build on their success. Their 'good conduct and elegance of this business' so impressed the bachelor miller John Crozier, that he transcribed the newspaper's description of the race week activities into his diary:

The first Ball which was given by Lord Waltham, who is adored by his constituents, was exceedingly brilliant.

The public breakfastings were crowded with people of the first distinction. Some excellent fireworks were play'd off every evening, under the worthy Master of Felix Hall.

[11] Chatsworth MSS 642, duchess of Devonshire to Lady Spencer [Chatsworth, 23–7 Aug. 1784].

The assemblage of beauties is not to be described; upwards of fifty couples danced at the last Ball, and every thing was conducted under the auspices of Lord and Lady Waltham with great harmony, whose affability and polite attention has gained them universal esteem.[12]

Since socializing among groups of people who shared few interests in common was necessary for political purposes, some artificial affability seems to have been acceptable. Open rudeness, however, was unforgivable. Women who felt that mixing with the local gentry was below them, and made this clear, could materially damage their husbands' political careers or their families' political interests. If both the husband and wife were arrogant and unsociable, the result could be political disaster, as Sir Watkin Williams Wynn found out to his chagrin in Wales in the 1770s:

Sr. Watkin has lost almost all his interest in Wales meerely by his & Ly. Williams in particular behaving rudely to their country neighbours as an example we were told of a Mr. & Mrs Mostyn Owen people of consequence in that country that went to dine with them during the dinner Sr. Watkin & Ly W——scarcely spoke to them & after dinner went out of the Room & left them, this behaviour displeas'd them so much that he was resolved to oppose Sr. Watkin as much as possible & got Ld. Powis to set him up against him & was elected Member; they say Lady Williams makes it a rule not to speak to any of the Country Squires; & in short Sr. Watkin who was King of Wales & whose Family has been so for a long time is now nothing very great.[13]

Maintaining good relations locally meant playing the part. Consequently, when clubs and groups asked women from local political families to act as 'Lady patronesses' and preside over their annual feasts or banquets, they tended to comply.[14] Their ceremonial services forged a connexion between the group and the family. When the Old Interest country gentlemen in Oxfordshire elected Sir Thomas Stapleton's sister as patroness for their annual feast of the High Borlace in 1753,[15] for

[12] ERO, T/A 387/1, Transcript of the diary of John Crozier, 1753–1788, ed. C. Willett Cunningham.

[13] Badminton Muniments, FmK 1/2/7, Lady Granby to duchess of Beaufort, Liverpool, 24 Sept. [1778?].

[14] BP, L.IV.7.B.30, Lady Susan Keck to Revd Thomas Bray, Great Tew, 21 Aug. 1753.

[15] The Oxfordshire gentlemen gathered together once a year on 18 August for the High Borlace. In the 1740s this annual feast had been marked by nostalgic Toryism and bibulous Jacobitism. Although the Jacobitism had dissipated by the mid-1750s, the Borlace was still the stronghold of the Tory-inclined Old Interest. The young woman who was chosen as 'Lady Patroness' appears to have been officially presented with a gift of plate in commemoration. Bodl., MS D. D. Dashwood (Bucks) B.11/12/32, Sir Thomas Stapleton to Sir Francis Dashwood, Oxford [the letter is undated, yet comments in the Bray Papers indicate

instance, Lady Susan Keck saw the political meaning of the appointment immediately. Local political gossip had placed Sir Thomas Stapleton high on the list of potential Old Interest candidates for Oxfordshire, and she interpreted his sister's appointment as a statement of 'Tory' intent.[16]

Between elections there may have been little need for extensive mixing with freeholders, but making the right gestures was important. When the Corporation at Cambridge granted the duke of Rutland the freedom of the borough at an 'overflowing meeting' in 1787, the duchess, who was managing the family interest while the duke was serving as lord-lieutenant in Ireland, supplied the meat for the mayor's feast. This made the right impression, inspired numerous toasts of gratitude and praise for the family, and was duly reported back to the duke.[17]

It is unlikely that the duchess attended this Feast, but women did varying amounts of 'burgessing', as the Cust family called it. Entertainments, which at times also included the aldermen's or freeholders' wives, were held in taverns, in rooms hired specially for the purpose, or in the home itself. They generally took place with varying degrees of formality over food and drink. Entertainments provided an opportunity to take the political temperature, conduct patronage negotiations, monitor the potential for opposition, or form new alliances. They also played a part in making plans for the future, as the life-expectancy of the aged, the ill, and the dying would be shrewdly estimated.[18] Developing skill in 'burgessing' took time and practice; it was part of a young woman's informal

that it must date from the summer of 1753]; R. J. Robson, *The Oxfordshire Election of 1754* (London, 1949), 11.

[16] Bodl., MS D. D. Dashwood (Bucks) B.11/12/32, Sir Thomas Stapleton to Sir Francis Dashwood, Oxford. Stapleton lists a group of the leading Old Interest gentlemen who had written to inform him of his sister's appointment as patroness; furthermore, he indicates that she would be chaperoned at the Borlace by Lady Litchfield, a member of one the foremost Old Interest families in the county. In 1761 Sir Thomas was still being flattered. A letter from the Revd Dr Leigh of Balliol College comments on a rumour that Stapleton was to be married, suggesting that if the rumour was correct the young lady would probably be appointed Patroness for the next meeting of the Borlace. Bodl., Beachcroft Coll. (hereafter Leigh MSS), Dep. C.577, fol. 36: Revd Dr Theophilus Leigh to Revd Dr Thomas Pardo, Balliol College, 16 Aug. 1761.

[17] 'John Butcher to Rutland, Cambridge, 30 Sept. 1787', in *HMC 36 Rutland*, 423.

[18] After being widowed, Lady Spencer continued to entertain the local Corporation at St Albans on her own or in conjunction with her son. She ensured that she remained on good terms with the aldermen and was always careful to keep her finger on the Corporation's pulse. Since she spent the majority of her time at Holywell House, close to St Albans, she was able to maintain regular contact and, as a result, was more likely to be aware of the state of Corporation politics than her son.

political education, and young women appear to have often found this sort of socializing stressful. They gained the necessary experience by accompanying their mothers, mothers-in-law, or other female relatives to such events, or by having more proficient women accompany them.

Mature, politically experienced women were the most effective burgessers: they understood what was expected of them and they knew the local notables and freeholders, their personalities, histories, and rivalries. In the Cust family the matriarch, Lady Cust, and her married daughter, Mrs Evelyn, were recognized as experts. An unmarried daughter, Lucie, was also well experienced. When a nephew's wife, Lady Brownlow, was called upon to act as hostess for the Grantham Corporation, Francis Cust reported to Mrs Evelyn that she had not gone alone: 'Lucie is going to assist Lady Brownlow in doing the Honrs. of the Table with the corporate Body, but as she does not pretend to shine like you in the Character of a Burgesser, I shall leave her to tell you in a Post-script how she has succeeded.' As the daughter of a London alderman, Lady Brownlow's family background might well have prepared her for such political duties, but she had married only a few weeks after turning 19. Lucie's presence might well have been reassuring, and her knowledge of the people and the personal politics of the area would undoubtedly have been useful. Burgessing was part of the business of politics, and a good burgesser was expected to be alert to any news that would have political implications for the family, as Francis's subsequent comment to his sister made clear: 'You know the Business of burgessing so well, that it may be scarce News to you that Mr. Barnes died on Saturday morning.'[19]

Lady Cust was a political figure of some standing in Grantham. She mangaged the Cust family interest at Grantham for her eldest son, Sir John, who was regularly away in London, first as a Member of Parliament and then later as speaker of the House of Commons. She also had some political interest of her own at Bishop's Castle in Shropshire.[20] In order to maintain the family interest, she treated accordingly. In 1762 she invited the members of the Grantham Corporation to celebrate the New Year, and had two of her younger sons act as hosts for the all-male gathering.

[19] BL, MS Coll. Jenkinson Loan 72, vol. 60, fol. 77, Francis Cust to Mrs Evelyn, Grantham, 20 Oct. [post-1776]. The letter in the British Library collection is undated, but must date from after 1776, as Brownlow Cust was not created Baron Brownlow until 20 May 1776. In 1775 he married, as his second wife, Frances Bankes, daughter of Henry Bankes, alderman, of London. See G. E. Cokayne, *The Complete Peerage . . .*, ed. Vicary Gibbs, 10 vols. (London, 1910–53) (hereafter GEC), ii. 347–8.

[20] Namier, *Structure of Politics*, 247–8.

During the afternoon she attended herself, accompanied by two of her daughters, thus devoting five members of the family to the Corporation at once. This made a statement about the worth of the Corporation to the family, and her efforts were duly rewarded with huzzas.[21] As Peregrine Cust later reported to his brother John, the evening had been a thorough success, and the aldermen had been sent off 'with their skins full of liquor'.[22]

Nearly thirty years later the progress of politeness had made it possible to move beyond the bumpers-and-beer approach to political entertaining. When the duchess of Rutland returned to England from Ireland in 1787, she turned her political attention to the borough of Scarborough and the Rutland family's rivalry with Lord Tyrconnel. With the 1788 general election looming, Tyrconnel planned to treat the Corporation to the traditional, hard-drinking election dinner. The duchess upstaged him by inviting the Corporation to her home for a play: 'Her Grace gives a play this evening to the Corporation, who are all admiration of her condescension and goodness, and I must take the liberty to acquaint your Grace that the Duchess's appearance here, with the prudence of the Lord Bishop of Ferns, will do more good than a hundred blind spies, or the whole house of Tyrconnel combined.'[23] While her choice of entertainment coincided with her personal preference for quiet, controlled socializing, even with her peers,[24] it also fitted in with a growing desire for a more respectable form of politics towards the end of the century.[25] The pride with which another participant reflected on a similar sort of evening—dinner and cards—hosted by Lady Portsmouth for the Andover Corporation in her home in 1789 reflects this. This 'very noble Entertainment indeed' saw the group partake of an excellent dinner, with the men spending no more than an hour at the table afterwards before dispersing for walks and then rejoining Lady Portsmouth (and possibly their wives or other female family members, although this is not indicated) in the library for cards. Moderation seems to have been the keynote

[21] 'Peregrine Cust to Sir John Cust [Belton, 9 Jan.] 1762', as quoted in *Records of the Cust Family*, ed. Cust, 3rd ser., 217.

[22] Ibid.

[23] 'Dr Robert Knox to Rutland, Scarborough, 20 Sept. 1787', in *HMC 36 Rutland*, 415.

[24] Lady Hester Stanhope remembered the duchess of Rutland's parties as being 'a heavy, dull business . . . a great deal of high breeding and bon ton; but there was, somehow, nothing to enliven you': *Memoirs of The Lady Hester Stanhope*, ed. Meryon, ii. 52–3.

[25] Langford, 'Politics and Manners from Sir Robert Walpole to Sir Robert Peel', *Proc. Brit. Acad.*, 103–25.

of the evening, which was reported as having been 'carried on with great good humour pleasantry & chearfulness'.[26]

Women in voters' families, especially wives, were assumed to have a significant amount of political influence. They were often courted during elections, but wise political families made a point of keeping channels open even between elections. Aldermanesses and the lady mayoress could be important local personages. While women were at times included in entertainments aimed at the Corporations, entertaining them fell more frequently to the lot of the women in MPs' or patrons' families. It was not entirely a one-way process, however: a dutiful lady mayoress was expected to call upon the women from the leading political families in her area, as a note in Lady Chatham's papers attest: 'The Mayoress of Exeter and Mrs Walker (Captain Hoods Sister) present their most respectful Compliments to Lady Chatham and they will do themselves the Honor of Waiting on Her Ladyship if it is Agreeable.'[27] The formality of the note is indicative of the nature of the call. Descriptions of this type of female socializing are limited and, while some of these interactions may have become increasingly personal with time, or may have served as an avenue to patronage or other political favours, elite women's desire to preserve differentials in social status must have kept the majority of these visits stiff and conventional, perhaps even insipid.

RACE-MEETS AND ASSIZES

Probably the most onerous events in the 'drudgery of pleasure',[28] as Lord Stormont termed politically tinged socializing in the country, were those associated with the assizes or the annual race-meets. They were the highlight of the summer social calendar, with the race-meets often drawing the largest audiences and being the most openly politicized.[29] During the 1768 races the Assembly Rooms at York attracted 496 members of the nobility and gentry, 163 of whom were women.[30] Race weeks were

[26] ERO, D/DBy C9/54, James Hayes to Lord Howard, Holyport, 13 Sept. 1789.

[27] PRO, 30/8/66, pt. 1, fol. 43, Mayoress of Exeter to Lady Chatham, Exeter, 22 Aug. 1771.

[28] 'Stormont to [Huntingdon], Wentworth, 30 Aug. 1754', in *HMC Hastings*, iii. 88.

[29] Langford, *Public Life and the Propertied Englishman*, 382.

[30] By publishing the names of the members of the political elite in attendance in local newspapers or on separate handbills, political visibility was assured. See 'List of the Nobility and Gentry Who appeared at the Assembly-Rooms at York, in the Race-Week, 1768', included in BL, MS Coll. Althorp, F. 169.

usually held in the county towns or market towns at any time from early July through September. They gathered the local political elite together with the more important non-resident landholders and a large crowd of others—freeholders and non-freeholders alike. As a result, they provided another important venue for political manoeuvre. They also provided political families with the opportunity to reinforce their standing in the locality through family presence, ostentatious display, and conscientious attention to civility and the paternalistic niceties of hospitality. Women usually went with other family members. Widows or women whose husbands were unable to attend might maintain family visibility by going with other local couples or with other women in similar circumstances; sometimes they went accompanied only by their children. Families that were actively cultivating their political interests were expected to attend the races and to take a prominent part in hosting the associated entertainments. In small communities, where people had long memories, a social or political gaffe was sure to be remembered, and young political wives approached their first race-meets with significant trepidation. Even a virago like Lavinia, Lady Spencer, appreciated her mother-in-law's advice when she was a young bride: 'I was frightened at first to think how I shoud go thro' all my ceremonies but I remembered your good instructions of last year & I got over them tollerably well.'[31]

Some of the complaints about race-meet-inspired exhaustion that run through women's correspondences were undoubtedly exaggerated, part of ongoing games of social oneupsmanship that women played with each other, but attendance could be genuinely wearing. Men complained of '*ennui*',[32] and women wrote of being 'so tir'd with those vile races',[33] but it was the continuous display and socializing that accompanied the races themselves that made them exhausting, as Lady Polwarth made clear: 'Kelso Races begin next Tuesday, & a tolerable fatiguing time it will be: three days of public Breakfasts, Races at Noon, public Dinners & Balls at Night. So if I drop down in a Country Dance ... you must Comfort yourself like Cato, when he says, "My boy has done his Duty!"'[34] The burden fell most heavily upon those who were the wives of county

[31] Spencer had been elected MP for Northampton in 1780 and in 1782 was elected MP for Surrey: BL, MS Coll. Althorp, F. 29, Lavinia, Lady Spencer to Lady Spencer, Althorp, 13 Sept. 1782.

[32] 'William Whitehead to Harcourt, Middleton Park, 14 July 1767', in *Harcourt Papers*, ed. Harcourt, vii. 271.

[33] BL, Add MS 45,911, fol. 1, duchess of Devonshire to Lady Melbourne, Chatsworth [1780?].

[34] WP, L30/9/60/32, Lady Polwarth to Marchioness Grey, Wrest, 19 May 1774.

members or leading political families, for, like Lady Sarah Bunbury, they often had to attend numerous race-meets: 'his being chosen for the county obliges them to that.'[35] Lady Sarah was temperamentally well suited to the task, but women who felt stifled by county society or found it wearingly unsophisticated could find even one race week a trial. Theresa Parker and her sister Anne Robinson had grown up in the cultured and worldly society of Empress Maria Theresa's court, and Theresa found society in Devonshire, where she was the wife of a hard-drinking, fox-hunting county Member, crude. A dutiful wife, she appeared conscientiously at race-meets, often accompanied by Anne, but even at the best of times she could rouse little enthusiasm for them: 'there was a good deal of Company at the races and they went off as well as those sort of things generally do.'[36] The importance of making an appearance should not be underestimated, however. Lord Rockingham's concerns about his wife's illness in 1770 and the steps that she took to ensure that she was present at York Races when it mattered most serve as a case in point:

> I got to Wentworth only about eight or nine days before York Races,—and of those days—the four or five last were uncomfortable as Lady Rockingham's state of Health, made it continually doubtful whether she would be able to go to York. In the end, she was able—and by only staying the first two days of the Race Week at York, and going away for three days and returning for the Last days, she was able to get through the week.[37]

Contemporaries knew how to read the political signals that were broadcast at race-meets and assizes. An impressive family presence, spiced with politically important guests and combined with generous sponsorship of public entertainments, was a measure of social status, political interest, and political intent. When race-meets took place under family patronage, the responsibility for organizing and hosting the various activities normally fell to the head of the family and his spouse. Occasionally they were shared among, or delegated to, other family members. When Newcastle found out that the duke of Richmond was bringing a large family group to the Lewes Races and Assizes in 1760, he sensed a potential political challenge and mobilized family forces to neutralize the Lennox family presence. He needed to, as he was operating

[35] 'Lady Holland to Lady Kildare, Holland House, 15 June [1762]', in *Correspondence of Emily, Duchess of Leinster*, ed. Fitzgerald, i. 330–1.

[36] BL, Add. MS 48,218, fol. 29, Anne Robinson to Frederick Robinson, Saltram, 2 Aug. 1772.

[37] 'Rockingham to Edmund Burke, Wentworth, 5 Sept. 1770', in *Correspondence of Edmund Burke*, ed. Copeland *et al.*, ii. 151.

at a distinct disadvantage. The Newcastles were at least a generation older than Richmond and his young, attractive female coterie (especially the teenaged Lady Sarah);[38] moreover, the duchess of Newcastle's health was too precarious to allow her to attend. As Newcastle informed his nephew Lord Sondes, the attendance of the younger members of the family was necessary:

I am now going to ask a Favor of you, & my Neice, to which I will not admit of a Refusal. The Duke & Dutchess of Richmond, Lady George, & Lady Sarah, Lady Fetherstone &c., all intend to be at Lewes Races. I should be very sorry, not to shew them all possible Respect. I am too old to entertain them Myself, without Help. There is Nobody but Mrs Pelham of Stanmer, & it will be too much for One. I must therefore beg, & insist, that you & Lady Sondes would come, & then I shall be easy.[39]

Anne Pelham was pregnant and the demands of the races might well have been too much for her. The Sondes agreed to do all in their power.[40] Newcastle's concerns increased when his favourite niece and the wife of his heir, Lady Lincoln, died at the end of July and mourning customs forbade his attendance. He deputized Thomas and Ann Pelham to act in his stead, and 'take care of the Ball, Supper & Every Thing at the Races'.[41] Her part in the races was reflected in their response: 'Your Grace may depend that Mrs Pelham (for she desires me to answer for her that she takes an equal share in ye whole) and I, will do every thing within our Power with respect to the Ball & Supper.'[42]

Such concerns were not limited to either southern England or the admittedly hypersensitive Newcastle. When, in 1765, the duke of Queensberry appeared at the assizes in Dumfries with the Percy and Lowther families, guests whose personal and political connexions were with Lord Bute, Lord Breadalbane's political sensors were alerted. As he told his daughter, Marchioness Grey, this was a declaration of political intent:

[38] The letters of the Fox, Lennox, and Fitzgerald families indicate that Lady Sarah caught the attention of the young prince of Wales in 1760, but it is impossible to determine whether his attachment was public knowledge before the winter of 1761. Her closeness to the Court and her movement in the highest social circles would nonetheless have made her an attraction at any county race-meet.

[39] BL, Add. MS 32,909, fols. 13–14, Newcastle to Sondes, 23 July 1760.

[40] Ibid., fol. 92, Sondes to Newcastle, Lees Court, 19 July 1760.

[41] Ibid., fol. 165, Newcastle to Ashburnham, Claremont, 31 July 1760; BL, Add. MS 33,067, fol. 186, Newcastle to Thomas Pelham, Claremont, 31 July 1760.

[42] Ibid., fol. 189, Thomas Pelham to Newcastle, Stanmer, 2 Aug. 1760. For genealogical information, see, Mark Antony Lower, *Historical and Genealogical Notices of the Pelham Family* (London, 1873), 55.

The *now* Earl Percy and his lady and Sir James Lowther and Lady were here two days ago, they had been at Drunlanrig the Duke of Queensberry's and went with him to the Assizes at Dumfries, where his Grace sat in the Court as Justice General of Scotland, and gave afterwards an entertainment and ball. These are political views of his Grace for the next elections.[43]

The appearance of an unexpected family representative at a race-meet could also raise political speculation. After a county election in Gloucestershire in 1776 that had ended in a petition to parliament, the duke of Beaufort was understandably suspicious when he learned that his mother's old political opponent, Lady Berkeley, was going to revive the Berkeley family presence at the Tetbury Races.[44]

POLITICAL PATRONAGE

Patronage was another way of securing or rewarding individual political support. Men and women from political families were regularly approached by their political supporters—usually, but not always, men—with requests based on past or potential political service. Decisions about which requests to forward were frequently taken on the basis of what would serve the best interests of the family or faction. The duchess of Rutland, when controlling the Rutland family interest after her husband's death, made numerous patronage requests to William Pitt, many of which seem to have been broached over dinners and during visits:

When I had the pleasure of dining with you at Lord Chathams I mentioned some Scarbro' Friends who have applied to me to make their requests to you one is Lieutenant Turner, who has always been a very steady supporter of our Family as well as all his family he is now a Lt. in the Marines, & wishes to get some Promotion in that line, but I beleive that is always done by succession, & if that is the case He wishes much to give up his Commission & to have some civil employment or Place under Government, but I fear his demands & expectations are rather unreasonable as He told me any thing under two Hundred pr. annum would be of no use to him, as He would then give up his Commission; He mentioned also that He hoped it might be some Place that would not prevent his having a Vote, & I should imagine the best thing to be done for him would be

43 WP, L30/9/17/98, Lord Breadalbane to Marchioness Grey, Edinburgh, 8 Oct. 1765.

44 Badminton Muniments, FmK 1/2/4/26, fol. 2, duke of Beaufort to dowager duchess of Beaufort, Badminton, 8 July 1777. Cannon, *Aristocratic Century*, 108.

to give him something He could hold with his Commission, so as to make up his Sallary nearly what he mentions.[45]

As someone who had known Pitt for years, she knew that he found patronage distasteful, but she also knew that it was electorally important and had to be attended to between, as well as during, elections. Three years before the 1788 election she was already taking steps to secure the Corporation at Scarborough by seeking a place for a man who had influence with the aldermen.[46] Then, as the 1790 election came closer, she reminded Pitt that this meant that the voters 'always expect more to be done':

it has been mentioned as a thing that would be very advantageous to the Interest to get Mr. Clarkson's Son into some Office in which he might rise by degrees, if this could be done before the Election it would secure more than one vote; if a small living also could be procured for Mr. Cleathing it would secure Mr. Travis who is a very leading Man at Scarbro.[47]

Similarly, in 1792, when Pitt was dragging his heels over a request from a distant relative of her late husband's, she pointed out the political benefits of granting a request from a man who was 'very anxious to unite his Interest to ours in Politicks', and whose support was worth having: 'he will be a great acquisition both to you & to us, as he is extreemly Rich, & by that means has great Interest both in Leicestershire & Lincolnshire.'[48]

Rumours of a dissolution or an unexpectedly vacant seat triggered numerous patronage requests. An experienced aristocratic matriarch who was determined to get her way could be a political force to contend with. The dowager Lady Howe was one of the most imperturbable. Reputedly the illegitimate daughter of George I, she had moved in the highest circles of the Court and political world all her life, and had the assured confidence to go with her birth.[49] By 1758 she had been part of the political world for close to forty years—as long as the duke of Newcastle himself.

[45] PRO, 30/8/174/2, fol. 239^{r-v}, duchess of Rutland to William Pitt, Albemarle Street, 4 July 1789.

[46] Ibid., fols. 261–3, duchess of Rutland to William Pitt, Albemarle Street, 4 Apr. 1795. She included the request from Thos. Philliskirk, Thos. Hinderwell Jr, and John Woodall that asked for her interest.

[47] Ibid., fol. 247^{r-v}, duchess of Rutland to William Pitt, Albemarle Street, 7 Apr. [1790].

[48] Ibid., fols. 251^{v}–2, duchess of Rutland to William Pitt, Albemarle Street, 14 Nov. 1792.

[49] Mary Sophia Charlotte von Kielmansegge (1695–1782) was the daughter of George I's favourite, the countess of Darlington. She married Emanuel Scrope Howe, 2nd Viscount Howe, in 1719, with a fortune of £5,000 and a pension of £1,500 p.a. They had 10 children,

Moreover, her political skills had been honed by controlling the family interest for ten years after she had been widowed in 1735, with eight children under the age of 12. When her eldest son, the MP for Nottingham, was killed at Ticonderoga in 1758, she reassumed control of the family's political interest, superseding the new Lord Howe. Consequently, it was she who responded to the letter of condolence and support sent by the Corporation as the head of the family.[50] It was also she who then designated that another son, Lieutenant-Colonel Howe, would succeed to the seat. Only after all of this had been done did she write to Newcastle for his endorsement.[51]

As recorder for the Corporation of Nottingham and the owner of Nottingham Castle, Newcastle had an important political interest in the county and was an old political opponent of the Howes. In 1722 he had unsuccessfully supported what was to be the last contest for a century against the Howe candidates.[52] Although he had supported the Howe family in the 1743 election,[53] Lady Howe appears to have had little trust in him. When nine days had passed and he had not responded to her letter, she took pre-emptive action: she had her son's candidacy declared in the newspapers. Only then did she tell Newcastle what she had done.[54] This elicited a quick and aggrieved response. Newcastle complained that he had only been waiting to hear back from his 'friends' in Nottingham before writing to her: 'But as your Ladyship has now thought it proper to

6 sons and 4 daughters, 8 of whom reached maturity. Lady Howe served as a lady of the bedchamber to Augusta, princess of Wales. Her own political position and her close connexion to the princess of Wales made Newcastle, whose relationship with Leicester House was tenuous at best, approach her with extreme courtesy. GEC, vi. 596–7, 600; *Collins's Peerage of England: Genealogical, Biographical and Historical*, ed. Sir Egerton Brydges, 6th edn., 9 vols. (London, 1812), viii. 143; BL, Add. MS 32,895, fols. 197–8, Newcastle to Lady Howe, Newcastle House, 5 Sept. 1759.

50 BL, Add. MS 32,883, fol. 186, Lady Charlotte Howe to the Corporation of Nottingham, n. pl., 30 Aug. 1758.

51 Ibid., fols. 308–9, Lady Howe to Newcastle, Battlesden, 5 Sept. 1758.

52 Browning, *Newcastle*, 30–2.

53 Namier, *Structure of Politics*, 91–4.

54 BL, Add. MS 32,883, fol. 452, Lady Howe to Newcastle, Albemarle Street, 14 Sept. 1758. That the declaration was in her own name finds support in a letter of Horace Walpole, who used the incident to make a characteristically snide comment about a contemporary of his, Lady Howe's daughter: 'I was really touched with my Lady Howe's advertisement, though I own at first it made me laugh, for seeing an address to the voters of Nottingham signed Charlotte Howe, I concluded (they are so manly a family) that Mrs Howe, who rides a fox chase and dines at the table d'hôte at Grantham, intended to stand for member of Parliament.' 'Horace Walpole to Henry Seymour Conway, Arlington Street, 19 Sept. 1758', in *Horace Walpole's Correspondence*, ed. Lewis, xxxvii. 571.

make This Public Declaration, I conclude you think it immaterial,—what my Opinion might be.'[55]

In fact, she had beaten him at his own game. He had been stalling, possibly in order to play the new Lord Howe against his mother, but certainly in order to scent out whether John Plumptre, the son of one of his oldest political connexions in the county (and Howe's second cousin), would have stood a chance. After receiving Lady Howe's letter, he had written to the new Lord Howe to discover if he was going to take the seat at Nottingham (and thus vacate the seat he held at Dartmouth). When he found out that Howe was not, he had gone on to encourage Plumptre to stand. Plumptre had wanted to stand for the seat in 1753, but when Newcastle had persuaded him to stand aside for Lord Howe he had promptly allied himself with the opposition. By the time that he was surprised by Lady Howe's announcement, Newcastle had already sent his agent out to see if the Corporation would support Plumptre's candidature.[56] It would not. While there is nothing in the surviving correspondence that indicates that Lady Howe knew of these machinations, it is highly unlikely that the Howe supporters in the Corporation would have remained silent about such developments for long. Newcastle's immediate response was to inform her, petulantly, that she could expect no further engagement from him if Lord Howe did not stand, but within a month he was forced to concede defeat. In the end, he pledged his support to Lieutenant-Colonel. Howe and advised Plumptre to support Howe's candidacy. Plumptre agreed, albeit sullenly. Lady Howe had outmanoeuvred them both.[57]

Attempting to make electoral influence pay dividends in terms of patronage for family members or other deserving individuals was part of the debt–obligation cycle of patronage. Politicians' correspondences demonstrate that both men and women with political interests used the system to their advantage. Katherine, 4th duchess of Gordon, and her

[55] BL, Add. MS 32,884, fol. 16^{v}, Newcastle to Lady Howe, Claremont, 17 Sept. 1758.

[56] Namier, *Structure of Politics*, 92–5.

[57] Ibid. Newcastle continued his efforts for Plumtpre, however, and succeeded in having him elected for Penryn before the end of the year. By 1761 Plumptre achieved his goal and was elected for Nottingham alongside General Howe. For Newcastle's correspondence over this episode, see esp. BL, Add. MS 32,884, fols. 232–3: Newcastle to John Plumptre, Newcastle House, 3 Oct. 175; for Plumptre's response, fols. 295–6, 8 Oct. 1758. For Newcastle's correspondence with Lord Howe and his agent, see BL, Add. MS 32,883, fols. 58–9, Newcastle to Howe, Newcastle House, 23 Aug. 1758; for Howe's response, fols. 190–1, Howe to Newcastle, London, 31 Aug. 1758; and fols. 388–9, Newcastle to J. S. Charlton, 9 Sept. 1758.

daughter-in-law Jane, the 5th duchess, were both excellent at securing patronage, but it was Katherine who, at mid-century, as a widow in charge of one of the most important political families in Scotland, specifically tied electoral support to familial gain in a way that her daughter-in-law would later take yet further.

Widowed in 1752, with four children under the age of 10, Katherine was determined to protect her son's interest from being eroded, especially by the family's chief political rivals, the administration-supporting Argylls. This entailed securing the support of George II by dispelling any lingering notions of Jacobitism (one of her husband's brothers having served in the army of Prince Charles Edward in 1745).[58] Within a month of being widowed she began to consolidate her political position. She wrote to Newcastle, declaring her firm allegiance to the king and Whig cause. She then reinforced this, as did some other Scottish widows from families of dubious loyalty, by seeking the king's directions about her children's education.[59] More pointedly, she demonstrated her allegiance by assisting government candidates and putting Gordon family seats at the behest of the administration in the 1754 election. She never let Newcastle forget that she controlled an important electoral interest. As early as 24 October 1758 she was seeking his support for candidates for the 1761 election: 'I am Strongly Solicited by different Candidates, and as I have always Acted in the way I thought was most agreable to Your Grace.'[60] Newcastle, in turn, knew that he needed her interest and that of her brother, Lord Aberdeen, if he wanted to field successful government candidates in Scotland.[61]

This intertwining of family interest, loyalty, and electoral politics would play a central part in her political correspondence for years to come. At the height of the Seven Years War she conducted a number of familial/political campaigns simultaneously. The longest-running of these saw her seeking the transfer of her second husband, Staats Long Morris, eventually Brigadier-General Morris, to the elite regiment of the

[58] Frank McLynn, *The Jacobites* (London, 1988), 67.

[59] Lady Margaret Macdonald provides perhaps the best example of a Scottish widow of questionable family loyalty who placed her heir's education in the hands of the king as a means of demonstrating the family's commitment to the Hanoverian succession: BL, Add. MS 32,855, fol. 248, Lady Margaret Macdonald to Newcastle, London, 29 May 1755; BL, Add. MS 32,861, fols. 528–9, A Memorial from Lady Margaret Macdonald and her son James [1755].

[60] BL, Add. MS 32,885, fol. 66, Katherine, duchess of Gordon, to Newcastle, Upper Grosvenor Street, 24 Oct. 1758.

[61] BL, Add. MS 32,903, fol. 110, Deskfoord to Newcastle, Banff Castle, 6 Mar. 1760.

Guards. She followed the request for electoral guidance cited above with a report on her progress on Morris's behalf. She had solicited military support by writing to Lords Barrington and Ligonier, and, as she reminded Newcastle pointedly, her brother Aberdeen had asked him personally for Morris's transfer before he left London. She then sought his support directly herself.[62]

A little over a year later she was trying to recoup a pension of £400 per annum that Henry Pelham had diverted from her to Lady Stair, with the promise that it would be returned to her when Lady Stair died. On 26 November 1759 she wrote two letters to Newcastle on the subject. In the first, she simply made her request and asserted her 'most true and sincere attachment for your Person and Government'. The second was more elaborate: she heaped praise on Pelham, claiming that his advice 'has been the rule of my conduct ever since, both in regard to the affairs in this Country and as to the Education of my Children', and went on to make calculated use of her dedication, and that of her family, to the service of king and country. After a little shrewd flattery—she would, of course, only apply to the king through Newcastle—she excused herself from waiting on him personally by claiming that, as she was raising a regiment in her son's name which would be commanded by Morris, she was too involved with her patriotic efforts to travel to London.[63] By 8 January 1760 she had succeeded in obtaining the pension and was having her son, Lord Adam, send her instructions to the lord register as to how best to speed the delivery of the money.[64]

It was in raising the regiment that she achieved her greatest coup. The duke of Gordon's Highlanders (89th Highland Regiment) was part of her ongoing strategy to win over the militarily inclined George II by demonstrating the Gordon family's patriotism and neutralizing any potential favouritism in support for the duke of Argyll. By placing the regiment under the direction of her second husband, she ensured that the Gordon family retained both military control and political visibility. In December 1759 the pay-list for the regiment recorded nine companies and over 1,000 men. However, when the regiment was unexpectedly posted to the East Indies in March 1760 local electoral concerns triumphed and she

[62] BL, Add. MS 32,885, fol. 66, duchess of Gordon to Newcastle, Upper Grosvenor Street, 24 Oct. 1758.

[63] BL, Add. MS 32,899, fols. 125–6, 128–9, duchess of Gordon to Newcastle, Gordon Castle, 26 Nov. 1759.

[64] BL, Add. MS 32,901, fols. 160–1, Lord Adam Gordon to Newcastle, Preston Hall, 8 Jan. 1760.

used every argument at her disposal to get it reassigned. She stressed that sending the regiment to the East Indies would influence her three sons, all officers in the regiment, negatively in 'this first Essay of their early Zeal for His Majestys Person & Government', and also that it would upset the tenants, which in an election year would have dire political consequences for the family and the Whig interest: 'I can assure your Grace no measure could be more hurtfull to Government in our Part of the World, as well as to my Sons Interest.'[65] In this case she failed, and the regiment went on to serve valiantly in India until 1765, when it returned to England and was disbanded. The Gordon family interest, however, was firmly established.

Described uncharitably by the family's historian as 'a most persuasive and unscrupulous wirepuller', whose actions were a combination of 'patriotism and blatant self-advancement',[66] the duchess's political activities need to be seen in context. She was driven by familial concerns and the need to protect the family interest. Her actions were politically appropriate, sophisticated, and ultimately successful. The estates and interest that her son finally inherited were undiminished: the Gordon family remained one of the most influential political families in Scotland, and under the sharp eyes of her daughter-in-law the family's alliance with the monarch and the administration, and its ability to benefit from patronage, would continue throughout the century.[67]

[65] BL, Add. MS 32,903, fols. 57–8, duchess of Gordon, to Newcastle, London, 3 Mar. 1760.

[66] George Gordon, *The Last Dukes of Gordon and their Consorts, 1743–1864* (Aberdeen, 1980), 23–4.

[67] See BL, Add. MS 32,737, fol. 44, Andrew Mitchell to Newcastle, Banff Castle, 5 Oct. [1754]; ibid., fols. 257–8, Deskfoord to Newcastle, Hopetoun House, 4 Nov. 1754; BL, Add. MS 32,899, fols. 128–9, duchess of Gordon to Newcastle, Gordon Castle, 26 Nov. 1759; Gordon, *Last Dukes of Gordon and their Consorts*, 25.

7

'Up to the Ears in Electioneering'[1]

Five months before the 1768 general election, Lord Breadalbane complained to his daughter, Marchioness Grey, that the 'Rage of Electioneering' had already infected Scotland and that the 'epidemical Madness' of the upcoming elections was more virulent than ever.[2] At the same time, in London, Mrs Sarah Osborn was observing wryly that 'Cards & Elections are the only Subjects',[3] and Lady Spencer, writing from Althorp, was remarking, 'we are all Election Mad just at present'.[4] As the polls approached, the subject of elections dominated elite society everywhere. Comments such as 'Elections is the subject of all conversation',[5] or 'Nothing is talk'd of but Elections',[6] form a refrain in women's letters from London during election years. Letters from women in the country echo with similar comments. Anne Robinson, writing from Devonshire in 1780, knew she was not alone when she wrote to Lord Grantham, 'we hear of nothing but Elections in this part of the world'.[7] When elections swept the country, they dominated conversation, personal correspondence, and the press. As national politicization was spurred on in the second half of the century by improvements in transportation and communication and a steady stream of highly politicized events, the peaks of political excitement became higher and more all-consuming. Images of disorder in the body politic—madness and fever caused by periodic, uncontrollable, and exceptionally virulent contagions—proliferated. Infection by election fever was considered almost inevitable; thus, people who were heavily involved in particularly heated campaigns might be characterized as acting under 'the influence of a strong delerium', as Lady

[1] WP, L30/9/97/36, Agneta Yorke to Marchioness Grey, Tittenhanger, 20 Oct. 1774.

[2] WP, L30/9/17/125, Lord Breadalbane to Marchioness Grey, Edinburgh, 10 Nov. 1767.

[3] Bodl., MS North d.11, fol. 94, Sarah Osborn to Guilford, Berkeley Square, 7 Nov. 1767.

[4] PRO, 30/29/4/3/43, fol. 348^v, Lady Spencer to Lady Susan Stewart, Althorp, 9 Nov. [1767].

[5] 'Journal, London, 15 Mar. 1768', in *Letters and Journals of Lady Mary Coke*, ii. 213–14.

[6] 'Journal, Notting Hill, 13 Oct. 1774', ibid., iv. 413.

[7] BL, Add. MS 48,218, fol. 58^v, Anne Robinson to Grantham, Saltram, 12 Sept. 1780.

Spencer presumed that her daughters were during the 1784 Westminster election.[8] This notion of elections as epidemics which resulted in temporary irrationality provided contemporaries with a vivid means of describing or complaining about the effects of periods of intense political excitement, and also allowed them to legitimate actions and behaviours which exceeded ordinary social sanctions. For women of the political elite, this extension of boundaries could provide the opportunity to be more active, assertive, authoritative, opinionated, and publicly recognized than at almost any other time. But even then they had to be careful; it was all-too-easy to overstep the limits.

While electoral organization became more sophisticated and efficient over the course of the eighteenth century, elections continued to centre primarily on parochial concerns and local candidates. A complex pattern of interdependence existed among patrons, candidates, committees, and networks of political agents. Although committees came to shoulder ever more responsibility for conducting campaigns, even to the point of directing candidates' activities and expenses, elections remained predominantly personal and familial throughout the eighteenth century.[9] By involving entire communities in an assortment of social and political events, and a variety of well-established rituals, they served a number of purposes. They provided periodic opportunities for celebration and spectacle, reaffirmed vertical connexions, vented community frustrations, and readjusted the status quo without threatening the fabric of society.[10] Moreover, the tendency towards more elaborate and ritualistic elections in the late eighteenth century, despite the political elite's growing discomfort with the social inversion necessary to win votes,[11] is itself a testimony to the continued importance of this transactional relationship between candidate and community.

Women added a female dimension to election campaigns and contests. They can be found taking part in any of a range of election entertainments, processions and parades, formal and informal canvasses, and assorted propaganda campaigns, even occasionally in print. Those who

[8] BL, MS Coll. Althorp, F. 38, fol. 307^{v}, Lady Spencer to Lady Duncannon [Holywell House], 2 May 1784.

[9] See e.g. Langford, *Polite and Commercial People*, 213, 591–4, 710–13; O'Gorman, *Voters, Patrons, and Parties*, 106–71; Namier and Brooke, *House of Commons*, vol. i.

[10] O'Gorman, 'Campaign Rituals and Ceremonies'. The following examination of women's place in the electoral process follows the general outline of the electoral process as delineated by Namier and Brooke and then elucidated by O'Gorman: Namier and Brooke, *House of Commons*, vol. i; O'Gorman, *Voters, Patrons, and Parties*, 106–71.

[11] Langford, *Public Life and the Propertied Englishman*, 269–76.

were directly involved in electioneering tended to act for family connexions out of tradition or duty, but there were always some women who campaigned for friends, lovers, or factions—out of loyalty and/or personal conviction. During elections, committees met in, and campaigns were run from, the homes of candidates and patrons. Women in these families might act as managers and administrators. Admittedly, some did little more than receive and dispatch information, acting as the links between men, but others co-ordinated people and events, managed correspondence networks, issued directions, and made decisions. When families were involved in multiple elections, women could become the family representatives in one borough while the men travelled around, or were based in, other boroughs. Local people and political concerns came to them. In some families multiple political interests were divided among family members, leaving women to co-ordinate and run certain campaigns.

Given the extent to which communities and social activities were politicized during elections, it would have been nearly impossible for women to have remained untouched by election fever. Indeed, the women of the political elite were not the only women politicized by elections or involved in elections or electioneering (either as subjects or objects). Campaigns could also touch the lives those women who were not personally involved in the contests themselves, or whose families' contests took place in distant boroughs. They were likely to read the newspapers, discuss the elections with their friends and correspondents, and/or attend politicized social events.

Individual family attitudes may have had more effect in terms of determining the extent of women's involvement in campaigns and contests than either personal preferences or ideological divisions. Women who were members of families that expected them to play a part were usually active; women who came from families without this tradition were seldom heavily involved. At mid-century the last remnants of the Whig–Tory divide that had driven party politics several decades earlier still existed in some locations, but they were destined to disappear quite rapidly. In 1750/1, for instance, party feeling was still strong enough in Tory-leaning Oxfordshire to prevent Lady Susan Keck from offering assistance to the Revd Theophilus Leigh and his son-in-law, Sir Edward Turner, on the grounds that being openly affiliated with 'me who you know was a Whig'[12] might have harmed Sir Edward's chances of election.

12 Leigh MSS, Dep. C.576/108, Lady Susan Keck to Revd Theophilus Leigh, Great Tew, 2 Feb. 1750/1.

Even after Turner lost the election, she warned Leigh to consider a social invitation carefully before accepting: 'whether coming to me will not do you ill, with one Party.'[13] For Lady Susan, the 1754 Oxfordshire election was still a party election. By the formation of the first Rockingham administration, however, faction had triumphed. Consequently, Lady Rockingham could chide Lady Susan Stewart for her 'Gr[envi]lle face', but she could also justify the exclusion of the duke of Bedford from the new ministry on factional grounds: 'if he was a Rose that could be pluck'd off without tearing ones flesh with the Briars that are about the tree I should think a Bouquet could not be better graced.'[14] Women's factional allegiance became especially marked during heated factional elections, the best-known example of which remains the actions of the female supporters of Charles James Fox during the 1784 Westminster election. Notions of Whig progressivism in the face of a conservative or reactionary proto-Toryism cannot be posited, however, or at least not with regard to women's involvement, as the activities of the rival Pittite Whig women were indistinguishable from those of the Foxites.

While diversities in borough franchises, sizes, wealth, and local community circumstances (including local political personalities and family rivalries) ensured that each campaign had its own idiosyncrasies, the election process itself followed an established routine. Canvassing and campaigning prior to a dissolution were widespread, and were as likely to occur in areas that did not eventually go to a poll as in those that did.[15] Upon the dissolution of a parliament, writs of summons for elections to a new parliament were issued and sent to the sheriffs in the counties, who in turn relayed them to the returning officers for all of the county seats. The returning officers then fixed the dates for the elections, which by law had to take place within eight days of the receipt of the writ.

This multi-stage process provided numerous opportunities for delay, favouritism and corruption, any of which could affect the eventual outcome. Participants and their supporters, therefore, did all they could to gain an edge on the opposition. Whenever an election was imminent and a dissolution was expected, correspondence networks buzzed as political men and women kept each other and themselves informed of

[13] Ibid., Dep. C.576/111, 4 Feb. 1750/1.

[14] GP, PRO, 30/29/4/2/65, fols. 247–8, Lady Rockingham to Lady Susan Stewart, Peterborough House, 6 Aug. [1765].

[15] According to McAdam, all elections where there was an open canvass should be considered as contested, as the amount of electioneering was nearly the same: D. McAdams, 'Politicians and the Electorate in the Late Eighteenth Century', Ph.D. dissertation, Duke University (1967), 179.

the latest 'News'. Having the latest News was particularly important to those who lived far away from the metropolis, like Lady Galloway in Scotland. Since advance warning of a dissolution could spell success at the polls or prevent a poll from taking place, she depended upon connexions in London, especially her politically active sister-in-law, at such times: 'I trouble You My Dear Lady Gower to inquire what You hear, *or rather think*, relative to the time it is probable the Parliament may, or may not, be dissolved, such intelligence wou'd be of material Consequence, as the success of the Stewartry Election will much depend upon that epoch.'[16]

Although counties often chose their candidates well in advance of a coming dissolution, candidates were usually only formally declared once election dates had been set. Open electioneering commenced with the publication and dissemination of the candidates' addresses or statements to the freeholders. In areas where a contest was a foregone conclusion, setting a date for the election might only accelerate and intensify campaigns that had already been long-established. In Oxfordshire, for instance, the struggle that culminated in the notorious 1754 election went on almost without a break from the time that the New Interest Whigs lost the by-election for a University seat in 1750.[17] By the time that the election had finally been officially called, the campaigning was frenzied.

Once campaigns were officially under way, they built up their own momentum. Election committees began to meet daily, and election agents and candidates crisscrossed the countryside. Formal canvassing began and flurries of publications inundated the electorate with propaganda. All sorts of election entertainments were staged, with the aim of winning votes and securing support. Some provided colour, sound, and spectacle; others aimed to satisfy the various appetites of the electorate; a few even touched upon the candidates' opinions. A close contest dominated local society: tempers frayed and political expediency supplanted politeness. Every possible opportunity was taken to secure outstanding votes. The election itself could last for weeks. It was only after the excesses of the 1784 Westminster election, when the polls opened on 1 April and did not

[16] GP, PRO, 30/29/4/3/93, fol. 451, Lady Galloway to Lady Gower, Galloway House, 27 Aug. [1780].

[17] It was Sir Edward Turner's loss in this by-election that resulted in Lady Susan Keck's dissatisfaction with the Whig leadership and her own managerial role in the county campaign. For Lady Susan's reasons for becoming involved, see her correspondence with the Revd Theophilus Leigh, in Feb. 1750/1: Leigh MSS, Dep. C.576, fols. 108–11; Robson, *Oxfordshire Election*, 13.

shut until 17 May, that polling was restricted by law to fifteen days, excluding Sundays.

ELECTION BALLS, FEASTS, AND TREATS

During election campaigns ordinary socio-political activities were politicized and split, or duplicated, along factional lines. Election treats might cater for men alone, but some were mixed. Balls 'for the ladies' were hosted by candidates and their wives or a close female family member.[18] They were expected by the freeholders and were part of most election campaigns.[19] When political feelings remained moderate or an amicable compromise had been achieved, they might even be co-sponsored by the candidates as a mark of their co-operation and good-will; when the opposite was the case, they became another field of competition, and rival events might be held in the same town at the same time. Election balls served a number of purposes: they gave patrons, candidates, and their families an additional social event at which to charm the voters, their wives, and daughters; balls supplied them with an additional forum for canvassing;[20] and balls served as yet another occasion where they could make a show of their generosity, hospitality, and civility, turning these traits to political purpose. Most importantly, however, balls testified to contemporary beliefs about female influence and the need to gain women's support in order to keep male votes. Election balls were only successful, though, if the members of the elite party were willing to accept the degree of social inversion that that they entailed.

For women in the host parties, this could mean making special efforts to impress the freeholders. At balls—and throughout election campaigns—women used their clothing and accessories to impress as well as to make

[18] They were also an acknowledged part of Corporation politics. When Lady Spencer was trying to persuade her son-in-law, Lord Duncannon, to get involved in Spencer family politics by taking up the next vacancy in the St Albans Corporation so as to ensure that the family interest was maintained, she noted that there were two 'inconveniences' associated with the nomination that he might feel would be an affront to his dignity: the necessity of serving once as mayor; and that, while serving, 'it will be necessary to give a Ball; to the Ladies residing in the Town—': BL, MS Coll. Althorp, F. 3, Lady Spencer to Lord Duncannon [Holywell?], 12 Dec. 1786.

[19] In 1784 even contested boroughs with less than 100 voters had the full panoply of parades, balls, dinners, and crowds: McAdams, 'Politicians and the Electorate in the Late Eighteenth Century', 99; O'Gorman, 'Campaign Rituals and Ceremonies', 86.

[20] WCRO, CR 1368/5/9, vol. 36, Mary [Mordaunt] to [John Mordaunt?], Wallington, 1 Aug. 1766.

political statements. While it was important to dress resplendently and appear at the height of fashion, women might also wear gowns in the family or faction's colours, or decorate their clothes or their coiffures with appropriately coloured ribbons, sashes, and cockades. This added to the spectacle, but it also provided a visual demonstration of allegiance. The fox's brush and the blue-and-buff costumes adopted by Charles James Fox's female followers in 1784 are probably the best-known examples of this, but they were not innovative. In 1753 an Oxfordshire Old Interest supporter gave backhanded support for the popularity of such practices when he tried to dismiss the opposition female presence at a race-meet by claiming that they had no more interest in the election 'than the Colour of their Ribands'.[21] The following year *The Connoisseur* poked fun at the custom that required political wives to wear gowns in their husbands' or faction's colours.[22] Elizabeth Montagu, writing in 1757, confirmed that this was not a figment of George Colman's satirical imagination. Henry Fox had claimed a narrow victory at Windsor after an election that had been marked by such mob violence that Fox himself had been physically assaulted and several others had been left dangerously ill. This prompted Montagu to remark acerbically that the peaceful sartorial politics of the women—Fox's female supporters having worn yellow and green gowns, those of his rival, blue—was a 'wise way of expressing their political principles', in comparison with that of the men, which had resulted in 'a great harvest of bruises and fractures'.[23]

Annual balls, such as those that accompanied the assizes or the races, also served as a litmus test for local political sentiment during election campaigns. Local and distant but desirable relatives were regularly inveigled into attending, and both men and women were expected to make a show of their civility by crossing social barriers and dancing, especially country dances. Young political wives were repeatedly reminded to fulfil this duty. A full ten years after her marriage, the duchess of Devonshire was still being chided by her mother for not having danced with enough of the duke's voters in Derbyshire.[24] Balls made similar demands on men. For a man like Lord Nuneham, who disliked politics only slightly less than mixing with the commonalty, dancing was something that he had to

[21] *Jackson's Oxford Journal*, 6 Oct. 1753.

[22] Colman, *et al.*, *The Connoisseur*, no. 20 (13 June 1754), i. 118.

[23] 'Mrs Elizabeth Montagu to Mr Montagu, Windsor Castle [ante-28 June 1757]', in *Elizabeth Montague*, ed. Climenson, ii. 103.

[24] 'Lady Spencer to duchess of Devonshire, n. pl., 26 Aug. 1784', in *Georgiana*, ed. Bessborough, 92.

be flattered into doing. The scene painted by his friend, William Whitehead, before the 1768 election, in an effort to entice him to do his duty, is worthy of a Jane Austen novel:

I am glad you are to be at the Mayor's feast, I am glad you are to be at Abingdon races, I hope you have been at the Oxford Act, & I wish you were obliged to attend all the Corporation dinners and horse-coursing work of the summer...

To be the first person in the place to be addressed with deference, & that deference mixed with a satisfaction of having the honour to address you at all; to see a glow of happiness playing on Mrs Mayoress's plenteous countenance when she gives both hands in the conclusion of the minuet, or receives her fan from some humble relation who can never aspire to equal dignity; to have every black silk gown with pink ribbons in the whole assembly bursting with desire to be taken notice of; to have half a word give pleasure, and whispers in every corner of the room of 'How charmingly he looks!' 'How delightfully he is dressed!' 'He is certainly the best bred man in England; you know, Madam, I always said it:'—these, my Lord, are gratifications which will repay the little trouble you may be at to gain them; &, I dare say, could I be invisible in the Abingdon ball-room, I should certainly see you enjoying most of them. I shall ask Lady Nuneham, the next time I have the honour of seeing her, how you have behaved yourself?[25]

Arrogance and pride lay behind Nuneham's inactivity, but these evenings were a trial of another sort for men who were shy or poor dancers. It is a mark of the importance placed on dancing at these balls that even the non-dancers danced. As Lady Chatham charitably remarked of Thomas Pitt's efforts after one such evening, politics, not pleasure, was the point: 'I hope the Ladies were duely sensible of their obligation on the occasion, and that it will be remember'd at a proper time.'[26]

Race-meets which took place during election campaigns were often openly aligned with certain candidates or factions. Attendance at one and not another was a statement of political allegiance. In Oxfordshire, the New Interest dominated the Burford Races, leaving the Old Interest unchallenged at the Oxford Races. When, in January 1753, Lady Susan Keck had heard rumours that 'Lord Litchfield and Party' were wooing the race-mad young squire, Robert Fettiplace, and that he was 'almost brought over to them', she passed the comments on to Marlborough. Although she believed that the rumours were exaggerated, she felt that the young man was a 'Simpleton', and told Marlborough that the proper

[25] 'William Whitehead to Lord Nuneham, Middleton Park, 14 July 1767', in *Harcourt Papers*, ed. Harcourt, vii. 271–2.

[26] BL, Add. MS 59,490, fols. 10^{v}–11, Lady Chatham to Anne Pitt, Burton Pynsent, 13 Sept. 1773.

way to guarantee his support would be to secure him through the women in his life. Fettiplace was probably used to getting directions from forceful women, as he was Lady Howe's son-in-law and had married her namesake: 'Lady How should writ to her Daughter.—for it is not every body that is fit to be trusted to themselves, no more is yt. [that] Cub.'[27] When, later that summer, Lady Susan heard that he might attend the race-meet at Oxford (where one of his horses would run and win),[28] she wrote a confidential letter of warning to him and sent it to the agent in Oxford, the Revd Thomas Bray. Should Fettiplace arrive in Oxford for the races, Bray was to pass it on to him immediately: 'as we are all absent, [his attendance] will make him look like one of them.'[29] To modern eyes this might seem excessive concern over a triviality, but race-meets were important statements of political sympathy and/or intent to contemporaries; moreover, the factions' practice of challenging each other to publish their attendance lists, as the New Interest would itself do after the Chipping Norton Races that year, so that 'the World may judge which Party has the most numerous and considerable supporters', meant that contemporaries knew that their presence was political. Lady Susan's concerns about Fettiplace proved justified: his indecision triumphed in the end, and he split his vote.[30]

Control of the race-meet at Chipping Norton was perceived to be an important marker of political strength in the county. Like the election, it too was contested and, according to *Jackson's Oxford Journal*, both groups rallied their supporters to make the best possible showing: 'There was by far the greatest Appearance of Ladies and Gentlemen (both in the Old and New Interest) that ever met together at any Races in this County before.'[31] The New Interest secured the political advantage by publishing its attendance list in the *Journal* on 8 September. The Old Interest refused to do the same. This reduced Old Interest hacks to spluttering ineffectually about the calibre and gender of the New Interest supporters. New Interest men were dismissed in one grand sweep as socially and politically inferior—'all the neighbouring Counties, have been ransack'd

[27] BL, Add. MS. 61,667, fol. 162v, Lady Susan Keck to Marlborough [Great Tew?], 29 Jan. 1753.

[28] *Jackson's Oxford Journal*, 8 Sept. 1753.

[29] See, BP, L.IV.7.B.30: Lady Susan Keck to Revd Thomas Bray, Great Tew, 21 Aug. 1753.

[30] *The Poll of the Freeholders of Oxfordshire, Taken at The County Court Held in Oxford on the 17th of April, 1754, By Tho. Blackall, Esq. High Sherriff* (Oxford, 1754), 13.

[31] *Jackson's Oxford Journal*, 22 Sept. 1754.

for *Colonels* and *Captains*, and dependent younger *Brothers*, without Title, Profession, or Fortune'.[32] New Interest women were dealt with similarly: forty-one of the eighty-seven people on the New Interest list were women. Their attendance was trivialized and devalued and, where that was impossible, as with Lady Susan, they were ridiculed and deemed unfeminine:

For though the Ladies are very Garniture for a Race, and are absolutely necessary to furnish out a Ball-Room, yet, I think it would be not great Compliment to suppose them concerned (any farther than the Colour of their Ribands) in the Affairs of the Election. However, if L——y S——K—— should make any Objection to this Observation, I should be willing (on her Account only) to correct the *Erratum*, and add her to the Number of the Gentlemen.[33]

While it is possible that women's names were included on the attendance list solely to boost New Interest numbers, the inclusion of women who were landholders and actively involved in the election makes it impossible to dismiss them as apolitical by gender. It is far more likely that they, like the men, were of varying levels of political interest, awareness, and involvement. All but fifteen of the women were members of family groups. Of these, Lady and Mrs Talbot, Lady Wheat and her two unmarried daughters, and Lady Dalkeith and Lady Jane Scot seem to have represented their families themselves. At least five of the unattached women had some political interest through property: Lady Paulet, Lady Wheat, and Lady Austin were widows with property; and Lady Talbot, although married, was legally separated from her husband and had property of her own.[34] Lady Talbot was also openly political and had been involved in the election contest on the New Interest side from the outset. Lord Harcourt included her with Lady Susan as early as December 1752: 'If the men of quality and distinction would do half what Lady Talbot & Lady Susan have done, towards the success of this affair, our enemies would have quitted the field before now.'[35] If anything, Lady Talbot's support for the New Interest was too enthusiastic: it led to the creation of some specious votes on her estates, four of which

[32] Ibid., 6 Oct. 1753. [33] Ibid.

[34] Analysis of Land Tax Assessments, *ex. info*. Paul Langford. Lady Talbot was a wealthy heiress, worth more than £70,000 at the time of her marriage; she received £3,000 p.a. after her separation from her husband in 1742 (when the duke of Beaufort started divorce proceedings over Lord Talbot's relationship with the duchess): GEC, vol. xii, p. 1, pp. 623–4.

[35] BP, L.IV.7.B.14, Harcourt to Revd Thomas Bray, Great Tew, 17 Dec. 1752.

were disallowed in the scrutiny, and generated complaints from the Old Interest during the parliamentary petition.[36]

Lady Dalkeith's interests were more complex than those of other women present, but she too would be active in the election. As the daughter and heiress of the widowed duchess of Argyll, who had a significant estate and political influence at Adderbury, she had a direct interest in her mother's estates. Although Lady Susan would later complain that Lady Dalkeith had been too lax in her canvassing at Adderbury and too trusting of her mother's agents, whom Lady Susan feared were Jacobites and Old Interest supporters in disguise, she *did* canvass.[37] Whether Lady Susan exaggerated the situation, or whether Lady Dalkeith's political strength did not rest in canvassing, is hard to tell; what is clear from her patronage requests to the duke of Newcastle in 1755 is that she was anything but lax in her efforts to protect the political interests of her 7-year-old son, the heir of the earl of Buccleuch.[38] At the races, therefore, she represented both her family of birth—for no one else from the Campbell family was there—and, together with her unmarried sister-in-law, Lady Jane Scot, her family by marriage.[39]

Women who were their husbands' political partners tended to capitalize on their personal strengths when taking part in the social aspects of electioneering. Some chose highly visible and physically demanding parts, while others chose less taxing, social roles. Marcia Pitt combined the two when her husband was involved simultaneously in elections at Dorchester and Wareham in 1754. As Richard Rigby told the duke of Bedford, 'Mrs Pitt tells me she has been a buck-hunting three days in the week at five o'clock in the morning, and drinking strong beer with the freeholders at that hour, to convince them she is an Englishwoman. She returns to-morrow to assist her worst half at the meeting of the seventh at

[36] Robson, *Oxfordshire Election*, 164, n. 1; WCRO, CR136 B.2524 B/8, Sir Roger Newdigate's Parliamentary notes on Oxfordshire Election of 1754, 11 Jan. 1755; ibid., B.2527, 7 Apr. 1755.

[37] BL, Add. MS 61,667, fol. 154^{v}, Lady Susan Keck to Marlborough [Great Tew], 25 Jan. [1754]; ibid., fols. 161–2, 29 Jan. 1753 [seemingly misdated by Lady Susan; it should be 1754].

[38] In requesting the position of sheriff for her candidate, she was protecting her son's interest: 'as my Son the Duke of Buccleuch, has a large property in that County, I look upon it, that his Interest is materially concerned in the appointment': BL, Add. MS 32,854, fol. 226, Lady Dalkeith to Newcastle, n. pl., 22 Apr. 1754.

[39] The only possible Argyll connexion among the men is the Revd Eddowes, who could possibly be the 'Mr Eddows' that Lady Susan Keck names as the duchess of Argyll's steward and a possible Jacobite/Tory supporter: BL, Add. MS 61,667, fol. 165^{r-v}, Lady Susan Keck to Marlborough, Great Tew, 30 Jan. 1753.

Dorchester.' Hunting was not one of the duchess of Bedford's strengths, but dancing was, and Rigby advised Bedford to 'inform your little candidate, that though she is not quite so robust as your Dorsetshire friend, that she must follow her example as far as she is able... dancing... you must insist upon'.[40]

Rigby may have been overstating Marcia Pitt's involvement, but hunting was not in itself extraordinary for women; moreover, her personal circumstances may well have encouraged her to make an extra effort. This election marked her debut as a political wife and, being Irish by birth, it may have been important for her to establish her 'English' credentials. The extent of her involvement most likely reflected the demands of political circumstance. Her husband's election at Dorchester was not contested, so her assistance there probably required little more than an appearance and some flattery. Obversely, the election at Wareham was hard fought and would eventually result in a double return.[41] In such circumstances, every family member and every opportunity to win votes mattered: other women might not have taken to hunting to woo the local gentlemen, but women played to their strengths, and it would have been surprising if she had not taken some part.

The importance that the political elite attached to voters and their families is reflected in the variety of appeals that were made to them. Treats for the gentlemen and freeholders were customary forms of electioneering, either in the form of the traditional election feast or the election breakfast, a more polite incarnation that became popular towards the end of the century.[42] Since successful treating and feasting were central to Lady Susan Keck's plans for a New Interest victory in Oxfordshire in the 1754 election,[43] the Kecks turned their home at Great Tew

[40] 'Richard Rigby to Bedford, London, 3 Aug. 1753', in *Correspondence of John, Fourth Duke of Bedford*, ed. Russell, ii. 131–2.

[41] *History of Parliament*, iii. 284.

[42] McAdam notes that few candidates in 1784 used public breakfasts, but that there were scores of them by 1790. During the 1790 election they were advertised in the *Public Advertiser*, and all the candidates but one in London held at least one breakfast a day throughout the poll. McAdam, 'Politicians and the Electorate', 187.

[43] The New Interest candidates were a local gentleman, Sir Edward Turner, and Lord Parker, the heir to the earl of Macclesfield. In addition to Lady Susan Keck and her husband, they were strongly supported by a group of local Whig peers with Court connexions, specifically the duke of Marlborough, Lord Harcourt, and Lord Macclesfield. The Old Interest candidates were both local country gentlemen, Lord Wenman and Sir James Dashwood. Of the two, Dashwood had the most influence, as he was a prominent landholder in the county. Their aristocratic supporters were local peers with previous Tory connexions, such as Lord Litchfield and Lord Abingdon. The election cost a legendary £20,000 per side. After a prolonged scrutiny and two spurious attempts to link the Old Interest to supposedly

into the New Interest's social and political headquarters. Lady Susan, who was the driving political force in the family,[44] was ideally suited by temperament for the rough-and-tumble of eighteenth-century electoral politics. She seemed unconcerned by even the most scurrilous publicity, and was always ready to laugh at herself. She was treating by as early as November 1752.[45] A description of her early campaigning, sent to her nephew, the young duke of Hamilton, sparkles with humour and reflects the public attention her involvement received and the emphasis that she placed on treating:

I am now paying you the greatest compliment that is to be imagined by favouring you with a letter. I am now a woman of the utmost consequence and I am sold in Gingerbread in all the Fairs, and I am satyrized by our enemys as a formidable opposer, and in short, I have not time to eat for my great importance. I live with all sorts of trades and dine with hundreds in the Hall and sit up till five of the morning, and everybody drunk round me even the squire. You see what it is to be of consequence, nothing goes so fast as my tongue, but our Bells, which never cease, everybody delighting in them and our Tap. Nobody names Bumpers but Hogsheads, there soon will be neither Rum nor Lemmons in England, and wine begins to be scarce. The smalest useful vessel in this house is the great cooper, or a quart Mug for the Drawn Cup. How do you like this, what are all your former Revelrys to my ancient Gambol, which will even make me extinct, but I shall make my exite in the midst of loud acclamations.[46]

Lady Susan knew that successful treats secured votes. When a conflict in scheduling made it impossible for the candidates to attend one of her feasts in 1753, she commented ruefully that it cost upwards of thirty votes.[47] She was astonished later that summer when she heard that one of

Jacobite plots, the New Interest candidates were finally declared elected by Parliament. For the most detailed examination of the election, see Robson, *Oxfordshire Election.*

[44] Lady Susan's well-known domination of him provided fodder for the Old Interest throughout the campaign. References to 'Hen-peck'd K——k', or variations thereon, are rife in Old Interest election doggerel. See e.g. 'The Rump-Worthies: or The New Interest Supporters in Their Own Colours', in *News Boys, News! or the Electioneering Journal with Improvements*..., no. 2. (Oxford, 1753), 33–4; 'A Hue and Cry After the Greens', in *The Election Magazine, or the Oxfordshire Register*... (Oxford, 1753), 76.

[45] Robson, *Oxfordshire Election*, 57. Robson identifies nine New Interest treats but only five Old Interest treats in 1752–3. By basing his information on published accounts in *Jackson's Oxford Journal* and the *London Evening Post* he appears to have missed some New Interest events, including the Keck's feasts in April and June 1753.

[46] 'Lady Susan Keck to Hamilton, Great Tew, 27 Dec. 1752', in *HMC Hamilton* (suppl.), 176–7. Unfortunately Lady Susan's prophecy was to prove too true; the election did mark her 'exite', as she died in June 1755, not long after the New Interest candidates for whom she had campaigned so ardently were finally seated on petition.

[47] BP, L.IV.7.B., fol. 22, Lady Susan Keck to Revd Thomas Bray [Great Tew], 12 Apr. [1753].

the Old Interest candidates was not treating: 'Lord Wenman's own conduct is very incomprehensible since no man that meant to be chosen Beadle, wou'd Lock up his House, and himself, while the thing was depending, therefore all these things consider'd at one view, can only arise from the highest pitch of Idiotism, and Ignorance of the effects of appearances, on the Multitude.'[48] She treated throughout the campaign, and regularly reminded both grandees and agents that out-performing the Old Interest socially would be remembered on the hustings: 'Should Sir James [Dashwood] come into Oxford or any of the Gang they must always be faced, out eat, out drank, and outdone. At the expence be what it will Command me.'[49]

When freeholders' womenfolk attended treats, they appear to have partaken with gusto. The tendency of some of Lady Susan's female guests to over-indulge prompted a criticism in *Jackson's Oxford Journal*—but it was criticism that simultaneously acknowledged the inevitability of female electoral involvement:

> I am far from thinking that the Ladies are unconcern'd in our Members, or that they should sit primm'd with their hands passively before 'em, and their Mouths drawn up like the Purse of an old Usurer, whilst we are engaged in this important Business; but then neither would I have them swagger amongst the Men, and Holla, and roar, and fill out Bumpers with an Air more becoming *Colonel Bully* than *Lady Dainty*. Much less would I have Ladies of Distinction, out of an intemperate Zeal for their Country, send away from their Houses, not only Men, but even Persons of their own Sex, so disguised with Liquor as to merit the Stocks as an Example.[50]

Neither were Oxfordshire women unique. William Tufnell discovered that Yorkshire women were equally avid participants when he treated the freemen of Beverley: 'I think I never saw so many women in all my life. The voters they brought their wives along with 'em & then they introduc'd some of their acquaintances who stay till they fell off their chairs.'[51] Women were not always this bacchanalian, however. Usually their attendance raised only passing comment: for example, Newcastle's agent at Seaford simply noted the presence of the wives at a feast in 1761; similarly, Edmund Burke mentioned to his wife in 1774 that the wives

[48] Ibid., fol. 30, 21 Aug. 1753.

[49] Ibid., fol. 52, Lady Susan Keck to Revd Thomas Bray [Great Tew] [?Dec. 1753].

[50] *Jackson's Oxford Journal*, 1 June 1753.

[51] 'William Tufnell to Samuel Tufnell, n. pl. [1754]', in *Samuel Tufnell of Langleys, 1682–1758: The Life and Times of an Essex Squire*, ed. Francis W. Steer (Chelmsford, 1960), 133.

of the men on his election committee had attended a dinner given by one of the Bristol aldermen.[52]

As the century progressed, the election breakfast and the election ball provided more polite entertainment than the traditional election feast.[53] Women regularly attended both. By the time that Lady Bessborough was campaigning with her brother, Lord Spencer, in the family borough of St Albans in 1796, a sedate respectability appears to have triumphed:

> [she went]... to do the civilities for him, but more to attend a morning ball and visit some freeholders' wives, whom he wanted to please. Conceive being dress'd out as fine as I could at eleven o'clock this morning, squeez'd into a hot assembly room at the Angel Inn, cramming fifty old Aldermen and their wives with hot rolls and butter, while John and Fred danced with the misses, playing at four-penny Commerce and tradille, and then visiting all about the gay town of St. Albans. Can you boast of anything to surpass this?[54]

Spencer's wife should have played the hostess, but she was temperamental and arrogant—ill-suited to electioneering.[55] His sister was a much better choice. She was charming and glamourous, highly political, and well experienced. She knew the people and the politics of St Albans and was known in return, having successfully canvassed the borough in the past.

Spencer, his sister, and sons from each of their families shared the electioneering tasks, acting together to achieve familial political goals. This intertwining of political, personal, and ornamental attributes underlines the multiplicity of levels on which elite women's electoral involvement operated. It also attests yet again to the belief that freeholders' womenfolk had political influence. The degree to which they were won over by such electoral entertainments and flattery must have varied immensely, but, as D. McAdams has argued, their inclusion was at the

[52] BL, Add. MSS 32,919, fol. 192, S. Shepherd to Newcastle, Bishopstone, 21 Feb. 1761; 'Edmund Burke to Jane Burke [Bristol], 8 Nov. 1774', in *Correspondence of Edmund Burke*, ed. Copeland *et al.*, iii. 74.

[53] For a satirical look at the election ball, see C. Anstey, *An Election Ball in Poetical Letters, in the Zomerzetshire Dialect, From Mr Inkle, a Freeman of Bath, to His Wife at Gloucester: With a Poetical Address to John Miller, Esq. at Batheaston Villa* (Bath, 1776).

[54] 'Lady Bessborough to Lord Granville Leveson Gower, Holywell House [1794–5?]', in *Letters of Lord Granville Leveson Gower*, ed. Granville, i. 98–9.

[55] As first lord of the Admiralty after 1794, Spencer carried on the custom of dining with all officers from the rank of captain upwards upon their appointment to new commands. Lavinia participated in these dinners, but made it a rule not to invite the officers' wives. Georgina Battiscombe gives a variation on this, maintaining that Lady Spencer did invite the women, but then refused to acknowledge them later: Georgina Battiscombe, *The Spencers of Althorp* (1984), 82.

very least preventative, balancing treats for voters and forestalling accusations of bribery.[56]

Flattering voters' self-importance was essential. Knowledge of the local people, their characters, idiosyncrasies, and family skeletons, and an appreciation of minute differences in status or local social rivalries could prevent mistakes that put votes at risk. The politicization of traditional female social activities—teas and visits, carriage rides and courtesies—reveals yet another female dimension of electioneering, one that has been largely unrecognized.[57] While these activities did not translate directly into votes, they were politically important. During the 1760 election campaign Elizabeth Montagu, who was decidedly smug about her performance as a political wife, had accompanied her husband to Newcastle. She stayed with a local political family, and her activities included visits to the Northumberland ladies, entertaining the ladies of the local Corporation to tea, and attending the local plays, concerts, and assemblies: 'I behave very prettily, make visits duly, and have been this evening to make my compliments to the wife of the sheriff elect; and I think if Mr. Montague had the honour to be made an alderman of Newcastle, I should become the station very well . . .'[58]

Such activities tended to be unpopular with women of the political elite. In part, it was fashionable to complain about the amount of time spent on freeholders' womenfolk. It gave women a socially acceptable way to advertise their dedication and fulfilment of wifely duties, allowed them to advertise their political involvement obliquely, and reinforced social solidarity and exclusivity. Complaints tended to depict an unbridgeable gap between the polite and cultured women of the political elite and the supposedly ill-bred, vulgar women of the electorate. *The Connoisseur* satirized this when detailing the horrors suffered by a

[56] McAdams, 'Politicians and the Electorate in the Late Eighteenth Century', 186. Satirical accounts of the political opinions of freeholders' wives and the power that they had over their husbands can be found throughout the eighteenth century. In *The Humours of a Country Election* (London, 1734), 20, the cobbler's wife, an alderman's wife, and the lady mayoress all assert their political power over their husbands. In a typical sexual inversion, the wives promise to beat their husbands if they do not vote as they are told. The poem ends with male submission: 'To keep our Skins whole, and preserve our dear Lives, | We both will submit, and agree with our Wives: | The rest said the same, and swore they would do it; | AMEN, says the *Clerk* and *Vicar* unto it.'

[57] Paul Langford has interpreted this type of interaction as male-directed and an example of wifely obedience: 'a lady . . . could only be pitied when she was compelled to submit herself to the small-mindedness of bourgeois society': *Public Life and the Propertied Englishman*, 274.

[58] *HMC Fortescue*, 144.

fashionable, urban woman forced to play the part of political wife in a contested county election: 'There is not a woman creature within twenty miles of the place that is fit company for my housekeeper, and yet I must be intimate with them all.' The demands of the election dictated her tea-table company—'Mrs Mayoress, a taylor's wife' and 'Mrs Alderman *Gascoyne* who sells pins and needles'—and her company of an evening: 'I am obliged to take them and their brats out an airing in my coach every evening; and am afterwards often doomed to sit down to whist and swabbers, or one and thirty bone-ace for farthings.'[59] Mrs Montagu's actual experiences would have been with women who were considerably more elevated, but more than a faint whiff of smugness still permeates her comments.

While social gaps may have been exaggerated, they did exist and undoubtedly made election-entertaining taxing—perhaps more so for women than for men. Most men's election entertaining was overtly political and took place in relatively large groups over food and drink, especially the latter. The custom of interminable toasting would have formalized and limited conversation, just as the amount of alcohol consumed would have lessened social inhibitions. Women's entertainments did not share the same advantages. While they might include some food and drink, women's gatherings tended to be small and the drink was largely tea, with all its formalities of service and emphasis on polite conversation. The fact that the socializing was a superficial or artificial cover for a political transaction would have been obvious to everyone, but it must have weighed especially heavily on the hostess, who had to try to make the activities and civilities appear natural and genuine.

'SO CHARMING A SOLICITRESS'[60]

The demands of electioneering also required a certain amount of mixing with freeholders. This was always potentially problematic for the women. The idea of elite women soliciting 'lowly' freeholders for their votes and securing them through a combination of personal charms and persuasive abilities implied a socio-sexual inversion that threatened social hierarchies and accepted modes of female behaviour. Not only were the boundaries between acceptable and unacceptable female behaviour ill-marked and

[59] *Connoisseur*, no. 20 (13 June 1754), i. 117–18.
[60] 'Sir William Musgrave to Carlisle, London, 20 Nov, 1767', in *HMC Carlisle 42*, 221.

variable when it came to canvassing, but it was also possible for a charismatic woman who was a skilled canvasser to outperform a male candidate and displace him in the public perception. This called into question the prevailing belief in a 'natural' male polity, and could result in the canvasser being subjected to a torrent of abuse and sexual slander.

Careful mixing was sanctioned, preferably with the women in safe, physically elevated or ceremonial positions. Given the dirt of the streets, the unpredictability of election crowds, and the turbulence of many contests, these qualifications also gave women a degree of comfort and safety, especially when canvassing on their own or with other women. Situations that were more informal, and particularly ones where women dealt with the freeholders face-to-face and on foot, were the most likely to be criticized. As a result, more women electioneered from the safety and distance—real and social—of their chairs, carriages, and cabriolets, or rode in parades and processions, than mixed with the crowds on foot alone or accompanied only by other women.

Lady Spencer, who tried continuously to get her daughters to be conventional, sent the newly married duchess of Devonshire an instructive description of acceptable electioneering in 1774:

that abominable Sir James Langham began canvassing North'ton on Wednesday and had so much more success than was expected that our friends took fright and little Clarke sent word that things looked ill, and as your Papa could not go into the town (because a Peer cannot interfere in an election after the writ is out) he wish'd I would; accordingly I set out on Thursday morning with Mrs Tollemache in my Cabriolet and four, in hope of putting a little spirit into our people . . . I succeeded much beyond my expectations, for I no sooner got to the George than a little mob surrounded us and insisted on taking off our horses and drawing us round the town. I consented to it, tho', by the by, I could not have prevented it if I had had the inclination to have done it, and in a very few minutes we had a mob of several hundd. people, screaming Spencer for ever—Tollemache and Robinson— No Langham. In this manner did they drag us about thro' every street in the town, and were so delighted with my talking to them and shewing no signs of fear at going wherever they chose, that it was with the utmost difficulty I could in the evening (for we din'd with the gentlemen at the George) prevent their drawing me quite home to Althorp. I went thro' the same ceremony again on Friday . . . it has had an extraordinary good effect in the election for it has ensur'd Mr. Tollemache a great majority, by putting such numbers of people in spirits and good humour who before were cross and sulking and would not vote because there was nothing to enliven them.[61]

[61] 'Lady Spencer to the duchess of Devonshire, Althorp, 9 Oct. 1774', in *Georgiana*, ed. Bessborough, 15–16.

Concerns about maintaining propriety aside, the demands of circumstance combined with her own inconsistency saw Lady Spencer take a more active part upon occasion. A letter from her closest friend, Mrs Howe, just after this election, reveals that Lady Spencer's involvement had gone significantly further than processions and dinners: 'I hear you harangued from the Belcony, pray tell me all how & about it.'[62] When the Spencer candidate won, the duchess of Devonshire paid tribute to her mother's efforts in a way that was to foreshadow compliments that would be paid to herself only ten years later: 'I really think Mr. Tollemache should allow you to go sometimes to the House of Commons in his stead as you certainly have done a great deal to ensure his success.'[63]

The duchess of Northumberland, who was both more secure of her rank and more exuberant by nature than Lady Spencer, spent far less time worrying about the niceties of her electioneering. During her son's contest in Westminster in 1774 she was involved throughout: she canvassed, took a hotel at Covent Garden overlooking the poll, and she made speeches to the crowd from her window.[64] Horace Walpole, who had long accused her of vulgarity, commented snidely on her 'Hail, fellow, well met!' approach to electioneering,[65] something that William Whitehead also noted disapprovingly: 'her Grace of Northumberland goes most condescendingly out of her sphere, shakes every basketwoman by the hand.'[66]—her 'sphere' in this case being one of class, not gender. While Whitehead also complained that she was miserly in not giving the electorate *douceurs*, neither of the men criticized her for electioneering itself. There was a fine line between being miserly and too profuse, however: the latter could all too easily lead to accusations of bribery: 'Lady Strathmore's conduct at Newcastle, in the election, is, perhaps not generally known. Her ladyship sits all day in the window at a public-house, from whence she sometimes lets fall some jewels or trinkets, which voters pick up, and then she gives them money for restoring them—a new kind of offering bribes.'[67]

[62] BL, MS Coll. Althorp, F. 53, Mrs Howe to Lady Spencer, Grafton Street, 14 Oct. [1774].

[63] Chatsworth MSS 33, duchess of Devonshire to Lady Spencer, 17 Oct. 1774.

[64] GP, PRO, 30/29/4/2/69, fol. 255^{v}, Lady Carlisle to Lady Gower, London, 13 Oct. 1774. See also Horace Walpole's letters to Henry Seymour Conway and Sir Horace Mann, 16 and 22 Oct. 1774, in *Horace Walpole's Correspondence*, ed. Lewis, xxxix., pp. vii, 196, 51–2.

[65] 'Horace Walpole to Henry Seymour Conway, Strawberry Hill, 16 Oct. 1774', ibid., xxxix. 196.

[66] 'William Whitehead to Nuneham, London, 1774', in *Harcourt Papers*, ed. Harcourt, vii. 315.

[67] 'Mrs Montagu to [unknown]', in *A Lady of the Last Century*, ed. Doran, 223.

Despite the furore raised by the duchess of Devonshire's canvassing in 1784, women's canvassing was neither innovatory in the second half of the century, nor was it usually controversial. It was much more likely to be taken for granted as one of the electoral responsibilities of women whose families were involved in elections. This is reflected by the way that it was simply mentioned in passing in letters. Thus: 'Lady Brandon is gone down to them [the Agars] about her brother Jemmy Agar's borough, which there is some violent fuss about between him, Mr. Flood and Mr. Wemyss';[68] or, 'the Duke and Duchess of Northumberland are gone down to Andover, to canvass the town for Sir Francis Delavel'.[69]

Contests that were resolved before or immediately after an initial canvass might require little effort from men or women. A long battle, on the other hand, could mean repeated canvassing, formally and informally. The formal canvass involved the procession of an impressive and numerous canvassing party around a chosen route, complete with strategically placed entertainments. The candidates, their patrons, and associates might solicit votes in person, but it was their presence and their ability (and willingness) to socialize affably and appear open and accessible that mattered: agents could handle the rest. The outcome of the formal canvass was crucial: poor support for a candidate could put an immediate end to a contest.[70]

Processions, parades and treats, public breakfasts and dinners, and balls and assemblies all provided other opportunities for canvassing. Moreover, informal, spontaneous canvassing could take place anywhere right up to the poll.[71] Members of the political elite were usually canvassed in writing or in person by the candidates and/or their patrons, or by relatives, friends, and neighbours. Once their political support was obtained, they were expected to use their influence with their tenants, or at least permit partisan electioneering on their estates. The extent to which freeholders were canvassed, and by whom, depended upon a variety of factors, including the intensity of the campaign. The more

[68] 'Lady Kildare to Kildare, Castletown, 23 [Dec. 1762]', in *Correspondence of Emily, Duchess of Leinster*, ed. Fitzgerald, i. 163.

[69] 'Gilly Williams to George Selwyn, White's [?1768]', in *George Selwyn and His Contemporaries*, ed. John Heneage Jesse, 4 vols. (London, 1843), ii. 279.

[70] See, McAdams, 'Politicians and the Electorate', 179; Karl von den Steinen, 'The Fabric of an Interest: The First Duke of Dorset and Kentish and Sussex Politics, 1705–1765', Ph.D. dissertation, University of California, Los Angeles (1969), 203–12; and, O'Gorman, *Voters, Patrons, and Parties*, 90–105.

[71] McAdam, 'Politicians and the Electorate', 179–87.

intense the campaign, the more likely freeholders were be to be canvassed by elite—and female—canvassers.

At times it was hard to tell where socializing ended and canvassing started. Francis Mackenzie's suspicions of Jane, duchess of Gordon, provide a case in point. In November 1789, during the struggle between the administration and opposition for control of the Northern (Tain) Burghs in Scotland, she travelled to Inverness at the instigation of her close friend, Henry Dundas. This caused consternation among the opposition politicians, who feared that, even if she did not canvass formally, she would secure votes just by her presence:

> I must tell you that the Gordon family who have as you know treated Inverness both shire & town a little cavalierly are at the instigation of Dundas altering their conduct & sweetening upon the good folks very quickly—The Dutchess escorted by Lenox & Sir Robert Sinclair was to be last week at Inverness to attend the Northern meeting a Society she has hitherto treated with marked contempt as I know this motion to be merely political I have a trusty friend to watch all her motions & if I learn anything will let you know—.[72]

Beautiful, vivacious, extroverted, and shrewd, the duchess was a political force to be reckoned with. Election poems and songs suggest that the ideal female canvasser was a beautiful, amiable, and charming young woman, politically astute and well connected. The social mixing involved in canvassing and its physical demands supposedly made it best suited to youth, as a poem from the 1754 Oxfordshire election made clear: 'Let younger Wenches Coax *Freeholders* | And Shake their Hands, and slap their Shoulders, | And ride about, and scold, and quarrel.'[73] Any election that could be described as one where 'an old woman may canvass for you with success', was assumed to be placid—a certain victory.[74]

As with any reconciliation of the ideal with the real, however, not all actual female canvassers were either young or beautiful. A brief

[72] 'Francis Humbertson Mackenzie to William Adam, Seaforth Lodge, 10 Nov. 1789', in Donald E. Ginter, *Whig Organization in the General Election of 1790: Selections from the Blair Adams Papers* (Berkeley 1967), 119. The Northern (Tain) burghs were Dornoch in Sutherlandshire, Wick in Caithness, Kirkwall in Orkney, and Tain and Dongwall in Ross. The government interest was in the countess of Sutherland and her husband Lord Gower, who were allied with Sir John Sinclair and controlled Dornoch and Wick. After 1786 they also controlled Tain and in 1790 were able to return a government candidate without a contest.

[73] 'Another New Song', in *The Oxfordshire Contest: or the Whole Controversy between the Old and New Interest* (Oxford, 1753), 51.

[74] An unidentified friend to John Strutt on his chance of winning the Maldon by-election in 1773, as quoted in Hon. Charles R. Strutt, *The Strutt Family of Terling, 1650–1873* (1939), 18.

examination of the canvassers in the 1754 Oxfordshire and 1784 Westminster elections reveals that they came in all ages, shapes, and sizes. Some were single, others were married; still others were separated or widowed. Their political experience, interest, and connexions varied similarly. Of the three women who can be identified as canvassing in Oxfordshire—Lady Susan Keck, Lady Talbot, and Lady Dalkeith—all were affiliated with the New Interest Whigs. Lady Susan was 48, married, and the mother of two daughters;[75] Lady Talbot was in her mid-thirties, separated from her husband, with one daughter; Lady Dalkeith was also in her thirties, widowed, and the mother of three children under 8.[76] In Westminster in 1784 at least twenty-five women can be identified. The Foxite Whig women who are mentioned by name ranged from duchesses down to a demi-rep: the duchesses of Devonshire and Portland; the Ladies Duncannon, Willoughby, Archer, Grosvenor, Dornhoff, Worsley, Beauchamp, Carlisle, Derby, and the Ladies Waldegrave; the Miss Keppels, Mrs Crewe, Mrs Bouverie, and Mrs Sheridan; and Mary 'Perdita' Robinson. The Pittite women appear to have been fewer in number, but not remarkably different socially: the duchesses of Rutland, Argyll, and Ancaster; the Ladies Salisbury, Buckinghamshire, and Talbot; and Mrs Hobart.[77] Given the larger number of participants in 1784, the range of women is correspondingly more diverse. Although most were married women in their twenties and thirties, the Waldegraves and the Keppels were unmarried. The canvassers included famous beauties like the duchesses of Rutland and Argyll; fashion-leaders and society hostesses, such as the duchess of Devonshire, Ladies Duncannon and Archer, and Mrs Crewe; and noted members of the artistic community in Mrs Sheridan and Perdita Robinson. Not all of them were remarkable for their beauty and grace either: Mrs Hobart, in particular, was continuously criticized for her obesity and awkwardness.

The outstanding canvassers in these two elections were Lady Susan Keck and the duchess of Devonshire. Of the two, Lady Susan's involvement was, if anything, more political and extensive than that of the duchess thirty years later. It also generated similar praise and scurrility,

[75] See my forthcoming *DNB* entry for Lady Susan. She was born in 1706. Comments in election poems allude to her grey hair and wrinkles: see e.g. *Advice from Horace to Lady S—s—n* (Oxford, 1753); and 'The Grey Mare The Better Horse: or, The Oxfordshire Freeholder's Choice', in *Jackson's Oxford Journal*, 6 Oct. 1753.

[76] Herbert Croft described her as fierce and dauntless: Herbert Croft, *The Abbey at Kilkhampton* (London, 1780), 27–8; GEC, ii. 368–70.

[77] See Hartley *et al.*, *History of the Westminster Election*; Grego, *History of Parliamentary Elections and Electioneering*, 269–93.

especially in the form of execrable doggerel full of sexual innuendo (often, in Lady Susan's case, associated with riding or the wearing of breeches), albeit, because it was Oxford and not London, on a smaller scale. Lady Susan's purported predilection for donning riding-boots and taking a horse from her husband's stables to go canvassing particularly fascinated Old Interest publicists, who dubbed her 'Lord Sue'. They pointedly reminded her that her activities were not good for her looks—'Think how such Exercise will peel Your Bum and your Complexion'[78]—or suitable for someone of her age.[79] She remained unconcerned, and so too did the New Interest hacks. Indeed, they positively flaunted her ability to 'unman' the opposition, and set her up as a rival to the leading candidate, Sir James Dashwood. Her own response may have been shaped in part by the generally more robust attitudes at mid-century, but she was primarily impervious because she believed in herself and what she was doing—she lacked the personal insecurities that would lay the duchess open to attack. When she was mockingly designated '*Patroness* right Antiblue' and the '*Guardian-Goddess* of the Crew', she was delighted and subsequently signed her next letter to the Revd Bray as 'Susan Antiblue'.[80]

Her sense of humour aside, Lady Susan took the election as seriously as any of the other New Interest peers. Her letters are full of detailed references to potential, problem, or promised votes. Her web of contacts provided her with information and she shot instructions out to whoever was the right person to handle the job: 'I have a notion that a man that keeps a shop opposit to St. Marys his name is something like Cront, is a vote, he had a part of an Estate at Radford with one Martyn, that is a minor. He is a Confectioner, pray enquire after him. The Confectioners name is Coast. Canvass him instantly.'[81] She kept a close watch on political developments and acted on her own initiative when she believed that votes were in danger. After complaining about the state of affairs at Adderbury, where she feared that the duchess of Argyll's agents were misdirecting votes, she conducted a canvass of her own: 'I have eight in her Town, who assures me they never were askt, four of them I got so late as the Banbury entertainment . . . I have a man now informing himself of

78 'Boots and Shoes: or, Advice to a Lady', in *The Oxfordshire Contest*, 43.

79 *Advice from Horace to Lady S—s—n.*

80 'The Rump Worthies: or The New-Interest Supporters in Their True Colours', in *Oxfordshire in an Uproar: or The Election Magazine* (Oxford, 1753), 34; BP, L.IV.7.B/49, Lady Susan Keck to Revd Bray [?Dec. 1753].

81 BP, L.IV.7.B/27, Lady Susan Keck to Revd Bray, 19 Aug. 1753.

the state of that Towne, I mean Aderbury in every particulare.'[82] Her efforts at Adderbury were successful in the long run, as the New Interest candidates were returned resoundingly there, but sometimes even her best efforts could be frustrated, especially when distance and a hostile wife intervened. After having done all she could to secure a freeholder named Wilson, she told Bray that she was afraid she would lose his vote in the end:

> I found whilst he was with me I cou'd do with him what I pleased, but that availeth little since as . . . he is married to another woman, he will again fall into her claws and then my power drops, I try'd to have stroak'd her, but she is a Viper, and told me she always was of the high party—at the same time I have his Word of Honour to do everything I shall command him, but as I may not meet with him this twelvemonth, and Letters will be Read and—Answered by his wife, in this case what signifies—honour and assurance's.[83]

In such a close contest, she undoubtedly contributed to the New Interest's campaign and to its candidates' eventual success. It is often difficult to determine the impact that women's canvassing made on votes, but poll results for the areas that Lady Susan canvassed are generally favourable. In addition to doing well at Adderbury, the New Interest won a small victory at Heath and trounced the Old Interest in Bodicot and Milton. The elections in Banbury and Wardington were near misses, but the results were close enough for the New Interest candidates to maintain their viability during the scrutiny and subsequent parliamentary petition.[84] Moreover, results at these last two places may have been affected by her tussle with Lord Guilford. This occurred because Lady Susan's agent and the duke of Marlborough's canvassed these areas without Guilford's prior approval. As a result, Guilford's agent's competence was called into question, and Guilford himself was incensed and his pride was damaged.[85]

Lady Susan had little patience with this, because she saw the New Interest cause as far more important than the individual. Her political commitment was firmly ideological. Although her husband was a New Interest Whig, his own election for Marlborough's pocket borough of New Woodstock was uncontested and appears not to have required her

[82] BL, Add. MS 61,667, fol. 154^{v}, Lady Susan Keck to Marlborough [Great Tew], 25 Jan. [1753; misdated by an archivist as 1754]; also ibid., fols. 161–2, 29 Jan. 1753.

[83] BP, L.IV.7.B/37, Lady Susan Keck to Revd Thomas Bray, Great Tew, 21 Oct. 1753.

[84] *Poll of the Freeholders of Oxfordshire*, 17–19, 24–5, 59–60, 89.

[85] The fuss with Guilford runs through Lady Susan's letters to Marlborough in BL, Add. MS 61,667.

energies. Instead, it was she who drove the family's involvement in the county election. While she was unusual in being so firmly ideological, and the majority of women who canvassed did so for family members and/or family-sponsored candidates, the dividing-line between dedication to family and to party or faction was not always boldly drawn.

When the duchess of Devonshire and Lady Duncannon canvassed St Albans in 1784, at their mother's request and for their brother's candidate, their involvement was decidedly familial. They out-performed the opposition's familial canvassers, Lady Salisbury and Lady Talbot, to secure the seat.[86] Indeed, they would have gone on to canvass Northampton as well if they could have got there in time.[87] Their more famous involvement in Charles James Fox's campaign in Westminster that year, and that of the other women who canvassed on both sides of that election, was more complicated. While there was a familial dimension to the duchess's canvassing, that of the other female canvassers was predominantly factional.[88]

The details of the duchess's canvassing are not outstanding in themselves; what is by far more interesting is what they reveal about the complicated interrelationship of political motivations and family expectations that could lie beneath the surface of women's electoral involvement. Caught between her widowed mother's notions of appropriate female electoral involvement and those of the Cavendish family and Foxite Whigs, the duchess was pulled in opposing directions. In canvassing for Fox, she was simultaneously supporting her friend (possibly her lover) and her faction, and fulfilling the expectations of her husbands' family.

It was not surprising that she attracted the most attention of all the women who canvassed in Westminster in 1784. Not only was she a public figure, as the wife of one of England's richest peers and a leader of the *ton* in her own right, but also her early predilection for outrageous fashions, her addiction to gambling, and her association with ne'er-do-well's such as Fox had made her the target of criticism and moralizing publications since her marriage.[89] Her political connexions and activities were also public knowledge. The Cavendish family was a pillar of the Whig aristocracy. Its support of the Foxite Whigs was active as well as financial.

[86] BL, MS Coll. Althorp, G. 276, Lady Spencer to Spencer [Holywell], 2 Apr. 1784.

[87] Lansberry, 'Politics and Government in St. Albans', 238.

[88] Colley, *Britons*, 244.

[89] See e.g. William Combe, *The First of April: or, The Triumphs of Folly: A Poem* (London, 1777); also *A Letter to Her Grace the Duchess of Devonshire* (London, 1777).

Furthermore, the duke of Devonshire's sister was married to the leading Foxite peer, the duke of Portland. The duchess of Devonshire had long been associated with the Foxites and, as the Whig hostess *extraordinaire*, she had turned Devonshire House into the unofficial headquarters of the Whig party, the centre of factional politics. If there was to be any criticism of Fox's female auxiliaries, she was the most obvious target.

Significantly, press criticism of the duchess and other Foxite women's canvassing only emerged when it became obvious that they were turning the election in Fox's favour. Their canvassing, often on foot among the lower sort of freeholders, generated a torrent of 'Newspaper abuse',[90] which combined sexuality, gender, and class in an attempt to drive them from the field. The disdain that the duchess showed for keeping a proper social distance, by entering freeholders' shops and homes, and by taking them into her carriage, made her as much of a target as her sexual allure. The political purpose behind the attacks resulted in a double standard of reporting: 'While the Duchess of Devonshire and her suite are rattling through the alleys on the one side, and the Duchess of Rutland on the other, the first is treated in a profligate morning print with all the *dirty* and *obscene cant* of a common *brothel*, and the second is treated in all the *other* newspapers, with the *gallantry* and *respect* due to *female beauty. Voila la difference!*'[91] Other writers identified the long-standing socio-sexual concerns that the women's canvassing raised. Central to this was the belief that female canvassers exerted undue (sexual) influence over men—most particularly over men from the lower orders. Intermeshed with this was a class concern: by canvassing freeholders face to face, female canvassers broke down class boundaries, undermining the 'natural' social hierarchy upon which eighteenth-century society rested. Most importantly, however, it was the duchess's skill and success that lay behind the attacks: she became an established political figure in her own right, threatening to displace Fox himself in the public eye. Her electoral involvement could not readily be explained away by casting her in the acceptable role of the dutiful female family member or even as subordinate to a man. The fact that her activities were deemed, if possible, yet more dangerous and more corrupt because she was not openly operating from within the recognized paradigm of familial politics

[90] BL, MS Coll. Althorp, G. 287, duchess of Devonshire to Spencer [London, 23 Apr. 1784]. For the most comprehensive contemporary collection of press clippings and other published material relating to the election see, Hartley *et al.*, *History of the Westminster Election.*

[91] Hartley, *et al.*, *History of the Westminster Election*, 312.

is in itself telling. By overstepping the limits as successfully as she did, she cast doubt on the 'natural' subordination of women to men and also challenged the assumptions which were used to define women as politically incompetent and the polity as male.

Lady Spencer was outraged at the press attacks on the duchess. She was especially fearful of the effect that they would have on the duchess's already precarious reputation—and, by reflection, on the Spencer family. For her, canvassing door-to-door exceeded that 'degree of dignity & delicacy which a Woman should never depart from'.[92] Believing that both the duchess and Lady Duncannon had temporarily lost their senses in the excitement of the election,[93] she tried to bring them back to sanity by chastising them severely. The duchess sulked about the unfairness of it all, and in particular about the accusations of exchanging kisses for votes which had been levelled at her: 'It is very hard they shd single me out when all the women of my side do as much . . . Dr Mama, I repent, as I often do, the part I have taken, tho' I don't see how I cd have done otherways. My Sr [Sister] and Lady H[?] were both kiss'd, so it's very hard I who was not shd have the reputation of it . . .'[94]

What the writers attacking her did not know at the time was how firmly her political participation was still embedded in familial politics, despite canvassing for Fox, and how close their campaign came to succeeding. By playing on the duchess's immaturity and insecurity—political and personal—her mother was able to persuade her in early April to flee London and stay with her in St Albans to escape the press.[95] She was only forced back to London in the middle of the month to continue canvassing by the exasperation of her sister-in-law, the duchess of Portland, the concerted efforts of her husband's uncle, and finally, the barely veiled commands of the leader of the Whigs in the Lords, her brother-in-law, the duke of Portland.

[92] BL, MS Coll. Althorp, F. 38, fol. 300, Lady Spencer to Lady Duncannon [Holywell], 13 Apr. 1784.

[93] Ibid., fol. 307^{v}, Lady Spencer to Lady Duncannon [Holywell], 2 May 1784.

[94] 'Duchess of Devonshire to Lady Spencer [London, Apr. 1784]', in *Georgiana*, ed. Bessborough, 79.

[95] Lady Spencer's relationships with her daughters are an interesting study in themselves. In this situation, once she had succeeded in getting the duchess to St Albans, she turned her attention to shaming Lady Duncannon into withdrawing from the political fray: 'if you knew what pain the Scandalous Lyes & abuse of you or rather of your Sister gives me, you would neither or you I am sure venture again upon a Conduct that subjects you to such insults—': BL, MS Coll. Althorp, F. 38, fol. 300, Lady Spencer to Lady Duncannon [Holywell], 13 Apr. 1784.

The duchess of Portland wrote first. The two women had never been particularly close, and in this instance her exasperation was obvious:

I do verily believe Mr. Fox will Succeed, every body seems to be of that Opinion if people will Continue to exert themselves—I am worn out almost & must beg of You to Come tomorrow There are a great many Votes that You can Command & No One else, & now if You only Stop at peoples doors it will be quite Sufficient, & really Your presence is quite expected—so tomorrow morning Pray be here early.[96]

The duchess continued to plead her mother's ill-health.[97] The duchess of Portland then made it clear that any continued absence would be interpreted as dereliction of duty and sheer selfishness: 'Every body is so anxious for your return that I do hope you will Come to town at latest tomorrow Evening, for if we should lose this (at last they will think) it is owing to your absence.'[98] For additional weight, a two-pronged attack followed the next day from the senior Whigs and family leaders, the duke of Portland and Lord John Cavendish. The duke had no time for Lady Spencer's fictional illness:

Every one is concerned that Your Exertions have produced the very material alteration which has happened in Foxs favor, & will continue to preserve & improve it into a decisive Majority, but be assured that if it could be imagined that Your absence was imputable to any other Cause than Your Affection to Lady Spencer & Your Anxiety (I hope perfectly unnecessary) for the State of Her health, & that a suspicion should arise of Your having withdrawn Yourself from the Election, a general Languor would prevail, Despondency would succeed, & the Triumph of the Court would be the inevitable Consequence. However it may seem, depend upon it, that this Representation is not exaggerated; & if You will give me credit in that respect, which I *seriously* assure You is due to me, I think We shall have the pleasure of seeing You in the course of tomorrow.[99]

Lord John Cavendish, who had known Lady Spencer most of his life, took another tack. He wrote to her, not the duchess, wisely blending persuasion with flattery. Recognizing that her underlying concerns were more personal than political, he hastened to reassure her that the Spencer family's social status (and specifically hers) had not been harmed by the duchess's activities. After reassuring her that the duchess would not

[96] Chatsworth MSS 610.4, duchess of Portland to duchess of Devonshire [London, Apr. 1784].

[97] There is nothing in the Althorp papers to suggest that Lady Spencer's illness was anything but fabricated.

[98] Chatsworth MSS 611, duchess of Portland to duchess of Devonshire [London], 13 Apr. 1784.

[99] Ibid., 612, Portland to duchess of Devonshire [London], 14 Apr. 1784.

canvass again on foot—'the Ladies never now quit their Coaches'—he reminded her that 'the manners & circumstances of the time' demanded that allowances be made. Finally, he flatteringly reassured her that the duchess's return was absolutely necessary to the outcome of the election, as no one else could possibly match the influence of her 'rank & engaging manners'.[100] Further dallying was impossible. As the duchess was later to tell her brother, the 'letters from the D & Dss & Ld John brought me back'.[101] While this resolution left Lady Spencer 'very unhappy', the duchess's return to the election found support from a surprising corner: her sister-in-law, Lavinia. For Lavinia, who usually disapproved wholeheartedly of both her sisters-in-law, the conclusion was simple and justified on familial grounds; nothing else mattered: 'the Dss is desired to do it by all the Caven:'s & that [is] vindication enough of her conduct.'[102]

The tension resulting from Lady Spencer's embarrassment, her desire to maintain control over her daughters, and the legitimate expectations of political involvement placed on them by their marriages, led her to try another approach in 1788. This time she started at the top by appealing directly to the duke of Devonshire. In an uneasy mixture of manipulation and conciliation, she attempted to persuade him to do what she wanted:

> Allow me to add a few words on another subject that gives me a good deal of uneasiness, I mean the Westminster election. I must think a business of so very publick a nature in such a place as London is better carried on by men than by women. What my daughters have already suffered from all the ill natured reflections that were cast upon them, when they before engaged in it, made me and, I conclude, made them very unhappy. If you see this in a different light and wish the Dutchess to subject herself to the same inconvenience again you have a right to direct her conduct which I shall never dispute, but if you see this matter in the light I do, let me entreat you to send her here or anywhere out of town 'till the election is over. If an excuse is wanting it may easily be said that one of the children is ill, (tho' I thank God, they are in perfect health) if to this you would add the additional service of persuading Lord Duncannon to consent to send Harriet here likewise you would make me happier than you can imagine.[103]

[100] BL, MS Coll. Althorp, F. 121, Lord John Cavendish to Lady Spencer [London, 14 Apr. 1784].

[101] BL, MS Coll Althorp, G. 287, duchess of Devonshire to Spencer [London 23 Apr. 1784].

[102] BL, MS Coll. Althorp, G. 289, Lavinia, Lady Spencer to Spencer, St Albans [received 24 Sept. 1784].

[103] 'Lady Spencer to Devonshire [Holywell, 22 July 1788]', in *Georgiana*, ed. Bessborough, 132.

Fortunately for her, the 1788 Westminster election turned out to be anticlimactic in comparison to 1784; consequently, women's involvement dropped back to normal. Some women canvassed; others did not. The duchess of Rutland canvassed as before for the Pittites, but the duchess of Devonshire focused her energies higher up the social scale. As Rachel Lloyd (no lover of the Foxites) commented sarcastically, the fact that she was not canvassing on the streets did not stop her from soliciting votes and being at the centre of the action: 'She only writes about fifty notes, and Sees fifty people every day. at Night the Heads of the party meet and Sup at Devonshire house and are So jolly and So eager that She Says its quite delightful.'[104]

WOMEN WITH POLITICAL INTERESTS

The duchess of Devonshire's situation would undoubtedly have been different had she been in control of a political interest. Since the value of a political interest did not vary according to the gender of the holder, candidates and patrons routinely approached women with political interests for support or permission to canvass their tenantry. Thus, in 1754 a successful candidate in Scotland grouped Katharine, duchess of Gordon, alongside other leading Whig peers when sending news back to the duke of Newcastle:

> One thing gives me sincere joy in this affair, which is, that upon my appearing to be protected by your Grace, I was assisted, in the most cordial manner, not only by Lord Findlater, & Deskfoord, but also by the Duchess of Gordon, Lord Braco, and His son Mr Duff, who is Member for this County, so that Your Grace's Recommendation, was supported by the most creditable appearance, that this Country affords.[105]

Later that year, when a dispute arose between Mr Duff and Lord Findlater over the appointment of a Sheriff for Banffshire, Lord Deskfoord deemed the duchess's preference important enough to use it to support his appeal to Newcastle: 'The Dutchess of Gordon too told me she wou'd recommend no other person, being perfectly pleased with the

[104] GP, PRO, 30/29/4/6/94, fol. 1139, Miss Rachel Lloyd to Lady Stafford [Holywell], 3 Aug. 1788.

[105] BL, Add. MSS 32,737, fol. 44, Andrew Mitchell to Newcastle, Banff Castle, 5 Oct. [1754].

choice My Lord Findlater had made.'[106] Then, in March 1760, when he informed Newcastle that there were rumours of an opposition to the pro-government candidate in Aberdeenshire, he made it clear that any action Newcastle might contemplate would need the duchess's support: 'Your Graces Friend the Dutchess of Gordon, and her brother Lord Aberdeen will be of Consequence in determing that Matter.'[107] Newcastle took this to heart. After a discussion with the duke of Argyll in June about the state of politics in Scotland, he noted in a memorandum that the duchess's support for the administration's candidate had to be obtained: 'My Lord Aberdeen to be desired to speak to His Sister, the Dutchess of Gordon, to support Lord Adam Gordon.'[108]

There were always some elite women who controlled significant political interests in the second half of the eighteenth century. Their political interests were integral to an area's political profile. In addition to widows like the duchesses of Gordon, Hamilton, Rutland, and Bedford, who managed some of the country's most important political interests for varying periods of time, there were also occasionally women who inherited significant interests. Few could compete with the countess of Sutherland, who inherited control over twenty-two of the thirty-four votes in Sutherlandshire, though—an 'almost insurmountable' influence.[109] There were also other women with less sweeping political interests. The dowager Lady Orford controlled both seats at Callington and one seat at Ashburton in the 1750s and 1760s;[110] Lady Bute held one seat

[106] Ibid., fols. 257–8, Deskfoord to Newcastle, Hopeton House, 4 Nov. 1754. A similar situation can be found nearly twenty years later, in 1773, when the duchess of Hamilton and Argyll was attempting to secure the Sheriffship of Lanarkshire in the interest of her son, the duke of Hamilton. She was less experienced politically than the duchess of Gordon and worked closely with her chief political agent, Andrew Stuart, to protect her son's political interest. Her long-term goal was to secure Lord North's support for a candidate in her son's interest, against that of the sitting member, for the upcoming election. Her short-term goal was to secure the appointment of the sheriff in Lanarkshire. While she carried on a correspondence with Lord Suffolk, the secretary of state for the Northern Department, to lay the groundwork for the former, Stuart raised the latter issue personally and successfully with Lord North: '[he]... authorised me to say that you may rest assured of the Sheriffship being given to the person you incline whenever the vacancy happens.' 'Andrew Stuart to the duchess of Argyll, London, 20 Aug. 1773', in *Intimate Society Letters of the Eighteenth Century*, ed. Argyll, i. 170; for the surrounding correspondence, see ibid. 155–72.

[107] BL, Add. MSS 32,903, fol. 110$^{r–v}$, Deskfoord to Newcastle, 6 Mar. 1760.

[108] BL, Add. MSS 32,999, fol. 15, Memds. with the Duke of Argyll.—The Whole List of Members gone thro' with His Grace, Newcastle House, 27 June 1760.

[109] 'William Robertson to William Adam, Edinburgh, 15 Feb. 1789', in *Whig Organization in the General Election of 1790*, ed. Ginter, 46–7.

[110] Newcastle's correspondence indicates that Callington was under Lady Orford's control in 1754 and that hers was the primary influence at Ashburton. Only Callington

at Bossiney throughout the period;[111] Harriot Pitt inherited one seat at Pontrefract in 1756, and retained it until her death in 1763;[112] Lady Irwin inherited a life interest in both seats at Horsham after her husband's death in 1778, and maintained it until her death in 1807;[113] Lady Andover was the patron of one seat at Castle Rising from the 1780s;[114] and so on. Others, such as Lady Downing, who fought unsuccessfully but continuously for control of Dunwich in Suffolk from 1764 until her death in 1778, are less historically visible.[115] And, of course, there were women, like men, whose estates gave them some local political interest but not actual control over a borough.

Even a small interest could be solicited assiduously. When a seat came open in Glamorgan in 1767, Lady Charlotte Edwin's interest was sought in turn by the candidate, by Lord and Lady Temple, and by George and Elizabeth Grenville.[116] As George Grenville reported to his brother, even

seems to have been under her complete control in 1760–1. Namier indicates that by 1761 she had reluctantly ceded control of Ashburton to her son. In commenting unfavourably on his nephew, Lord Orford's, sanity in 1774, Horace Walpole remarked that the dowager had given him control of both boroughs at some unspecified time prior to the dissolution. See BL, Add. MS 33,061, fol. 206^{r-v}, Mr Harris' State of the Case of the Burrough of Ashburton for Sr Wm Yonge, [1753–4]; BL, Add. MS 32,995, fol. 76, Present State of Elections for England & Wales [1754]; BL, Add. MS 32,999, fol. 301, Cornish Boroughs and the Principal Interests [1760–1]; Namier, *Structure of Politics*, 145; 'Horace Walpole to Sir Horace Mann, Strawberry Hill, 6 Oct. 1774', in *Horace Walpole's Correspondence*, ed. Lewis, xxiv. 46–7.

111 The extent of Lady Bute's actual involvement in the politics of the borough is debatable.

112 Namier, *Structure of Politics*, 147.

113 WSRO, Add. MSS 5190–203.

114 Cannon, *Aristocratic Century*, 110.

115 Margaret, Lady Downing, took over the Downing family interest in Dunwich after her husband's death in 1764. His arrogant and authoritarian approach to the freemen had already alienated them, and Lady Downing's approach was no more conciliatory. When the freemen looked to the Barne and Vanneck families as a way to break the Downings' control and Lady Downing refused to agree to any sort of compromise, a full-fledged battle ensued. She threatened the freemen with lawsuits for breaking the bonds that her husband had insisted they sign, had them all arrested and ejected, and was generally untactful and spiteful to them and their wives. Unsurprisingly, she lost control of the borough; however, she continued to fight to regain it for the next fourteen years. See A. R. Childs, 'Politics and Elections in Suffolk Burroughs in the Late Eighteenth and Early Nineteenth Centuries', M.Phil. thesis, University of Reading (1974), 9–29.

116 BL, Add. MS 57,804, fol. 165, Temple to George Grenville [London?], 18 Oct. 1767. Lady Charlotte was Lady Susan Keck's sister. The Grenvilles' attentions to Lady Charlotte were not new. Her position at Court, as a long-standing and influential lady of the bedchamber to the princess (later princess dowager) of Wales, had elicited their mindfulness in the past. In 1755, when William Pitt was rumoured to have offered his services to Leicester House, George Bubb Dodington assumed that Lady Charlotte had acted as Pitt's agent and had approached the princess for him, especially as he noted that all the Grenville and Temple women had been paying court to Lady Charlotte throughout the

this concerted attempt to win her over had not convinced her: 'I have Spoken to Lady Charlotte Edwin for her Interest in Glamorganshire in favor of Mr Aubrey, but I cannot yet Say with So much Success as I wish for She Still Seems desirous to keep herself unengaged till She Sees farther, but I hope my good Offices have had the Effect of disposing her towards Him.'[117] In actuality, the Grenvilles' attempt in October may have already been too late. Correspondence between the duchess of Hamilton and her agent indicates that they had been taking steps in September to secure a letter of support from Lady Charlotte, who was, after all, the duchess's aunt by marriage.[118]

For women, just as for men, the amount of energy that was expended on political interests varied with the size of the interest and the commitment of the individual. Women who found politics exciting or wanted to protect family interests might exercise their political influence in any number of ways; women who were uninterested in politics, had no heirs, or preferred to keep their electoral involvement to a minimum, needed to do little more than decide how to bestow their interest and then channel their instructions and all possible election business through a steward or agent. Elizabeth Montagu's approach to an election at Newcastle not long after her husband's death is illustrative. As a childless widow, her electoral involvement was the result of interest, not duty. While she preferred to remain above the electoral fray, she did have distinct political opinions, and consequently used her political influence at Newcastle to support the candidate of her choice. She then sat back to await the results: 'What little interest I have I gave to Sir John Trevelyan, who, we hope, will carry the election by a good majority. My steward tells me he is very weary of the bustle and treating the voters.'[119]

Given that women could be involved throughout campaigns, it is not surprising to find that they might also be present at the poll. It is difficult to ascertain what influence the presence of elite women might have had over outcomes, but the continued need to entertain voters and secure doubtful votes ensured some involvement with freeholders during the

winter: 'Diary, 21 July 1755', in *The Political Journal of George Bubb Dodington*, ed. John Carswell and Lewis Arnold Dralle (Oxford, 1965), 310–11.

[117] BL, Add. MS 57,804, fol. 167, George Grenville to Lord Temple, Wotton, 23 Oct. 1767.

[118] Note also that this provides an example of women with political interests approaching each other for support. See 'Andrew Stuart to duchess of Hamilton, Torrance, 13 Sept. 1767', in *Intimate Society Letters of the Eighteenth Century*, ed. Argyll, i. 119–21.

[119] 'Mrs Montagu to [unknown], n. pl. [?1777]', in *Lady of the Last Century*, ed. Doran, 223.

election itself. The daily events of elections—parades and processions, as well as meals—were well suited to women who enjoyed the spectacle and theatre of the occasions. Someone with a flair for the dramatic, like Lady Melbourne, was sure to make an impact. Agneta Yorke recounted her victory procession in 1774: 'I find Lady Melborne and Mrs Brand entered the Town in Triumph at the Head of the Melbourne Party with an open Landau filled with Musicians playing before them.'[120]

Those elite women who came to see the poll generally did so from the windows of surrounding buildings, or from their carriages, which they positioned on their candidate's side of the hustings.[121] By the last quarter of the century though, the candidates' pre-eminent female advocates might be found on the hustings themselves. While the duchess of Devonshire's presence on the hustings during the 1784 Westminster election has often been noted, Fox had already had female supporters, including the duchess, with him when he was re-elected for Westminster in April 1782.[122] A bevy of pretty, young, elite women was sure to be popular with the crowds. Their involvement could also extend beyond waving their riding-hats and joining in the cheers.[123] Thomas Wenman Coke's wife, for instance, is purported to have spoken to such effect from the hustings that her persuasive powers became legendary in the Coke family.[124]

Elite women were not the only ones who attended elections. As popular, if raucous, community events, elections gave women of all ranks a chance to socialize, show off their finery, and to express their political allegiances, if any. Those who attended the 1784 Norwich election left Sylas Neville appreciative: 'A number of fine country girls on the hill &c & a great show of beauty at the windows of the market place.'[125] They were, indeed, such a requisite part of election tableaux that contemporary dramatists included them in stage directions for election scenes: 'Windows, full of ladies, holding out their handkerchiefs.'[126]

[120] WP, L30/9/97/36, fol. 1^{v}, Agneta Yorke to Marchioness Grey, n. pl., 25 Oct. 1774.

[121] In 1784 this provided another excuse for poetry: 'On seeing Lady BEAUCHAMP, Lady CARLISLE, and Lady DERBY, in their Carriages, on Mr. FOX's Side of the Hustings', in Hartley *et al.*, *History of the Westminster Election*, 483.

[122] After his appointment as secretary of state. See Basil Cozens-Hardy, *The History of Letheringsett . . . With Extracts From the Diary of Mary Hardy (1773–1809)* (Norwich, 1957), 291.

[123] Ibid.

[124] A. M. W. Stirling, *Coke of Norfolk and his Friends* (London, 1912), 146.

[125] *The Diary of Sylas Neville, 1767–1788*, ed. Basil Cozens-Hardy (London, 1950), 316.

[126] See Trusler, *The Country Election*; for a visual representation, see Hogarth's *Election* series.

Dressed in party colours or ornamented with cockades and ribbons, they added to the spectacle as they cheered and waved their favourites on.

When candidates were finally chaired, or victory processions were staged, women were once again both spectators and performers. Lady Spencer's description of the Spencers' triumphal entry into Northampton after the rigours of the 1768 election provides a sense of the event:

> we were met by vast numbers of Men on Horseback all with Blue Cockades in their hats the whole way upon the road from Newport Pagnell, particularly at Horton where there was a Body of Men 200 of them . . . at Queens Cross there was a much larger number of them, with several Gentlemen & the principal people of the Town, there your Papa & Mr. Howe got out of their post Chaise & proceeded slowly on to the Town on Horseback. at the entrance to the Town there was a vast Crowd of people, with a Flag on which was wrote in great gold letters *Justice Triumphant* & several other Flags, the Company of Woolstapler[s] all drest very prettily in Blue & white, a Band of Musick, & the Chair which they insisted upon Mr. Howes getting in to . . . the Crowd was so great in the Streets that we were above three Quarters of an hour driving up the great Street.[127]

Fox's victory procession in 1784 included banners commemorating the Foxite women's contributions, as well as the carriages of the duchesses of Devonshire and Portland.[128]

RESTORING HARMONY

After elections were finally over, barring scrutinies and petitions to parliament, the political excitement subsided rapidly and society resumed its normal patterns. The task of smoothing ruffled feathers and restoring harmony fell, at least in part, to women. This did not always come naturally. After having Lady Salisbury nearly steal St Albans from her grasp in 1784, Lady Spencer found it difficult to bury her feelings, especially as she did not believe that Lady Salisbury had been properly humbled by her loss. Lord Jersey's comments did little to help: 'Ly Salisbury gave us a larger kind of Supper on Tuesday: she endeavors to

[127] BL, MS Coll. Althorp, F. 37, fols. 155–6, Lady Spencer to her children, Althorp [1769].

[128] Hartley *et al.*, *History of the Westminster Election*, 278; *Chelmsford Chronicle*, 21 May 1784. The conservative reaction that was set off by the French Revolution does not seem to have prevented Mary Hardy, a Foxite supporter and a thoroughly respectable and staunchly religious freeman's wife, from attending the chairing of the member in Norwich after the contested election of 1806: Cozens-Hardy, *History of Letheringsett*, 80.

laugh off the St Albans Business, but rather, I think, from what I hear, seems to claim much honor & merit from having made so extraordinary a Stand & so difficult a Contest: indeed the Advertisement tells as much.'[129]

When elections were fiercely contested, scrutinies and petitions to parliament could extend the election battles for weeks or even months. When this happened, women who had been active in the campaign might turn their attention to locating and sending witnesses to 'regularify' votes.[130] Women from the ranks of the freeholders and below might well act as witnesses.[131] Before women's removal from parliament, those who had a stake in the outcome of the election through their membership of political families or because of their factional allegiances might even attend the petition.[132] In 1762, for instance, during a petition that concerned the Richmond family, the duchess of Richmond and her sister-in-law, Lady George Lennox, accompanied by the wives of the two candidates in question, attended 'as constantly as the men'.[133]

[129] BL. MS Coll. Althorp, F. 109, Jersey to Lady Spencer, Grosvenor Square [10 Apr. 1784].

[130] BP, L.IV.7.C/76, Lady Parker to Revd Thomas Bray, St James's Square, 21 Dec. 1754. See also my 'The Rag Plot: The Politics of Influence in Oxford, 1754', in Rosemary Sweet and Penelope Lane (eds.), *Women and Urban Life in Eighteenth-Century England: On the Town* (Leicester, 2003).

[131] See my 'Women, Electoral Privilege and Practice', in Gleadle and Richardson (eds.), *Women in British Politics*, 30–4.

[132] Jupp acknowledges, but says little about, eighteenth-century women's attendance. He maintains that women's attendance in the Commons and the Lords increased after the end of the war in 1815, and was particularly marked during the debates on Catholic emancipation and parliamentary reform. P. J. Jupp, 'The Roles of Royal and Aristocratic Women in British Politics, c. 1782–1832', in Mary O'Dowd and Sabine Wichert (eds.), *Chattel, Servant or Citizen: Women's Status in Church, State and Society* (Belfast, 1995), 106–7.

[133] 'Lady Caroline Fox to Lady Kildare [London, 1762]', in *Correspondence of Emily, Duchess of Leinster*, i. 317.

8

Conclusion

What conclusions, then, can we draw about women's involvement in political life in the second half of the eighteenth century? Several points spring to mind. The first is that, while by no means all women were politically active, given the institutional and cultural discrimination and disqualifications under which they operated at the time, and while it may well have been easier for women than for men to opt themselves out of participating directly in politics by adopting strands of contemporary thought that were hostile to their involvement, the personal and familial nature of eighteenth-century politics and the interpenetration of the social and political arenas ensured that, on the whole, women were an integral part of political life. Women who were members of the most politically active families on the local and national stages would have been hard pressed to live lives untouched by politics, especially during a period marked by national crises, wars, and heated general elections. Even those women who were further from the centre, geographically, socially, or politically, often found themselves politicized in similar ways—through family members and personal networks, and through the intricacies of patronage or the manoeuvrings of the social arena. All of these could provide women with formal and informal points of contact and reasons for engagement.

Women's political involvement highlights the degree to which eighteenth-century politics was familial and families could be political units. It grew out of women's traditional female roles as wives/widows, mothers, daughters, and sisters. Women from politically active families grew up with politics, absorbed its rituals, had their socializing inflected by it, and frequently even had the shapes of their lives dictated by its annual patterns. Young women were schooled in politics informally, often by their mothers and mothers-in-law. They gathered political knowledge and learned the niceties of politicized socializing at home and also as they moved into society, especially in London, where every social venue and encounter had the potential to take on a political edge when sentiments ran high.

Although women's involvement in political life was always potentially more problematic than men's, given contemporary concerns about the links between sex, politics, and corruption, most of women's political involvement was taken as a matter of course. As long as their activities could be explained by recourse to a familial model which defined women's activities as subordinate to and supportive of men's, inspired by family and personal duty, then their involvement in social politics, patronage, or electoral politics could be justified and accepted, even demanded. Exactly where the boundary fell between acceptable and unacceptable involvement depended largely upon individual beliefs and the demands of particular political circumstances. The more important the cause or the more heated the campaign, the more women, like men, were able to stretch the conventions which regulated ordinary social interactions. If, however, they went too far, overstepping this invisible and highly variable boundary by coming to be seen as themselves the leading political actors in a cause, and not men's seconds or representatives—or were perceived to be so by moralists and critics—then they became the target of torrents of often sexualized criticism designed to shame them back into their subordinate political roles.

Eighteenth-century elite women, even the most active, tended to be politically and socially conventional: they were not seeking a larger political role for themselves, neither were they wanting to overthrow the status quo. While their critics worried that they posed a threat to the male polity, they were largely unconscious of this themselves. What made their political participation threatening was that they proved, by their actions, that women were not politically incompetent, that they could play the same political games as men—and win. In other words, they demonstrated that gender was not a reason for political exclusion.

There is little doubt that the dividing-line between acceptable and unacceptable female political behaviours was drawn more sharply from the last quarter of the eighteenth century onwards, as concerns rose about political corruption and demands for parliamentary reform increased, both of which targeted the kind of personalized political dealings and unaccountable influence that were associated with women. The deeply conservative drive for a purified, more respectable, and uniquely male polity was then emphasized by the conservative response to the French Revolution, but there is little to suggest that it spelled the end of women's involvement in political life. Indeed, for those women of the political elite who were willing to negotiate the political shoals and work creatively within the familial model, political activity remained a possibility throughout the eighteenth and, arguably, the nineteenth centuries. While the reform of parliament, the growth of a more meritocratic civil service, and the development of party politics saw women's opportunities for certain forms of political involvement constrained, at the level of the political elite nineteenth-century women existed who operated in much the same way as their eighteenth-century ancestors, and for the same reasons. Thus, traditional family-focused political involvement continued to be important, even while a new strand of individualist feminist politics was beginning to take shape. The two strands of female political thinking ran parallel; they were not necessarily causal, neither did they quickly converge.

But did women's political involvement matter? Did it make a difference? While it is true that women did not pass laws or set the policies which guided the development of the state through the complexities of successive eighteenth-century wars, and while it is also true that there were both men and women who found the idea of women's participation in politics abhorrent, there is little question but that, by adopting a wider definition of politics—one that looked at the means by which government in its widest sense took place—women played an important, if subtle and often unquantifiable, part in creating and maintaining a society that was in itself highly politicized; and that they were seen by their contemporaries to be doing so. While their social contributions to politics cannot be readily disentangled and measured, they should not be underestimated or trivialized either.

It is, understandably, the grand aristocratic hostesses of the great factional houses, and the formidable or incontrovertibly outstanding female canvassers, who remain fixed in our memories when we think in passing about women's political involvement in this period. While the importance of the leading hostesses and 'fixers'—women such as Lady Hervey, Lady Stafford, and the duchess of Devonshire—or consummate brokers and campaign managers, such as Lady Katherine Pelham and Lady Susan Keck, should not be dismissed, it is by extending our knowledge of women's political involvement to include those less immediately obvious women, who were perhaps also less socially elevated or more closely confined to one specific locality, that we gain a more comprehensive understanding of the range and extent of women's involvement in political life, and the ways in which they contributed to eighteenth-century English political culture.

To determine whether women could make a 'difference', we need to recognize and not trivialize the political potential of the dinner-table, the assembly, and the ball, and of the women who used these venues to political advantage. We need to look at the range of political women and the variety of forms that their involvement took. This means recognizing the contributions of female witnesses in controverted elections cases, the unquestioned electoral interest of female burgage-holders, and the genuine potential for influence held by urban women with customary electoral privileges due to birth, who were the means for men to become voters. It means taking seriously, as contemporary politicians and canvassers did, that multitude of wives who influenced their husbands, landladies who influenced their tenants, and so on. We need to pay more attention to that wide assortment of female clients, brokers, and patrons who made the patronage system work for themselves and for others, and to the political implications of their activities. And we need to acknowledge that women could be recognized as political forces within their own communities and beyond, and that they were dealt with as such. Every place obtained, every vote won, every reluctant supporter secured, made a difference.

The nature of politics in the eighteenth century combined with the pervasive understanding that women should dedicate themselves to forwarding the interests of their husbands and families to encourage and facilitate female political involvement. As Lady Stafford told her daughter Charlotte, it had been her goal as a young woman to be the best of daughters, and then later, when married, to become the best of wives.[1] In both cases this meant devoting her life to serving and forwarding the interests of her families of birth and marriage—and that, in her case, made political involvement inevitable. There was probably little praise more satisfying to political women like her than that accorded her by her stepson-in-law in 1783—even though the patronage bid he was thanking her for had been unsuccessful: 'I never in my Life knew a stronger instance of true attachment to a husbands family, & the resolute performance of duty, than that to which you allude, for which I have ever admired you.'[2]

[1] BUL, MSS 14/v, no. 93, Lady Stafford to Lady Worcester, n. pl., *c.*1800.

[2] PRO, 30/29/4/5/38, fol. 692, Archibald Macdonald to Lady Gower, *c.*1783.

BIBLIOGRAPHY

MANUSCRIPT SOURCES

Bedfordshire County Record Office, Bedford

Wrest Park (Lucas Papers)

Bodleian Library, Oxford

Assorted election addresses: MS Top Oxon. d.251
Beachcroft Collection (Leigh MSS)
City of Oxford Election Intelligence, 1765–96: MS Top Oxon. c. 280
Dashwood MSS
Extracts from Oxford and London Newspapers . . . &c., relating chiefly to Oxford and Woodstock, 1730–1820: MS Top Oxon. d. 174
Gough Oxf. 39
Greville, Fulke, letterbook: MS Eng. Hist. c. 190.
MS Don. b. 19, C. 164, E.165.
MS Eng. lett. c. 223, C. 239, D.85.
Poll book, Preston election commencing 11 Sept. 1780: MS Eng. Misc. c. 120
Carteret, Lady Sophia, letters of, 1744–62, [n. d.]: MS Lyell Empt. 34–5
Napier MSS: MS Eng. Lett. c. 239
North MSS

Birmingham University Library, Special Collections

Stafford Letters: MSS 14/v

British Library, London

Adair Papers of James Adair: BL, Add. MS 53,803
Althorp Papers: BL, MS Coll. Althorp Papers, F. 6–7, F. 11–16, F. 29, F. 37–40, F. 42–43, F. 53–5, F. 100–3, F. 105, F. 107, F. 109, F. 112, F. 114, F. 119–21, F. 123–4, F. 130–1, F. 169, F. 174, G. 276–7, G. 287–9
Anglesey Papers: BL, Add. MS 31,889
Auckland Papers: BL, Add. MS 34, 419, 34,424, 34,429–30
Bathurst Family Papers: BL, MS Coll. Bathurst, Loan 57, vols. 75–6, 103–6
Birch MSS, BL Add. MS 4,222

Blenheim Papers: BL, Add. MS 61,667–70
Bute, earl of: register of correspondence, 1739–1762; copies of correspondence, 1756–1765: BL, Add. MS 36,796–7
Calcraft Papers: BL, Add. MS 17,493–6, 43,771
Canning–Clanricarde Papers: BL, Add. MS 47,469
Charlotte, Queen: Correspondence: BL, Add. MS 33,131
Chesterfield, Lord: notes on Hanoverian Personalities: BL, Stowe MS 308
Dropmore Papers: BL Add Ms 59,486–7, 59,490–1, 69,042–3, 69,046, 69,065, 69,074, 69,289, 69,292
Egmont Papers: BL, Add. MS 47,012A, 1075B
Essex Papers: BL Add. Ms 27,733
Fairfax Papers: BL, Add. MS 11,325
Farnborough: Papers of English Statesmen, 1660–1847: BL, Eg. MS 2,136–7
Foster, Lady Elizabeth: Journal of events of my own times, 1788: BL, Add. MS 41,579
Fox Papers: BL, Add. MS 47,568, 47,580, 51,467
Francis Papers: BL, Add. MS 40,762–4
Grenville Papers: BL, Add. MS 42,083–5, 42,087, 57,804, 57,806–7, 57,821–4, 57,828
Hardwicke Papers: BL, Add. MS 35,349, 35,359, 35,369, 35,376, 35,386, 35,388–9, 35,395, 35,414–17, 35,511, 35,592–7, 35,604, 35,639, 35,692, 36,189
Hertford Papers: BL, Eg. MS 3,260
Holdernesse Papers: BL, Eg. MS 3,440
Holland House Papers: BL, Add. MS 51,337, 51,340, 51,345, 51,353–4, 51,385, 51,397, 51,402, 51,404, 51,415–16, 51,420–1, 51,424, 51,426, 51,436, 51,520
Jenkinson Papers: BL, MS Coll. Jenkinson, Loan 72, vols. 53, 58, 60
Lamb Papers: BL, Add. MS 45,548, 45,911
Leeds Papers: BL, Eg. MS 3,434, 3,441, 3,505
Liverpool Papers: BL, Add. MS. 38,197–201, 38,204, 38,222, 38,233; 38,307, 38,457–8, 38,469–71
Lord Chamberlain's Papers: BL Add. MS 42,940
Martin Papers: BL, Add. MS 41,357
Morley Papers: BL, Add. MS 48,218
Napier Papers: BL, Add. MS 49,090
Newcastle Papers: BL, Add. MS 32,734–7, 32,848, 32,852–952, 32,955–6, 32,958, 32,964, 32,968, 32,982, 32,989, 32,995–9, 33,044, 33,061, 33,066–8, 33,075–6, 33,082
North (Sheffield Park) Papers: BL, Add. MS 61,867–8, 61,874
Northumberland Papers (Syon House MSS): BL, Microfilm M/295–7, M/302, M/307

Northumberland, duchess of: correspondence with Bishop Percy, 1764–76: BL, Add. MS 32,334
Pelham Papers: BL, Add. MS 33,091, 33,100, 33,124
Public Advertiser: original contributions to: BL, Add. MS 27,777
Robinson Papers at Bridge Castle, rotographs: BL, MS Facs. 340 (1–3)
Sheridan, R. B.: correspondence and papers, 1770–1827: BL, Add. MS 35,118
Suffolk Papers: BL, Add. MS 22,628–9
Tamworth Pollbook, 1765 [but 1764 handwritten on cover]: BL, Add. MS 41,152
Townshend Papers: BL. Add. MS 50,005
Thurlow, Lord Chancellor: transcripts of letters, June 1778–June 1783; Dec. 1783–June 1792: BL, Eg. MS 2,232

Bristol Archives

Ashton Court Papers: AC/C123/1–16: Letters to Sir John Hugh Smyth, 1747–1801

Buckinghamshire Record Office, Aylesbury

Lee Papers, Hartwell II: D/LE/D1/1–40, D/LE/E1/1–15, D/LE/E1/16–28, D/LE/E1/29–40, D/LE/E2/1–62, D/LE/E3/1–39, D/LE/E4, D/LE/F/1–5
Spencer Bernard MSS: D/SB/P12/1–15, D/SB/P4/1–14, D/SB/P11/1–43, D/SB/P16/1–43, D/SB/P17/1–18, D/SB/P7/1–17, D/SB/P8/1–21, D/SB/P9/1–9, D/SB/PFE1/1, D/SB/PFE2/1–3b, D/SB/PFE6/1–15, D/SB/P14/1–13

Centre for Kentish Studies, Maidstone

Camden Papers: Pratt MSS U840
Stanhope of Chevening MSS: U1590

Chatsworth House, Derbyshire

Devonshire Papers, 5th Duke's Group: 238–369, 370–455, 456–569, 570–700, 701–829, 830–937, 938–1077, 1173–12001, 1201–26, 1321–44

East Sussex Record Office, Lewes

Ashburnham Papers: ASH 934–6, 3226–35
Sayer MSS: 523–31, 557–79.

Essex Record Office, Chelmsford

Account of poll, 1763: D/DM Z4

Audley End Papers: D/DBy C3/1–43, D/DBy C1–3, C5, C8, C9, C42; D/DBy F30, F57
Belhus Estate Papers. Barrett–Lennard family: D/DL C43/3/199–286, D/DL C43/4, D/DL C51–4, D/DL Z22
Crozier, John: transcript of diary, 1753–1788, ed. C. Willett Cunningham: T/A 387/1
Diary (probably kept by a sister of Charlotte Brydges), 1769–76: D/DRu F10
Du Cane Papers: D/DDc F6
Election poems, 1763: D/DPr 566
Essex Election pamphlets, 1774: D/DU 65/86
Essex Freeholders Book, 1759: Q/RJ 1/2
Fairclough Papers: D/DB 950
Harwich, parliamentary representation of 1754–61: T/P 86/16
Miscellaneous correspondence, 1713–1869: D/DJs F6
Political Papers, Essex, 1769–80: D/DBe Z2
Porter Family MSS: D/DPo C1
Savill Papers: D/DCd C2–8
Smyth Papers: D/DFg F4, Z1
White of Bulphan Papers: D/DZg 1–17, 30–4
Willson Family Papers: D/DU 66/23

Exeter College Archives, Oxford

Bray Papers. L.IV.7.B–L.IV.7.C: Oxfordshire Parliamentary Election, 1752–5

Gloucester Record Office

Badminton Muniments: FmK1/1/6, FmK1/2/4, FmK 1/2/7, FmK 1/2/15, FmK 4/3/1–5
Bragge Bathurst Papers: D421 C5, C7–9, F17

Horsham Museum Archives

Browne Papers
Hill (Irwin) Papers: MS 795, 798, 801–2, B6 B23/55
Horsham Election: MSS 3, 4.1

John Rylands Library, Manchester

Henry Bilson Legge Correspondence: Eng. MS 668
Melville Papers: MS Eng. 678, 699
Pitt Papers: MS Eng. 1272/1–72

Lancashire Record Office, Preston

Canvassing Book, 1768: DDPr/131/7a
Preston Election, 1768: DDPr/131/8

Leicestershire Record Office, Leicester

Finch MSS DG7 Bundle 30

National Record Office of Scotland, Edinburgh

Diary of Lady Mary Coke: 95/54

Nottinghamshire Archives, Nottingham

Foljambe of Osberton Papers: DD.FJ 11/1/4/180

Oxfordshire Archives, Oxford

Beaufort: DIL. XX/a/5a
Bucks. Election, 1784: Thame II/ii/8
Jersey Papers: JXXVIIF, JXXV16/4
Oxfordshire 1754 election papers: QSX 1
Printed Bills, Acts of Parliament, etc. 1701–81: DIL. XXV/1–15
Tadmarton patronage, 1775–6: Misc. Ey III/9–12

Public Record Office, London

Chatham Papers, 1st series: PRO, 30/8/19, 29, 39, 54, 48, 60, 63, 66
Chatham Papers, 2nd series: PRO, 30/8/107–9, 135, 139, 146–7, 152, 154, 175, 180, 183
Cornwallis Papers: PRO, 30/11/277
Ellenborough Papers: PRO, 30/12/1/2, 2/1, 2/3, 17/3, 17/7
Granville Papers: PRO, 30/29/1/14, 1/17; 30/29/4/1–8, 30/29/5/1–3, 30/29/8/1
Rodney Papers: PRO, 30/20/20/1–2, 30/20/21/1

Sheffield Archives

Wentworth Woodhouse Muniments: Microfilm (WWM M/F27) R1, R134–153; (WWM M/F 28) R154–169

Somerset Record Office, Taunton

Carew of Crowcombe Papers
Wells Elections 1765–8: DD/TD Box 6

University of Nottingham

Portland Papers: PwF, PwG

Warwick Record Office

Election Broadsides and Lampoons, Warwick and Oxford, 1753–4, n. d.: CR1291/655/1–18
Mordaunt Papers: CR1368/5/9, CR1534
Mordaunt Papers: CR1368/5/9, CR1534 [Book 2]
Newdigate Papers: CR136 A./554–6, A.[584], CR136 B.37/3687–90, CR136 B.40/4459–60, CR136 B./1398–1772, CR136 B./2524B.–B.2529, CR136 B./2705–3011
Sanderson Miller Papers: CR125
West Suffolk Record Office
Grafton Papers: 423/264

West Sussex Record Office, Bury St Edmunds

Goodwood MSS: 192, 355, 1078, 1170–3, 1175, 1919, 1975
Horsham Election, 1790: Add. Mss. 5190–5203

Unpublished Theses

BARKER, H. J., 'Press, Politics and Reform, 1779–1785', D.Phil. thesis, University of Oxford (1994).

BLOY, MARJORIE, 'Rockingham and Yorkshire: The Political, Economic and Social Role of Charles Watson-Wentworth, 2nd Marquess of Rockingham', Ph.D. thesis, University of Sheffield (1987).

CHILDS, A. R., 'Politics and Elections in Suffolk Burroughs (*sic*) During the Late Eighteenth and Early Nineteenth Centuries', M.Phil. thesis, University of Reading (1974).

CONNORS, R. T., 'Pelham, Parliament and Public Policy, 1746–1754', Ph.D. thesis, University of Cambridge (1993).

D'CRUZE, SHANI, 'The Middling Sort in Provincial England: Politics and Social Relations in Colchester, 1730–1800', Ph.D. thesis, University of Essex (1990).

DUNCAN, A. I. M., 'A Study of the Life and Public Career of Frederick Howard, Fifth Earl of Carlisle, 1748–1825', D.Phil. thesis, University of Oxford (1981).

FARRELL, STEPHEN, 'Divisions, Debates and "Dis-Ease": The Rockingham Whig Party and the House of Lords, 1760–1785', Ph.D. thesis, University of Cambridge (1993).

FORRESTER, ERIC G., 'Northamptonshire County Elections and Electioneering (1695–1832), Based Mainly on the Isham and Cartwright Muniments', B.Litt. thesis, University of Oxford (1939).

HARDY, ALAN, 'The Duke of Newcastle and His Friends in Opposition, 1762–1765', MA thesis, University of Manchester (1956).

LANSBERRY, H. C. F., 'Politics and Government in St. Albans, 1685–1835', Ph.D. thesis, University of London (1964).

LEE, J. M., 'Stanford and the Cecils, 1700–1885: A Study in Political Control', B.Litt. thesis, University of Oxford (1957).

LOWE, STEPHEN, 'Hampshire County Elections and Electioneering, 1734–1830', M.Phil. thesis, University of Southampton (1971).

LUFF, P. A., 'Henry Fox, the Duke of Cumberland, and Pelhamite Politics, 1748–1757', D.Phil. thesis, University of Oxford (1981).

MCADAMS, D., 'Politicians and the Electorate in the Late Eighteenth Century', Ph.D. dissertation, Duke University (1967).

MCKELVEY, JAMES L., 'Lord Bute and George III: The Leicester House Years', Ph.D. dissertation, Northwestern University (1965).

PICKERSGILL, A., 'Parliamentary Elections in Essex (excluding Harwich) from 1759 to 1774', MA thesis, University of Manchester (1953).

POTTLE, M. C., 'Loyalty and Patriotism in Nottingham, 1792–1816', D.Phil. thesis, University of Oxford (1988).

ROBERTS, KIM, 'The English County Members of Parliament, 1784–1832', B.Litt. thesis, University of Oxford (1974).

ROSS, DAVID F., 'William Henry Cavendish, Third Duke of Portland: The Years in Opposition, 1738–1794', Ph.D. thesis, University of Chicago (1980).

SMITH, JOHN RAYMOND, 'The Borough of Maldon, 1688–1768', M.Phil. thesis, University of Leicester (1981).

STEINEN, KARL VON DEN, 'The Fabric of an Interest: The First Duke of Dorset and Kentish and Sussex Politics, 1705–1765', Ph.D. dissertation, University of California, Los Angeles (1969).

TURNER, D. J., 'George III and the Whig Opposition (1760–1794)', Ph.D. thesis, University of Nottingham (1953).

PRINTED SOURCES

Contemporary Books, Pamphlets, Prints, Poems, Collections, etc.

AIRLIE, MABELL, *In Whig Society, 1775–1818* (London, 1921).

A Lady's Address to the Ladies, to Maintain their antient Liberty [n.d.].

A Letter from a Gentleman at Bampton to his Friend at Oxford ([Oxford?] Apr. 1754).

A New Election Song [n.d.: 1753–4].

A New Election Song [1753–4].

A Prime Minister and His Son, ed. Hon. Mrs E. Stuart Wortley (London, 1925).

A Series of Letters of the First Earl of Malmesbury, His Family and Friends from 1745 to 1820, ed. Malmesbury, 2 vols. (London, 1870).

Address to the Freeholders of the County of Oxford on the Subject of the Present Election (London, 1753).

Address to the Gentlemen of the Grand-Jury for the County of Oxford, On Their Late Presentment of a Libel Against His Majesty's Person and Government (London, 1754).

Advice from Horace to Lady S-s-n (Oxford, 1753).

ALBEMARLE, earl of, *Memoirs of the Marquis of Rockingham and his Contemporaries*, 2 vols. (London, 1852).

ALEXANDER, WILLIAM, *The History of Women, From the Earliest Antiquity, to the Present Time* 2 vols. (London, 1779).

An Eighteenth-Century Correspondence, ed. Lilian Dickins and Mary Stanton (London, 1910).

An Entire and Impartial Collection of all the Papers &c Published on Both Sides, concerning the Late Election at Liverpool, for Members to serve in Parliament (London, 1761).

An History of the Late Important period, from the beginning of His Majesty's Illness, to the Settlement of the Executive Government, in the Appointment of a Regent (London, 1789).

ANDREWS, JOHN, *Remarks on the French and English Ladies, in a Series of Letters: Interspersed with Various Anecdotes, and Additional Matter, Arising from the Subject* (London, 1783).

Anecdotes of the House of Bedford from the Norman Conquest to the Present Period (London, 1797).

Announcement of Guidelines for Election (Oxford, 1754).

Annual Register: 1783, 1874, 1788 (London, 1784, 1785, 1789).

Another New Election Song: By a Lady (Newcastle, 1777).

ANSON, CAPT. W. V., *The Life of Lord Anson: The Father of the British Navy, 1697–1762* (London, 1912).

ANSPACH, Margravine of [Craven, Elizabeth], *Memoirs of the Margravine of Anspach*, 2 vols. (London, 1826).

ANSTEY, C., *An Election Ball in Poetical Letters, in the Zomerzetshire Dialect, From Mr. Inkle, a Freeman of Bath, to His Wife at Gloucester: With a Poetical Address to John Miller, Esq. at Batheaston Villa* (Bath, 1776).

Apotheosis of the Dutchess (London, 1784).

APPLETON, ELIZABETH, *Private Education; or A Practical Plan For The Studies of Young Ladies: With an Address to Parents, Private Governesses, and Young Ladies* (London, 1816).

ARBUTHNOT, JOHN, *Kiss my A—— is no Treason: or, An Historican and Critical dissertation upon the art of Selling Bargains* (London, 1728).

Aristocratic Women: The Social, Political and Cultural History of Rich and Powerful Women: Part 2: The Correspondence and Diaries of Charlotte Georgiana, Lady Bedingfield (formerly Jerningham) c.1779–1833, together with the letters of Anna Seward, c.1791–1804 and Lady Stafford, c.1774–1837 (Marlborough, 1997).

ASQUITH, MARGOT, *More Memories* (London, 1933).

—— *Off the Record* (London, 1943).

AUSTEN, JANE, *Pride and Prejudice* (London, 1813).

Autobiography and Correspondence of Mary Granville, Mrs. Delany: With Interesting Reminiscences of King George the Third and Queen Charlotte, ed. Lady Llanover, 2nd ser., 3 vols. (London, 1862).

Autobiography and Political Correspondence of Augustus Henry Third Duke of Grafton, ed. Sir William R. Anson, Bt. (London, 1898).

BANTOCK, ANTON, *The Later Smyths of Ashton Court From Their Letters, 1741–1802* (n.pl., 1984).

BARNARD, LADY ANNE, 'Extracts from the Journal of a Residence at the Cape of Good Hope . . . ', in Lord Lindsay, *Lives of the Lindsays: or, A Memoir of the Houses of Craford and Balcarres*, 3 vols. (London, 1849), vol. iii.

BARROW, SIR JOHN, Bt., *The Life of George Lord Anson* (London, 1839).

BELLAMY, DANIEL, *The Rival Priests: or, The Female Politician* (London, 1732).

BELLAMY, GEORGE ANNE, *An Apology for the Life of George Anne Bellamy, Late of Covent Garden Theatre*, 2nd edn., 3 vols. (Dublin, 1785).

BERCHTOLD, LEOPOLD, Graf von, *An Essay to Direct and Extend the Inquiries of Patriotic Travellers* (London, 1789).

Betsy Sheridan's Journal, ed. William Lefanu (Oxford, 1986).

Boswell's London Journal 1762–1763, ed. Frederick A. Pottle (London, 1950).

Bristol Contest: Being a Collection of All the Papers Published by Both Parties, on the Election, 1754 (Bristol [1754?]).

Bristol Poll-Book: Being a List of the Freeholders and Freemen, Who Votes at the General Election for Members to Serve in Parliament for the City and County of Bristol, (Begun at the Guildhall of the Said City Wednesday the 17th of April, 1754, and Ended Wednesday the 1st of May Following) (Bristol [1754?]).

Bristol Poll-Book: Being a List of the Freeholders and Freemen, Who Votes at the General Election for Members to Serve in Parliament for the City and County of Bristol, [Begun at the Guildhall on Friday October the 7th, and Ended Thursday, November the 3d, 1774.] (Bristol [1774?]).

BROWN, JOHN, *An Estimate on the Manners and Principles of the Times* (London, 1757).

—— *The Real Character of the Age* (London, 1757).

Canvassing, All the Ton (London, 1784).

CAREY, W. P., *Address to the Free Uninfluenced and Independent Electors of Westminster* (London, 1784).

CAVENDISH, LOUISE FREDERICKE AUGUSTE, 'Selections From the Letters of Georgiana, Duchess of Devonshire', *Anglo-Saxon Review*, 1–2 (June, Sept., 1899).

CHAPONE, HESTER, *The Works of Mrs. Chapone*, 4 vols. (London, 1807).

Chelmsford Chronicle.

Cheverels of Cheverel Manor, ed. Lady Newdigate-Newdegate (London, 1898).

Clergyman's Intelligencer: or, A Compleat Alphabetical List of all the Patrons in England and Wales, With the Dignities, Livings, and Benefices in their Gift, and their Valuations Annex'd (London, 1745).

COKE, LADY MARY, *The Letters and Journals of Lady Mary Coke*, 4 vols. (Edinburgh, 1889–96).

Collection of Letters on Patronage and Popular Election (Edinburgh, 1783).

Collection of Odes, Songs, and Epigrams, Against the Whigs, Alias the Blue and Buff (London, 1790).

Collection of Papers, Addresses, Songs &c. Printed on all Sides, During the Contest for Representatives in Parliament for the Borough of Liverpool, Between Bamber Cascoyne, Jun., Richard Pennant, and Henry Rawlinson, Esquires, Which began on Tuesday, September 12, and ended September the 16th, 1780 (Liverpool, 1780).

Collection of Tracts on the Proposed Regency (London, 1789).

COLMAN, GEORGE and DAVID GARRICK, *The Clandestine Marriage* (London, 1766).

—— *et al.*, *The Connoisseur: By Mr. Town, Critic and Censor-General*, 2 vols. (1755–6).

COMBE, WILLIAM, *A Letter from a Country Gentleman, to a Member of Parliament on the Present State of Public Affairs*, 2nd edn. (London, 1789).

—— *A Letter to Her Grace the Duchess of Devonshire* (London, 1777).

—— *An Answer to the Country Gentleman's Letter to a Member of Parliament; with a Review of the Characters of the Dukes of Norfolk, Portland, and Northumberland* (London, 1789).

—— *The First of April: or, The Triumphs of Folly: A Poem* (London, 1777).

Commons Journals.

Complete Works of George Savile, First Marquess of Halifax, ed. and intro. Walter Raleigh (Oxford, 1912).

Correspondence Between the Right Honble. William Pitt and Charles Duke of Rutland, Lord Lieutenant of Ireland, 1781–1787 (London, 1890).

Correspondence of Charles, First Marquis Cornwallis, ed. Charles Ross, 3 vols. (London, 1859).

Correspondence of Edmund Burke, ed. T. W. Copeland *et al.*, 10 vols. (Cambridge, 1958–78).

Correspondence of Emily, Duchess of Leinster (1731–1814), ed. Brian Fitzgerald, 3 vols. (Dublin, 1949–57).

Correspondence of George, Prince of Wales, 1770–1812: Vol. 1: *1770–January 1789*, ed. A. Aspinall (London, 1963).

Correspondence of John, Fourth Duke of Bedford: Selected from the Originals at Woburn Abbey, ed. Lord John Russell, 3 vols. (London, 1842).

Correspondence of King George the Third from 1760 to December 1783, ed. Hon. Sir John Fortescue, 6 vols. (London, 1927).

Correspondence of William Pitt, Earl of Chatham, 4 vols. (London, 1838).

COWLEY, J. *Orders and Resolutions of the House of Commons on Controverted Elections and Returns*, 2nd edn. (London, 1736).

COXE, WILLIAM, *Memoirs of the Administration of the Right Honourable Henry Pelham, Collected from the Family Papers and Other Original Documents*, 2 vols. (London, 1829).

COZENS-HARDY, BASIL, *The History of Letheringsett . . . With Extracts From the Diary of Mary Hardy (1773–1809)* (Norwich, 1957).

Creevey Papers, ed. John Gore (London, 1963).

CROFT, SIR HERBERT, *The Abbey of Kilkhampton*, 3rd edn. (London, 1780).

CUNNINGHAM, T., *An Historical Account of the Rights of Election of the Several Counties, Cities and Boroughs of Great Britain* (London, 1783).

CUST, ELIZABETH, Lady, *et al.*, *Records of the Cust Family*, 3rd ser. (London, 1898–1927).

DELANY, MARY, *Letters from Mrs. Delany (widow of Doctor Patrick Delany) to Mrs. Frances Hamilton, From the Year 1779, to the Year 1788; Comprising Many Unpublished and Interesting Anecdotes of Their Late Majesties and the Royal Family*, 2nd edn. (London, 1820).

DENT, WILLIAM, *The Duchess Canvassing for her Favourite Member* (13 Apr. 1784).

Diaries and Correspondence of James Harris, First Earl of Malmesbury, ed. Malmesbury, 4 vols. (London, 1844).

Diaries and Correspondence of the Right Hon. George Rose, ed. the Revd Leveson Vernon Harcourt, 2 vols. (London, 1860).

Diary of Frances Lady Shelley, 1818–1873, ed. Richard Edgcumbe, 2 vols. (London, 1912–13).

Diary of Sylas Neville, 1767–1788, ed. Basil Cozens-Hardy (London, 1950).

DORAN, JOHN, *A Lady of the Last Century* (London, 1873).

Early Journals and Letters of Fanny Burney, ed. Lars. E. Troide, 2 vols. (Oxford, 1988).

ECTON, JOHN, *Thesaurus Rerum Ecclesiasticarum: Being an Account of the Valuations of all the Ecclesiastical Benefices in the Several Dioceses of Engand and Wales*, updated by Browne Willis, 2nd edn. (London, 1754).

Election Magazine, or the Oxfordshire Register (Oxford, 1753).

Elizabeth, Lady Holland to her Son, 1821–1845, ed. Ilchester (London, 1946).

Elizabeth Montague: The Queen of the Blue-Stockings, ed. Emily J. Climenson, 2 vols. (London, 1906).

Evidence . . . in the Trial Wherein the Rt. Hon. John, Earl of Sandwich, was Plaintiff, and J. Miller, Defendant (London, 1773).

Female Ægis; or, The Duties of Women from Childhood to Old Age, and in Most Situations of Life, Exemplified (London, 1798).

Female Guardian, 2nd edn. (London, 1787).

Female Liberty Regained: A New Song (London, 1790).

Female Restoration, by a Moral and Physical Vindication of Female Talents: in Opposition to all Dogmatical Assertions Relative to Disparity in the Sexes: By a Lady (London, 1780).

Female Rights Vindicated: or The Equality of the Sexes Morally and Physically Proved By a Lady (London, 1758).

Female Taste: A Satire, In Two Epistles: Inscribed to a Modern Polite Lady, By a Barrister of the Middle Temple (London, 1755).

Female Virtues: A Poem (London, 1787).

FITZROY, AUGUSTUS HENRY, *Autobiography and Political Correspondence of Augustus Henry, Third Duke of Grafton*, ed. Sir William R. Anson, Bt. (London, 1898).

FORDYCE, JAMES, *The Character and Conduct of the Female Sex, and the Advantages to be Derived by Young Men from the Society of Virtuous Women* (London, 1776).

Four Genuine Letters Which Lately Passed Between a Noble Lord and a Young Woman of Fashion (London, 1762).

General Correspondence of James Boswell, 1766–1769. Vol. 1: *1766–1767*, ed. Richard C. Cole (Edinburgh, 1993).

Gentleman's Magazine.

Georgiana: Extracts From the Correspondence of Georgiana, Duchess of Devonshire, ed. Bessborough (London, 1955).

GISBORNE, THOMAS, *An Enquiry into the Duties of the Female Sex* (London, 1797).

GLASSE, SAMUEL, *Advice from a Lady of Quality to her Children* (London, 1779).

GODWIN, WILLIAM, *Instructions to a Statesman* (1784), in *Four Early Pamphlets by William Godwin* (Gainesville, Fla., 1966).

GOLDSMITH, OLIVER, *She Stoops to Conquer* (London, 1773).

—— *The Good Natur'd Man* (London, 1768).

GORDON, JANE, *An Autobiographical Chapter in the Life of Jane, Duchess of Gordon* (Glasgow, 1864).

Grenville Papers, Being the Correspondence of Richard Grenville, Earl Temple, K.G., and the Right Hon. George Grenville, their Friends and Contemporaries, ed. William James Smith, 4 vols. (London, 1852–3).

HAMPDEN, JOHN (ed.), *Plays of the Eighteenth Century* (London, 1928).

HANSARD, T. C., *Cobbett's Parliamentary History of England to 1803*, 36 vols. (London, 1806–20).

Harcourt Papers, ed. Edward William Harcourt, 14 vols. (Oxford, 1876–1905).

HARDY, FRANCIS, *Memoirs of the Political and Private Life of James Caulfield, Earl of Charlemont* (London, 1810).

HARTLEY, J. *et al.*, *History of the Westminster Election, Containing Every Material Occurrence, from its Commencement on the First of April, to the Final Close of the Poll, on the 17th of May* (London, 1784).

Hary-O: The Letters of Harriet Cavendish, 1796–1809, ed. Sir George Leveson Gower and Iris Palmer (London, 1940).

HATSELL, JOHN, *Precedents of Proceedings in the House of Commons, Under Separate Titles, With Observations* (London, 1781).

HAYWOOD, E. *et al.*, *The Female Spectator*, 4 vols. (1755).

Heber Letters, 1782–1832, ed. R. H. Cholmondeley (London, 1950).

Henry, Elizabeth and George, 1734–80, ed. Herbert (London, 1939).

HERVEY, MARY, *Letters, with a Memoir and Illustrative Notes* (London, 1821).

Historical Manuscripts Commission (for full details, see HMSO Sectional List 17), *8th, 9th, 10th, 11th, 12th, 13th, 14th, 15th Reports*; *Abergavenny MSS*, *Ailesbury MSS*, *Bath MSS*, *Bathurst MSS*, *Beaufort MSS*, *Buccleuch MSS*, *Buckinghamshire MSS*, *Carlisle MSS*, *Charlemont MSS*, *Dartmouth MSS*, *Fortescue MSS*, *Hamilton MSS*, *Hastings MSS*, *Home MSS*, *Kenyon MSS*, *Laing MSS*, *Lonsdale MSS*, *Palk MSS*, *Polwarth MSS*, *Round MSS*, *Rutland MSS*, *Stopford-Sackville MSS*, *Townshend MSS*, *Weston Underwood MSS*, *Various Collections and Verulam (Gorhambury) MSS*.

History of the Late Important Period, From the Beginning of His Majesty's Illness, to the Settlement of the Executive Government, in the Appointment of a Regent (1789).

HOWARD, HENRIETTA, *Letters to and from Henrietta, Countess of Suffolk, and Her Second Husband, the Hon. George Berkeley: from 1712 to 1767*, 2 vols. (London, 1824).

HOWARD, ISABELLA [Countess Dowager of Carlisle], *Thoughts in the Form of Maxims Addressed to Young Ladies on their first Establishment in the World* (London, 1789).

Humours of a Country Election (London, 1734).

Informations and Other Papers Relating to the TreasonableVerses Found at Oxford, July 17. 1754 (Oxford, 1755).

Intimate Society Letters of the Eighteenth Century, ed. Argyll, 2 vols. (London, 1910).

Jackson's Oxford Journal.

JEBB, JOHN, *The Works Theological, Medical, Political, and Miscellaneous, of John Jebb, M.D. F.R.S. with Memoirs of the Life of the Author*, 3 vols. (London, 1787).

Jenkinson Papers, ed. Ninetta S. Jucker (London, 1949).

Jerningham Letters, 1780–1843, ed. Egerton Castle, 2 vols. (London, 1896).

JESSE, JOHN HENEAGE, *George Selwyn and His Contemporaries*, 4 vols. (London, 1843).

Journal and Correspondence of William, Lord Auckland, ed. Robert J. Eden, Bishop of Bath and Wells, 2 vols. (London, 1861).

KENYON, Hon. G., *The Life of Lloyd, First Lord Kenyon* (London, 1873).

Lady Bessborough and her Family Circle, ed. Bessborough and A. Aspinall (London, 1940).

Lady's Address to the Ladies, to Maintain Their Antient Liberty [n.pl., n.d.].

Lady's Magazine; or, Entertaining Companion for the Fair Sex . . ., 15 (1784).

Later Correspondence of George III, ed. A. Aspinall, 5 vols. (Cambridge, 1962).

Laws Respecting Women, as They Regard Their Natural Rights, or Their Connexions and Conduct (London, 1777).

'Leicester House Politics, 1750–60, from the Papers of John, Second Earl of Egmont' ed. Aubrey N. Newman, *Camden Miscellany xxiii*, Camden Soc., 4th ser., 7 (London, 1969), 85–228.

Lesser English Comedies of the Eighteenth Century, ed. Allardyce Nicoll [n.d.].

Letter From a Gentleman at Bampton to his Friend at Oxford (London, 1754).

Letter-Journal of George Canning, 1793–1795, ed. Peter Jupp, Camden Soc., 4th ser., 41 (London, 1991).

Letters Addressed to Two Young Married Ladies, on the Most Interesting Subjects, 2 vols. (London, 1782).

Letters from George III to Lord Bute, 1756–1766, ed. Romney Sedgwick (London, 1939).

Letters of Bysshe and Timothy Shelley, and other Documents, ed. Susan Cabell Djabri and Jeremy Knight (Horsham, 2000).

Letters of Harriet, Countess Granville, 1810–1845, ed. Hon. F. Leveson Gower, 2 vols. (London, 1894).

Letters and Journals of Lady Mary Coke, 4 vols. (privately printed, Edinburgh, 1889–96).

Letters of Lady Palmerston, ed. Trevsham Lever (London, 1957).

Letters of Mrs. Elizabeth Montagu, with Some of the Letters of her Correspondents, ed. Matthew Montagu, Esq., 4 vols. (London, 1809–13).

Letters of Philip Dormer Stanhope, 4th Earl of Chesterfield, ed. Bonamy Dobrée, 6 vols. (London, 1932).

Letters to Henry Fox, Lord Holland, ed. Ilchester (London, 1915).

Life and Letters of Lady Sarah Lennox, 1745–1826, ed. Lady Ilchester and Lord Stavordale, 2 vols. (London, 1901).
Life and Letters of Sir Gilbert Elliot First Earl of Minto from 1751 to 1806, ed. Nina, Lady Minto, 3 vols. (London, 1874).
Life of the Late Most Noble Francis Duke of Bedford Including the Speech of the Hon. Charles James Fox in the House of Commons, March 16, 1802 &c. (London, 1802).
London Chronicle.
London Evening Post.
Lord Granville Leveson Gower (First Earl Granville), Private Correspondence, 1781–1821, ed. Castalia, Lady Granville, 2 vols. (London, 1916).
LUDERS, ALEXANDER, *Reports of the Proceedings in Committees of the House of Commons upon Controverted Elections (1785–1790)*, 3 vols. (London, 1825).
LYSONS, Revd DANIEL and SAMUEL, *Magna Britannia: being a concise topographical account of the several counties of Great Britain* (London, 1806).
MACFARLANE, ROBERT, *The History of the Reign of George the Third, 1760 to 1770*, 2nd. edn (London, 1773).
Masters of Extraordinary Merit, Or all the Recommendations and Qualifications of the Candidates of the Old Interest, as They are Made Public and Assisted, by their Secretary D.G. of Burford, in His Letter to the Freeholders of Oxfordshire (1754).
Memoirs and Correspondence (Official and Familiar) of Sir Robert Murray Keith, K.B., ed. Amelia Smyth, 2 vols. (London, 1849).
Memoirs of a Highland Lady, ed. Lady Strachey (London, 1911).
Memoirs of the Court and Cabinets of George III, ed. Buckingham and Chandos, 2 vols. (London, 1853).
Memoirs of the Lady Hester Stanhope, as Related by Herself in Conversations with her Physician, ed. Charles Meryon, 3 vols. (London, 1845).
Memoirs of the Marquis of Rockingham and his Contemporaries, ed. Albemarle, 2 vols. (London, 1852).
Memorials and Correspondence of Charles James Fox, ed. Lord John Russell, 4 vols. (London, 1853).
Memorials, Personal and Historical of Admiral Lord Gambier, ed. Lady Georgiana Chatterton, 2 vols. (London, 1861).
Modern Characters for 1778: By Shakespear, 2nd edn. (London, 1778).
MORITZ, CARL PHILIP, *Journeys of a German in England*, trans. with introduction by Reginald Nettel (London, 1983).
—— *Travels through Several Parts of England in 1782*, intro. P. E. Matheson (London, 1924).
Mr. Boots's Apology for the Conduct of the late H——h Sh——ff; In answer to a late Infamous Libel, intituled, The Blackest of all Black Jokes [London 1754?].
Mrs Jordan and Her Family, Being the Unpublished Correspondence of Mrs Jordan and the Duke of Clarence, Later William IV, ed. A. Aspinall (London, 1951).
News Boys, News! or the Electioneering Journal with Improvements . . ., no. 2. (Oxford, 1753).

Nineteenth-Century Constitution: Documents and Commentary, ed. H. J. Hanham, (Cambridge, 1969).

NUGENT, CLAUD, *Memoir of Robert, Earl Nugent* (London, 1898).

Old and New Interest: or a Sequel to the Oxfordshire Contest (London, 1753).

OLDFIELD, T. B., *The Representative History of Great Britain and Ireland: Being a History of the House of Commons and the Counties, Cities, and Boroughs of the United Kingdom from the Earliest Period*, 6 vols. (London, 1816).

Olive v. *Ingram*, Hilary term, George II, 7 Mod. 263, *English Reports*, 87 (Edinburgh, 1932).

Orange-Girl at Foote's to Sally Harris: or, the Town to the Country Pomona: An Heroic Epistle (London, 1773).

OSBALDESTON, GEORGE, *Squire Osbaldeston: His Autobiography* (London, 1926).

Oxford Rag-Plot: or, A Rag-a-muffin Song or Tag, Rag, and Bob-Tail (1754).

Oxfordshire Contest: or The Whole Controversy Between the Old and New Interest (1753).

Oxfordshire in an Uproar; or The Election Magazine (Oxford, 1753).

PALEY, WILLIAM, *The Principles of Moral and Political Philosophy*, 2nd edn., Bk. 6 (London, 1785).

'Parliamentary Diaries of Nathaniel Ryder, 1764–7', ed. P. D. G. Thomas, in *Camden Miscellany, xxiii*, Camden Soc., 4th ser., 7 (London, 1969), 229–351.

Parliamentary History of England, from the Earliest Period to the Year 1803 (London, 1813).

Parliamentary Papers of John Robinson, 1774–1784, ed. William Thomas Laprade, Camden Soc., 3rd ser., 33 (London, 1922).

Pembroke Papers (1780–1794), ed. Herbert (London, 1950).

PIGOTT, CHARLES, *The Female Jockey Club, or A Sketch of the Manners of the Age*, 2nd edn. (London, 1794).

—— *The Jockey Club, or A Sketch of the Manners of the Age*, 4th edn. (London, 1792).

—— *The Whig Club, or A Sketch of the Manners of the Age* (London, 1794).

Plays of the Restoration and Eighteenth Century, ed. Dougald MacMillan and Howard Mumford Jones (London, 1931).

Political and Military Episodes in the Latter Half of the Eighteenth Century: Derived from the Life and Correspondence of The Right Hon. John Burgoyne, General, Statesman, Dramatist, ed. Edward Barrington de Fonblanque (London, 1876).

Political Journal of George Bubb Dodington, ed. John Carswell and Lewis Arnold Dralle (Oxford, 1965).

Political Memoranda of Francis Fifth Duke of Leeds, Camden Soc., NS, 35 (London, 1884).

Political Society: A Poetical Essay, Addressed to John Wilkes, Esq. (London, 1769).

Poll for Members of Parliament for the Borough of Colchester in the County of Essex; taken before Samuel Ennew, Esq; Mayor, On Wednesday the 16th of March 1768 (1768).

Poll of the Freeholders of Oxfordshire, Taken at Oxford, on the 17th, 18th, 19th, 20th, 21st, 22nd, and 23rd of April 1754 (Oxford, 1754).

Poll of the Freeholders of Oxfordshire, taken at the County Court Held in Oxford on the 17th of April, 1754, By Tho. Blackall, Esq. High Sherriff (Oxford, 1754).

Poll of the Freeholders of Oxfordshire, Taken at Oxford, on the 17th, 18th, 19th, 20th, 22nd, and 23rd of April 1754 (Oxford, 1754).

Poll of the Freeholders of Oxfordshire (Oxford, 1754).

Poll taken at the Town-Hall, in the City of Borough of Wells, Thursday, the 26th December, 1765 . . . for Peter Taylor, Esq. (1765).

Poll taken by the Mayor, at the Assize-Hall, After his Secession from the Town-Hall, for Robert Child, Esq. (1765).

PORT, MICHAEL (ed.), *The Houses of Parliament* (New Haven, Conn., 1976).

'Private Journal of the Fourth Duke of Bedford', ed. J. Wright, in *Sir Henry Cavendish's Debates of the House of Commons*, 7 pts. (London, 1841–3).

Private Letters of Princess Lieven to Prince Metternich, 1820–1826, ed. Peter Quennell (London, 1948).

Rag Plot: Informations and other Papers Relating to the Treasonable Verses Found at Oxford July 17, 1754 (Oxford, 1755).

Ragged Uproar: or, The Oxford Roratory: A new Dramatic Satire [1755?].

RIDLEY, JANE and CLAYRE PERCY (eds.), *The Letters of Arthur Balfour and Lady Elcho, 1885–1917* (London, 1992).

ROCHEFOUCAULD, FRANÇOIS DE LA, *A Frenchman in England: 1784*, trans. S. C. Roberts (Cambridge, 1933).

RODGER, N. A. M., *The Insatiable Earl: A Life of John Montagu, 4th Earl of Sandwich* (London, 1993).

ROUSE, W. H. D. (ed.), *Election Scenes in Fiction* (London, 1929).

ROWLANDSON, THOMAS, *Two Patriotic Duchess's on their Canvass* (3 Apr. 1784).

Royal Kalendar of Complete and Correct Annual Register . . . for the Year 1770 (London, [1770?]).

SAVILE, GEORGE, 'The Lady's New-Year's-Gift: or, Advice to a Daughter' (London, 1750), in *The Complete Works of George Savile, First Marquess of Halifax*, ed. and intro. Walter Raleigh (Oxford, 1912).

SECKER, THOMAS, *The Autobiography of Thomas Secker Archbishop of Canterbury*, ed. J. S. Macauley and R. W. Greaves (Lawrence, Kan., 1988).

Selections from the Letters and Correspondence of Sir James Bland Burges, Bart., ed. James Hutton (London, 1885).

SEYMOUR, A. C. H., *The Life and Times of Selina Countess of Huntingdon*, 2 vols. (London, 1839).

SEYMOUR, FRANCES, *Select Letters between the Late Duchess of Somerset . . . and Others*, 2 vols. (London, 1778).

SHERIDAN, R. B., *The School for Scandal* (London, 1777).

SHERSON, ERROLL, *The Lively Lady Townshend and Her Friends* (London, 1926).
Short Review of Proceedings (Nottingham, 1820).
SICHEL, WALTER, *Sheridan . . . Including a Manuscript Diary by Georgiana Duchess of Devonshire*, 2 vols. (London, 1909).
STEER, FRANCIS W., *Samuel Tufnell of Langleys, 1682–1758: The Life and Times of an Essex Squire* (Chelmsford, 1960).
STIRLING, A. M. W., *Coke of Norfolk and His Friends* (London, 1912).
STRUTT, HON. CHARLES R., *The Strutt Family of Terling, 1650–1873* (London, 1939).
STUART, LADY LOUISA, *Gleanings From an Old Portfolio*, ed. Mrs Godfrey Clark, 3 vols. (Edinburgh, 1895–8).
—— *Some Account of John Duke of Argyll and His Family* (London, 1863).
The Beautiful Lady Craven, ed. A. M. Broadley, and Lewis Melville, 2 vols. (London, 1914)
The Devonshire Diary: William Cavendish, 4th Duke of Devonshire, Memoranda on State of Affairs, 1759–1762, ed. Peter D. Brown and Karl W. Schweizer, Camden Soc., 4th ser., 27 (London, 1982).
The Noels and the Milbankes: Their Letters for Twenty-Five Years, 1767–1792, ed. Malcolm Elwin (London, 1967).
The Soliloquoy of Reynard . . . To which is added, a Devonshire Lamentation! [n.pl., n.d.].
The Spy, or Pasquin at Oxford (London, 1755).
Thraliana: The Diary of Mrs. Hester Lynch Thrale (Later Mrs. Piozzi), ed. Katharine C. Balderston, 2nd edn., 2 vols. (Oxford, 1951).
Tit for Tat, A Comedy in Three Acts (London, 1788).
TROLLOPE, ANTHONY, *Phineas Finn* (London, 1869).
—— *Phineas Redux* (London, 1873).
True Blue: Or, A Letter to the Gentlemen of the Old Interest in the County of Oxford (London, 1754).
TRUSLER, JOHN, *The Country Election* (London, 1788).
Two Duchesses: Georgiana Duchess of Devonshire: Elizabeth Duchess of Devonshire, ed. Vere Foster (London, 1898).
Universal Passion: Satire V: On Women (1727).
Victoria County History: *Bucks*; *Herts.*; *Oxon.*; *Wilts.*
Votes of the House of Commons (London, 1754–5).
WADE, JOHN, *The Black Book; or, Corruption Unmasked* (London, 1820).
WALDEGRAVE, M. H., *Waldegrave Family History*, 4 pts. (London, 1974–8).
WALLACE, EGLANTINE, *The Ton; or Follies of Fashion* (London, 1788).
WALPOLE, HORACE, *The Last Journals of Horace Walpole During the Reign of George III, from 1771–1763*, ed. J. Doran and A. F. Steuart, 2 vols. (London, 1910).

WALPOLE, HORACE, *Memoirs of the Reign of King George II*, ed. John Brooke, 3 vols. (London, 1985).

Westminster Election: Fair Statement of Public Services [London, 1788].

Whig Organization in the General Election of 1790: Selections from the Blair Adams Papers, ed. Donald E. Ginter (Berkeley, 1967).

WILDE, OSCAR, *An Ideal Husband* (London, 1895).

Windham Papers, 2 vols. (London, 1913).

WRAXALL, NATHANIEL, *Historical Memoirs of My Own Time*, 2 vols. (London, 1815).

WRAXALL, NATHANIEL, *Posthumous Memoirs of His Own Time*, 3 vols. (London, 1836).

Yale Edition of Horace Walpole's Correspondence, ed. W. S. Lewis, 48 vols. (London, 1937–83).

SECONDARY SOURCES

Books, Essays, Collections, etc.

ABSHAGEN, KARL HEINZ, *King, Lords and Gentlemen: Influence and Power of the English Upper Classes*, trans. E. W. Dickes (London, 1939).

ADAMSON, DONALD and PETER BEAUCLERK DEWAR, *The House of Nell Gwyn: The Fortunes of the Beauclerk Family, 1670–1974* (London, 1974).

ALBERY, WILLIAM, *A Parliamentary History of the Ancient Borough of Horsham, 1295–1885, With Some Account of Every Contested Election, and so Far as can be Ascertained, a List of Members Returned*, intro. Hilaire Belloc (London, 1927).

ALLEN, ROBERT J., *Life in Eighteenth Century England* (Boston, 1941).

ALLGOR, CATHERINE, *Parlor Politics: In Which the Ladies of Washington Help Build a City and a Government* (Charlottesville, Va., 2001).

ANDERSON, BONNIE S. and JUDITH P. ZINSSER, *A History of Their Own*, 2 vols. (New York, 1988).

ANDREW, DONNA, *London Debating Societies, 1776–1799*, London Record Soc., 30 (London, 1994).

—— '"The Passion for Public Speaking": Women's Debating Societies', in Valerie Frith (ed.), *Women and History: Voices of Early Modern England* (Toronto, 1995).

APPLEWHITE, HARRIET B. and DARLINE G. LEVY (eds.), *Women and Politics in the Age of the Democratic Revolution* (Ann Arbor, 1990).

Aristocratic Women: The Social, Political and Cultural History of Rich and Powerful Women, pt. 1: *The Correspondence of Jemima, Marchioness Grey (1722–97) and her Circle*, Bedfordshire County Record Office (Marlborough, 1995).

B., Ll. C. W., *Memoirs of the Family of Bullock of Berkshire, Essex, and Other Counties* (London, 1905).

Bagley, J. J., *The Earls of Derby, 1485–1985* (London, 1985).

Balfour Paul, Sir James (ed.), *The Scots Peerage*, 9 vols. (Edinburgh, 1909–14).

Barker, Hannah, *Newspapers, Politics and Public Opinion in Late Eighteenth-Century England* (Oxford, 1998).

—— and Elaine Chalus (eds.), *Gender in Eighteenth-Century England: Roles, Representations and Responsibilities* (Harlow, 1997).

Barker-Benfield, G. J., *The Culture of Sensibility: Sex and Society in Eighteenth-Century Britain* (London, 1992).

Barrett-Lennard, Thomas, *An Account of the Families of Lennard and Barrett* (London, 1908).

Battiscombe, Georgina, *The Spencers of Althorp* (London, 1984).

Beastall, T. W., *A North Country Estate: The Lumleys and Saundersons as Landowners, 1600–1900* (London, 1975).

Becker, Marvin B., *The Emergence of Civil Society in the Eighteenth Century: A Privileged Moment in the History of England, Scotland and France* (Bloomington, Ind., 1994).

Beckett, J. V., *The Aristocracy in England, 1660–1914* (Oxford, 1986).

Beckett, John, *The Rise and Fall of the Grenvilles: Dukes of Buckingham and Chandos, 1710 to 1921* (Manchester, 1994).

Berg, Maxine, *The Age of Manufactures, 1700–1820*, 2nd edn. (London, 1994).

Biddulph, Violet, *Kitty, Duchess of Queensberry* (London, 1935).

—— *The Three Ladies Waldegrave (and their Mother)* (London, 1938).

Black, Jeremy (ed.), *British Politics and Society from Walpole to Pitt, 1742–1789* (London, 1990).

Blodgett, Harriet, *Centuries of Female Days: Englishwomen's Private Diaries* (Gloucester, 1989).

Boissevain, Jeremy, *Friend of Friends: Networks, Manipulators and Coalitions* (Oxford, 1974).

Bonsall, Brian, *Sir James Lowther and Cumberland & Westmorland Elections, 1754–1775* (Manchester, 1960).

Bourne, J. M., *Patronage and Society in Nineteenth-Century England* (London, 1986).

Brewer, John, *Party Ideology and Popular Politics at the Accession of George III* (Cambridge, 1976).

—— *The Sinews of Power: War, Money and the English State, 1688–1783* (London, 1989).

—— 'This, That and the Other: Public, Social and Private in the Seventeenth and Eighteenth Centuries', in Dario Castiglione and Lesley Sharpe (eds.), *Shifting the Boundaries: Transformations of the Language of Public and Private in the Eighteenth Century* (Exeter, 1995).

BREWER, JOHN, *The Pleasures of the Imagination: English Culture in the Eighteenth Century* (London, 1997).
BROOKE, JOHN, *The Chatham Administration, 1766–1768* (London, 1956).
BROUGHAM, HENRY, *Historical Sketches of Statesmen who Flourished in the Time of George III*, 3rd ser. (London, 1843).
BROWNE, ALICE, *The Eighteenth Century Feminist Mind* (Brighton, 1987).
BROWNING, REED, *The Duke of Newcastle* (London, 1975).
BRYSON, ANNA, *From Courtesy to Civility* (Oxford, 1998).
BUCHOLZ, R. O., *The Augustan Court: Queen Anne and the Decline of Court Culture* (Stanford, Calif., 1993).
BURKOLTER, VERENA, *The Patronage System: Some Theoretical Remarks* (Basel, 1976).
CALLAN, HILARY and SHIRLEY ARDENER (eds.), *The Incorporated Wife* (London, 1984).
CANNON, JOHN, *The Fox–North Coalition: Crisis of the Constitution, 1782–4* (Cambridge, 1969).
—— *Parliamentary Reform, 1640–1832* (Cambridge, 1973).
—— *Aristocratic Century: The Peerage of Eighteenth-Century England* (Cambridge, 1987).
CARTER, PHILIP, *Men and the Emergence of Polite Society, Britain 1660–1800* (Harlow, 2001).
CECIL, LORD DAVID, *Melbourne* (London, 1955).
—— *The Cecils of Hatfield House: A Portrait of an English Ruling Family* (London, 1975).
CHALUS, ELAINE, 'Kisses for Votes: The Kiss and Corruption in Eighteenth-Century English Elections', in Karen Harvey (ed.), *The Kiss in History* (Manchester, 2005).
CHARTIER, ROGER (ed.), *A History of Private Life*, Vol. 3: *Passions of the Renaissance* (London, 1989).
CHILDE-PEMBERTON, WILLIAM S., *The Earl Bishop*, 2 vols. (London, 1924).
CHRISTIE, I. R., *The End of North's Ministry: 1780–1782* (London, 1958).
—— *Wilkes, Wyvill and Reform* (London, 1962).
—— *Wars and Revolutions: Britain, 1760–1815* (Cambridge, Mass., 1982).
CLARK, ANNA, *The Struggle of the Breeches: Gender and the Making of the British Working Class* (London, 1995).
CLARKE, NORMA, *Dr Johnson's Women* (London, 2000).
COKAYNE, G. E, *The Complete Peerage of England, Scotland, Ireland, Great Britain and the United Kingdom*, ed. Vicary Gibbs *et al.*, 12 vols. (London, 1910–53).
—— *The Complete Baronetage*, microprint edn. (Gloucester, 1983).
COLLEY, LINDA, *Britons: Forging the Nation, 1707–1837* (London, 1992).
Collins's Peerage of England: Genealogical, Biographical and Historical, edn. Sir Egerton Brydges, 6th edn., 9 vols. (London, 1812).

COLLINSON, PATRICK, *De Republica Anglorum: or, History with the Politics Put Back* (Cambridge, 1990).

CONNELL, BRIAN, *Portrait of a Whig Peer: Compiled from the Papers of the Second Viscount Palmerston, 1739–1802* (London, 1957).

CRUICKSHANKS, E. and J. BLACK (eds.), *The Jacobite Challenge* (Edinburgh, 1988).

CULLEY, LORRAINE, *Women and Power* (Leicester, 1986).

DAVIDOFF, LEONORE, *The Best Circles: 'Society', Etiquette and the Season* (London, 1986).

—— *Worlds Between: Historical Perspectives on Gender and Class* (Cambridge, 1995).

—— and CATHERINE HALL, *Family Fortunes: Men and Women of the English Middle Class, 1780–1850* (London, 1992).

DAVIS, I. M., *The Harlot and the Statesman: The Story of Elizabeth Armistead and Charles James Fox* (Bourne End, 1986).

DAVIS, NATALIE ZEMON, 'Women in Politics', in id. and Arlette Farge (eds.), *A History of Women in the West*, Vol. 3: *Renaissance and Enlightenment Paradoxes* (Cambridge, Mass., 1993).

DE COURCY, ANNE, *Circe: The Life of Edith, Marchioness of Londonderry* (London, 1992).

DE RIENCOURT, AMAURY, *Woman and Power in History* (Bath, 1974).

DERRY, JOHN W., *The Regency Crisis and the Whigs, 1788–88* (Cambridge, 1963).

Dictionary of National Biography.

EASTWOOD, D. S., *Governing Rural England: Tradition and Transformation in Local Government, 1780–1840* (Oxford, 1994).

—— *Government and Community in the English Provinces, 1700–1870* (London, 1997).

EHRMAN, JOHN, *The Younger Pitt: The Years of Acclaim* (London, 1969).

EISENSTADT, S. N. and LUIS RONIGER, *Patrons, Clients and Friends: Interpersonal Relations and the Structure of Trust in Society* (Cambridge, 1984).

ELLIOT, HON. GEORGE F. S., *The Border Elliots and the Family of Minto* (Edinburgh, 1897).

ELSHTAIN, JEAN BETHKE, *Public Man, Private Woman: Women in Social and Political Thought* (Oxford, 1981).

ERICKSON, AMY LOUISE, *Women and Property in Early Modern England* (London, 1993).

EVANS, ERIC J., *The Forging of the Modern State: Early Industrial Britain, 1783–1870* (London, 1983).

EYCK, ERICH, *Pitt versus Fox: Father and Son, 1735–1806* (London, 1950).

EZELL, MARGARET J. M., *The Patriarch's Wife: Literary Evidence and the History of the Family* (London, 1987).

FALK, BERNARD, *The Berkeleys of Berkeley Square and Some of their Kinsfolk* (London, 1944).
FLETCHER, ANTHONY, *Gender, Sex and Subordination in England, 1500–1800* (London, 1995).
FOREMAN, AMANDA, *Georgiana: Duchess of Devonshire* (London, 1998).
FORRESTER, ERIC G., *Northamptonshire County Elections and Electioneering, 1695–1832* (Oxford, 1941).
FOTHERGILL, ARTHUR B., *The Mitred Earl: An Eighteenth-Century Eccentric* (London, 1974).
GEORGE, DOROTHY, 'London and the Life of the Town', in A. S. Turberville (ed.), *Johnson's England: An Account of the Life and Manners of his Age* (Oxford, 1952).
GILBERT, MARTIN, *Churchill: The Man Behind the Legend* (London, 1998).
GLEADLE, KATHRYN, *British Women in the Nineteenth Century* (Basingstoke, 2001).
—— and SARAH RICHARDSON (eds.), *Women in British Politics, 1760–1860: The Power of the Petticoat* (Basingstoke, 2000).
GLUBB, A. DE C., *When Cornwall Had 44 MPs* (Truro, 1934).
GODBER, JOYCE, *The Marchioness Grey of Wrest Park*, Bedfordshire Historical Record Soc., 47 (1968).
GOODY, JACK, JOAN THIRSK, and E. P. THOMPSON (eds.), *Family and Inheritance: Rural Society in Western Europe, 1200–1800* (Cambridge, 1976).
GORDON, GEORGE, *The Last Dukes of Gordon and their Consorts, 1743–1864* (Aberdeen, 1980).
GREAVES, R. W., *The Corporation of Leicester 1689–1836* (1939; Leicester, 1970).
GREGO, J., *History of Parliamentary Elections and Electioneering in the Old Days* (London, 1886).
GUEST, HARRIET, *Small Change: Women, Learning and Patriotism, 1750–1810* (London, 2000).
GUTTSMAN, W. L., 'The British Political Élite and the Class Structure', in Philip Stanworth and Anthony Giddens (eds.), *Elites and Power in British Society* (Cambridge, 1974).
HABAKKUK, JOHN, *Marriage, Debt and the Estates System: English Landownership, 1650–1950* (Oxford, 1994).
HALL, CATHERINE, 'Private Persons versus Public Someones: Class, Gender and Politics in England', in id., *White, Male and Middle Class: Explorations in Feminism and History* (Cambridge, 1992), 151–71.
HAMILTON, ELIZABETH, *The Mordaunts: An Eighteenth-Century Family* (London, 1965).
Hardwicke of Derbyshire: By a Scion of the House (London, 1908).
HARLING, PHILIP, *The Waning of 'Old Corruption': The Politics of Economical Reform in Britain, 1779–1846* (Oxford, 1996).

HARRIS, FRANCES, *A Passion for Government: The Life of Sarah Duchess of Marlborough* (Oxford, 1991).

HARRISON, BRIAN, *Separate Spheres: The Opposition to Women's Suffrage in Britain* (London, 1978).

HATTON, RAGNILD, 'George I as an English and a European Figure', in Paul Fritz and David Williams (eds.), *The Triumph of Culture: 18th Century Perspectives* (Toronto, 1972).

HAY, DOUGLAS and NICHOLAS ROGERS, *Eighteenth-Century English Society: Shuttles and Swords* (Oxford, 1997).

HELLMUTH, ECKHART (ed.), *The Transformation of Political Culture: England and Germany in the Late Eighteenth Century* (Oxford, 1990).

HELLY, DOROTHY O. and SUSAN M. REVERBY (eds.), *Gendered Domains: Re-thinking Public and Private in Women's History: Essays from the Seventh Berkshire Conference on the History of Women* (London, 1992).

HILL, BRIDGET, *The Republican Virago: The Life and Times of Catharine Macaulay, Historian* (Oxford, 1992).

HIRST, DEREK, *The Representative of the People? Voters and Voting in England Under the Early Stuarts* (Cambridge, 1975).

History of Northumberland, 15 vols. (Newcastle, 1893–1940).

HODGSON, JOHN, *A History of Northumberland in Three Parts*, 3 vols. (Newcastle, 1827–40).

HOLLIS, PATRICIA, *Ladies Elect: Women in English Local Government, 1865–1914* (Oxford, 1989).

HOLMES, GEOFFREY, *Augustan England: Professions, State and Society, 1680–1730* (London, 1982).

—— *The Making of a Great Power: Later Stuart and Early Georgian Britain, 1660–1722* (London, 1993).

—— and DANIEL SZECHI, *The Age of Oligarchy: Pre-Industrial Britain, 1722–1783* (London, 1993).

HUDSON, PAT, *The Industrial Revolution* (London, 1992).

HUFTON, OLWEN, *The Prospect Before Her: A History of Women in Western Europe*, Vol. 1: *1500–1800* (London, 1995).

HUGHES, A. F. and J. KNIGHT, *Hills: Horshams Lost Stately Home and Garden* (Horsham, 1999).

HUNT, MARGARET, *The Middling Sort: Commerce, Gender and the Family in England, 1680–1780* (London, 1996).

HUXLEY, GERVAS, *Lady Elizabeth and the Grosvenors: Life in a Whig Family, 1822–1839* (London, 1965).

JALLAND, PAT, *Women, Marriage and Politics, 1860–1914* (Oxford, 1986).

JENKINS, PHILIP, *The Making of a Ruling Class: The Glamorgan Gentry, 1640–1790* (Cambridge, 1983).

JENKINS, ROY, *Churchill* (London, 2001).

JONES, VIVIEN (ed.), *Women in the Eighteenth Century: Constructions of Femininity* (London, 1990).

JUDD, G. P., *Members of Parliament, 1734–1832* (New Haven, 1955).

JUPP, P. J., 'The Roles of Royal and Aristocratic Women in British Politics, *c.*1782–1832', in Mary O'Dowd and Sabine Wichert (eds.), *Chattel, Servant or Citizen: Women's Status in Church, State and Society*, Historical Studies, 19 (Belfast, 1995).

KEAST, JOHN, *A History of East and West Looe* (Phillimore, 1989).

KELCH, RAY, *Newcastle: A Duke Without Money: Thomas Pelham-Holles, 1693–1768* (London, 1974).

KELLY, GARY, *Revolutionary Feminism: The Mind and Career of Mary Wollstonecraft* (Basingstoke, 1991).

KELLY, JOAN, 'Did Women Have a Renaissance?' in id., *Women, History, and Theory: The Essays of Joan Kelly* (London, 1984).

KENT, SUSAN KINGSLEY, *Gender and Power in Britain, 1640–1990* (London, 1999).

KETTERING, SHARON, *Patrons, Brokers, and Clients in Seventeenth-Century France* (New York, 1986).

KLEIN, LAWRENCE E., 'Gender, Conversation and the Public Sphere in Early Eighteenth-Century England', in Judith Still and Michael Worton (eds.), *Textuality and Sexuality: Reading Theories and Practices* (Manchester, 1993).

LANDES, JOAN, *Women and the Public Sphere in the Age of the French Revolution* (Ithaca, NY, 1988).

LANGFORD, PAUL, *The First Rockingham Administration, 1765–1766* (Oxford, 1973).

—— *A Polite and Commercial People: England, 1727–1783* (Oxford, 1990).

—— *Public Life and the Propertied Englishman, 1689–1798* (Oxford, 1991).

LAURENCE, ANNE, *Women in England, 1500–1800: A Social History* (London, 1994).

LAWSON, PHILIP, *George Grenville: A Political Life* (Oxford, 1984).

LOVENDUSKI, JONI and PIPPA NORRIS (eds.), *Women in Politics* (Oxford, 1996).

LOWER, MARK ANTONY, *Historical and Genealogical Notices of the Pelham Family* (London, 1873).

LUMMIS, TREVOR and JAN MARSH, *The Woman's Domain: Women and the English Country House* (London, 1993).

MCDOWELL, L. and R. PRINGLE (eds.), *Defining Women: Social Institutions and Gender Divisions* (Cambridge, 1992).

MCLYNN, FRANK, *The Jacobites* (London, 1988).

MANDLER, PETER, *Aristocratic Government in the Age of Reform: Whigs and Liberals, 1830–1852* (Oxford, 1990).

MARSHALL, DOROTHY, *Eighteenth-Century England*, 2nd edn. (Harlow, 1989).

MASTERS, BRIAN, *Great Hostesses* (London, 1982).

—— *The Dukes: The Origins, Ennoblement and History of 26 Families* (London, 1988).

MAY, SIR THOMAS ERSKINE, *The Constitutional History of England Since the Accession of George III*, 3rd edn., 3 vols. (London, 1871).

MAYFIELD, SUE, *Timeline: Women and Power* (London, 1988).

MELVILLE, LEWIS, *Regency Ladies* (London, 1926).

MIDDLETON, R., *The Bells of Victory: The Pitt-Newcastle Ministry and the Conduct of the Seven Years' War, 1757–1762* (Cambridge, 1985).

MIDGLEY, C., *Women Against Slavery: The British Campaigns, 1780–1870* (London, 1992).

MILES, R., *Women and Power* (London, 1985).

MINGAY, G. E., *English Landed Society in the Eighteenth Century* (London, 1963).

MINTO, NINA [Lady Minto], *Notes from Minto Manuscripts* (Edinburgh, 1861).

MITCHELL, L. G., *Charles James Fox and the Disintegration of the Whig Party, 1782–1794* (Oxford, 1971).

—— *Holland House* (London, 1980).

—— *Charles James Fox* (Oxford, 1992).

MYERS, SYLVIA HARCSTARK, *The Bluestocking Circle: Women, Friendship, and the Life of the Mind in Eighteenth-Century England* (Oxford, 1990).

NAMIER, LEWIS, *The Structure of Politics at the Accession of George III* (1929; 2nd edn., London, 1960).

—— *England in the Age of the American Revolution*, 2nd edn. (London, 1961).

—— *Crossroads of Power: Essays on Eighteenth-Century England* (London, 1962).

—— 'The Social Foundations', in Daniel A. Baugh (ed.), *Aristocratic Government and Society in Eighteenth-Century England: The Foundations of Stability* (New York, 1975).

—— and JOHN BROOKE, *The House of Commons, 1754–1790*, 3 vols. (London, 1964).

NEWBOULD, I., *Whiggery and Reform, 1830–41: The Politics of Government* (Basingstoke, 1990).

NICHOLSON, L. J., *Gender and History: The Limits of Social Theory in the Age of the Family* (New York, 1986).

NUSSBAUM, FELICITY A., *The Autobiographical Subject: Gender and Ideology in Eighteenth-Century England* (London, 1989).

O'GORMAN, FRANK, *The Rise of Party in England: The Rockingham Whigs, 1760–82* (London, 1975).

—— *Voters, Patrons, and Parties: The Unreformed Electoral System of Hanoverian England, 1734–1832* (Oxford, 1991).

—— *the Long Eighteenth Century: British Political and Social History, 1688–1832* (London, 1997).

OKIN, SUSAN MOLLER, *Women in Western Political Thought* (Princeton, 1979).

OLSON, ALISON GILBERT, *The Radical Duke: Career and Correspondence of Charles Lennox, Third Duke of Richmond* (Oxford, 1961).

Owen, J. B., *The Rise of the Pelhams* (London, 1957).

—— 'Political Patronage in 18th Century England', in Paul Fritz and David Williams (eds.) *The Triumph of Culture: 18th Century Perspectives* (Toronto, 1972).

Oxfordshire County Council, *The Oxfordshire Election of 1754*, Record Publication No. 6 (Oxford, 1970).

Parker, R. A. C., *Coke of Norfolk: A Financial and Agricultural Study, 1707–1842* (Oxford, 1975).

Pearson, John, *Stags and Serpents: The Story of the House of Cavendish and the Dukes of Devonshire* (London, 1983).

Peck, Linda Levy, 'Benefits, Brokers and Beneficiaries: The Culture of Exchange in Seventeenth-Century England', in B. Y. Kunze and D. D. Brautigam (eds.), *Court, Country and Culture: Essays on Early Modern British History in Honor of Perez Zagorin* (Rochester, 1992).

—— *Court Patronage and Corruption in Early Stuart England* (London, 1993).

Perkin, Harold, *Origins of Modern English Society* (London, 1991).

Perrot, Michelle (ed.), *A History of Private Life*, Vol. 5: *From the Fires of Revolution to the Great War*, trans. Arthur Goldhammer (London, 1990).

Perry, Ruth, *The Celebrated Mary Astell: An Early English Feminist* (London, 1986).

Phillips, John A., *Electoral Behavior in Unreformed England: Plumpers, Splitters, and Straights* (Princeton, 1982).

Plumb, J. H., *Sir Robert Walpole*, 2 vols. (London, 1956).

—— *The Growth of Political Stability in England, 1675–1725* (London, 1967).

—— 'Political Man', in James L. Clifford (ed.), *Man Versus Society in Eighteenth-Century Britain: Six Points of View* (Cambridge, 1968).

—— 'The Woman's Burden', in id., *In the Light of History* (London, 1972).

—— *Georgian Delights* (London, 1980).

—— *The First Four Georges* (London, 1987).

Porritt, Edward and Annie G. Porritt, *The Unreformed House of Commons: Parliamentary Representation before 1832*, 2 vols. (Cambridge, 1903).

Porter, Roy, *Enlightenment: Britain and the Creation of the Modern World* (London, 2001).

Reay, Barry, *Popular Cultures in England, 1550–1750* (Harlow, 1998).

Rendall, Jane, *The Origins of Modern Feminism: Women in Britain, France and the United States, 1780–1869* (Chicago, 1985).

Reynolds, K. D., *Aristocratic Women and Political Society in Victorian Britain* (Oxford, 1998).

Rizzo, Betty, *Companions Without Vows: Relationships Among Eighteenth-Century Women* (1994).

Robbins, Caroline, *The Eighteenth-Century Commonwealthman* (Cambridge, Mass, 1959).

ROBERTSON, SIR CHARLES GRANT, *England Under the Hanoverians*, 15th edn. (London, 1948).

ROBSON, R. J., *The Oxfordshire Election of 1754* (Oxford, 1949).

ROGERS, KATHERINE M., *Feminism in Eighteenth-Century England* (Urbana, Ill., 1982).

ROGERS, NICHOLAS, *Whigs and Cities: Popular Politics in the Age of Walpole and Pitt* (Oxford, 1989).

—— *Crowds, Culture and Politics in Georgian Britain* (Oxford, 1998).

RONIGER, LUIS and AYSE GÜNES-AYATA (eds.), *Democracy, Clientelism, and Civil Society* (London, 1994).

ROSALDO, MICHELLE ZIMBALIST and LOUISE LAMPHERE (eds.), *Women, Culture, and Society*. (Stanford, Calif., 1974).

ROWSE A. L., *The Later Churchills* (London, 1958).

RUDÉ, GEORGE, *Hanoverian London, 1714–1808* (London, 1971).

SAXONHOUSE, ARLENE W., *Women in the History of Political Thought: Ancient Greece to Machiavelli* (New York, 1985).

SEELEY, L. B., *Mrs. Thrale Afterwards Mrs. Piozzi* (London, 1908).

SHAPIRO, ANN-LOUISE (ed.), *Feminists* Revision *History* (New Brunswick, 1994).

SHARPE, KEVIN, *Faction and Parliament* (Oxford, 1978).

SHARPE, PAMELA, *Adapting to Capitalism: Working Women in the English Economy, 1700–1850* (Basingstoke, 1996).

SHEVELOW, KATHRYN, *Women and Print Culture: The Construction of Femininity in the Early Periodical* (London, 1989).

SHIACH, MORAG, *Discourse on Popular Culture: Class, Gender and History in Cultural Analysis, 1730 to the Present* (Oxford, 1989).

SHKOLNIK, ESTHER SIMON, *Leading Ladies: A Study of Eight Late Victorian and Edwardian Political Wives* (London, 1987).

SMITH, E. A. *Whig Principles and Party Politics: Earl Fitzwilliam and the Whig Party, 1748–1833* (Manchester, 1975).

—— *A Queen on Trial: The Affair of Queen Caroline* (Stroud, 1993).

SMITH, HILDA L. (ed.), *Women Writers and the Early Modern British Political Tradition* (Cambridge, 1998).

SPACKS, PATRICIA MEYER, *Gossip* (New York, 1985).

SPENCER, SAMIA I. (ed.), *French Women and the Age of Enlightenment* (Bloomington, 2nd., 1984).

SPRING, EILEEN, *Law, Land, & Family: Aristocratic Inheritance in England, 1300–1800* (London, 1993).

STEINEN, KARL VON DEN, 'The Discovery of Women in Eighteenth-Century English Political Life', in Barbara Kanner (ed.), *The Women of England From Anglo-Saxon Times to the Present* (Hamden, Conn., 1979).

STIRLING, A. M. W., *Annals of a Yorkshire House: From the Papers of a Macaroni and His Kindred*, 2 vols. (London, 1911).

STONE, LAWRENCE, *The Family, Sex and Marriage in England, 1500–1800*, abridged edn. (London, 1979).

SWEET, ROSEMARY and PENELOPE LANE (eds.), *Women and Urban Life in Eighteenth-Century England: On the Town* (Leicester, 2003).

SUNTER, RONALD M., *Patronage and Politics in Scotland, 1707–1832* (Edinburgh, 1986).

SUTHERLAND, LUCY S., 'Political Respectability, 1751–1771,' in L. S. Sutherland and L. G. Mitchell (eds.), *The History of the University of Oxford: The Eighteenth Century: Vol. 5* (Oxford, 1986).

TADMOR, NAOMI, *Family and Friends in Eighteenth-Century England: Household, Kinship and Patronage* (Cambridge, 2001).

TAYLOR, STEPHEN, RICHARD CONNORS, and CLYVE JONES, *Hanoverian Britain and Empire: Essays in Memory of Philip Lawson* (Cambridge, 1998).

THOMAS, P. D. G., *The House of Commons in the Eighteenth Century* (Oxford, 1971).

THOMPSON, E. P., *The Making of the English Working Class* (Markham, Ont., 1986).

THOMPSON, F. M. L. (ed.), *The Cambridge Social History of Britain*. Vol 2: *1750–1950* (Cambridge, 1990).

TILLYARD, STELLA, *Aristocrats: Caroline, Emily, Louisa and Sarah Lennox, 1740–1832* (London, 1994).

TOMALIN, CLAIRE, *The Life and Death of Mary Wollstonecraft*, revised edn. (London, 1992).

TRETHEWEY, RACHEL, *Mistress of the Arts: The Passionate Life of Georgiana, Duchess of Bedford* (London, 2002).

TREVELYAN, G. M., *English Social History* (London, 1944).

VALENZE, DEBORAH, *The First Industrial Woman* (Oxford, 1995).

VERNON, JAMES, *Politics and the People: A Study in English Political Culture, c.1815–1867* (Cambridge, 1993).

VICKERY, AMANDA, *The Gentleman's Daughter: Women's Lives in Georgian England* (London, 1998).

—— (ed.), *Women, Privilege and Power:British Politics 1750 to the Present* (Stanford, 2001).

Victoria County Histories: Essex, Hertfordshire, Oxford.

WARD, W. R., *Georgian Oxford* (Oxford, 1958).

WATTS, RUTH, *Gender, Power and the Unitarians in England, 1760–1860* (Harlow, 1998).

WEIL, RACHEL, *Political Passions: Gender, the Family and Political Argument in England, 1680–1714* (Manchester, 1999).

WELCH, STEPHEN, *The Concept of Political Culture* (1993).

WHYMAN, SUSAN, *Sociability and Power in Late Stuart England: The Cultural Worlds of the Verneys, 1660–1720* (Oxford, 1999).

WIFFEN, J. L., *Historical Memoirs of the House of Russell, from the Time of the Norman Conquest*, 2 vols. (London, 1833).

WIGGIN, LEWIS M., *The Faction of Cousins: A Political Account of the Grenvilles, 1733–1763* (New Haven, Conn., 1958).

WILENTZ, SEAN (ed.), *Rites of Power: Symbolism, Ritual, and Politics Since the Middle Ages* (Philadelphia, 1985).

WILLIAMS, BASIL, *The Whig Supremacy, 1714–1760* (Oxford, 1939).

WILLIAMS, W.R., *The Parliamentary History of Oxfordshire from the Earliest Times to the Present Day: 1213–1898* (1898).

WILSON, KATHLEEN, 'Empire of Virtue: The Imperial Project and Hanoverian Culture *c.*1720–1785', in Lawrence Stone (ed.), *The Imperial State at War: Britain from 1689–1815* (London, 1994).

—— *The Sense of the People: Politics, Culture and Imperialism in England, 1715–1785* (Cambridge, 1995).

—— *The Island Race: Englishness, Empire and Gender in the 18th Century* (London, 2002).

WING, WILLIAM, *Oxfordshire in the Eighteenth Century and the County Election of 1754* (repr. from the *Bicester Herald*, 1881).

—— *The Great Oxfordshire Election of 1754* (repr. from the *Oxford Chronicle*, 1881).

WRIGLEY, E. A. and R. S. SCHOFIELD, *The Population History of England, 1541–1871: A Reconstruction* (Cambridge, 1989).

Articles

ADAMS, SIMON, 'Faction, Clientage, and Party, English Politics, 1550–1603', *Hist. Today*, 32 (1982), 33–9.

BATESON, MARY, 'Clerical Preferment Under the Duke of Newcastle', *Eng. Hist. Rev.*, 7 (1892), 685–96.

BENNETT, JUDITH M., 'Women's History: A Study in Continuity and Change', *Women's Hist. Rev.*, 2 (1993), 173–84.

BLACK, JEREMY, 'Eighteenth-Century English Politics: Recent Work and Current Problems', *Albion*, 25 (1993), 419–42.

BONHAM CARTER, VIOLET, 'The Souls', *The Listener* (30 Oct. 1947), 769–70.

CANNADINE, DAVID, 'Through the Keyhole', *New York Review of Books*, 21 Nov. 1991.

CHALUS, ELAINE, 'Elite Women, Social Politics and the Political World of Late Eighteenth-Century England', *Hist. Jl.*, 43 (2000), 669–97.

—— 'How Lady Susan Wooed the Voters', *BBC History Magazine*, 2 (June 2001), 44–6.

CLARK, ANNA (Sept. 1998), Review of Amanda Vickery, *The Gentleman's Daughter: Women in Georgian England* (London, 1998): http://www.history.ac.uk/reviews/paper/anna.html.

Colley, Linda, *Sunday Times*, 17 Apr. 1994.

Copelman, Dina M., 'Liberal Ideology, Sexual Difference, and the Lives of Women: Recent Works in British History', *Jl. Modern Hist.*, 62 (1990), 315–45.

Deutsch, Phyllis, 'Moral Trespass in Georgian London: Gaming, Gender and Electoral Politics in the Age of George III, *Hist. Jl.*, 39 (1996), 637–56.

Fergusson, James, ' "Making Interest" in Scottish County Elections', *Scottish Hist. Rev.*, 26 (1947), 119–33.

Gould, Eliga H., 'American Independence and the Cosmopolitan Foundations of Britain's First Counter-Revolution', *Past & Present*, 153 (Feb. 1997), 107–41.

Habakkuk, John, 'The Rise and Fall of English Landed Families, 1600–1800: II', *Trans. Royal Hist. Soc.*, 5th ser. (London, 1980), 199–221.

Haffenden, Philip, 'Colonial Appointments and Patronage Under the Duke of Newcastle, 1724–1739', *Eng. Hist. Rev.*, 78 (1963), 417–35.

Harris, Barbara J., 'Property, Power, and Personal Relations: Élite Mothers and Sons in Yorkist and Early Tudor England', *Signs*, 15 (1990), 606–32.

—— 'Women and Politics in Early Tudor England.' *Hist. Jl.*, 32 (1990), 259–81.

Hill, Bridget, 'Women's History: A Study in Change, Continuity or Standing Still?', *Women's Hist. Rev.*, 2 (1993), 5–22.

Hufton, Olwen, 'Women Without Men: Widows and Spinsters in Britain and France in the Eighteenth Century', *Jl. Family Hist.*, 9 (1984), 355–76.

Hunt, Tamara L., 'Morality and Monarchy in the Queen Caroline Affair', *Albion*, 23 (1991), 697–722.

Jeune, Lady, 'A Century of Women', *Anglo-Saxon Review*, 4 (Mar. 1900), 197–209.

Jones, Clyve and Frances Harris, ' "A Question . . . Carried by Bishops, Pensioners, Place-men, Idiots": Sarah, Duchess of Marlborough and the Lords' Division over the Spanish Convention, 1 March 1739', *Parliamentary Hist.*, 11 (1992), 254–77.

Kent, Joan R., 'The Centre and the Localities: State Formation and Parish Government in England, circa 1640–1740', *Hist. Jl.*, 38 (1995), 363–404.

Kettering, Sharon, 'Gift-Giving and Patronage in Early Modern France', *French Hist.*, 2 (1988), 131–51.

—— 'The Historical Development of Political Clientelism', *Jl. Interdisciplinary Hist.*, 18 (1988), 419–47.

—— 'The Patronage Power of Early Modern French Noblewomen', *Hist. Jl.*, 32 (1989), 817–41.

Klein, Lawrence E., 'Gender and the Public/Private Distinction in the Eighteenth Century: Some Questions About Evidence and Analytic Procedure', *Eighteenth-Century Studies*, 29 (1995), 92–109.

Lana, Renata, 'Women and Foxite Strategy in the Westminster Election of 1784', *Eighteenth-Century Life*, 26 (Winter 2002), 46–69.

LANGFORD, PAUL, 'Property and "virtual Representation" in Eighteenth-Century England', *Hist. Jl.*, 31 (1988), 83–115.

—— 'Politics and Manners from Sir Robert Walpole to Sir Robert Peel', *Proc. Brit. Acad.*, 94 (London, 1997).

LAQUEUR, T. W., 'The Queen Caroline Affair: Politics as Art in the Reign of George IV', *Jl. Modern Hist.*, 54 (1982), 417–66.

LEVIS, R. B., 'Sir James Lowther and the Political Tactics of the Cumberland Election of 1768', *Northern Hist.*, 19 (1983), 108–27.

MANDLER, PETER, 'Namier in Petticoats?' (Feb. 1999), review of K. D. Reynolds, *Aristocratic Women and Political Society in Victorian Britain* (Oxford, 1998): http://www.history.ac.uk/ihr/Focus/Victorians/mandler.html.

MCCAHILL, M. W., 'Peers, Patronage and the Industrial Revolution, 1760–1800', *Jl. of Brit. Studies*, 16 (1976), 84–107.

MIDDLETON, RICHARD, 'The Duke of Newcastle and the Conduct of Patronage During the Seven Years' War', *Brit. Jl. Eighteenth-Century Studies*, 7 (1989), 175–86.

NAMIER, L. B., 'Three Eighteenth-Century Politicians', *Eng. Hist. Rev.*, 42 (July 1927), 408–13.

O'GORMAN, FRANK, 'The Unreformed Electorate of Hanoverian England: The Mid-18th Century to 1832', *Social Hist.*, 11 (1986), 33–52.

—— 'Campaign Rituals and Ceremonies: The Social Meaning of Elections in England, 1780–1860', *Past & Present*, 135 (May 1992), 79–115.

PALAZZI, MAURA, 'Female Solitude and Patrilineage: Unmarried Women and Widows in the Eighteenth and Nineteenth Centuries', *Jl. Family Hist.*, 15 (1990), 443–59.

QUENNELL, PETER, 'Hogarth's Election Series', *Hist. Today*, 3 (1953), 221–32.

RICHARDSON, SARAH, 'The Role of Women in Electoral Politics in Yorkshire During the 1830s', *Northern Hist.*, 32 (1996)

RUBENSTEIN, W. D., 'The End of "Old Corruption" in Britain, 1780–1860', *Past & Present*, 101 (Nov. 1983), 55–86.

SACK, JAMES J., 'The House of Lords and Parliamentary Patronage in Great Britain 1802–1832,' *Hist. Jl.*, 23 (1980), 913–38.

SHARPE, KEVIN, 'Faction at the Early Stuart Court', *Hist. Today*, 33 (1983), 39–46.

SHARPE, PAMELA, 'Continuity and Change: Women's History and Economic History in Britain', *Econ. Hist. Rev.*, 48 (1995), 353–69.

SMITH, E. A., 'The Yorkshire Elections of 1806 and 1807: A Study in Electoral Management', *Northern Hist.*, 2 (1967), 62–90.

—— 'The Election Agent in English Politics, 1734–1832', *Eng. Hist. Rev.*, 330 (1969), 12–35.

SOMERSET, H. V. F., 'Burke and the Cavendishes', *Eng. Hist. Rev.*, 47 (Apr. 1932), 280–6.

STARKEY, DAVID, 'From Feud to Faction: English Politics Circa 1450–1550', *Hist. Today*, 32 (1982), 16–21.

STOTT, ANNE, ' "Female Patriotism": Georgiana, Duchess of Devonshire, and the Westminster Election of 1784', *Eighteenth-Century Life*, 17 (Nov. 1993), 60–84.

SWEET, ROSEMARY, 'Freemen and Independence in English Borough Politics, *c.*1770–1830', *Past & Present*, 161 (Nov. 1998), 84–115.

SYKES, NORMAN, 'The Duke of Newcastle as Ecclesiastical Minister', *Eng. Hist. Rev.*, 57 (Jan. 1942), 59–84.

TADMOR, NAOMI, 'The Concept of the Household-Family in Eighteenth-Century England', *Past & Present*, 151 (May 1996), 111–40.

THOMPSON, E. P., 'The Moral Economy of the English Crowd in the Eighteenth Century', *Past & Present*, 50 (Feb. 1971), 76–136.

VICKERY, AMANDA, 'The Neglected Century: Writing the History of Eighteenth-Century Women', *Gender and Hist.*, 3 (1991), 211–19.

—— 'Golden Age to Separate Spheres? A Review of the Categories and Chronology of English Women's History', *Hist. Jl.*, 36 (1993), 383–414.

—— 'Shaking the Separate Spheres: Did Women Really Descend into Graceful Indolence?', *TLS*, 12 Mar. 1993.

WALL, RICHARD, 'Women Alone in English Society', *Annales de démographie historique*, 141 (1981), 303–14.

WASSON, E. A., 'The House of Commons, 1660–1945: Parliamentary Families and the Political Élite', *Eng. Hist. Rev.*, 106 (1991), 635–51.

WILSON, KATHLEEN, 'Citizenship, Empire, and Modernity in the English Provinces, *c.*1720–1790', *Eighteenth-Century Studies*, 29 (1995–6), 69–96.

WOOLF, D., 'A Feminist Past? Gender, Genre and Historical Knowledge in England, 1500–1800', *American Hist. Review*, 102 (1997), 645–79.

INDEX